Western Garden Annual

1997 EDITION

By the Editors of *Sunset Magazine* and Sunset Books

Iris douglasiana and hybrids (page 87)

NORMAN A. PLATE

Sunset Books Inc. ■ **Menlo Park, California**

SPRING FLOWER BOUQUET *includes annuals, perennials, and bulbs, plus feather grass and nandina foliage as filler (see page 100).*

The Gardening Year in Review

This *Western Garden Annual,* the fourth edition, places between two covers the entire body of 1996 gardening and outdoor living material from *Sunset Magazine.* Its format, with minor variations, reflects that of its predecessors: twelve chapters each address a single month of the year and contain all of the garden-related material for that month from the various regional editions of the magazine.

Leading off each chapter are the Garden Guide's mini-articles: short pieces on diverse points of interest relevant to the month or to the gardening period just ahead. Garden Notebooks offer personal tips and anecdotes from the *Sunset* garden editors who cover the West; a question-and-answer feature in each notebook focuses on garden problem-solving. Checklists for each region then remind readers of garden activities that might—or should—be undertaken that month. Concluding each chapter's offerings are longer feature articles, colorfully illustrated to entice and inspire.

In all of these monthly features, plant performance and gardening activities are often keyed to numbered climate zones. These zones—24 in all, covering the entire West—are described and mapped in the sixth edition of the *Sunset Western Garden Book,* published in 1995.

SUNSET BOOKS INC.

President and Publisher
Susan J. Maruyama
Director, Sales & Marketing
Richard A. Smeby
Editorial Director
Bob Doyle
Production Director
Lory Day
Retail Sales Development Manager
Becky Ellis
Art Director
Vasken Guiragossian

STAFF FOR THIS BOOK

Coordinating Editor
Suzanne Normand Eyre
Contributing Editors
Philip Edinger
Helen Sweetland
Cornelia Fogle
Indexer
Pamela Evans
Production Coordinator
Patricia S. Williams

SUNSET PUBLISHING CORPORATION

President/Chief Executive Officer
Steve Seabolt
VP, Chief Financial Officer
James E. Mitchell
VP, Publisher, *Sunset* Magazine
Anthony P. Glaves
VP, Consumer Marketing Director
Robert I. Gursha
Director of Finance
Lawrence J. Diamond
VP, Manufacturing Director
Lorinda Reichert
VP, Editor-in-Chief, *Sunset* Magazine
Rosalie Muller Wright
Managing Editor
Carol Hoffman
Executive Editor
Melissa Houtte
Senior Editor, Gardening
Kathleen Norris Brenzel

Cover: 'Ville de Lyon' hybrid clematis (see page 80). Design by Susan Bryant Caron. Photography by Michael S. Thompson.

Back cover: Container planting of colorful annuals surrounding a spiky dracaena. Photography by Kathleen N. Brenzel.

Endpapers (hardcover edition): *Tulipa saxatilis,* Norman A. Plate

All material in this book originally appeared in the 1996 issues of *Sunset Magazine.*

Sunset Western Garden Annual was produced by Sunset Books Inc. If you have comments or suggestions, please let us hear from you. Write us at:

Sunset Books Inc.
Garden Book Editorial
80 Willow Road
Menlo Park, CA 94025

If you would like to order additional copies of any of our books, call us at 1-800-643-8030 extension 544 or check with your local bookstore. For special sales, bulk orders, and premium sales information, call (415) 324-5789.

First printing March 1997
Copyright © 1997 Sunset Books Inc., Menlo Park, CA 94025.
First edition. All rights reserved, including the right of reproduction in whole or in part in any form.

ISSN 1073-5089
Hardcover edition: ISBN 0-376-03863-2
Softcover edition: ISBN 0-376-03861-6

Printed in the United States.

Contents

Introduction 4

Sunset's *Western Garden Annual* celebrates the glories of Western gardening

January 6

Colorful winter gardens, wonderful rugosa roses, hardy orchids, great shrubs for mild climates

February 30

Blooming branches indoors, dwarf conifers, camellias with extended bloom, Asian pears

March 50

Beginners' great gardens, vegetables in raised beds, trial garden for rhododendrons, guide to clematis

April 82

Cutting gardens, specialty nurseries, organic gardening tips, lavenders, bloom-again irises

May 118

Window boxes, propagating perennials, bellflower choices, well-behaved palms, lingonberries, pawpaws

June 144

Beautiful pot plantings, terra-cotta containers, choosing the right potting mix, thyme varieties

July 168

Fresh-flower wreaths, garden for the senses, lovely stewartias, South African landscape ideas

August 192

Unforgettable garden fragrances, favorite heathers, bananas in your landscape

September 216

Garden masters' secrets, species tulips year after year, drying hydrangeas, garlic revival, CDs for gardeners

October 248

Community gardens, smoke trees, Asiatic and Oriental lilies, preserving herbs, unusual annuals from seed

November 272

Growing wildflowers in small beds and pots, diminutive daffodils perfect for tiny spaces

December 292

Wreaths from seasonal materials, table decorations, shipping fruit, tabletop trees, indoor bamboos

Indexes 317

Article Titles Index on page 317, General Subject Index on page 318

The Oracle of Western Gardening

Where in the world can you find another region as diverse and hospitable as the West? Here you have the ultimate in scenic beauties and contrasts: the mighty Pacific Ocean with its beach-studded, craggy coastline; major mountain ranges (Sierra Nevada, Cascade, Rockies) and lesser ones as well; vast, fertile valleys and thickly timbered hills; and desert territory from panoramic to awe-inspiring. And everywhere, people reveling in the special glories that combine to produce a uniquely Western lifestyle.

For over 60 years, *Sunset Magazine* has served as chronicler and nurturer of that lifestyle and of one of the West's greatest opportunities: gardening. Generations of readers have looked to the pages of *Sunset* for the knowledge that would let them take full advantage of the West's amazingly varied gardening potential. Perpetually introduced are new plants, new products, and new gardening techniques. Readers are also kept abreast of sources for the unusual (experimentation is a Western pastime), books to advance their gardening skills, and special sites to visit for gardening inspiration. Culinary tips, too, in-

evitably intermingle in these pages, to satisfy gardeners' ambitions to use their marvelous array of exotic and familiar edibles in unusual and creative ways.

In 1996 our editors "beat the bushes" to come up with a variety of reader-worthy topics. In the realm of worthwhile plants—some new, others simply overlooked—we presented the rugged, carefree rugosa roses; bearded irises boasting two bloom periods a year; lavenders especially suited to mildest-winter regions; and heretofore unsung species tulips for year-after-year performance. Connoisseurs of garden edibles discovered *Sunset*'s taste-tested pick of Asian pears; watermelons for the smaller garden; even pawpaws! Garlic aficionados were treated to an exposition of varieties different from our supermarket standbys. In June, container gardeners were inspired by "Beautiful Pots," then tantalized by a variety of designer terra-cotta vessels crafted by regional artisans, and finally instructed on how to select the "perfect" potting mix. Not overlooked among readers were true garden romantics, who learned of the 18 flowers judged most memorably fragrant.

In short, these 320 pages contain not only solid information and inspiration but also proof of the dynamic Western gardening life—a pastime, even obsession, made exciting and challenging by the very diversity of conditions this great region offers.

SHADY REST STOP *nestles among carefully chosen assortment of perennials and annuals. Contrasting foliage types and colors make dynamic combination throughout the growing season (see page 187).*

DAVID FALCONER

A cloud of double pink flowers covers this 10-year-old 'Royal Burgundy' cherry tree in spring. For details on this red-leafed beauty, see page 9.

JANUARY

Garden guide 8

Checklists & garden notebooks . . 12

It's gloating time! 16

"Wild" and wonderful rugosas . . . 22

Hardy exotics 25

Four fabulous shrubs 26

Natural soil enrichers 29

SUNSET'S
GARDEN
Guide

Aloes ... the reliable winter color makers

Southern California's not exactly a "dead of winter" kind of place, yet gardens there do go a bit dull in January. Fortunately for the color-hungry among us, aloes oblige. These easy-to-grow succulents, native primarily to South Africa's arid veld, explode in spiky blooms of hot orange, vermilion, and yellow starting in December.

Aloe arborescens (pictured at right at Franceschi Park in Santa Barbara) is one of 200 species, ranging from container-size dwarfs to trees. It starts flowering in December and peters out in February. Two other large species—*A. bainesii,* with rose pink flowers, and *A. africana,* with yellow to orange-yellow flowers—bloom from December through January. Coral aloe (*A. striata*), with coral pink to orange flowers, and Cape aloe (*A. ferox*), with scarlet or orange flowers, are smaller plants with similar flowering periods. For even smaller spaces or pots, try torch plant (*A. aristata*) or partridge-breast aloe (*A. variegata*); both bear flowers in reddish shades in winter.

Not all aloes bloom in winter, so you need to choose plants carefully. Combine them with winter-blooming shrubs such as primrose jasmine (*Jasminum mesnyi*), Cape honeysuckle (*Tecomaria capensis*), or acacia. Avoid going overboard with aloes; a garden with more than one species can look

Bright vermilion blooms, which seem to glow like torches, give this aloe (*A. arborescens*) one of its many

like a plant collection.

Aloes like excellent drainage and rocky soil; surprisingly, they also appreciate soil rich in minerals and

organic matter. They take full sun in coastal areas and light shade inland. The foliage of *A. arborescens* is damaged by frost at 29°;

other aloes vary in hardiness. Some will even tolerate salt spray in coastal gardens. They also tolerate drought.

Franceschi Park is at the

JANUARY '96

- Aloes for winter color
- Meet the new All-Americas
- Not-so-red radishes
- Prechilled tulips
- Growing fuchsias inland
- Root pruning for container plants

common names: candelabra aloe.

corner of Mission Ridge and Franceschi roads on Santa Barbara's Riviera. Hours are 8 to sunset daily; admission is free.

Two petunias and a salvia are rookies of the year

Sports leagues honor the best new players with rookie-of-the-year awards. The seed industry honors the best new flowers and vegetables by naming them All-America Selections. Although no vegetable winners were named again this year, three flowers earned 1996 AAS awards, reflecting their outstanding performances in trial beds across the country, including *Sunset*'s gardens in Menlo Park, California.

Petunias. 'Fantasy Pink Morn' represents a new class of petunia called milliflora. This plant produces masses of 1-inch-wide blooms and grows only half as tall as standard petunias. Flowers are pink with white centers. Because of its size and spreading habit, it's the first petunia we'd recommend for use in the rock garden as well as the flower bed.

'Heavenly Lavender' also produces masses of flowers over a long period, but they're double and much larger (as wide as 3 inches). Unlike most lavender petunias, these blooms have no veins. We liked this plant's looks and performance very

Bicolored flower spikes distinguish *Salvia farinacea* 'Strata'.

much, both in nursery trials and after two or three months in the field.

Salvia. *S. farinacea* 'Strata' rounds out the AAS awards. This plant's blue-and-white flowers make it the first bicolored mealy-cup sage. The 6-inch-tall flower spikes rise above a knee-high plant with gray-green leaves, and the flowers are useful both fresh and dried. 'Strata' is a perennial, most often grown as an annual. It handles heat and drought with aplomb, but freezing causes it to die back.

A pink-flowering cherry with deep red leaves

Nothing says spring has arrived more than a spectacular Japanese flowering cherry in full bloom. One of the most dramatic bloomers is *Prunus serrulata* 'Kwanzan', with double pink flowers followed by red foliage. Unfortunately, the beautiful red foliage of 'Kwanzan' and other red-leafed cherries turns green by midsummer.

But now a new cherry is available, with foliage that stays brilliant purple-red all summer long. *Prunus serrulata* 'Royal Burgundy' (pictured on page 6) bears double pink flowers on red stems—similar to those of 'Kwanzan' but slightly smaller (about 1½ inches in diameter). The dark leaves appear about the same time as the flowers, and they accentuate the pink blooms. In fall, the foliage of this tree turns a gorgeous red-orange.

'Royal Burgundy' grows at a moderate rate to about 20 feet tall by 15 feet wide, and makes a fine accent tree or shade tree over a patio.

Japanese flowering cherries are cold-hardy enough to grow in *Sunset Western Garden Book* zones 2 and 3 if you protect them from winter winds. Plant them in full sun and well-drained soil. If your soil is heavy clay, plant them in raised beds.

Trees are available now at many nurseries. If you can't find one, ask your nursery to order for you from L. E. Cooke (wholesale only), Visalia, California.

A medley of radishes to grow from seed

Round red radishes are standard fare in grocery stores. But when you grow your own, you have many more types to choose from. We grew a slew of different kinds in our test garden last season. Some of our favorites are pictured at right.

Nontraditional colors. 'Easter Egg II' is a favorite with kids; one packet of seeds yields red, white, purple, and violet radishes. 'Hailstone' is a large white-skinned radish that's tender and sweet. 'Snow Belle', another white, grows a bit smaller. 'Sparkler' is a bicolor red with a white tip and is particularly flavorful when harvested small. And 'Plum Purple' is unusual both in color and in its resistance to pithiness.

Traditional round red. Dutch 'Gala' resists splitting, and even large radishes

Radishes range from round to oblong, from red to white.

NORMAN A. PLATE

are tender. 'Red King' is resistant to fusarium and club root (both are soilborne diseases).

Nontraditional shapes. 'Flamboyant' is a 3-inch-long cylindrical white-tipped radish considered a

delicacy in France. 'Long Black Spanish' grows 10 inches long and has spicy white flesh; it's best grown in fall.

Radishes are quick and easy to grow during cool weather in early spring or fall. Scatter a thin row of seeds, cover with ½ inch of soil, and keep the soil moist, and you'll get leaves in as soon as four days. Thin seedlings to 1½ inches apart, and in just three to four weeks, you'll be sinking your teeth into crunchy, succulent radishes.

You can buy seeds of the above varieties from the following mail-order suppliers. All sell 'Easter Egg II'. *Nichols Garden Nursery,* (541) 928-9280, sells 'Hailstone', 'Long Black Spanish', and 'Sparkler'. *Park Seed Co.,* (800) 845-3369, sells 'Plum Purple' and 'Snow Belle'. *Shepherd's Garden Seeds,* (408) 335-6910, sells 'Flamboyant'and 'Gala'. *Territorial Seed Co.,* (541) 942-9547, sells 'Red King'.

Taste test reveals flavorful fruit

For the last three years, Dave Wilson Nursery, a wholesale grower of fruit trees in Hickman, California (south of Modesto), has conducted seven taste tests of locally grown fruit varieties. Nurserymen and horticulturists judged the fruit on appearance, texture, sugar and acid content, flavor, and overall quality.

Don't overlook the following 10 highest-scoring varieties when you're shopping for bare-root fruit trees this month.

'Flavor King' pluot (a plum-apricot hybrid) is the highest scorer, followed by 'Flavor Supreme' pluot, 'Arctic Supreme' white-fleshed peach, 'Heavenly

White' nectarine, 'O'Henry' peach, 'Loring' peach, 'Arctic Glo' white-fleshed nectarine, 'Weeping Santa Rosa' plum, 'Hosui' Asian pear, and 'Fantasia' nectarine.

Not all of the above varieties were at peak tree-ripe quality on the taste-test dates. (Tree-ripened fruits always taste the best.)

Tulips for Southern California procrastinators

For a dozen years, professional growers of cut flowers have had access to prechilled tulip bulbs. Now Flamingo Gardens is offering the same bulbs to home gardeners. If you haven't

bought and prechilled your tulip bulbs yet (planting time is running out), you can buy tulip (also hyacinth and daffodil) bulbs from company coolers at most Home Depot and Nurseryland stores in San Diego County and selected Nurseryland stores in Orange and Los Angeles counties. To find the store nearest you, call (619) 734-1033. Expect to pay as much as 50 percent more than you would for non-chilled bulbs.

It's time to spray those roses

Last spring's late rainfall created ideal conditions for many rose diseases. Rust

and black spot ran rampant in many areas, even on some varieties normally considered disease resistant. Now's the time to take action to prevent these diseases from coming back this year.

If you haven't yet pruned your roses, do so soon. Prune to keep the center of the plants open for good air circulation. If any old leaves still cling to the plant, remove them. Rake up any debris beneath the plants and destroy or discard all prunings and plant debris.

Once the plants are pruned and the ground is clean beneath them, spray plants and the ground beneath them with a combination of dormant oil (to smother overwintering insect eggs) and lime sulfur (to kill dormant disease organisms); follow label instructions.

Fuchsia season flip-flop

Contrary to popular opinion, gardeners living outside of California's coastal fog belt *can* grow fuchsias successfully. "If you live in an inland area with hot summers," says fuchsia specialist Evelyn Weidner of Weidners' Gardens in Encinitas, California, "the trick is to pretend that January is summer, and Christmas is in July." In other words, in *Sunset Western Garden Book* zones 18 through 21, do just the opposite of what you'd do along the coast: grow fuchsias in the winter rather than summer, and treat summer, not winter, as the plants' resting period.

After years of selling fuchsias to inland gardeners, Weidner has learned that the cool, breezy, sunny days that Pasadena, Pomona, and Poway enjoy in the winter are as agreeable to fuchsias as foggy summer days along the coast. Fuchsias will bloom happily in these locations now through spring. When summer weather heats up, cut plants back by half. Don't withhold water. Through summer, pinch new growth to encourage bushiness. Then let plants bloom again in early fall.

This ploy, however, won't work with every fuchsia. Most varieties need spring's increase in daylight hours to trigger blooms. But Weidner and her inland customers have discovered at least a dozen varieties that are not dependent on day length to flower. They're the ones you're likely to find flowering in nurseries now, including 'Angel's Flight', 'Bicentennial', 'Dark Eyes', 'Dollar Princess', 'Fluffy Ruffles', 'Hula Girl', 'Miss California', 'Pink Marshmallow', and 'Voodoo'.

Controlling insects with spray oils

Insects must breathe to live. That includes dormant and active insects, larvae, and eggs. Smother them with horticultural oil any time of year and they die. The only trick is in matching the right oil to the right season, which isn't as complicated as it once was.

The earliest horticultural oils were rather heavy and impure, and while they could kill aphid eggs, mealybugs, mites, scale, and whiteflies, they were also toxic enough to burn or kill leaves. For that reason, they were applied only during winter, when dormant deciduous trees have no leaves. That's why they were called dormant oils.

You can still buy dormant oils, but most are refined enough to control insects without damaging most kinds of plants any time of year. Make sure the label says "Supreme-type," "Superior," or "Dormant and summer oil." These are still best applied in winter, when there are no leaves to shield insect eggs, larvae, or adults. After winter pruning, spray each tree thoroughly, especially any cracks in the bark, where pests like to overwinter.

Read labels closely so that you don't mistake a bottle of dormant spray (usually a fungicide such as lime sulfur) for dormant oil.

You can also buy "sticker" or "spray aid" horticultural oils that help herbicides, insecticides, and fungicides stick to leaves and branches.

A buyer's guide to bare-root roses

Millions of roses hit the markets this month, with retailers from discount stores to nurseries selling bare-root plants with and without packaging. The following tips can help you avoid buying duds.

Roots. Unpackaged bare-root roses are still your best bet, since you can lift them from nursery beds and inspect the roots before you buy. Healthy roots are fibrous and evenly spread, with tiny white root hairs.

You can't check the roots of roses sold in bags or boxes, but the packaging provides some clues to what you're likely to find inside. Roses in plastic bags, commonly sold by mass merchandisers, often hold fewer roots, since the roots are trimmed to fit the bag. Buy these early in the season, before the roots have a chance to dry out. Ask for a money-back guarantee. Roses in ready-to-plant boxes have plenty of room for roots, and since they're easy for the seller to water, the roots are less likely to be dry when you buy them.

Top growth. Hybrid tea roses should have three to five substantial, unbroken canes, about equally spread, to produce a lush, well-balanced bush the first year. Avoid packaged bare-root roses that have begun to leaf out.

Pruning the roots of potted plants

If you plan to keep deciduous or evergreen shrubs or trees growing outdoors in big pots, you need to prune their roots every three years. Since the plants are dormant in winter, January is a good month to do this job in climate zones 4 through 7, but wait until spring in cold-winter areas (zones 1, 2, and 3). You can use this technique to prune the roots of house plants such as ficus.

Roll the pot over on its side and pull the plant out of its container. On the outer edges of the rootball you'll

Cut roots back by a third to a half using shears or a saw.

find big roots that have wound around the inside of the pot. As you pull these out and untangle them, lots of soil will fall away from the rootball. Then use a pruning saw or shears to cut the big roots back by a third to a half. When spring comes, a new network of fine feeder roots will sprout from the cut ends.

Scrub the inside of the pot with a stiff brush (you may want to use a dilute solution of household bleach). Add a layer of fresh potting mix to the bottom of the container. Place the plant back in the pot and add more soil to cover the roots. Leave at least an inch between the soil line and the top rim of the pot. Water well. In spring and summer, fertilize the plant at about half the normal rate until it becomes reestablished, then resume regular feeding.

By Steven R. Lorton,
Jim McCausland,
Lauren Bonar Swezey

PACIFIC NORTHWEST
CHECKLIST
JANUARY

PLANTING AND PLANNING

☐ **BARE-ROOT STOCK.** In climate zones 4–7, shop for bare-root plants, including berries, grapes, fruit and shade trees, ornamental shrubs, roses, and vegetables (asparagus, horseradish, and rhubarb).

☐ **HARDY PERENNIALS.** Sow seeds of hardy perennials such as delphiniums, hellebores, veronicas, and violas now in coldframes or greenhouses. About a month prior to the last expected frost, you can set seedlings outside in the ground once they have two or three sets of true leaves.

☐ **WINTER-FLOWERING SHRUBS.** In climate zones 4–7, your choices include Chinese witch hazel, hybrid camellias, stachyurus, and wintersweet. Buy plants in bloom and slip them into decorative pots for display on a deck, or set them in the ground immediately.

☐ **ORDER SEEDS.** Seed catalogs are out now by the dozens. Order flowers and vegetables early—by mail, telephone, or fax.

MAINTENANCE

☐ **CARE FOR HOUSE PLANTS.** Feed only those plants that produce fruit or flowers in winter. Water only when the top ½ inch of soil is dry to the touch. Snip off yellowing leaves. If leaves are covered with a layer of house dust, set

Vancouver
Victoria
BRITISH COLUMBIA
Seattle
Spokane
WASHINGTON
Olympia
Yakima
Portland
Pendleton
Salem
OREGON
Bend
Eugene
Medford

Sunset Western Garden Book CLIMATE ZONES

☐ 1-3 ☐ 4-7

them in the shower and gently spray them clean with tepid water.

☐ **CHECK STORED BULBS.** Check corms and tubers. Sprinkle water on any that are shriveled and they should rehydrate. Throw out ones that show signs of rot. Dahlia tubers are the exception: cut out any bad spots, dust with sulfur, and store them apart from the rest.

☐ **FERTILIZE ASPARAGUS.** Top-dress plants with well-rotted manure or sprinkle a complete granular fertilizer.

☐ **PRUNE FRUIT TREES.** In zones 4–7, prune fruit trees this month. Choose a day when temperatures are well above freezing. Cut out dead, diseased, closely parallel, or crossing branches. Then prune for shape. In cold-winter climate zones 1–3, hold off on pruning until spring, when hard freezes won't kill back cut ends.

☐ **PRUNE ROSES.** In zones 4–7, prune roses this month. Prune hybrid teas to a vase shape made up of the three to five strongest canes. Cut back top growth by about a third.

PEST AND WEED CONTROL

☐ **BAIT FOR SLUGS.** When the weather warms, the slug army marches. When good weather hits, spread bait around rocks, under big leaves, and through ground covers. When spring arrives and you set out tender annuals, perennials, and vegetables, you'll be glad that you fought the battle early. Take care not to let pets or children get into the poison bait.

☐ **PULL WEEDS.** Now that many plants are leafless, weeds are easier to spot. If you see a dead weed stalk with small rosettes of leaves sprouting at the base, get the roots out of the ground now.

I have a love-hate relationship with blackberries. The fruit is delicious and the foliage quite handsome, but these plants are frightfully aggressive—they'll spread 10 feet a year if you don't control them. So around New Year's Day, at my Skagit Valley house, I'll start whacking them back. I'll cut the big, ornery old canes down to the ground and drag them off to the burn pile atop the dormant vegetable patch. In some cases, I'll use a shovel to dig out the roots. I'll leave enough plants behind to produce a good crop of berries next summer.

Now through February is a good time to tame blackberries this way. It's hard, prickly work, and you must dress for war—heavy gloves, long sleeves, and a hood or stocking cap to cover your head.

•

I've always admired the sight of old bald cypress trees (*Taxodium distichum*) that rise out of the Southern swamps, showing off their rugged bark and ferny foliage. Even though *Sunset Western Garden Book* says these trees are hardy enough to grow in all but the coldest winter climate in the Northwest (zone 1), I was dubious about their success in milder parts of the Northwest. But I wanted to try, so

PACIFIC NORTHWEST
Garden Notebook
BY STEVEN R. LORTON

three years ago I obtained a bald cypress in a 1-gallon can and planted it by the edge of my garden pond in zone 4. It's doing fine (one winter the pond even froze solid around it). Occasionally you can find this plant at a nursery. If you can't, ask your nursery to order it from a wholesaler in the South.

THAT'S A GOOD QUESTION

Q: I see roses advertised as "grown on their own roots." What else would they be grown on?

A: Most modern roses are budded to the rootstock of a hardy and vigorous rose such as 'Dr. Huey'. The budded roots ensure that the hybrid rose will be productive and better able to withstand dry spells and differences in soil. Occasionally the rootstock may send up a vigorous shoot of its own (remove soil to expose its base and pull the shoot off with a downward motion). Or if the hybrid rose canes die back to the ground, the shoots that may arise from the rootstock won't be the rose you want. With roses grown on their own roots, you won't have these problems, but the plants may be less robust initially than budded plants. Which is better? It's pretty much a trade-off—go with your own personal preference.

NORTHERN CALIFORNIA
CHECKLIST
JANUARY

PLANTING

❏ **ORDER SEEDS.** You should have received your new vegetable and flower catalogs by now. Take this opportunity to thumb through them and order varieties you can't find on seed racks.

❏ **PLANT BARE-ROOT.** Zones 7–9, 14–17: This is the prime month to buy and plant dormant roses, fruit and shade trees, shrubs, and vines. These bare-root plants cost less and adapt more quickly. It's best to plant immediately upon arriving home from the nursery, but if you can't, temporarily lay plants on their sides in a shallow trench and cover with moist sawdust or soil (called heeling in).

MAINTENANCE

❏ **CARE FOR GIFT PLANTS.** Zones 7–9, 14–17: After bloom, snip off spent blossoms and move hardier plants such as azaleas, cyclamen, and cymbidiums to a protected spot outdoors. Keep tender plants such as amaryllis and kalanchoe indoors in a well-lighted spot. Water regularly. Repot if plants are rootbound and dry out quickly. Fertilize amaryllis and azaleas after bloom finishes. Fertilize cymbidiums with half-strength fertilizer every week, other plants every two to three weeks. Zones 1–2: Keep all plants indoors until after the last hard freeze.

❏ **FEED PLANTS.** Zones 7–9, 14–17:

Sunset Western Garden Book CLIMATE ZONES

- Mountain (1–2)
- Valley (7–9)
- Inland (14)
- Coastal (15–17)

Fertilize annuals, vegetables, and cool-season lawns. Feed citrus trees six to eight weeks before they bloom, according to their age: give trees planted last season (2-year-old trees) ¼ pound of actual nitrogen, 3-year-old trees ½ pound, 4-year-old trees ¾ pound, 5-year-old trees 1 pound, and trees more than 5 years old 1 to 1½ pounds. Feed citrus all at once or in two feedings (January and February). In very sandy soil, divide into once-a-month feedings.

❏ **PROTECT PLANTS FROM FROST.** Zones 7–9, 14–17: Be on the lookout for dry, still nights when the sky is clear; listen to the weather forecast. If frost is predicted, move tender container plants, such as citrus, cymbidiums, hibiscus, and mandevilla, beneath overhangs or into the garage. Protect other frost-tender plants (in the ground or in containers too large to move) with burlap or cloth coverings; do not let the cover touch the leaves. Remove the cover first thing in the morning.

❏ **PRUNE.** Zones 7–9, 14–17: This is prime time for pruning many dormant deciduous plants, such as flowering vines, fruit and shade trees, grapes, and roses. For plants such as Japanese snowbell and lilacs that bloom only in spring, prune after they bloom.

❏ **WATER.** Zones 7–9, 14–17: If rains have been light or nonexistent, water plants periodically, especially ones planted last fall, which still have small root systems. Drought-stressed plants are more susceptible to freeze damage.

PEST CONTROL

❏ **SPRAY FOR PEACH LEAF CURL.** Zones 7–9, 14–17: To prevent this fungus from distorting peach leaves and destroying the fruit, spray with lime sulfur now and again as buds swell but before they have opened. Use a spreader-sticker to improve coverage, and do not spray when rain is predicted.

I t's that thorny time of year again when nurseries are overflowing with bare-root rose bushes. Plants are usually accompanied by glossy photographs of a beautiful rose bloom—either on the package or stapled to stakes nearby. It's easy to succumb to those promising photographs. I'm not a rose fanatic like my sister, but I've found myself oohing and aahing over pictures of exquisite flowers such as those of old-fashioned 'Souvenir de la Malmaison'. I have to restrain myself from purchasing even one more plant, though, because I realize I don't have room for another rose if I want to give it optimal growing conditions—6 hours of full sun.

When I walk around my neighborhood in Palo Alto, I see that some rose lovers don't restrain themselves. The result? They end up with too many bushes that are either crowded together in one sunny patch or spilling over into shade. Crowded bushes are much more prone to diseases such as rust and powdery mildew. Plants in too much shade are wimpy and produce few blooms, and also are prone to disease. So next time you're tempted by a gorgeous rose, make sure you can give it the growing conditions it needs—full sun, plenty of air circulation, and well-drained soil.

NORTHERN CALIFORNIA
Garden Notebook
BY LAUREN BONAR SWEZEY

It's January. That means it's time to think tomatoes and peppers. But wait! It's midwinter, you say. That's right. This is when I plan and order seeds of varieties I'd like to experiment with in our test gardens here at *Sunset*. By the time seeds arrive, it's February—the best month to start tomato and pepper seeds in the mild-winter climates of Northern California. Seedlings will be ready to set out in the garden in eight weeks, well after the last frost has passed. What looks interesting? 'Miracle Sweet' tomato (Tomato Growers Supply Co.) and 'Red Savina' habanero pepper (Shepherd's Garden Seeds).

THAT'S A GOOD QUESTION

Q: I like to brighten up my home in winter with roses from the florist, but why do cut roses sometimes wilt before or just after they open?
A: According to Jennifer Sparks of the American Floral Marketing Council, the condition is called bent neck. It is caused by air in the stem, which blocks water from being translocated up the stem to the neck. Without water, the neck wilts. If the rose is still fairly fresh (this won't work for a rose that is wilting from old age), you can probably get the stem to absorb water again. Partially fill a sink with warm water, recut the stem at an angle under water, and then submerge the stem for 45 to 90 minutes. Remove from the water and rearrange.

CHECKLIST
JANUARY

PLANTING

☐ **PLANT BARE-ROOT.** Most nurseries offer peak supplies of healthy rose plants now. You'll also find perennial vegetables such as artichokes, asparagus, horseradish, and rhubarb; fruits, including cane berries, grapes, and strawberries; and ornamentals such as hardy perennials, shade trees, shrubs, and vines, including wisteria.

☐ **PLANT CAMELLIAS.** Since so many camellias are blooming this month, it's a good time to shop for the flower types and colors you prefer. Whether or not they're flowering, plant them right away in a location that provides good soil drainage and afternoon shade.

☐ **PLANT SUMMER BULBS.** Nurseries now have supplies of summer-blooming bulbs, such as canna, crocosmia, dahlia, gladiolus, homeria, lilies, tigridia, tuberose, and tuberous begonias.

☐ **PLANT WINTER COLOR.** It's not too late, especially in coastal areas, to plant annuals and perennials for bloom now and into spring. Try calendulas, cinerarias (these are frost-tender), dianthus, English daisies, Iceland poppies, larkspur, pansies, primroses, snapdragons, stock, sweet alyssum, sweet peas, and violas. In the low desert (Zone 13), you can also plant petunias.

MAINTENANCE

☐ **DO DORMANT-SEASON PRUNING.** Before new growth begins this month,

Sunset
Western Garden Book
CLIMATE ZONES

1-3 7-9 11 13 14-24

prune deciduous roses, shrubs, trees, and vines. Make sure saws, loppers, and shears are sharp before starting. Wait until late spring, after flowers fade, to prune trees and shrubs grown primarily for their spring flowers.

☐ **CARE FOR BARE-ROOT PLANTS.** On bare-root roses, trees, and vines, keep roots moist before and after planting. If you can't set out the plants right away, cover their roots with moist soil or mulch until you set them out. While dig-

ging the plant hole, soak bare roots in a bucket of water.

☐ **WATER.** If rains have been light or nonexistent, water drought-tolerant plants. Also irrigate young, unestablished native plants. This is the season when they can best absorb and store water for summer. Plants set out in fall also need regular deep soaking.

PEST AND WEED CONTROL

☐ **GROOM CAMELLIAS.** If your plants are afflicted with petal blight (petals turn brown and rot in the center), pick infected flowers from plant. Also keep the soil beneath plants clean by removing fallen flowers and leaves promptly.

☐ **MANAGE WEEDS.** Mulch or remulch around vegetable and flower beds, shrubs, and trees. That's the best way to stay ahead of the weeds that come with winter's coolness and moisture.

☐ **SPRAY DORMANT PLANTS.** Inland (zones 18–21): To prevent or reduce pest problems next winter, spray leafless and dormant fruit trees and roses. Insects such as aphids and scale and diseases such as peach leaf curl are readily controlled now with sprays of horticultural oil, alone or combined with either lime sulfur or fixed copper (follow label directions). Most nurseries carry all three products. Nearer the coast (zones 22–24): If plants (notably 'Anna' apple) aren't leafless, withhold water to force dormancy before spraying.

SOUTHERN CALIFORNIA Garden Notebook
BY SHARON COHOON

I f this January is anything like the last one, it will be too wet to do much gardening. For once I'll be able to curl up with a good gardening book without the slightest pang of conscience. I won't waste the opportunity on a soufflé-weight summer read. Such a rare occasion will call for a book as rich, dense, and satisfying as a chocolate truffle. Something along the lines of *California's Changing Landscapes* (Sacramento, 1994; $24.95 paperback).

This California Native Plant Society publication tells the story of the state's amazingly diverse plant communities, the forces that created them, and the pressures threatening to destroy them. It does so in language that is both accessible and eloquent. You leave it with a deeper understanding of your local native landscape. And that understanding can't help but make you a better gardener.

If you can't find *California's Changing Landscapes* at your library or bookstore, order it from CNPS at (916) 447-2677.

•

Speaking of rain, I saw a nifty device called the Rain Drain at Pat Welsh's garden in Del Mar. It solves the problem of washed-out plants under downspouts. (If you've read *Pat Welsh's Southern California Gardening*, you know she has a knack for finding practical solutions to common gardening problems.) The Rain Drain is a 12-foot vinyl sleeve—perforated with tiny holes—that you tie onto the downspout. When it rains, the force of the water from the spout unfurls the sleeve like a New Year's Eve noisemaker, dispersing the rainwater evenly along its length. When the rain stops, you roll up the sleeve again on the plastic cylinder that comes with it. If you don't find the device at your retail nursery or home improvement center, check an irrigation supply store.

THAT'S A GOOD QUESTION

Q: What do I do if my newly planted shrubs topple after the rains, like my neighbor's did last year?

A: The combination of water-saturated woody stems and rain-softened soil can cause shrubs to lose their grip. But the plants can usually be salvaged if their roots haven't pulled out completely, says Steve Stewart of Earthscaping Designs in Laguna Beach. Here's his advice: Right the plants, fill in fissures with fresh dirt, and tamp down firmly. Add 1- by 1-inch nursery stakes beside small shrubs, 2-inch nursery stakes beside larger ones. Tie branches to the supports with nursery tape loosely enough to allow some play. Keep stakes in place for six to eight months, until roots have repaired completely.

CHECKLIST
JANUARY

PLANTING

☐ **HARDY PERENNIALS.** Start seeds of perennials such as delphinium, hellebore, veronica, and viola in a coldframe or greenhouse for planting when at least two sets of true leaves appear and after soil has warmed up.

☐ **ORDER SEEDS, PLANTS.** For best selection, order seeds and plants early.

PLANTING, ZONES 12 AND 13

☐ **BARE-ROOT STOCK.** In mild-winter areas, nurseries have berries, fruit trees, roses, and shade trees now. Plant immediately and water in well.

☐ **PRECHILLED BULBS.** If you bought spring flower bulbs in November and refrigerated them to provide preplanting chill, set them out now.

☐ **WINTER COLOR.** Nurseries offer plenty of winter color, including bachelor's button, calendula, cineraria, cyclamen, English daisy, pansy, primrose, and sweet alyssum.

☐ **VEGETABLES.** Sow vegetables such as eggplant, melons, peppers, and tomatoes now for transplant outside when the weather warms up.

MAINTENANCE

☐ **CARE FOR GIFT PLANTS.** After Christmas, rinse them off in a lukewarm shower, fertilize those with fruit or flowers, and put in a bright place away from drafts.

Sunset Western Garden Book CLIMATE ZONES
☐ 1-3
☐ 10-11
☐ 12-13

☐ **CARE FOR LIVING CHRISTMAS TREES.** Right after the holidays, move the trees to an outside location that's shaded from midday and afternoon sun (under a tree, for example), moving them into full sun two weeks later.

☐ **WATER HOUSE PLANTS.** Water when the top ½ inch of soil has dried out. Snip off yellowing leaves.

☐ **FERTILIZE ASPARAGUS.** Top-dress with well-rotted manure or organic mulch mixed with a complete fertilizer.

☐ **PRUNE ROSES.** Cut hybrid tea roses back to the three to five strongest canes, removing at least the top third of growth.

☐ **CARE FOR CITRUS TREES.** Zones 12 and 13: A day after watering, apply ammonium sulfate at 2½ pounds for grapefruit, 4 pounds for oranges and tangerines, and 5 pounds for lemon trees. Water again after application.

If temperatures below 28° are predicted, cover trees each night with a cloth (old sheets are fine). A temperature drop below 25° for more than 2 hours damages most citrus fruits. Pick and juice freeze-damaged fruit within 24 hours.

☐ **MULCH.** Zones 12 and 13: To keep weeds down and conserve water, mulch around shrubs and trees and in vegetable and flower beds.

☐ **WATER.** Zones 12 and 13: Deep-water trees and shrubs every two or three weeks if the rain doesn't do it for you. Don't waste water on acacia and cactus in cold weather, however, since their roots won't take up water when it's cold.

☐ **CHECK STORED BULBS.** Examine stored corms and tubers. Plump up shriveled ones by sprinkling with a little water. Discard bulbs that show signs of decay, except dahlia tubers: cut out bad spots, dust with sulfur, and store these tubers apart from the rest.

As a star-watcher, I always feel the year has turned the corner after Christmas. And so it has: from the winter solstice on, the days grow longer, buds on many shrubs and trees start swelling, and the impetuous spears of spring-flowering bulbs begin to peek out of the ground.

When I see these signs, I climb into my fruit trees with saw and sécateurs (pruning shears) and start working. Since I've never had much luck following pruning diagrams in books (you know the ones that show where to cut on an artist's perfectly symmetrical idea of a tree), I follow a much simpler method: First I cut out everything that's dead, injured, or diseased (last year that alone wiped out one whole apple tree). Then I remove all but one of any branches that run closely parallel or cross each other, especially if they rub. Then I stand back, size the tree up, and prune for shape.

Be cautious when pruning trees that bear stone fruits. Apricots, plums, and prunes bear some fruit on last year's wood and some on spurs, so you should leave a fair amount of last season's wood for next summer's crop. Nectarines and peaches bear virtually all their fruit on last year's wood, so save only as much older wood as you need for structure, and leave as much of last season's wood as possible. Cherries bear fruit on spurs that last for years, but they don't like hard pruning; try not to take more than 10 percent of the branches.

INLAND WESTERN STATES
Garden Notebook
BY JIM McCAUSLAND

One nurseryman I know stopped selling bare-root plants altogether because he had to reimburse so many customers for their losses—mostly caused, he guesses, by roots that were allowed to dry out between nursery and garden. When I buy bare-root plants, I always ask the nursery to wrap the roots in damp burlap or pack them in damp sawdust. Nothing dries out faster than tiny exposed roots on a dry day, and nothing dies faster than a bare-root plant with dry roots. Get bare-root stock in the ground as quickly as you can. If soil or weather conditions delay planting, then heel plants in: lay them on their sides and cover them with damp soil or sawdust. Just be sure to plant them upright before buds open.

THAT'S A GOOD QUESTION

Q: Are Christmas gift plants worth saving?

A: It depends on what they are. For ornamental peppers, poinsettias, and azaleas, the answer is no—they'll never again achieve their compact, bright beauty growing in your house. If you live in Arizona's low desert, however, you can plant poinsettias outside at the back of a shrub bed. Forced mums won't rebloom at Christmas again, but you can cut them back after bloom and plant them in the perennial bed for normal summer-fall bloom. Christmas cactus, cyclamen, and kalanchoe can do well and rebloom for years with normal care.

it's gloating time!

January 20, 1995—

Where were you on this day last winter? We were out in the garden, admiring Pam Morgan's poppies in Pasadena, Dan Hinkley's redtwig dogwood near Seattle, Kent Gullickson's grasses in Oakland, and Jan Frieder's gaillardia in Phoenix. While folks in Fargo were shivering in temperatures that ranged from 1° to a balmy 15°, we were taking pictures of four glorious winter gardens—in some cases in our shirtsleeves. That's the great thing about living in the West: even in January, when the days are short and the nights are long, you can still get out those gardening gloves, pull on a pair of rubber boots, and feel like a gardener.

By Sharon Cohoon,
Steven R. Lorton,
Lauren Bonar Swezey

paradise in Pasadena

WINTER BLOOM IN PAM MORGAN'S GARDEN IS AN ANNUAL EVENT

Other than a clump of *Salvia leucantha* (upper left), the color in Morgan's winter garden is provided by annuals planted amid society garlic and other perennials.

Iceland poppies blooming in winter are a sure sign of a temperate climate. The ones in Pam Morgan's Southern California garden were planted in October.

CHAD SLATTERY

lan in September, plant in October, gloat in January. That's gardening in Southern California for you. Planting spring flowers in fall for winter color would be sheer folly in most of the country. But in the benign climate of Southern California, this strategy makes perfect sense. Winter here is like spring elsewhere: cool air, cool soil, lots of rain. Forget the calendar. Pansies and poppies know better. New Year's Eve parties and white sales notwithstanding, weatherwise it's April.

Following this gardening regime was initially difficult for Minnesota transplant Pam Morgan. Everything about it went against the grain. But as her 5-year-old garden demonstrates, she has now mastered the switch.

The process begins in the middle of September, typically the hottest month of the year. Morgan takes stock and tries to imagine her garden in January.

"After I cut back my perennials, remulch, and neaten everything up, I can see the structure of the garden again," she says. "Then it's easy to decide what to keep, what to yank, and what I need to fill the gaps."

Annuals by the hundreds are the main source of color in Morgan's winter garden. They are tucked in along the front of the meandering border that edges a lawn, filling in gaps where the summer dahlias used to be or brightening up dark spots.

Planning early ensures that Morgan will be able to buy the colors she wants in the quantities she needs. 'Antique Shades' pansies and pink Iceland poppies, for example, figured prominently in her 1995 color scheme. "If I hadn't started early, I would have had to make do with mixed flats," she says. "And the effect wouldn't have been nearly as pretty, would it?"

October brings a marathon planting session. By November, the garden is settling in. And by January, when those 10,000 lakes back in Minnesota are frozen solid, Morgan's garden is alive with spring flowers.

That, as we said, is gardening in Southern California in the so-called dead of winter. It may be a bit goofy, but, Lord, ain't it grand?

Now starring in Southern California...

Although annuals such as English daisy (*Bellis perennis*), Iceland poppy (*Papaver nudicaule*), and pansy (*Viola wittrockiana*) are the most colorful stars of Pam Morgan's garden, showy perennials and colorful shrubs play important supporting roles.

■ **Front-of-the-border perennials.** African daisy (*Arctotis* hybrids), variegated society garlic (*Tulbaghia violacea*), yarrow (*Achillea*).

■ **Midborder perennials.** *Agapanthus*, reblooming daylily (*Hemerocallis* 'Midnight Magic').

■ **Winter and everblooming shrubs.** *Anisodontea hypomandarum, Camellia japonica, Lavatera maritima.*

■ **Evergreen shrubs and foliage plants.** Fortnight lily (*Dietes vegeta*), sword fern (*Nephrolepis*), Texas privet (*Ligustrum japonicum* 'Texanum').

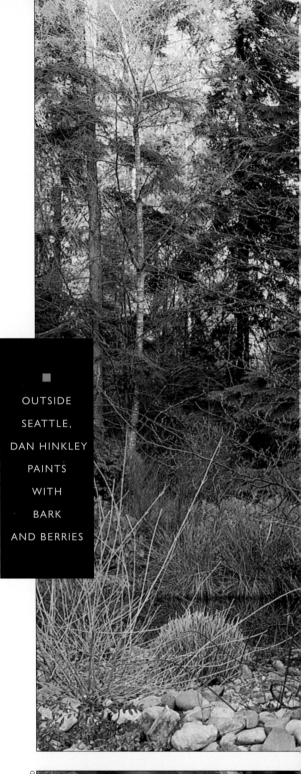

bark & berries
in Washington

Visitors to the Northwest are often amazed to hear us Northwesterners expound on the beauty of our winter gardens. To outsiders, January is a cold, gray, uninviting month. But we find the chill bracing, the wet a sign of renewal and growth. Mosses that had been brown and dry plump up, becoming glistening green jewels that line tree limbs and race through the cracks between bricks. Raindrops shimmer in rows on twigs and blades of grass, catching and reflecting the soft winter light. And since most human activity is driven indoors, the outside is remarkably quiet, save for the wind music: the rustle of bamboo, the clatter of evergreen leaves, the whispers of pines.

Dan Hinkley of Kingston, Washington, knows the winter garden well. Indeed, he approaches his as a painter does a canvas, which in this case means a steel gray or ice blue sky fronted by dark green walls of cedar and fir. First he applies the black and gray lines of Japanese and vine maples, deciduous magnolias, stewartias, and styrax. Then he adds broad strokes: clusters of hybrid camellias, fatsias, ivies, nandinas, pieris, rhododendrons, and viburnums. Next come the precise brush strokes of colorful barks—redtwig and yellowtwig dogwoods, bright yellow willows, the rusty, mottled bark of *Stewartia pseudocamellia*. Last, Hinkley dots the canvas with stranvaesia, for its jewel-like berries, and Chinese witch hazel, whose fragrant yellow blooms fairly explode at this time of year.

As an artist, Hinkley is fascinated by the unusual and exotic, but he is equally dedicated to using Northwest staples. Thus, his garden includes hydrangea for its rugged bark, and several varieties of holly for their brilliant red fruit. For this artist, anyway, the possibilities for the Northwest garden appear to be inexhaustible. Even in winter.

The Northwest color wheel

"Flowers in January? Who needs 'em?" That's the attitude we Northwesterners project. We have nothing against color, as our fondness for Chinese witch hazel (*Hamamelis mollis*) attests. It's just that up here, color has got to be tough, which is why, like bears, we feed on bark and berries.

■ **Barks.** Himalayan birch (*Betula jacquemontii*) has smooth, bone white bark on straight trunks. Dogwoods with red and yellow twigs include *Cornus alba* (red), *C. sanguinea* (red), and *C. stolonifera* 'Flaviramea' (yellow). The nice thing about *Stewartia pseudocamellia* is the way its bark flakes off like a sycamore's, leaving patches of brown, gray, and orange.

■ **Berries.** *Ilex aquifolium* 'September Gem' is a holly with bright orange-red fruit. *I. verticillata* 'Sunset' is a deciduous variety with brilliant red fruit.

One of the most appealing berry-bearing plants in Hinkley's garden is stranvaesia (left), whose evergreen leaves add depth and texture to the landscape.

Dark conifers are the backdrop for a forest of redtwig and yellowtwig dogwoods, as well as vivid green *Kerria japonica*. Chinese witch hazel (left) sports fragrant golden tassels.

time-out
in Oakland

Kent Gullickson's garden can be a busy place in spring. That's when the perennials and succulents around his hillside home come into bloom so fast and furiously, it's sometimes hard to keep up with it all.

Which is why Gullickson looks forward to winter. "The winter garden is a revelation," he says. "There are fewer distractions. When plants go dormant, the garden's structure is exposed. And the plants that remain are often very architectural."

Seen from an upstairs window of Gullickson's house, the garden is a medley of textures and forms, with only a hint of flower color here and there. "Evergreen plants make up the framework of my garden," Gullickson says. "The interplay of leaf textures is a lot easier to appreciate when you're not distracted by an abundance of flowers."

Along with the bold architectural look of evergreens such as *Doryanthes palmeri* and *Melianthus major*, shapely grasses are a prominent presence here. Even the deciduous grasses that turn brown in winter, such as *Miscanthus sinensis* 'Silver Fern', remain standing. They provide structure and texture, and "their color is an indication it's winter," says Gullickson. When they finally get beaten over from wind and rain, he cuts them to the ground.

Of course, Gullickson also appreciates his winter garden because the maintenance is much more reasonable. "There are always things to be done in the garden—95 percent of it is grooming—but you don't have this frantic growth like in spring. Winter is a time to take time."

> ■
>
> GREEN MEANS "SLOW DOWN" IN KENT GULLICKSON'S NORTHERN CALIFORNIA GARDEN

Greens and grasses in Northern California

Except for the odd winter-blooming plant (*Aloe senegalense, Bergenia crassifolia,* and *Phlomis russeliana*), Gullickson's garden is composed of textures and foliage colors.

■ **Architectural evergreens.** *Agave attenuata, Aloe bainesii, Furcraea foetida, Phormium tenax* 'Sundowner', *Puya violacea.*

■ **Grasses.** *Carex buchananii, C. comans* 'Frosty Curls', *Festuca ovina* 'Glauca', *Stipa tenuissima.*

■ **Plants for texture.** *Echeveria elegans* (and hybrids), *Euphorbia rigida, Helichrysum petiolare* 'Limelight', *Hesperaloe parviflora.*

CHARLES McGRATH

Kent Gullickson's Oakland garden is all about textures and hues of green, including large-leafed blue-green *Melianthus major* at the top of the steps. At left is *Aloe arborescens,* one of the few spots of color in the garden.

courting color **in Phoenix**

■

SHELTERING

SPACES GIVE

JAN FRIEDER'S

GARDEN A

JUMP-START

ON SPRING

Seasons are different in the desert. When winter arrives and folks in most parts of the country are hunkered down in front of a warm fire, Phoenicians have turned off their air conditioners and are outdoors enjoying the refreshingly mild temperatures.

That's where you'll find Jan Frieder. "January through April are the highlights of the year in terms of gardening," says Frieder, who, with her husband, Bill, used to live in Michigan, where the winter months were gray and depressing. "You never have that feeling here," she says. "The trees all have leaves. Everything is green."

The Frieders' 1920s adobe home in Paradise Valley is actually three buildings connected by a courtyard. The courtyard functions as another living space, especially in the winter months, when the Frieders entertain friends and family.

To accentuate the feeling of being inside a room, Phoenix landscape architect Christine Ten Eyck paved the courtyard and planted blue palo verde and ironwood trees to create a ceiling. Trees were planted beyond the courtyard walls, too, to heighten the home's oasis quality. "The gnarly branches look beautiful silhouetted against the adobe walls," says Ten Eyck. Below and around the trees are flowering perennials and succulents. The result is a lush desert garden with lots of shade and year-round color.

Of course, Phoenix does get cold in the winter—in some areas frosts can kill fragile plants. But the courtyard environment and the trees protect plants, and since the plants are less likely to freeze, they tend to bloom longer or start earlier than is typical. Gaillardia, one of Jan's favorites, blooms nearly all year. And when the gaillardia starts looking tired? Well, Frieder just takes a break from her winter entertaining, pulls it up, and lets the young seedlings below take over. ■

Winter color for Southwest gardens

As in other warm climates around the West, annuals are a fine choice for winter color in the Southwest—and Jan Frieder grows plenty of them in her kitchen cutting garden. But the courtyard and surrounding desert garden are better suited to tougher plants that thrive in the arid environment. Many of these beauties have the benefit of blooming in winter, too.

■ **Perennials and shrubs.** *Baileya multira-diata, Gaillardia pul-chella,* geraniums, *Justicia californica, Penstemon eatonii, Salvia coccinea, Tagetes lemmonii.*

■ **Succulents.** *Aloe chabaudii, A. saponaria, Opuntia ficus-indica, O. violacea* 'Santa Rita'.

CHARLES MANN

Desert marigold (*Baileya multiradiata*) and *Verbena pulchella gracilior* thrive under a gnarly old ironwood tree that was transplanted into the garden. At left is *Gaillardia aristata.*

The "wild," wonderful, and robust rugosas

They stand up to wind and cold. But still these tough roses bear colorful flowers (many of them fragrant) and bright hips

I F YOU GARDEN ALONG THE COAST, where plants—like tough old sea dogs—must constantly battle salt spray and wind, or if you live where winter temperatures regularly plummet below zero, you may already be familiar with rugosa roses. But to many gardeners, this hardy clan is still somewhat mysterious.

Rugosa roses are not as refined or flamboyant as their better-known rose relatives; like country cousins, they usually take a back seat to the glitz and glamour of the hybrid teas. But if you ask fans of rugosa roses to explain why they grow them, be prepared to hang around awhile as they tick off the reasons.

John Clements, co-owner of Heirloom Old Garden Roses in St. Paul, Oregon, has the largest collection of rugosas in the country (well over 50). He declares them "magnificent." While many have a wild-rose look unsuitable for a formal rose garden, they shine as landscape shrubs and hedges. All rugosas have dark green, glossy leaves that are highly resistant to disease and indifferent to salt and wind; classic rugose foliage is wrinkled or deeply veined. The best of the rugosas are repeat bloomers. And late spring through fall, most plants produce highly decorative bright orange or red rose hips, some as large as crabapples (hips don't inhibit flowering on rugosas as they do on other roses). These hips are extremely high in vitamin C, and they make good jam and syrup.

Christine Hart, greenhouse manager at Heirloom Old Garden Roses, says, "Fragrance is important in my book when growing roses, and many of the rugosas have a wonderfully spicy fragrance."

Are rugosas for everyone? Most rugosas don't hold up well as cut flowers. Also many of the older varieties and species are vigorous growers, and can sprawl 6 feet or more. So if you have a small garden, you may want to shy away from them. (But some of the new hybrids, such as the Pavement Series from Europe, are only 2½ to 3 feet tall.)

According to reports from Southern California, many rugosas don't perform well there, possibly because of the warmer climate and alkaline soils and water. But hybridizer Ralph Moore of Visalia has developed two outstanding hybrids—'Linda Campbell' (6 feet tall by at least 8 feet wide with red flowers) and 'Topaz Jewel' (5 feet by 5 feet, yellow flowers)—that thrive and bloom profusely there, although 'Linda Campbell' can mildew right on the coast. Two other favorites of Moore's that also do well in Southern California are 'Belle Poitevine' (soft pink flowers) and 'Rugosa Magnifica' (purplish red flowers).

A RUGOSA FOR EVERY GARDEN

The rugosa clan consists of three general groups. First are the species with the classic wrinkled foliage, recurrent single blooms, vigorous growth, hardiness, and beautiful hips. Several varieties spread by underground runners, though they're easy to dig up or pull. *Rosa rugosa, R. r.* 'Alba', *R. r.* 'Rubra', and 'Scabrosa' (a selected seedling) are most commonly available.

Then there are the mixed-heritage rugosas that have most or all of the rugosa characteristics. Typical examples are 'Corylus' and the Pavement Series ('Pirette', 'Purple', 'Snow Owl').

The last category of rugosas comprises hybrids that may be missing typical rugosa characteristics, particularly the rugose foliage (or they may have just a hint of it) and possibly extreme hardiness. Examples are 'Pink Robusta', 'Rugelda', and 'Topaz Jewel'.

All of these rugosas make good gar-

THE MOST BEAUTIFUL *of all roses according to some fans, 'Pink Robusta' bears semidouble flowers.*

MICHAEL THOMPSON

ROSA RUGOSA *blooms continually in Janet Byers's garden in Aptos, California; hips the size of cherry tomatoes develop after blooms fade.*

den plants. Which you choose to grow depends on the look you want, your climate, and where you plan to place them.

HOW TO GROW RUGOSAS

Rugosas prefer full sun and moderate water, but the species can take a bit more drought than can the hybrids. Janet Byers of Aptos, California, waters her species rugosa (shown at left) once every two weeks except in late summer when the temperature is in the 90s; then she waters twice a week. Rugosas also like well-drained soil.

Rugosas absolutely do not like to be sprayed with chemicals, including dormant oil and soap sprays (spraying will discolor or defoliate them). Fortunately, they generally don't need it, but sometimes spider mites attack them. Your best bet is to just rinse off the lower and upper leaf surfaces with blasts of water from the hose. Also, don't fertilize plants heavily; it promotes rank growth.

WHERE TO BUY PLANTS

Many mail-order suppliers sell rugosas. For a large selection, write to Heirloom Old Garden Roses, 24062 N.E. Riverside Dr., St. Paul, OR 97137; (503) 538-1576. Catalog is $5. ∎

By Lauren Bonar Swezey

A DOZEN OF THE BEST

Clements, who has been growing and testing roses for 35 years and rugosas for 10, has some definite favorites; these are his top 12.

'Basye's Purple Rose'. Bushy, upright plant with gray-green foliage; fragrant, velvety, deep purple blooms with stamens edged in gold. Grows 4 to 6 feet tall by 4 feet wide. "The blooms are magnificent."

'Charles Albanel'. Spreading plant with bright green foliage; semidouble medium-red flowers have strong fragrance. Grows 4 feet by 4 feet. "Superb rose."

'Corylus'. Shiny, bright green, rugose leaves; fragrant silvery-pink blooms; bright orange hips. Grows 4 to 5 feet by 4 to 6 feet. "Beautiful landscape plant even without blooms."

'Delicata'. Compact, bushy plant with rugose foliage; extremely fragrant semidouble lilac flowers with creamy yellow stamens. Grows 3 feet by 3 feet. "Very hardy, even in Montana."

'Pink Robusta'. Magnificent glossy, disease-resistant foliage; semidouble pink flowers good for cutting; always in bloom. Grows 7 feet by 7 feet (prune to keep lower). "In the top 10 to 20 of all roses in existence."

'Purple Pavement'. Rugose foliage on rounded shrub; fragrant semidouble crimson-purple flowers with gold stamens. Grows 3 feet by 3 feet. "I counted 47 buds and blooms on one plant."

R. rugosa. Original species from Japan; vigorous plant with thick, prickly stems and classic rugose foliage; very fragrant reddish purple flowers followed by huge hips. Grows as tall as 7 feet by 7 feet.

R. r. 'Alba'. Similar to species but with very fragrant pure white flowers and gold stamens; huge hips. Grows 6 feet by 6 feet.

'Rose à Parfum d l'Haÿ'. Vigorous, bushy plant without the rugose foliage; large, fully double cherry red flowers (no hips). Grows 5 feet by 5 feet. "Outstanding fragrance."

'Scabrosa'. Very fragrant 5-inch-wide single crimson blooms; handsome specimen plant; huge hips that birds love. Grows 6 feet by 4 feet. "My favorite of all true rugosas."

'Snow Owl' (Pavement Series). Compact plant with rugose foliage; white blooms tinted with lilac. Grows 3 feet by 3 feet.

'Thérèse Bugnet'. Upright growth with a hint of rugose foliage; fragrant old-fashioned-looking, ruffled double lilac-pink flowers. Grows 5 to 6 feet by 4 feet. "Hardiest rose in the world. Top rugosa for cut flowers."

Clements also suggests a few rugosas to avoid: 'Conrad Ferdinand Meyer' ("It's a rust bucket in my garden") and the Grootendorsts—'F. J. Grootendorst' and 'Pink Grootendorst' ("The flower is unusual, but the plants are rangy and prone to disease").

BEAUTIFUL BLOOMERS: *Oncidium ornithorhynchum (left) and two dendrobium hybrids.*

Hardy exotics

Five orchids (besides cymbidiums) take to life outdoors near the California coast

I F YOU CAN GROW CYMBIDIUMS outdoors in your climate, you can grow a variety of other orchids just as easily," says Lauris Rose, proprietor of Cal-Orchid, Inc., in Santa Barbara. "I call them cymbidium companions."

Five other orchids thrive in about the same conditions as cymbidiums. They come in a wide range of shapes and sizes, from *Oncidium ornithorhynchum,* which produces dozens of ½- to 1-inch-wide, deep lilac flowers on 16-inch spikes, to reed-stemmed epidendrums, which can grow as tall as 4 feet. Only *Laelia anceps* can match cymbidiums in bloom size, but the show from a large clump of dendrobiums can be just as dramatic. All five bloom from fall to early spring.

The right climate for growing these orchids includes a large portion of coastal California from the San Francisco Bay Area south to San Diego.

Elsewhere, grow them outdoors spring through fall, then bring them indoors when the weather turns cold.

FIVE ORCHIDS TO GROW OUTDOORS

Dendrobium hybrids. Stems of 1½- to 2-inch-wide starlike flowers appear from tips of 8- to 15-inch-tall canes with stiff leaves. Flower colors include yellow, pale yellow with red spots, white, white with red spots, white with purple margins, and lavender. Many hybrids have a sweet floral perfume. Cost: $15 to $20 for a 4-inch pot.

Laelias. Laelia anceps produces lavender or white 3- to 4-inch-wide flowers in groups of two to four on 2- to 3-foot-long spikes. The newest introductions from tissue culture have bigger flowers; they're very pricey ($500 or more apiece), but the cost should come down as supplies increase. Most other varieties cost $15 to $40 each; they're sold in 4-inch pots or on bark mounts and can be grown on a tree (attach the pseudobulbs firmly to the tree's bark with staples, or tie them on with fishline). *Laelia purpurata* has 5- to 6-inch-wide flowers and handles heat and cold better than *L. anceps*. It costs $35 for a blooming-size plant.

Oncidiums. These include *O. incurvum, O. leucochilum, O. ornithorhynchum,* and their hybrids, such as Sharry Baby. Lavender flowers grow on spikes 1- to 1½-feet long. All types are sweetly fragrant, like potpourri. Cost: $15 to $25 for a 4-inch pot.

Reed-stemmed epidendrums. Succulent leaves grow horizontally and alternately on canes. Orange, red, or purple 1-inch-wide flowers appear in clusters on stems that continue to elongate and produce flowers over a long period. Plantlets appear along the stem; to grow new plants, snap them off when roots are 2 to 3 inches long. Plants are often grown directly in the ground. Cost: $10 to $15 for a 4-inch pot.

Zygopetalums. Tall flower spikes are covered with 2- to 3-inch-wide flowers, each with green petals striped or spotted with chocolate (solid chocolate in some selections) and a white lip heavily marked with purple. Spicy-sweet fragrance can perfume a room. Cost: $15 to $35 for a 4-inch pot.

HOW TO GROW THESE ORCHIDS

Give plants the same growing conditions as cymbidiums—filtered or

Zygopetalum

Laelia anceps

Reed-stemmed epidendrum

dappled light but no midday sun, and regular water (evenly moist but not wet). Laelias can handle slightly brighter light and less water.

Fertilize with a half-strength solution of a balanced fertilizer such as 20-10-20 every two weeks or so.

Most plants handle cold down to about 28°. If colder weather is predicted, move plants into a protected area. Laelias are hardy to about 26°.

WHERE TO BUY PLANTS

Cal-Orchid, Inc., 1251 Orchid Dr., Santa Barbara 93111; (805) 967-1312.

Santa Barbara Orchid Estate, 1250 Orchid Dr., Santa Barbara 93111; (800) 553-3387.

Stewart Orchids, Box 550, Carpinteria, CA 93014; (805) 684-5448. ∎

By Lauren Bonar Swezey

Four fabulous shrubs

They're tailor-made for Southern California gardens: tough, unthirsty, and good-looking. And they bloom in winter

THE "FAB FOUR" IS CRISTIN Fusano's description of coleonema, erica, leptospermum, and westringia. "Romantic" is Pasadena landscape architect Denis Kurutz's word for them.

What makes these shrubs fabulous?

"They're all winter-blooming and sun-loving," says Fusano, general manager of

Roger's Gardens in Corona del Mar, "and that combination makes them extremely useful." Although azaleas and camellias are Southern California's traditional winter shrubs, they need shade to be at their best. For sunny gardens, sun-lovers like the Fab Four provide more reliable winter color.

They're also easier to care for than camellias and azaleas. They need less water, less fertilizer, and slightly less fussing. "For hardly any effort, they give you lots of winter color," Fusano says. "What more could you ask?"

A bit of romance, perhaps? Well, these four deliver here, too. Their open, graceful growth habits make them excellent shrubs for today's less formal, more nat-ural landscaping. They grow into billowy clouds of fine-textured foliage. "But it's their ability to catch the wind that is most appealing," says Kurutz. "That's what makes them romantic."

Practicality plus romance in one package *is* pretty fabulous. But as you'll see on the next page, there's a lot more to the Fab Four.

Erica canaliculata 'Rosea'

This tall (6 to 10 feet) South African shrub is the showiest of the lot. From late fall through early spring, its dark green needle-like foliage is nearly obscured by small, cup-shaped rose-pink flowers; the best bloom occurs during the coldest part of the year. Set out plants singly, or in groups of three or more to create a gorgeous hedge. Or train into a small (8- to 12-foot) tree.

'Rosea', like all ericas, likes loose, well-draining soil, so work in lots of compost. Water deeply but infrequently during summer once established.

Westringia 'Wynyabbie Gem'

Big and billowy best describes the character of this 4- to 6-foot-tall shrub with gray-green leaves. It's rarely without flowers, but its small light mauve blooms are most profuse and intense in cold weather. "A great addition to a gray garden," says Fusano. Give it plenty of room to grow because "shearing destroys its character." For contrast, pair it with a denser-foliaged plant like pittosporum.

'Wynyabbie Gem' endures clay soil and coastal winds. Though drought-tolerant once established, this plant can tolerate regular summer irrigation.

Leptospermum scoparium (New Zealand tea tree)

This shrub is a bit like Heathcliff, the character in *Wuthering Heights*. All varieties are unparalleled at lending a dark, brooding, romantic quality to the landscape. But, like Heathcliff, they're a trifle sensitive and demand some special treatment.

A New Zealand tea tree can be as showy as an erica; it bears along its stems many single or double flowers in shades of red, pink, or white, depending on variety, off and on throughout the year. Peak bloom often occurs in winter. But if neglected, it can look like a column of dead brown twigs. Proper irrigation makes the difference. *Leptospermum scoparium* doesn't wilt to warn you when it's thirsty. If allowed to dry out, it may not recover. It needs regular water until it's established, then infrequent but deep watering. Plants are susceptible to chlorosis due to iron deficiency. If leaves turn beige-pink, feed the plant with chelated iron according to package instructions.

Although the plant needs a bit of attention during its formative years, it's worth the effort. With age, it becomes as low-maintenance as the rest of these shrubs.

"An old 'Ruby Glow' about 12 feet tall and just as wide that has been trained into a multitrunked tree is a spectacular sight," says Kurutz. In fact, he says, there's just one word to describe it: romantic.

Coleonema pulchrum (Pink breath of heaven)

Though its branches and foliage are so lightweight that the plant shivers in the slightest breeze, its delicacy is a ruse. This South African native is one tough shrub. It needs little or no supplemental water once established, and only a yearly feeding, if that. But it requires good drainage. Slopes or hillsides are ideal. In other locations, lighten the soil with compost.

Coleonema pulchrum, also sold as pink disoma, has soft-textured, bright green foliage and a profusion of small pink flowers from winter through spring. It usually tops out at about 6 feet. To keep it shapely, prune it back by half after bloom is through. A white form is another option but is not considered as graceful. A compact form that reaches 3 feet tall is another option. All varieties are good along paths, where you can break off a twig to enjoy the foliage's lavender-licorice fragrance.

CARE AND MAINTENANCE OF THE FABULOUS FOUR

To keep water from collecting around the trunk, which can lead to fungal root rot, set any of these shrubs slightly (½ to 1 inch) higher than the surrounding soil. These plants need a light feeding annually at most. ∎

By Sharon Cohoon

A guide to natural soil enrichers

How to choose and use organic materials

TROWELS HOLD *six amendments; from left are municipal compost, peat moss, mushroom compost, worm castings, bat guano, and chicken manure.*

DECIDING WHICH natural soil amendment to use can seem like a mystery, especially when you're facing the stacks of bagged materials sold at nurseries and garden centers. Most natural amendments improve the soil's texture and ability to retain moisture. Many of them make good mulches. And some have good nutritional value, although they may contain widely varying amounts of the three essential nutrients: nitrogen (N), phosphorus (P), and potassium (K).

(By "natural" or "organic" soil amendments, we mean ones derived from living or once-living organisms, be they cows or worms, trees or other plants.)

Commercially packaged soil amendments come from a number of sources, including the agricultural industry. Some cities collect and compost yard waste, then package it for retail sale or let residents pick it up free in bulk.

READ THE LABELS

Some manufacturers list the materials' nutritive values on the package label; others do not. If the label describes the material as "ground," "screened," or "aged," you know you're getting something that wasn't just scraped off the barn floor and put in a bag. As Don Knipp of Bandini Fertilizer Company puts it, "Grinding gives it a uniform texture. Screening sifts out all the rocks and big chunks. Aging lets the organic material to break down so that it doesn't rob the soil of nitrogen as it decomposes and the animal urines have time to leach out."

One way to avoid using a manure that's too strong, or "hot," is to sniff the stuff. If the material has a strong smell of ammonia, let it sit in a pile for six weeks, turning it periodically, before you spread it on beds.

MANURES

Cattle manure (from steers and dairy cows) may contain as much as 1 or 2 percent nitrogen, 0.3 to 0.5 percent phosphorus, and 0.5 to 1 percent potassium. Dairy cow manure tends to have fewer salts than steer manure does. Well-aged manure is a good amendment for vegetables, annuals, and perennials.

Chicken manure is a rich, fertile amendment with nutrient values that can run up to 3 percent nitrogen, 4 percent phosphorus, and 3 percent potassium. It can be strong smelling. It can also burn plants, so don't use it on sensitive or shallow-rooted plants. If used properly, it gets annuals and vegetables off to a fast start. To avoid burning plants, spread it no more than 1 inch thick, and till it as deep as you can.

Guano and exotic droppings include bat guano, which typically has an N-P-K rating of 10-3-1, the highest nitrogen content of the amendments we list. Because of its potency, guano is the most likely to burn plants. Use it sparingly as a top-dressing.

Some zoos collect and package manure from various animals. Elephant manure is most commonly sold; the huge vegetarians produce a gentle substance that is on par with cow manure.

CONDITIONERS

Municipal compost is often made from grass clippings, leaves, and tree prunings gathered and composted by municipal agencies, then given free to residents or sold in packages or bulk quantities. Compost improves soil texture and water retention as it slowly releases nutrients. Nutritional values vary: Seattle-based Cedar Grove Composting, for example, rates its compost at 1.3 to 1.5 percent nitrogen, 0.15 to 0.22 percent phosphorus, and 0.44 to 0.60 percent potassium.

Mushroom compost, a byproduct of commercial mushroom farming, is low in nitrogen and phosphorus but quite high in potassium. This alkaline amendment works best in areas where it helps balance acid soils. It makes a fine top-dressing for roses.

Peat and sphagnum moss are great for holding moisture in the soil and loosening up dense soils. Peat moss increases soil acidity, so it's the amendment of choice for azaleas, rhododendrons, and other plants that thrive in acid soil. The moss is difficult to get wet initially. Suppliers suggest that you lay the plastic bag it comes in on its side, make a small slit in the plastic, insert a hose, and let it drip into the bag for a day or so before you dig the peat moss into the soil. Most peat moss comes from Canada, and there is some controversy concerning the depletion of this natural resource.

Redwood soil conditioner, made from the bark and sawdust of redwood trees and treated with nitrogen and iron, is a mainstay in California for loosening up hardpan soil. It decomposes slowly.

Worm castings are available packaged (although you can produce them at home with a vermicomposter). Their nutritive value is low, but castings aerate the soil and improve its ability to retain and release nutrients.

Rice hulls and other agricultural byproducts may be available in areas where crops are grown. All are worthy amendments, provided they are well aged and don't have heavy concentrations of animal urines.

USING THE AMENDMENTS

Fall through late winter is a good time to dig or till organic amendments into your planting beds. Work amendments into the soil to a depth of at least 1 foot. In sandy soil, they can help bind the loose particles together and increase water retention. They can break up the heavy texture of clay soil and allow better root penetration.

You can also spread a top-dressing of 1 to 2 inches of amendment over established beds and just let it sit. When spring arrives, plants will grow up through the mulch.■

By Steven R. Lorton

Sword ferns and Douglas iris in shades of cream and lavender fill this Southern California ravine designed by Carole McElwee, shown with Aussie. For details, see page 34.

FEBRUARY

Garden guide 32

Checklists & garden notebooks 37

Blooming branches for indoors 42

Conifers that won't outgrow you . . . 44

Camellias for a longer show 47

The juicy-crunch pears 48

GARDEN
Guide

A tropical paradise for indoor plants

It may be cold, gray, rainy, or snowy outside, but some lucky gardeners can pretend that winter doesn't exist by stepping into their greenhouses. The conservatory shown here belongs to George Little and David Lewis of Bainbridge Island, Washington. While it represents indoor gardening on a grand scale, their achievement can provide ideas for much smaller spaces.

In the middle of their custom-built conservatory, Little and Lewis dug a 9- by 16- by 2-foot pool sealed with a rubber pool liner. In the pond, a number of plants—including tropical water lilies and several species of tropical thalia—grow in containers, along with floating plants such as water hyacinths. Around the room are pots of angel's trumpet (*Brugmansia*), bougainvillea, ferns, orchids, and passion vine.

A thermostatically controlled propane space heater maintains the air temperature at 65° during the day and 55° at night. Goldfish in the pond keep the water clean and free of insects.

If you don't have space for a greenhouse, try growing water plants in pots set in a south- or west-facing window. It's easiest to grow these plants in plastic nursery cans set into larger ceramic pots that are filled with water.

Jungle-lush plants thrive in and around a conservatory pool.

FEBRUARY '96

- Chocolate-scented orchid
- Hazelnut hybrids for cold climates
- New seed catalog from a grand old firm
- Bite-size peppers with big-time flavor
- A spray tank that pumps up with a hose

JAMES FREDERICK HOUSEL

GIFT IDEA

A no-calorie chocolate for Valentine's Day

Oncidium Sharry Baby 'Sweet Fragrance' smells just like a box of freshly opened chocolates. But it doesn't contain a single gram of fat—finally, a "chocolate" that won't ruin your waistline. No wonder this orchid's a hit.

'Sweet Fragrance' first gained attention in 1989, when it won the Award of Merit from the American Orchid Society. But until recently, there weren't enough plants around to reach the general public. Now this oncidium is widely available at prices comparable to those of cymbidiums. Four- to 5-inch pots cost $25 to $35, depending on the number of flower spikes. Blooms last two to three months.

This orchid is easy to grow as a house plant. Place it where it will get a few hours of direct morning sunlight or medium to bright filtered light. Water once a week, and feed once a month with a water-soluble fertilizer. When danger of frost is clearly past, you can move the plant outdoors into filtered sunlight to spend the summer.

CLAIRE CURRAN

A flower spike of Sharry Baby 'Sweet Fragrance' orchid can reach 36 to 48 inches tall.

PLANTING OPPORTUNITIES

Hazelnut hybrids for cold country

At their commercial best in the valleys between the Cascades and the Pacific, standard hazelnuts have a hard time surviving in cold-winter parts of the West (*Sunset Western Garden Book* climate zones 1, 2, and 3). However, two promising new hybrids, called filazels and trazels, may make cold-climate hazelnuts possible. Both can

survive to -25°. One is a shrub; the other is a tree.

Filazels combine genes of the West's wild native filbert (*Corylus cornuta*) with those of a standard hazelnut (*C. avellana*). The result is a shrubby, drought-tolerant, early-maturing hybrid.

Trazels have one Turkish hazelnut (*C. colurna*) parent and one *C. avellana* parent. The hybrid offspring grow into drought-tolerant trees that also mature early.

For pollination, both filazels and trazels have to be planted in pairs (two filazel seedlings or two

trazel seedlings). Or you can mix one filazel with one *C. cornuta* or one trazel with one *C. colurna*.

Because this breeding is still in its infancy (and because all the hybrids are seedlings, not clones), the size and quantity of nuts are variable.

You can order filazels and trazels from Bear Creek Nursery, Box 4114, Northport, WA 99157, (509) 732-6219, catalog $1; and Raintree Nursery, 391 Butts Rd., Morton, WA 98356, (360) 496-6400, catalog free.

Dwarfing root-stocks for sweet cherries

Sweet cherries normally grow on large trees (to 30 feet), making the fruit difficult to protect from birds and the trees difficult to squeeze into a city garden (especially if you need a second tree as a pollenizer). That's why news of a new dwarf cherry rootstock that keeps trees at 12 to 15 feet sounds so good. But is it?

The rootstock, called Gisela (or Giessen, for its German city of origin), actually isn't just one rootstock; it comes in several numbered forms. Greg Lang at Washington State University's Prosser research center, where Gisela rootstocks have been grown since 1987, considers one of them—Gisela 5 (Giessen 148-2)—a "promising dwarfing rootstock." Trees grown on it reach 10 to 12 feet, start producing in two or three years, and set lots of fruit.

But Lang and his colleagues have recently discovered that several other Gisela rootstocks are hypersensitive to pollen-borne viruses. And one of these, Gisela 1 (GI 172-9), is still available to home gardeners.

Lang thinks that a cherry on Gisela 5 rootstock (which hasn't shown sensitivity to viruses) would be better in the home garden. Nurseryman Josef Biringer of Mount Vernon, Washington, recommends Gisela 7 (GI 148-8) but also Gisela 1 (if you don't live near an orchard where virus is a problem), for its productiveness and small size (trees grow 6 to 8 feet tall).

Tree availability is limited. You should be able to get Gisela 7 this year from Raintree Nursery; (360) 496-6400. Gisela 5 will be available during the 1996–97 season.

Wild arugula: The zesty, lemony green

Italian wild rustic arugula is to cultivated arugula as Cabernet Sauvignon is to beaujolais. All four are palate pleasers. But the wild arugula and the Cabernet have deeper, more complex flavors than their counterparts. Use rustic arugula like regular arugula to jazz up green salads. Or mince it finely, as the Italians do, and sprinkle it over hearty pasta

Perennial arugula thrives in a wide patio container.

dishes, pizza, or focaccia.

Regular arugula is an annual, and a short-lived one at that. (The English call it rocket salad, presumably for the speed with which it sprouts, then sets seed.) But *Arugula selvatica,* its wild parent, is a perennial and develops at a more leisurely pace. Treat it as an herb if you like, pinching back leaves and flowers regularly to promote fresh growth. In areas subject to hard freezes, enjoy the plants until frost, then reseed the next spring.

Arugula selvatica seeds are available from Shepherd's Garden Seeds. Call (408) 335-6910.

This coastal ravine is a haven for native plants

Where others saw a problem, Wally Moore saw an opportunity. Rather than filling in the ravine that bisected his San Juan Capistrano, California, property to make his yard level, Moore decided to treat the natural drainage pattern as a landscaping feature.

"The ravine that scared everyone away from this lot is just what attracted me to it," he says. "I immediately pictured a bridge across it and sycamores around it. I'd always wanted sycamore trees, and thought they'd look at home here."

After the sycamores, though, Moore got stuck. Various landscape architects drew up plans for the ravine, but none of the plans satisfied him. "They all looked like landscaping," he says. "I wanted something that looked more like nature."

Finally, Moore met a kindred spirit, garden designer Carole McElwee, who understood his vision. First she visited Santa Barbara Botanic Garden and Strybing Arboretum and Botanical Gardens in San Francisco to see their manmade dry creek beds. And then, as is her style, she plunged in.

"I planted every shade-tolerant native I could think of," says McElwee. "Coral bells, carpenteria, meadow rue, ribes, hummingbird sage, and sword fern (*Polystichum munitum*)."

The results, shown on page 30, exceeded Moore's dreams. "I love the ravine now," he says.

Tune-up time for ornamental grass

Perennial ornamental grasses have become familiar sights in Western gardens during the last 5 to 10 years. Their graceful forms and wide range of textures and colors provide handsome foils to shrubs and perennials.

They require very little maintenance, but they do benefit from an annual cleanup each winter. What is needed depends on the type of grass.

Most grasses fit into two basic groups: warm-season (winter-dormant) and cool-season (evergreen). But grasses can perform differently depending on the climate (in cold climates, an evergreen grass may freeze to the ground each year).

Warm-season grasses include arundo, miscanthus (most), molinia, panicum, and pennisetum. They grow from spring through summer, flower in fall, then go dormant. Even though plants turn brown in fall as they go dormant, they remain attractive through winter. The best time to cut them back is just before new growth emerges (starting in early spring, check plants periodically for new growth, since weather can affect emergence time). Using pruning shears, cut them down to within a few inches of the ground. Try not to cut new shoots, but if you nip a few, you won't hurt the plant.

Cool-season grasses include carex, deschampsia, elymus, festuca, *Helictotrichon sempervirens,* and sesleria. They begin new growth in fall, bloom in early spring (sometimes winter), and are usually evergreen (some are semi-evergreen). These grasses don't need cutting back every year; cut them back to two-thirds of their size only when they start looking ragged. Clean up plants by removing any dead foliage (you can run your fingers through fine-bladed grasses like carex to comb out old growth). Divide plants every few years when they die back from the center; discard dead sections. Elymus can be sheared back twice (late winter and early fall) to encourage new foliage.

NEW PLANT REPORT

A reliable new strawberry

June-bearing strawberries produce bigger, more flavorful fruits than ever-bearing kinds do. Now a new June bearer called 'Puget Reliance' produces large, juicy fruit comparable to those of the old 'Hood'.

'Puget Reliance', developed by Washington State University, yields heavy crops, and since the tart berries come all at once, they're perfect for preserves or freezing.

This berry has excellent resistance to virus, so it should perform well for years in home gardens. Because this plant is so new, its cold tolerance is not yet well known. It is being grown east of the Cascades, but the planting site at Prosser hasn't yet had a winter severe enough to test the plant's hardiness.

Look for bare-root plants of 'Puget Reliance' at nurseries this winter and spring.

Thousands of yellow daffodils glow under the blooming branches of old apricot trees in Saratoga, California.

Daffodils run wild in a Bay Area garden

Daffodil Hill in the foothills of the Sierra is famous for its dramatic display of daffodils every year. But you don't have to live in a chilly-winter climate to get an annual show that rivals the best of them.

The wild-looking planting pictured below dates back eight years ago when the Bird family bought the daffodil bulbs, a naturalizing mix, by the bushel from Van Bourgondien Bros.; (800) 622-9997. The five members of the Bird family spent about two months planting more than 6,000 daffodil bulbs, one by one, in an old apricot orchard on their Saratoga, California, property. After planting, they watered the bulbs to get them started. It was a lot of work to begin with, but it was well worth it.

A few years later, the Zemke family bought the property, and the daffodil show has continued to grow. It's particularly impressive when the trees and bulbs are in peak bloom at the same time, as they were last year (bloom times vary due to weather conditions).

Every two years or so in late spring (just when the foliage dies to the ground), the Zemkes divide the bulbs and replant them in the open spaces on the hill. Julia Zemke says that other than dividing, the daffodils require no work.

To start a show like this, plant bulbs as soon as they become available in fall.

Veteran seed grower resumes catalog sales

Though gardeners have been growing Ferry-Morse seeds for 140 years, they've had to buy them off seed racks since the company dropped its mail-order catalog during the 1960s. But now the catalog is back, offering a full line of vegetables, flowers, summer-flowering bulbs, and perennial roots.

As is true of most seed catalogs, Ferry-Morse's offers a wider selection of seeds, including a number of high-performing hybrids, than you'll find on seed racks. For a free copy, call Ferry-Morse Seeds at (800) 283-3400.

NORMAN A. PLATE

Minipeppers are big in flavor

'**B**ig Bertha', stand aside. Here come the minipeppers. You won't find any big, chunky peppers in this group. These diminutive jewels—called 'Cherrytime', 'Jingle Bells', and 'Little Dipper'—grow only 1½ to 2 inches long and wide.

They may be small in stature, but they're big in flavor, particularly when red-ripe and sweet. The peppers mature as much as three weeks earlier than a standard-size variety like 'California Wonder'. Plants of these varieties are also very productive.

'Cherrytime' sweet pepper is only 1½ to 2 inches wide.

Minipeppers are perfect in dips and salads, on shish kebabs, and stuffed as hors d'oeuvres. Harvest some to serve green, and let others mature to shiny red.

Sow seeds in flats. To hasten seed germination, use bottom heat (try setting flats on a water heater). After germination, make sure young seedlings get plenty of light so they don't get leggy. Before planting the seedlings, gradually acclimate them to ever-brighter sunlight over a week, then plant them in full sun.

Order seeds from one of these sources: Johnny's Selected Seeds, Foss Hill Rd., Albion, ME 04910; (207) 437-4301 (sells 'Cherrytime'). Nichols Garden Nursery, 1190 N. Pacific Highway, Albany, OR 97321; (503) 928-9280 (sells 'Jingle Bells'). W. Atlee Burpee & Co., Warminster, PA 18974; (800) 888-1447 (sells 'Little Dipper').

A spray tank that cuts pumping

Pump-up tank sprayers make dormant spraying easy, except that you have to pump them all the time. Now a new kind of sprayer uses water from the garden hose to pressurize the air.

The spray tank looks unremarkable except for a quick-coupler valve that fits into its top. You pour undiluted chemical into the 2-gallon polyethylene tank, thread in the hand pump, snap on the garden hose, then add water. As water fills the tank, it compresses the air inside. The one-way valve prevents chemicals from flowing back into the hose.

The Pumpless Sprayer, made by H. D. Hudson Manufacturing Co., comes with a spray wand. It's sold at garden centers and hardware stores. Cost is about $40.

A drive-in nursery

You might feel like a kid in a candy store when you visit a well-stocked nursery—especially if you're about to tackle a big landscaping project and need lots of plants. But when it comes time to lug your discoveries back to the checkout stand, you can feel more like a slave hauling stones to build pyramids.

Drive-in nurseries let you do the kid part without the slave part by opening nursery roads to cars.

One such nursery is Evergreen Nursery in Del Mar, California. Stop at the main entrance to pick up a map and price sheet, then drive down miles of nursery roads, stopping at plant groups that interest you, be they pines, tropicals, palms, or hibiscus. Search for the ones you want, load the containers into your car, then drive back to the cashier to pay.

Plants are priced by container size. If you need help making selections, stop at an information kiosk.

Evergreen Nursery is at 7150 Black Mountain Road in Del Mar. Exit Interstate 5 at Del Mar Heights Road, and drive east about a mile. Turn left on Lansdale Drive, which becomes Black Mountain Road, and drive 3¼ miles to the nursery. Call (619) 481-0622 for directions to the other Evergreen drive-in nursery, in Spring Valley, east of San Diego.

The rose you grow for its thorns

What first attracts your attention to this rose is neither its pretty, cream-colored single flowers nor its rather ferny foliage. What makes *Rosa sericea pteracantha* stand out in the landscape is the translucent crimson thorns that line each cane like teeth on a giant ripsaw.

This deciduous shrub rose grows in *Sunset Western Garden Book* climate zones 4 through 22. The plant's habit is generally upright, with arching canes reaching 6 to 9 feet. The thorns can be as wide as an inch at the base and half as tall.

This rose is made to be

Winglike thorns of *Rosa sericea pteracantha* demand attention.

pruned, since only the young thorns are crimson. After the first year, thorns turn gray and woody. That's when you prune back older stems to produce new growth.

This thorny conversation piece is sold as a container-ized plant by Forest Farm, 990 Tetherow Rd., Williams, OR 97544; (503) 846-7269. Cost is $8 per plant, plus shipping.

*By Steven R. Lorton,
Jim McCausland,
Lauren Bonar Swezey*

PLANTING

☐ **PEAS.** In zones 4–7, peas can be planted outside this month. To give them a head start, first soak the seeds overnight in warm water. Then, place the seeds between layers of paper towel on a cookie sheet and set them aside in a warm place. Once the seeds have sprouted, plant them in the ground.

☐ **PRIMROSES.** Blooming plants in 4-inch pots will be everywhere this month. They're great for valentine gifts. Pop them into decorative pots and baskets. Keep them well watered: one good way is to set the plastic pots in a sink or dishpan full of water and let them soak for several hours or overnight. Pick off blooms as they fade. Give plants a complete liquid plant food (12-12-12 is a good choice) diluted to half-strength to encourage a second and third crop of flowers. When flowering ceases, set out plants in the ground in a shady spot.

☐ **ORDER PLANTS, SEEDS.** Spring planting time isn't far away. Order seeds and plants now to ensure that the supplier won't be sold out. Most companies take credit cards and have toll-free numbers, making ordering very easy. Make a list of the plants you order, and determine where they'll go in the

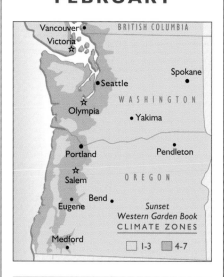

garden. That way, when the plants arrive you won't be wondering where you're going to put them.

MAINTENANCE

☐ **FEED HOUSE PLANTS.** Fertilize ones that are blooming, fruiting, or showing signs of growth (feed others between April and the end of October). With short days and low winter light, plants don't need much—it's best to mix a liquid plant food to half-strength.

☐ **PRUNE ROSES.** In zones 4–7, around midmonth is the time to prune hybrid tea roses. Remove injured or dead canes, then cut remaining canes back to one third to one half their length. Finally, shape plants so that canes stretch up and out in a vase shape. In zones 1–3, delay pruning until early April.

☐ **CHECK STORED BULBS.** Inspect bulbs that you've stored for winter. If any show signs of rot, toss them out. If any are shriveled, sprinkle a bit of water on them to plump them up.

PEST AND WEED CONTROL

☐ **BAIT FOR SLUGS.** The war never ends. You can reduce the future population by getting slugs now so they won't be around to reproduce. Broadcast bait liberally around the garden. Don't miss slugs' hiding places: near rocks, along house foundations, and under decking. Be careful to keep pets and children away from bait.

☐ **WEED.** Get weeds out now so they won't compete with desirable plants by gobbling up soil nutrients. Add the weeds you pluck to the compost pile, except for deadly nightshade, morning glory, and thistle; throw them in the trash instead.

Bare-root season is a magical time for me. When I pull those ugly roots from the sawdust of nursery bins, and later as I plant them in my garden, I wonder how these lifeless-looking roots can possibly grow into beautiful trees and vines, much less bear delicious fruit. But I've learned to harness the natural magic of dormant deciduous plants. In the orchard of my country garden in Washington's Skagit Valley, every one of the 14 fruit trees was grown from bare roots that I put into the ground on a cold, wet February day. There they sat for two months, then *pop!* They leafed out and started growing up. This year, those trees are almost twice as tall as I am, and they've begun bearing crops of apples, apricots, cherries, peaches, and pears.

I'm a bare-root convert. If you're still a skeptic, just try one bare-root plant this winter. I'll bet you one of my apples that you'll be planting more next year.

•

Spring planting isn't far off, and I've already put in my order for a dozen plants of the daylily 'Stella de Oro'. I'd always snubbed this one because it was available everywhere. Forgive me, Stella, you deserve your popularity. I tried growing one, and now I want to border a whole walkway with them. One of the smaller members of the genus *Hemerocallis*, 'Stella de Oro' forms a dense mound of grassy leaves 18 to 24 inches tall. From mid-June into late summer, golden yellow

PACIFIC NORTHWEST
Garden Notebook
BY STEVEN R. LORTON

flowers about 2½ inches across cover the plants. The flowers stay close to the foliage so you can really see the contrast of yellow blooms and green leaves.

•

I've mentioned before that I fertilize on holidays. This month, I'll celebrate Valentine's Day by tossing granular fertilizer around my garden like rice at a wedding. At this time of year, when the soil is moist and plants are just coming out of dormancy, they can handle a stronger dose of nutrients; I use a potent 20-20-20 blend. (For April Fools', Memorial Day, and the Fourth of July, I'll apply a milder 12-12-12 formulation.)

THAT'S A GOOD QUESTION

Q: I keep hearing that the timing for cutting off the old leaves of epimedium is tricky. Why?

A: This noble ground cover keeps its heart-shaped leaflets through all but the most brutally cold winters. They acquire a reddish blush in cold weather. Often, by season's end the leaves are battered, so you want them off when the new leaves arrive. More important, in early spring epimedium sends up lots of delicate little flowers on 8-inch stems in shades of red, pink, cream, yellow, or white. These would be lost in a thicket of old leaves. So cut back epimedium this month and you'll be able to enjoy the flower show in a few weeks.

CHECKLIST
FEBRUARY

Eureka

Redding

CALIFORNIA

NEVADA

Mendocino

Sacramento

Santa Rosa

San Francisco

San Jose

Fresno

Monterey

Sunset Western Garden Book
CLIMATE ZONES

☐ Mountain (1-2)
☐ Valley (7-9)
☐ Inland (14)
☐ Coastal (15-17)

PLANTING

☐ **FLOWERING PLANTS.** Zones 7–9, 14–17: Nurseries now have the best choice of container-grown early spring–blooming shrubs and vines—azalea, camellia, Carolina jessamine, daphne, flowering quince, forsythia, hardenbergia, heath, and primrose jasmine.

☐ **PLANT LILACS.** The most economical way to purchase lilacs is to buy them bare-root. Call nurseries this month to find ones that still have them in stock.

☐ **PLANT GLADIOLUS.** Zones 7–9, 14–17: For flowers from spring through fall, begin planting gladiolus this month and make successive plantings every 15 to 25 days through July.

☐ **PLANT VEGETABLES.** Zones 7–9, 14–17: Set out artichokes and asparagus, and seedlings of broccoli, cabbage, cauliflower, celery (only in zones 15–17), green onion, kohlrabi, and lettuce. From seed, plant beets, carrots, chard, lettuce, peas, and spinach. Sow seeds of eggplant, pepper, and tomato indoors; allow six to eight weeks to reach transplant size.

Zones 1, 2: To get a jump on the season, start seeds of broccoli, cabbage, and cauliflower indoors or in a greenhouse at the end of the month. When seedlings are ready to plant (in six to eight weeks), set out and drape with floating row covers.

MAINTENANCE

☐ **FERTILIZE.** Zones 7–9, 14–17: Feed fall-planted annuals and perennials, and established trees and shrubs, if they lack vigor or leaves look pale. Wait to feed azaleas, camellias, and rhododendrons until after bloom. Fertilize lawns later this month.

☐ **PRUNE TREES AND SHRUBS.** Zones 7–9, 14–17: Finish pruning deciduous fruit and ornamental trees, grapes, roses, and wisteria by midmonth. Wait to prune spring-flowering plants until after bloom. Zones 1, 2: Wait to prune until toward the end of the dormant season but before growth starts.

☐ **REPOT CYMBIDIUMS.** It's time to repot cymbidium orchids if they're bulging out of their containers. Do this between mid-February and early July. Repotting later will prevent bloom and also may make outdoor cymbidiums more susceptible to cold.

☐ **WATER.** Zones 7–9, 14–17: If winter rains are light or infrequent, deep-water plants when the soil is dry.

PEST CONTROL

☐ **PICK UP OLD BLOSSOMS.** Azaleas and camellias are both prone to petal blight diseases (caused by different organisms). Brown lesions develop, and the flowers rot. Azalea flowers cling to the leaves or stems; camellias drop from the plant. The only means of control are to discard infected blossoms and to avoid overhead watering. Apply 4 inches of organic mulch beneath camellias to reduce spore survival.

☐ **CONTROL SLUGS AND SNAILS.** Zones 7–9, 14–17: As nighttime temperatures rise, snails and slugs become more active. Go on a search-and-destroy mission at night when these pests appear, or use beer traps or commercial bait (keep away from pets).

On one of our warm Indian summer days last October, my husband and I were doing chores (I was deadheading roses while he was washing our curly-coated retriever). Suddenly he noticed how healthy our 'Southern Rose' dwarf peach looked. "It doesn't have any wrinkled foliage," he exclaimed. *Wrinkled* wasn't exactly the right technical term, but I knew just what he meant—peach leaf curl, a fungus that puckers and distorts new leaves and destroys the fruit.

In past years, this poor tree had had serious cases of this disease. I had asked myself why I was growing a fruit tree if it never bore fruit. So last winter I had finally gotten motivated to spray my tree. The books say the most effective way to control the fungus is with one spray of lime sulfur (with a spreader sticker to improve coverage) in fall after leaves have fallen, followed by another spray in late winter when buds swell but before green tissue shows. I was lucky to get in the one late-winter spray last year. And guess what? It worked—no puckered foliage. Unfortunately, it was pouring rain when the tree was in full bloom, so fruit production was limited again.

•

There's nothing more frightening than the thought of my child chewing on a plant that could be poisonous. So I was glad to find a

NORTHERN CALIFORNIA
Garden Notebook
BY LAUREN BONAR SWEZEY

book that addresses the subject with common sense and care. *Baby-Safe Houseplants & Cut Flowers: A Guide to Keeping Children and Plants Safely Under the Same Roof,* by John I. Alber and Delores M. Alber (Storey Communications, Box 445, Pownal, VT 05261, 800/441-5700, 1993; $12.95), provides concise information about plants and their toxins, and recommends dozens of plants that can safely be grown or displayed indoors. At the back of the book is a list of some poison control centers to call in case of an emergency (check them against those in your local phone book to make sure they are current).

THAT'S A GOOD QUESTION

Q. I love climbing roses, but haven't had much luck with them. The ones I've tried get terribly diseased. Do you know of any disease-resistant varieties?

A. Santa Clara County Rose Society recommends the following climbers: 'Altissimo' (medium red large-flowered climber), 'Cl. Cécile Brunner' (light pink climbing polyantha), 'Clair Matin' (medium pink large-flowered climber), 'Handel' (red-blend large-flowered climber), 'Jeanne Lajoie' (medium pink climbing miniature), 'Rosarium Uetersen' (deep pink large-flowered climber), and 'Sombreuil' (white climbing tea).

PLANTING

☐ **PLANT ANNUALS.** In coastal (zones 22–24) and inland (zones 18–21) areas, fill in bare spots with calendula, Iceland poppy, nemesia, pansy, primrose, snapdragon, stock, sweet pea, viola, and other cool-season annuals.

☐ **PLANT BARE-ROOT.** There's still time to plant bare-root cane berries, fruit and shade trees, grapevines, roses, strawberries, and perennial vegetables such as artichokes and asparagus.

☐ **PLANT SUMMER BULBS.** In coastal and inland areas, plant caladium, calla lily, canna, crocosmia, dahlia, gladiolus, gloxinia, tigridia, tuberose, and tuberous begonia. Glads planted now will bloom before thrips attack in summer.

☐ **PLANT WINTER VEGETABLES.** Coastal, inland, and high-desert (zone 11) gardeners can still sow seeds of cool-season plants like beets, carrots, celery, kale, head and salad greens, onions, early peas, potatoes, radishes, spinach, Swiss chard, and turnips. Broccoli, cauliflower, and other cabbage-family vegetables are best planted from seedlings this late in the season. In the low desert (zone 13), many warm-season vegetables, including peppers and tomatoes, can go into the ground after midmonth.

MAINTENANCE

☐ **AMEND SOIL.** Before planting, add compost to vegetable and flower beds. Work in 20 to 30 percent compost by volume; add a complete high-nitrogen fertilizer (see package directions).

Sunset
Western Garden Book
CLIMATE ZONES

1-3 7-9 11 13 14-24

☐ **FERTILIZE CITRUS.** Gardeners in low desert zone 13 should feed mature trees this month with a complete citrus food according to package directions. If not done last month, coastal gardeners should fertilize citrus now as well.

☐ **FERTILIZE PLANTS.** In coastal, inland, and low-desert gardens, feed deciduous fruit trees with a complete fertilizer two to three weeks before bloom is expected. Feed spring-blooming flowers with a complete fertilizer as well.

☐ **TEND LAWNS.** Fertilize cool-season lawns every six weeks, and water if rains are inadequate; mow with blades set at 1½ to 2 inches. Warm-season lawns will begin to grow midmonth along the coast and early next month inland; they should be dethatched, fertilized, and watered thoroughly.

☐ **PRUNE DORMANT PLANTS.** Before weather warms and growth begins, prune deciduous trees, fruit trees, grapes, roses, shrubs, and vines.

☐ **PRUNE FUCHSIAS AND BEGONIAS.** Hard pruning now will result in shapelier plants later in the season. Cut back hanging-basket plants to container's edge, and garden-planted fuchsias by half or more. Cut cane and angel-wing begonias to pot level or three or four nodes from the ground. Prune wax begonias to 1 to 2 inches from the ground.

PEST AND WEED CONTROL

☐ **PREVENT CRABGRASS.** To control crabgrass in lawns, apply a preemergence weed killer this month.

☐ **SPRAY DORMANT OIL.** In coastal, inland, and high-desert areas, apply dormant oil to kill mealybugs, spider mites, and scale on deciduous shrubs and trees. Follow label directions.

☐ **PROTECT PLANTS AGAINST FIRE-BLIGHT.** Evergreen pear, pyracantha, and many plants in the rose family are susceptible to this bacterial disease that causes leaves and stems to wilt, curl, darken, and dehydrate. To protect susceptible plants, apply a fixed-copper spray every four or five days during bloom period.

If dinner guests leave my table under the illusion that I'm a swell cook, I credit cream of sorrel soup (I substitute sorrel for spinach in a good cream of spinach soup recipe). It's a first course that never fails to please, so I serve it often. Start the evening with this guaranteed hit, I've learned, and a few errors in the courses that follow will be forgiven and forgotten.

There's just one trick to this soup—finding the main ingredient. Sorrel is rarely available in grocery stores or even at farmers' markets. The reason must be that not enough people know about it to create a demand. It's certainly not that sorrel's difficult to grow. My 4-year-old plant is tough as a weed. All I do is dig in a little compost around it now and then and water it in the months it doesn't rain. The only difficulty with sorrel is learning to live with a culinary reputation you don't deserve.

You can usually find sorrel in 4-inch pots in the herb section of a nursery. If you don't, visit Herban Garden in Rainbow (call 619/723-2967 or 800/407-5268 for directions) or order plants from Mountain Valley Growers (209/338-2775).

SOUTHERN CALIFORNIA
Garden Notebook
BY SHARON COHOON

A lot of rosarians seem to be into alfalfa these days. Not alfalfa sprouts, but alfalfa pellets or meal for their shrubs. Tom Carruth, Weeks Roses's hybridizer, has been using alfalfa as a fertilizer and soil amendment for 10 years and swears by it. "It's a nice gentle form of nitrogen, it adds organic material to the soil, and earthworms love it," he says. Apply a cup of pellets or meal around big shrubs and a half-cup around miniatures this month, he advises. Water in well, as you would any fertilizer. Farm supply stores are a good source for alfalfa.

THAT'S A GOOD QUESTION

Q. "Can I prune my mandevilla, and if so, when?"

A. The temptation to cut back 'Alice du Pont' is strong in the winter when this vine goes semidormant and looks homely, says Evelyn Weidner of Weidners' Gardens in Encinitas. But, she says, please resist. Cutting 'Alice' back when it is not in an active growth period could kill it. Wait to prune until you see new leaves emerge—usually late March. 'Red Riding Hood' and 'My Fair Lady', on the other hand, can be pinched back year-round. For more severe pruning, again, wait until March.

CHECKLIST
FEBRUARY

PLANTING

❑ **ORDER SEED.** Place your seed orders for spring planting this month, before suppliers run out of popular and unusual varieties.

❑ **BARE-ROOT PLANTS.** If soil can be worked where you live, now is the time to plant bare-root stock. Nurseries carry small fruits like grapes and strawberries; cane fruits like blackberries and raspberries; all kinds of ornamental, fruit, and shade trees; and even vegetables such as asparagus and horseradish.

❑ **VEGETABLES.** Indoors or in a greenhouse, start seeds of cool-season vegetables, including broccoli, cabbage, cauliflower, Chinese vegetables, kale, and lettuce, about six weeks before planting time in your area. In many areas, the time for such indoor sowing will be late this month.

❑ **WILDFLOWERS.** Sow seeds of hardy wildflowers suited to your area in prepared, weeded soil. Most will bloom this season, but some of the perennials and biennials common to most wildflower mixes won't bloom until their second growing season.

❑ **PREPARE BEDS.** As soon as the ground can be worked, dig or till compost or other organic matter into the soil to prepare flower and vegetable beds for spring planting. If you live where spring comes late, you can even dig in manure that's not yet fully rotted; by planting time, it will have mellowed enough to fertilize plants without burning them.

Sunset
Western Garden Book
CLIMATE ZONES

❑ 1-3   ❑ 10-11

MAINTENANCE

❑ **CLEAN HOUSE PLANTS.** Sponge off big leaves to remove dust. For small plants in pots, cover the soil with plastic wrap, put pots in the shower, and spray with lukewarm water. Prune out yellowing and dead leaves. If plants are losing too many leaves, short days are likely the problem: consider installing artificial light.

❑ **FEED BEARDED IRISES.** Late in the month, sprinkle a complete fertilizer on the soil over iris rhizomes. Water the fertilizer in well.

❑ **FEED ROSES.** Pick a day in late February when nighttime temperatures are forecast to remain above freezing. Water established plants, let the soil drain, apply a complete fertilizer, and water again.

❑ **TIDY UP GREENHOUSES.** Before you start spring-flowering vegetables and flowers, wash pots and flats with a mild mixture of household bleach and water. Replace potting soil and check heating cables, heaters, vents, weatherstripping, and glazing. There's still time to order parts and make repairs before sowing.

❑ **PREPARE FOR LATE FROST.** In the coldest parts of the West, late frost can come anytime and nip tender seedlings. Order cloches or row covers now so you'll have them when you need them. Windbreaks are also essential to keep tender seedlings from drying out; to protect your garden plot, plant a double row of Siberian peashrub (*Caragana arborescens*) and pines on the windward side of the area you want to protect.

PEST CONTROL

❑ **MONITOR HOUSE PLANTS.** Inspect leaves for aphids, telltale webs of spider mites, and the sticky honeydew that signals scale insects. Spray pests off leaves with lukewarm water; scrape off scale insects if necessary. If you choose to spray with an insecticide, first cover the plant with a plastic garment bag (the kind you get from dry cleaners) to confine the spray.

INLAND WESTERN STATES
Garden Notebook
BY JIM McCAUSLAND

Sherlock Holmes once explained, "You see, but you do not observe." That's a charge I try not to be guilty of, since close observation is as important in gardening as in detective work. It helps me understand why parts of my garden work visually, and why other parts don't.

This time of year, with fewer leaves blocking the view, I can see where plants are growing too close together or out of proportion, or in the wrong place altogether. I respond by ripping out tired old plants, installing new ones, and moving trees and shrubs from place to place. By late spring, when the dormant plants leaf out, they cover the evidence of my remodeling so well that it's hard to tell whodunit.

●

I'm always amazed at how big a plant I can move successfully and relatively easily. But before I move anything, I dig the planting hole (always much wider than deep). Then I dig a trench around the roots of the plant. To move a chest-high, 4-foot-diameter false cypress, I dug the trench 16 to 18 inches out from the trunk, then down barely deeper than the shovel blade. I finished by undercutting the root-

ball with sharp jabs from the spade, then sliding the plant (balanced atop the spade blade) onto an old blanket. A friend and I dragged it to its new hole, eased it in, pulled out the blanket, and watered it well. The plant never missed a beat.

●

To help prepare any small tree or shrub for transplanting in autumn, late winter or early spring is the time to cut a circle around the plant's root zone with vertical thrusts of a shovel. Don't remove any soil: you're just cutting roots to concentrate this year's new root growth inside the circle. By fall, the plant will have a much more concentrated root mass that will hold together better in the move.

THAT'S A GOOD QUESTION

Q: My Chinese evergreen (*Aglaonema modestum*) is getting lots of trunk growth with few leaves on top. It wants to look like a Dr. Seuss plant, but I want it to look lush and full, as it was when I bought it.
A: Be brutal. Cut the stems off about 3 inches above soil level, and they'll sprout and regrow as full plants.

PLANTING

❑ **BARE-ROOT PLANTS.** In zone 11 (Las Vegas), this is the last good month for bare-root planting, while in colder zones 1 and 2, bare-root season is just getting started. Nurseries carry bare-root grapes, strawberries, blackberries, and raspberries; ornamental, fruit, and shade trees; and asparagus and horseradish.

❑ **GROUND COVERS, VINES.** In zone 11, set out Hall's honeysuckle, *Vinca major*, or *V. minor*. In zones 12 and 13, set out these as well as perennial verbena, star jasmine, and trailing indigo bush (*Dalea greggii*).

❑ **PERENNIAL WILDFLOWERS.** In zones 12 and 13, set out evening primrose, desert marigold, paperflower (*Psilostrophe cooperi*), penstemon, and salvia for bloom this spring. You can still scatter wildflower mixes in cold-winter zones now for bloom this summer.

❑ **VEGETABLES.** In zones 11, 12, and 13, start seeds of cucumbers, eggplant, melons, peppers, squash, and tomatoes indoors for transplanting after danger of hard frost is past. Sow seeds of root crops (beets, carrots, radishes), peas, and spinach in prepared garden soil. In zone 10 and milder parts of zone 2, sow broccoli, cabbage, cauliflower, Chinese vegetables, and lettuce indoors late in the month. In zones 1 and 2, order seed now for sowing when the weather warms up.

SOUTHWEST
CHECKLISTS
FEBRUARY

Sunset Western Garden Book CLIMATE ZONES
1-3   10-11   12-13

MAINTENANCE

❑ **FEED BEARDED IRISES.** Late in the month, sprinkle a complete fertilizer on the soil over iris rhizomes, and water it in well.

❑ **FEED CITRUS TREES.** In zones 12 and 13, scatter a complete fertilizer over the entire root zone, and water it in well, if you didn't do it last month.

❑ **FEED ROSES.** Pick a day in late February when nighttime temperatures are forecast to remain above freezing. Water established plants, let the soil drain, apply a complete fertilizer, and water again.

❑ **FEED WINTER RYE LAWNS.** In zones 12 and 13, apply 2½ pounds of ammonium sulfate per 1,000 square feet of lawn, and water it in well.

❑ **PREPARE BEDS.** Dig compost or other organic matter into planting beds to improve the soil's texture and water- and nutrient-holding capacity. Lower the pH of alkaline soil and increase fertility by adding 2 pounds of ammonium phosphate and 3 pounds of soil sulfur per 100 square feet. Because of the poor soil quality in the Las Vegas area, the county extension office recommends planting in raised beds of imported soil.

PEST CONTROL

❑ **CONTROL APHIDS.** In zones 12 and 13, check tender new growth for aphids. When you see them, blast them off with a jet of water, and if necessary, spray with insecticidal soap.

❑ **MONITOR HOUSE PLANTS.** Inspect leaves for aphids, telltale webs of spider mites, and the sticky honeydew that signals scale insects. Spray pests off leaves with lukewarm water; scrape off scale insects. If you spray with an insecticide, first cover the plant with a plastic garment bag to confine the spray.

TEXAS

PLANTING

❑ **BARE-ROOT PLANTS.** Plant bare-root grapes, strawberries, blackberries, and raspberries; ornamental, fruit, and shade trees; and asparagus and horseradish.

❑ **GROUND COVERS, VINES.** In South Texas (San Antonio), plant Baja evening primrose (*Oenothera stubbei*), Hall's honeysuckle, prostrate myoporum, dwarf periwinkle (*Vinca minor*), star jasmine, and perennial verbena.

❑ **PERENNIAL WILDFLOWERS.** There's still time to scatter wildflower seed mixes. Most kinds will bloom this spring, summer, or fall, but some perennials won't show flowers for another year.

❑ **VEGETABLES.** As soon as you're within six weeks of the average date of

your area's last killing frost, start seeds of warm-season crops (cucumbers, eggplant, melons, peppers, squash, tomatoes) indoors for transplanting later. In prepared soil, sow seeds of beets, carrots, radishes, plus spinach, and peas.

MAINTENANCE

❑ **PREPARE SOIL.** Get flower and vegetable beds ready for spring planting by digging compost or well-aged steer manure into the soil.

❑ **DIVIDE PERENNIALS.** In North Texas (Dallas/Forth Worth) and West Texas (El Paso, Midland), divide overcrowded clumping perennials like chrysanthemums and daylilies to promote vigorous growth and flowering next summer and fall.

❑ **FEED IRISES.** In South Texas and the Houston area, sprinkle a complete fertilizer on the soil over iris rhizomes late in the month. Water well.

❑ **FEED ROSES.** In South Texas, fertilize roses late this month when night temperatures are expected to remain above freezing. Water established plants, let the soil drain, apply a complete fertilizer, and water again.

Blooming branches
for winter bouquets

BIG WINTER BOUQUETS are strutting new blooms these days. And the blooms are not from the flower garden: they're from trees and shrubs—deciduous ones such as flowering cherry and forsythia. When they erupt with pink, white, or yellow blooms, they're the crowning glory of the garden. Snip a few small branches when their buds are swelling, bring them indoors and put them in a vase of water, and they'll continue to unfurl just as they would on the plant.

Florists are now offering many types of flowering branches from deciduous fruit trees, ornamental trees, and shrubs to use in arrangements. These branches all come from fabulous landscape plants we can grow in the West.

For your own supply of blooming branches to enjoy both indoors and out, plant one or several of the trees and shrubs listed at right.

BEST BRANCHES FOR GROWING AND CUTTING

Most of these plants grow in a wide variety of climates. Use the *Sunset Western Garden Book* climate zones to choose the best plants for your garden.

Acacia (*A. baileyana*): Often called mimosa when sold by the branch. Bright yellow blossoms from this 20- to 30-foot, sometimes multi-trunked tree are great in bouquets as long as you're not allergic to their pollen. Branches last about five days. Zones 7, 8, and 9, 13 to 24 (borderline zone 6).

Flowering quince (*Chaenomeles*): This is one of the first shrubs to bloom, and named varieties come in coral, orange, many shades of pink, red, and white. Most are thorny and vigorous (6 to 10 feet tall, although some reach only 2 to 3 feet), and benefit from pruning. Zones 1 to 21.

Forsythia: All types make good cut flowers, but the most common are varieties of *F. intermedia*. Plants generally grow 7 to 10 feet tall and produce arching branches covered with yellow flowers. Branches last as long as two weeks if cut when only a few flowers are opening. Zones 2 to 16, 18, 19.

Fruit trees: When most people think of cutting branches to bring indoors, they think of flowering fruit trees first. But fruiting varieties can be just as handsome. Whether flowering or fruiting, the trees make wonderful garden plants. In bouquets, they last five to seven days if you cut them before buds open.

Choices include apple (white flowers), apricot (white), cherry (pink or white), crabapple (pink, red, or white), nectarine (pink), peach (pink, red, white, or striped), and plum (pink or white). What you can grow varies by zone, but in each zone you can succeed with at least several.

DECIDUOUS TREES AND SHRUBS *are a bouquet maker's dream. A few choice clippings are pictured below. At right, delicate coral blooms of flowering quince make a lovely arrangement.*

Plum
Apple
Apricot
Forsythia
Acacia
Pussy willow

NORMAN A. PLATE

42

ANDY FREEBERG

Magnolia: The showiest of the flowering branches are the deciduous magnolias. Their huge blooms add drama to a living or dining room. Florists generally carry branches of saucer and star magnolia, but many other garden kinds are good for cutting, including *M. denudata* and *M.* 'Galaxy'.

Magnolia flowers bruise easily—even when laid on a counter—so handle with care. Flowers last four to five days in water. Zones vary, but every zone except 11 can grow at least several.

Pussy willow: Well known and loved for its fuzzy, pearly gray buds (actually catkins). The most common pussy willow is *Salix discolor* (to 20 feet), but gardeners can also grow French pussy willow (*S. caprea*), which grows to 25 feet and has woolly pinkish gray catkins. All zones.

CUT THE BRANCHES WHEN BUDS SHOW COLOR

For longest-lasting bloom, cut stems either when the first buds are just showing color or when they have just opened; the buds will continue to open. If branches are cut when blooms are totally open, they last only a couple of days.

Follow proper pruning practices when cutting off branches. Prune to thin or shape the tree or shrub; don't hack branches off indiscriminately. And always prune back to a side branch; never leave stubs.

DISPLAY BRANCHES TO SHOW OFF EVERY ANGLE

"The best way to display flowering branches is in a deep container full of water, not oasis (florist's foam)," says Jeffrey Adair of J. Floral Art in Menlo Park, California. "Otherwise they dry out." The exception? "One time for a party I tied fruit tree branches on a chandelier that hung above a buffet table. It was like standing under a flowering tree that grew indoors. The blossoms even started falling on the floor. Since the branches only lasted for the party, it was temporary beauty."

Before selecting a vase, choose the location where you'll display the branches. Adair sets big galvanized French buckets by a front door and tall, slender, clear glass vases to frame a mirror over a mantle. He also sets water-filled containers into tall baskets. Vases with flared necks don't work as well for cut branches, although Adair suggests a remedy for them: "Stuff the top of the vase with camellia or evergreen magnolia foliage for support."

Adair arranges the branches so he can see the line of each one twisting and turning. He doesn't cram a lot of branches into one container. To determine the correct height to cut the branches, Adair follows this rule for all arrangements: they should be about 1½ times the height of the container. "But you can push it to the extreme and cut the branches taller, if the size looks right where they'll be displayed," he says.

Before arranging the branches, Adair strips from the bark any flowers or buds that will sit below water. This helps keep the water cleaner, which is especially important in a clear vase (as is changing the water every two days). Then he cuts the stems at a deep angle with pruning shears. If you don't have sharp pruning shears, smash the stem ends with a hammer.

Does Adair ever mix flowering branches with other flowers? "Flowering fruit trees look beautiful with long-stemmed French tulips or lilies. And yellow forsythia looks wonderful with white lilac or tall white tulips. Forsythia arranged with red, yellow and green parrot tulips is so dramatic." ∎

By Lauren Bonar Swezey

Conifers that won't outgrow you

The selection of vertically challenged plants includes firs, hemlock, junipers, pines, and spruces

MUCH OF THE WEST IS prime country for conifers, and winter is the season when we fully appreciate just how much they contribute to our landscape. But many conifers are forest giants, and growing them in your garden is like trying to keep a whale in a bathtub.

Fortunately, a group of smaller plants—the dwarf conifers—is ideally suited for home gardens. This month, many nurseries will be well stocked with these plants in 1- and 5-gallon cans. You can plant them in the ground anytime the soil is workable.

Nurseries typically classify conifers into four sizes: *mini-ature* (plants that seldom grow taller than a foot); *dwarf* (plants that will be between 3 and 6 feet tall in 10 years); *intermediate* (6 to 15 feet); and *large* (more than 15 feet tall).

The dwarf plants are the easiest to use in most home gardens. They stay compact and fit well into the landscape

A COLORFUL PALETTE *of conifers: around the rim from top left are yellow Chamaecyparis obtusa 'Nana Lutea', steel blue Abies lasiocarpa 'Glauca Compacta', bluish green Picea sitchensis 'Tenas/Papoose', Pinus strobus 'Blue Shag', golden Juniperus horizontalis 'Mother Lode', orange and gold Thuja occidentalis 'Rheingold', and slate blue Picea pungens 'R. H. Montgomery'. In the center are green Thuja occidentalis 'Hetz Midget' and 'Blue Star' juniper. On opposite page, a gardener loosens up the rootball of a dwarf blue spruce before planting.*

FROSTY BLUE *Abies procera 'Glauca Prostrata' (above) in the foreground plays off white-tipped Chamaecyparis obtusa 'Snowkist' in the background. The spidery form of blue Cedrus deodora 'Prostrate Beauty' (below right) contrasts in shape and color with umbrella pine (Sciadopitys verticillata) behind it.*

a low, spreading form and typical dark green needles.

Hemlock. *Tsuga canadensis* 'Cole's Prostrate' is a mounding ground cover; its foliage keeps its dark green color best in partial shade.

Japanese cryptomeria. *C. japonica* 'Tansu' grows into an irregular pyramid of green foliage that takes a bronze hue in winter.

Mugho pine. *Pinus mugo* 'Sherwood Compact' maintains its globular form and has dark green needles.

GOLDEN HUES

Arborvitae. *Thuja occidentalis* 'Rheingold' has a globular form and ferny sprays of foliage that are yellow-orange in summer, turning dark copper-orange after the first hard frost.

False cypress. *Chamaecyparis obtusa* 'Nana Lutea' is a slow grower with an upright form and golden yellow foliage.

Juniper. *Juniperus horizontalis* 'Mother Lode' is a tough, sprawling ground cover with brilliant gold needles.

Spruce. *Picea glauca* 'Rainbow's End' grows into an upright cone of fine green foliage that sports creamy yellow new growth in summer.

SHADES OF BLUE

Alpine fir. *Abies lasiocarpa* 'Glauca Compacta' has a dense pyramidal form and rich steel blue needles.

Colorado spruce. *Picea pungens* 'R. H. Montgomery' is a compact, globe-shaped plant in its youth, stretching into a pyramid as it matures. Its needles are slate blue.

Junipers. *Juniperus communis* 'Compressa' forms a narrow column of bluish green needles with a silvery cast. *J. squamata* 'Blue Star' has a compact, irregular globe shape and sparkling deep turquoise blue needles. ■

By Steven R. Lorton

or a container. They are long-lived and relatively free of disease and pests.

When choosing conifers for your landscape, consider plant form and color. Do you want a plant that grows upright, or one that cascades or sprawls near the ground? Do you want foliage that's green, gold, or blue?

Before you dig a hole, set the plant in different places around the garden to see where it will work best. Consider the seasonal colors of neighboring plants: a 'Blue Star' juniper or a golden cedar may be a handsome focal point in a winter landscape but would look insipid in summer surrounded by pink petunias.

Most conifers grow happily in any light from full sun to partial shade. Give them rich, loose, well-drained soil. Once plants are established, they'll take summer drought in stride in much of the West. Fertilize most of them lightly in spring to promote strong, healthy new growth. Pines are the exception: most don't like to be fertilized at all.

Most of the conifers listed below grow well in *Sunset Western Garden Book* climate zones 1–7; with the exception of junipers, they are not recommended for desert zones 10–13.

GREAT GREENS

Arborvitae. *Thuja occidentalis* 'Hetz Midget' is globular in form with soft green foliage.

Douglas fir. *Pseudotsuga menziesii* 'Loggerhead' is a garden-size Douglas fir with

MICHAEL THOMPSON

'DONATION' *bears clusters of delicate pink flowers. 'Freedom Bell' (bottom right) has rich red flowers of moderate size.*

Camellias for a longer flower show

These 10 plants offer extended bloom in a variety of colors

ALTHOUGH MANY camellias will reward you by flowering for a few weeks, some overachievers can go on blooming for as long as five months. The keys to an extended flower show are to pick the right plants and to grow them in the right conditions.

We list 10 long-blooming camellias in a range of flower colors. Unless noted, these are japonica camellias, which flower from midwinter through spring. Sasanqua camellias flower in fall and winter, and hybrids bloom in winter.

Camellias grow well in *Sunset Western Garden Book*

climate zones 4 through 9, 12, and 14 through 24. They bloom longest in mild climates with long, cool springs. Hard winters can delay spring bloom, while early heat can shut it down. With that in mind, plant under high-arching trees to take the edge off winter cold and summer heat. That also gives plants the filtered sunlight they need to thrive (some tolerate full sun, as noted in our list).

Buy camellias in bloom this month, and set plants out right away. Be patient: camellias bloom longer as they mature.

'*Ace O'Hearts*' produces large red flowers at midseason. Takes full sun.

'*Conrad Hilton*' is a white-flowered child of 'High Hat' (next column) with peony-shaped blooms. Flowering starts very early.

'*Covina*' starts producing 3-inch red flowers in midseason. Takes full sun.

'*Daikagura*' bears peony-shaped rose red flowers splotched with white. This early bloomer has lots of long-flowering descendants.

'*Debutante*' bears medium-size light pink flowers in early and midseason. Grow this one for long-term success: plants may not set any flowers at all until they're 7 or 8 years old.

'*Donation*' bears medium-size orchid pink semidouble flowers at midseason. Bloomtime lengthens as plants age.

'*Freedom Bell*' hybrid bears bright red small to medium bell-shaped flowers.

LYNNE HARRISON

Bloom starts early and continues into midseason.

'*Garden Glory*' hybrid produces masses of medium-size orchid pink double flowers from early to late in the season.

'*High Hat*' is an early-flowering, light pink sport of 'Daikagura'.

'*Shibori Egao*' normally blooms for four months in Southern California. It has variegated foliage and semi-double variegated pink-and-white flowers. It blooms late for a sasanqua, early for a japonica (it's probably a hybrid of the two). If you don't like variegated foliage or flowers, try its parent, 'Egao', with pure pink blooms.

SOURCES

Many nurseries sell these camellias in 1-, 2-, and 5-gallon cans. One grower who sells all the varieties listed here by mail is Nuccio's Nurseries, Box 6160, Altadena, CA 91003; (818) 794-3383; free catalog.

CARING FOR PLANTS

When flowering starts, scatter a tight handful of low-nitrogen (2-10-10) granular fertilizer over the root zone of each mature plant every three weeks until bloom is finished.

After flowering, prune camellias to open plants up to light and air, and to stimulate growth.

All camellias are susceptible to camellia petal blight, a fungus disease that turns petals brown. There is no known cure for this blight (the American Camellia Society is offering a $20,000 reward for the person who discovers one). To help prevent reinfection, remove blighted blossoms, rake up fallen flowers and petals, and send the plant debris out with the trash. ■

By Jim McCausland

KEVIN CANDLAND

YELLOW-GREEN *or russeted skin and a round apple shape are typical of Asian pears. They're the size of large apples, too.*

The juicy-crunch pears
that look like funny apples

Asian pears are making news again. Which are the most flavorful varieties you can grow? Tasters share their favorites

R OUND AND JUICY LIKE APPLES, Asian pears made headlines in *Sunset* more than a decade ago when they began showing up in grocery stores and produce markets.

These crisp, crunchy pears with yellow or russeted skin have long been known to Asians. But until the mid-'80s, most Westerners were unfamiliar with them. What has happened to Asian pears since our story first introduced them to *Sunset* readers?

Plenty. We interviewed growers from two California wholesale nurseries that specialize in Asian pears, a few home gardeners, and researchers at the Washington State University Experiment Station in Mount Vernon. And we conducted taste tests at *Sunset*. The bottom line: while few new varieties were introduced during the last decade, a handful of them have emerged as clear winners for flavor.

'HOSUI': #1 CHOICE OF GROWERS

The all-time flavor favorite among growers in California is 'Hosui' (in the Puget Sound area, this variety often succumbs to a bacterial disease called pseudomonas). "It's the benchmark for flavor," says George Jackson of Kingsburg Apple Packers, which grows a large percentage of all Asian pears in California.

"It has a uniquely sweet flavor and is wonderful when dried," says home gardener Chester Aaron of Occidental, who has grown five varieties of Asian pear. He finds 'Hosui' the best-tasting. "There's no comparison to the other varieties," he says. "I'm cutting those trees down."

'Seuri' is another tasty pear; Jackson's employees say it's tops for flavor. "You can drive by the orchard and smell the wonderful aroma," says Jackson. Its one drawback is its short storage life (about four weeks).

Several varieties have fallen out of favor since our last story. 'Chojuro', 'Ichiban' (not listed in our previous story), 'Kosui', 'Niitaka', and 'Shinseiki' are now generally considered bland. 'Twentieth Century' (a yellow-skin type) was highly rated in our old story and is still the Asian pear most commonly sold in grocery stores. Jackson has eliminated 'Twentieth Century' from his 520 acres of trees. "It just doesn't have the flavor of the others," he says.

But time of harvest greatly affects flavor, according to Lorin Amsberry of Fowler Nurseries in Newcastle, which grows and sells Asian pear trees. "'Twentieth Century' usually is picked too green," says Amsberry. "It's fairly good-tasting if picked when yellow starts to show through the green mottling."

Climate affects flavor, too. In general, Asian pears are sweetest where weather is warm (flavor won't be as good right on the coast, in *Sunset Western Garden Book* zones 5 and 17 for example). Gary Moulton of Washington State University Experiment Station has been growing and testing Asian pears for several years. He considers 'Chojuro' very well adapted to the Puget Sound area and

'Shinseiki' the best adapted of the yellow-skinned varieties, with good, sweet flavor. Promising varieties include 'Yoinashi' and 'Ichiban Nashi'.

TOPS WITH *SUNSET* TASTERS? 'HOSUI' AND FIVE OTHERS

Six tasters gathered on two afternoons to try 11 varieties. Most tasters agreed on the top six varieties, although they ranked them differently. Ripening dates will be later in cool climates.

'Hosui', a golden brown russet with white tart-sweet flesh, captured the most votes for flavor. This tree is weeping and spreading. Fruit is ready to harvest from late July to mid-August; it stores well for about three months.

'Kikusui' came in close behind 'Hosui'. This large yellow-green pear has tart-sweet white flesh that some tasters compare to a 'Golden Delicious' apple. Harvest fruit in early to late August; it keeps for six to seven weeks.

'Seuri' is a round Chinese pear (the rest are Japanese varieties) with bright white flesh and unattractive yellow and brown mottled skin. The tree is vigorous. Harvest fruit in early to mid-September. This low-chill variety is especially suitable for coastal Southern California.

'Yoinashi' came out on top in the first tasting and rated fourth in the second crop. The tan fruit has very sweet white flesh with good pear flavor. Harvest from early August to early September; fruit lasts about three months in storage. The tree appears to resist pseudomonas.

'Shinsui' (not pictured because of its early ripening date) is a green-brown to orange-brown russet with sweet, spicy white flesh. The tree is vigorous. Harvest in early to mid-July; it keeps for about six weeks.

'Shinko' was rated highly by some tasters, but others reported a bitter aftertaste. The fruit is brown to golden brown russet with yellow-white flesh. The tree is resistant to fireblight (see below). Harvest from mid-August to mid-September; fruit stores for three to four months.

HOW TO GROW ASIAN PEARS

All Asian pear trees need or benefit from a pollenizer ('Hosui' and 'Shinseiki' are partially self-fruitful).

Select any two trees listed at left to pollinate one another. Two exceptions: 'Hosui' and 'Shinsui' are not compatible with one another, and 'Seuri' must be pollinated by 'Ya Li' (these two varieties can be purchased as a multiple-grafted tree).

Plant Asian pear trees in full sun where they will get plenty of air circulation. Since most of them are vigorous growers, allow enough room for them to grow and spread (they can be maintained with pruning at 12 to 15 feet tall). Water them regularly during dry months.

Trees generally start bearing the second or third year after planting. Most trees produce a huge crop of flowers in spring (every bud makes five blooms). The profusion of blooms is beautiful, but the fruits that follow them will need to be thinned if each one of them is to become sizeable. The best practice is to remove all but one pear per cluster when the fruit reaches an inch or so wide.

Harvest pears when they are sweet and flavorful (test by picking and tasting one). Be careful when picking thin-skinned types such as 'Kikusui', which bruise more easily than thicker russet types.

Fireblight can be a serious problem, especially in areas such as parts of California's Central Valley where temperatures regularly climb above 65° during periods of rainfall. In these areas, stick to 'Shinko', which resists the disease, or follow a fireblight-control program: at four- to five-day intervals during the bloom period, spray the tree with fixed copper or agricultural streptomycin (if available).

In the Northwest, prune trees only from March to September in order to avoid infection by pseudomonas bacteria. And apply a copper spray in October (before heavy rains), again in January, and finally just before blossoms open in March.

WHERE TO BUY TREES

Look for bare-root Asian pear trees at nurseries, or order by mail (not all sources carry every variety).

Northwoods Retail Nursery, 27635 S. Oglesby Rd., Canby, OR 97013; (503) 266-5432.

Raintree Nursery, 391 Butts Rd., Morton, WA 98356; (360) 496-6400. ∎

By Lauren Bonar Swezey

Ornamentals and edibles are handsome companions in Rosalind Creasy's front-yard garden in Los Altos, California. For details on this medley of flowers and gourmet vegetables, see page 55.

DARROW M. WATT

MARCH

Garden guide 52

Checklists & garden notebooks 57

First gardens 62

California "geology" garden 71

Raise a bed of great vegetables 72

'Seascape' strawberry 75

A trial garden for rhodies 76

Easy-care herb pot 79

Clematis: A three-season guide 80

GARDEN
Guide

"Painted" by a gardener in Laguna Beach

Looking down on Sharon McErlane's back garden from her upstairs landing is like peering down at four giant paintings by the Dutch baroque master Jan Davidsz de Heem. McErlane's garden and Heem's paintings have the same exuberant mixture of flowers and vegetables so brimming with vitality they need the restriction of frames to keep them in check. Maybe it's the tufted mondo grass that frames the four planting beds that creates the effect. Or maybe it's the Heem-like combination of edibles and ornamentals within them.

McErlane inherited the mondo grass "frames." But the pictures inside are all hers. She replaced naturalized violets with a medley of food and flowers: Swiss chard and lettuce cheek by jowl with ranunculus and larkspur one season; pole beans and eggplant sharing quarters with delphiniums and nasturtiums the next.

"I like visual surprises in the garden, which is one of the reasons I started tucking in vegetables with the flowers," says McErlane. "But growing our own food turned out to be so much fun that now the ratio is the reverse."

The frames provide a discipline that helps pull everything together, she says. "All you have to do is create a pretty picture in each one, and four pictures that look pretty together, and you're finished."

Red geraniums, pink foxglove, and other flowers spice this vegetable garden with color.

MARCH '96

- Pansy bouquets that shimmer

- A glorious new purple verbena ground cover

- 'Señorita': The gentler jalapeño pepper with a hint of heat

- New fast-acting herbicide

CLAIRE CURRAN

GARDEN ART

A pool of floating pansy blossoms

Cut flowers are not just for indoor bouquets. Rugged arrangements can brighten a garden with their own outdoor grace and style. Take the pansy blossoms in the photo at right, for instance. They float in a water-filled ceramic pot, which sits on a garden bench. The wide-rimmed pot beautifully frames the blossoms and their shimmery water backdrop. The bench raises the pot so you can see the blossoms up close as you stroll by.

Displayed in a cool, lightly shaded part of the garden, the pansies can last a week or so in water. And picking pansies, at the same time you're removing faded blooms from the plants, keeps more flowers coming.

Look for blooming plants in 4-inch pots in nurseries to take home and pop into containers or plant along walkways or at the edges of raised beds. Offerings are wide, from the rich colors and panda faces of classic varieties to the soft pastels currently popular with hybridizers.

NORMAN A. PLATE

Pansies float on the water's surface; dark pot enhances their color.

'Accord Mix' and 'Universal Mix' pansies float in the pot shown. Choose 'Accord Mix' for large, abundant flowers on short stems (allowing blossoms to stand up well in spring rains). For earliest bloom and intense colors, look for 'Universal Mix'.

BOOK REVIEW

A celebration of gardens and gardening

At the age of 5 and in the company of Viney, her grandparents' gardener, Pat Welsh "breathed in the magical odor of sweet moist compost and understood without words that it was both the end and the beginning of all growing things."

Welsh, who lives and gardens in Del Mar, describes her introduction to gardening, and gardens she has known and loved, in *All My*

Edens: A Gardener's Memoir (Chronicle Books, San Francisco, 1996; $24.95). This delightful book weaves together Welsh's memories of her early years in England, and in the eastern United States and Southern California, with garden observations and advice.

It's a delicious read. Welsh describes a garden toad, for example, as a "treasure," beneficial insects as "diminutive garden sentries," and orange Iceland poppies, planted in front of a clump of Spanish lavender, as a "stream of sunshine

breaking up a gray day." And the book is peopled with memorable characters: her Victorian-era grandparents and movie star mother, and, of course, old Viney ("When I am in the garden, I often hear Viney's voice," she writes).

But practical gardening tips are sprinkled throughout the book, too. Among them: how to chill ladybugs before releasing them in the garden, and how to bring the garden alive with "a splash of red." The book is heavily illustrated with photos, letters, and memorabilia that give it scrapbook appeal.

A compact gaura with rose pink blooms

Gaura lindheimeri, a native Western perennial, fills summer gardens with clouds of white flowers. This long-lived, drought-tolerant plant requires little care, and it grows in all Western climate zones.

Now there's a new form, *G. l.* 'Siskiyou Pink', with glowing rose pink blossoms that unfold from wine red buds. A profusion of inch-wide flowers covers the plant over a long bloom period. Green leaves are spotted with dark purple. 'Siskiyou Pink' doesn't grow much above 30 inches tall (the species typically reaches 4 feet).

Give this plant full sun and quick-draining soil. Shear the plant periodically to promote compactness,

'Siskiyou Pink' gaura bears inch-wide blooms.

and cut it back to the ground after the first hard frost. It self-sows freely, so keep spent flower stems snipped off unless you want it to naturalize.

Plants cost $9.95 each, plus shipping, from Siskiyou Rare Plant Nursery, 2825 Cummings Rd., Medford, OR 97501; (541) 772-6846 (catalog $3).

Five tempting choices

Every year as we pore over the latest crop of catalogs, the new plant offerings test our self-control. Here are five choices we couldn't resist.

Aquilegia fragrans. This columbine has cream-colored cups with purple-blue outer petals and spurs. Its soft fragrance is reminiscent of apples. Cost is $2.99 for 40 seeds, from Thompson & Morgan, Box 1308, Jackson, NJ 08527.

***Ilex* 'September Gem'.** This evergreen holly eventually forms a dense pyramid (to 6 feet tall, 3½ feet wide) of dark green foliage that's loaded with bright red berries from September through winter. Cost is $6

per plant, from Heronswood Nursery, 7530 288th St. N.E., Kingston, WA 98346.

***Impatiens* 'Rose Parade'.** Compact plants have double flowers in white, red, rose, bicolor red and white, or burgundy. Leaves are dark green. Cost is $14.95 for 12 plants, from W. Atlee Burpee & Co., Warminster, PA 18974. Seeds are also available.

***Nasturtium* 'Jewel of Africa'.** These 4- to 6-foot trailing plants have variegated foliage, and flowers in vibrant yellow, red, peach-pink, and cream. Cost is $2.65 for 25 seeds, also from Thompson & Morgan.

***Tree peony* 'Black Panther'.** This hybrid bears fragrant, almost black-red semidouble flowers. Cost is $50 per plant, from Caprice Farm Nursery, 15425 S.W. Pleasant Hill Rd., Sherwood, OR 97140.

Hot peppers for cool-summer places

Like tomatoes, chili peppers are tropical plants, and they can be finicky about temperatures. If it's too cold, seeds may not germinate and plants may not set fruit. So it's important to choose varieties that do well where summers are short and cool.

If you like hot to very hot chilies, try jalapeño varieties such as 'Early Jalapeño' (60 to 70 days) and 'Ole' (jumbo fruits, 60 to 65 days) or slightly milder 'TAM Jalapeño' (70 days). Mild to

medium-hot New Mexican types include 'Anaheim' (70 to 75 days), 'Española Improved' (70 days), and 'NuMex Joe E. Parker' (65 days). Note that seed packets usually state the number of days to harvest based on the date you set transplants out in the garden.

Start seeds indoors six to eight weeks before you intend to set out seedlings in the garden. Plant them outdoors only after all danger of frost is past and when the soil has thoroughly warmed. Plant peppers through black plastic and use floating row covers to hold in warmth (many peppers will not set fruit if night temperatures fall below 50°).

A ground cover for nearly nonstop bloom

Few ground covers can claim to bloom almost nonstop, but *Verbena canadensis* 'Homestead Purple' is one of them. Starting in winter or early spring, the plant is covered in a glorious show of purple blooms.

The 'Homestead Purple' shown in the photograph below grows in landscape designer Page Sanders's Palo Alto, California, garden. Sanders started with one small plant in a raised

bed. A year later, the plant tumbled to the ground in a sea of color.

This low-growing plant reaches about a foot tall and spreads 2 to 3 feet in one season. It thrives in full sun, takes little water (but grows more lushly with moderate water), and stays evergreen in mild climates.

To keep new flowers coming, remove old blooms regularly. Once a year, after peak bloom is through (usually early summer), cut the plant back by about half or more to stimulate new growth. If you wait too long to cut it back, the stems get overly woody and the plant doesn't recover as well.

'Homestead Purple' verbena is blanketed with blossoms in spring.

A butterfly bush with silver leaves, lilac flowers

Nothing lights up the garden like silver foliage. Most of the silver-leafed plants (such as artemisias) rarely grow much taller than 1 to 3 feet. But if you want a sterling shrub that can stretch up 6 to 10 feet with an almost equal width, consider *Buddleia crispa,* a species of butterfly bush native to the Himalaya. *B. crispa* took a long time to reach this country, but at last a few specialty nurseries in the West are offering it.

Buddleia crispa is hardy in *Sunset Western Garden Book* climate zones 4 through 7 (in cold-winter areas, you may want to grow it in a pot and move it into a freezeproof place during the coldest months). Its deeply cut leaves range from 1 to 5 inches long. The foliage and stems are covered with a silvery white felt. The fragrant flowers are a soft lilac color with an orange, sometimes white, throat. The flowers form clusters about 4 inches long, with bloom peaking in late summer.

This plant has plenty of good uses in the landscape. It's stunning when grown as a background for a cloud of pink cosmos or filling up a sunny corner entangled with the old-fashioned shrub rose *Rosa rubrifolia.*

Give *B. crispa* full sun. It's not fussy about soil but does need good drainage. Many gardeners like to let buddleias grow up through a single season, then cut them to the ground in late winter to come up again in spring.

One source for *B. crispa* is Mountain Valley Growers, 38325 Pepperweed Rd., Squaw Valley, CA 93675; (209) 338-2775.

NORMAN A. PLATE

Himalayan butterfly bush bears fragrant 4-inch blooms.

Vegetables replace the front lawn

When you have a shady backyard but you love to grow vegetables, where do you grow them? In the front yard, of course.

Landscape designer and author Rosalind Creasy does this well. In her front yard in Los Altos, California, she grows an ever-changing medley of flowers and gourmet vegetables. She started in the mid-'70s, when she was researching *The Complete Book of Edible Landscaping.* To make room for vegetables, she first removed a large bent grass lawn, old junipers, and two dying apricot trees. Then she dug the rock-hard adobe soil deeply, added truckloads of organic amendments (mushroom compost, chicken manure, redwood soil conditioner, oakleaf mold, and homemade compost), and built planting beds and brick paths.

Every planting season, Creasy adds a 2- to 3-inch layer of compost to the planting beds. Now the soil is so rich and deep that "you can put your hand in it up to your elbow," she says.

The summer garden, shown in the photograph on page 50, was partially planted for research on sweet and hot peppers. The center beds were filled with about 20 varieties. Creasy's favorite sweet types are 'Corno di Toro' red, 'Corno di Toro' yellow, and 'Pimento' ("great for roasting, since it sears and peels easily"). For chilies, she likes poblano (sold as 'Ancho'), "which has so much more flavor than 'Anaheim'," and 'Alma' paprika pepper, which is great for drying and grinding. The pepper seeds were started in late February and planted out in April.

In the rest of the garden, she grew artichokes, fennel, herbs, mesclun salad mix, and flowers such as white cosmos. 'Crystal Palace' lobelia edged the path.

She waters the garden by ooze tubing, except for new plantings of greens, carrots, and other root vegetables. These get irrigated by drip misters until established.

If your dirt is downright bad

Some of the West's worst garden soil is in the Las Vegas area, where salt concentrations are sometimes 25 times higher than it takes to kill most garden plants. Plant-damaging levels of boron and sodium are also usually present. How do you deal with bad soil?

Clark County Cooperative Extension agent Bob Morris offers two suggestions for local gardeners that will also work in other areas where saline soil is a problem.

• When you're planting a tree or a shrub, dig the hole, then fill it with at least a foot of water and let it drain to leach the salts out of the root zone before planting.

• If you want to grow vegetables or non-native flowers in beds, forget trying to grow them in native soil. Instead, build raised beds and fill them with imported soil. Remember, though, that many soil mixes have practically no nutritive value, so you should mix in plenty of well-aged manure at planting time, and fertilize regularly.

A jalapeño for gringos

"New 'Señorita' hybrid jalapeño pepper… great jalapeño flavor without the pain," announced the press release. The new pepper sounded interesting, so we tried it in *Sunset*'s Menlo Park, California, test garden.

We sowed the seeds last spring and grew the plants through the summer and fall. They reached about 2 feet tall and proved to be extremely productive. They also remained green and bushy throughout the season. The press release said

'Señorita' pepper ripens from green to bright red. Both stages are tasty.

NORMAN A. PLATE

they'd be very disease resistant. They were.

'Señorita' peppers grow about 3 inches long and 1½ inches wide and look just like traditional jalapeños— wider at the neck and tapering to the tip. They are green at first and then mature to red.

When we tasted 'Señorita', we discovered its surprising flavor. Most of the pepper tastes extremely mild, like a green pepper. But a bit of heat *is* there—at the very top of the pepper

next to the stem.

If you like your chili peppers mild, give 'Señorita' a try. You won't be disappointed by its flavor or production. Seeds are available from Tomato Growers Supply Co., Box 2237, Fort Myers, FL 33902; (813) 768-1119. But if you prefer your peppers *hot,* stick with the much hotter old-fashioned jalapeño.

High-potency, low-residue herbicide

Herbicides are useful for regaining control of gardens where weeds run amok. Once you've cleaned the slate chemically, it's easy to keep up with handweeding. Many gardeners use glyphosate-based herbicides because the chemical kills nearly everything it touches but breaks down harmlessly when it hits soil. They complain, however, that glyphosate doesn't have much visible effect for several days after application.

A new herbicide called Finale may give glyphosate a run for its money. Finale, which is made of glufosinate-ammonium, kills a wide spectrum of weeds, roots and all, in one to four days. It degrades into carbon dioxide, nitrogen, and water after it hits the soil. When we used it, we saw weeds start to die about three days after application. Because plant roots don't take up Finale, nearby ornamentals aren't likely to be damaged as long as spray doesn't touch their leaves. To keep the spray from drifting, apply it when the air is still.

Finale is sold by nurseries and garden centers as ready-to-use liquid in quarts and gallons and as concentrate in smaller containers.

Small trees with broad appeal

A small tree is the kind of plant you live with up close, so it needs to look good, if not spectacular, for as long as possible. Here are five that grow well throughout most of Northern California. All have appeal in more than one season. For specific cultural needs, check the *Sunset Western Garden Book.*

Crape myrtle (*Lagerstroemia indica*). Trees can reach 25 to 30 feet tall. Shiny brown bark. Spectacular clusters of white, pink, red, or purple flowers in summer. Yellow to red fall color. Grows best in hot-summer areas (zones 7, 8, 9, and 14).

In cooler areas, choose mildew-resistant varieties.

Eastern redbud (*Cercis canadensis*). Usually stays less than 25 feet tall. Rosy pink flowers in spring. Bright green heart-shaped leaves turn yellow in fall.

Evergreen pear (*Pyrus kawakamii*). Grows 20 to 25 feet tall. White flowers in spring. In frosty areas, handsome green foliage turns red.

Flowering dogwood (*Cornus florida*). Grows about 20 feet tall. Beautiful white or pink flowers in spring. Bright red leaves in fall. Red berries often last into winter.

Washington thorn (*Crataegus phaenopyrum*). Reaches 25 feet tall. White flowers in spring, red fruit in autumn. Glossy lobed leaves turn orange to red in fall.

Protect paperbark maple from picky passersby

If you've ever seen the glistening cinnamon-colored bark of paperbark maple (*Acer griseum*) peeling away from the trunk of this tree in large, tissue-thin flakes, you understand why people admire it so much. This native to China, hardy in all Northwest climate zones, eventually grows to a height of 25 feet with upright limbs that form a narrow to rounded crown. Its bare limbs are very handsome in winter. In autumn, its coarse-toothed leaflets turn brilliant red.

The key to displaying this tree is to plant it where low morning or afternoon light shines through the bark. For maximum glow, place it in front of a window, away from the house and other structures that cast shadows.

Don't plant one near a sidewalk. As Skagit Valley gardener Jackie Lundberg learned, the bark is so interesting that passersby pick at it and pull it off. This diminishes the attractive flaky effect and sometimes damages the tree.

Lundberg moved her tree well away from the sidewalk. Then, to foil the few brazen bark-pickers who persisted in walking onto her lawn, she planted thorny Japanese barberry (*Berberis thunbergii*) between the tree and the sidewalk. She chose *B. t.* 'Cherry Bomb', a variety with big, dark maroon leaves that grows to about 4 feet tall. The maple and barberry make a handsome combination, and the arboreal vandalism has stopped.

Nurseries commonly sell *A. griseum* in 5- and 15-gallon cans for $50 to $90. Occasionally, you'll find it in 1-gallon cans for as little as $10. Buy plants now, and put them in the ground immediately.

By Debra Lee Baldwin, Sharon Cohoon, Steven R. Lorton, Jim McCausland, Lauren Bonar Swezey, and Lance Walheim

PLANTING

☐ **SOW COOL-SEASON CROPS.** In zones 4–7, sow beets, carrots, lettuce, peas, radishes, spinach, and most members of the cabbage family.

☐ **START WARM-SEASON CROPS.** In all Northwest climate zones, start seeds of tomatoes, peppers, and other warm-season crops indoors—on windowsills or in a greenhouse or sunroom—for planting out when the weather warms.

☐ **SOW HARDY PERENNIALS.** In zones 4–7, arabis, calendula, columbine, coral bells, delphinium, pansies, sweet alyssum, sweet peas, veronica, and others can all be sown directly in the ground. In zones 1–3, hold off until the threat of heavy freeze has ended.

☐ **PLANT NEW LAWNS.** In all Northwest climate zones, you can start a new lawn now. Spade and rake the top 6 to 12 inches of soil to a fine consistency, and amend it with organic matter. Next, lay sod or rake in a seed mix of bent, blue, fescue, and rye grasses. In zones 4–7, bluegrass should be a minor part of the mix; in zones 1–3, it should be the predominant seed. Water the newly planted lawn regularly.

MAINTENANCE

☐ **DIVIDE PERENNIALS.** In climate zones 4–7, dig, divide, and replant summer- and fall-blooming perennials such as asters, chrysanthemums, and coral bells. A sharp spade or knife will cut the

PACIFIC NORTHWEST
CHECKLIST
MARCH

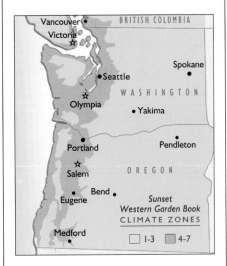

Vancouver
Victoria
BRITISH COLUMBIA
☆
● Spokane
● Seattle
WASHINGTON
☆
Olympia
● Yakima
Portland
● Pendleton
☆
Salem
OREGON
● Bend
Eugene ●
Sunset
Western Garden Book
CLIMATE ZONES
☐ 1-3 ▨ 4-7
Medford

clumps into pieces: a dinner plate–size clump will divide into three or four. In zones 1–3, wait another month to divide these perennials.

☐ **FERTILIZE LAWNS.** Anywhere in the Northwest, give lawns their first feeding of the year. Apply ½ pound of actual nitrogen per 1,000 square feet of turf. The fertilizer should have a 3-1-2 ratio of nitrogen, phosphorus, and potassium.

☐ **PRUNE DAMAGED BRANCHES.** Make a sweep through the garden to check for branches that were damaged by ice, snow, or wind. If a branch is broken, remove it or cut it back to a point where growth buds will emerge and new shoots will grow into a handsome continuation of the old branch.

☐ **TEND FUCHSIAS, GERANIUMS.** In zones 4–7, you'll be setting these plants out in early May, so bring out those that have been overwintering and put them in a warm, bright room or a greenhouse. Water and fertilize lightly to get them going. By mid-April you'll have leafy plants that will give you a jump on summer greenery and bloom.

PEST & WEED CONTROL

☐ **BAIT FOR SLUGS.** As weather warms, slugs become more active. Get them early and you'll have fewer laying eggs later in the year. When a stretch of dry weather is forecast, bait liberally through ground covers, along house foundations, and around rocks, paving, and containers. Be very careful to keep pets and children away from the poisonous bait.

☐ **CONTROL WEEDS.** They're easier to pull when they are little and the ground is moist. Get dandelions and other early bloomers out so they won't produce and cast seed. Hoe out the weed seedlings when the soil is dry. Put seed-free plants on the compost pile. Put the garden monsters, such as morning glory and deadly nightshade, in the garbage can.

No store-bought potatoes can produce the delicious ecstasy you get from eating homegrown new potatoes. If the soil is dry enough to till this month, I'll plant a row of seed potatoes. And I'll keep planting consecutively every two weeks into May. 'Norgold' and 'Yellow Finn' go in around March 23, depending on the wetness of the soil. Later on, I'll put in 'Yukon Gold', 'Red Norland', 'Nooksack', 'Bison' (a beautiful new red potato), and 'Purple Peruvian'. My favorite source is Ronniger's Seed Potatoes, Star Route 6, Moyie Springs, ID 83845 (catalog $2).

All of the many varieties available are easy to grow. Dig a furrow 4 to 6 inches deep (pushing the excess soil up on each side). Plant the seed potatoes whole, or place cut segments with eyes up; cover with soil. As the potatoes grow, fill in the furrow with soil from the sides, eventually mounding soil up around the plants.

Last August, I invited guests at my Skagit Valley house to dig some potatoes to boil for dinner. They lumbered out to the garden and began to dig into the soft, warm mounds with their hands. When the first spud popped out of the ground, potato fever struck them, and they looked like a trio of pirates digging into Treasure Island. They boiled a big potful and gobbled them up without a drop of butter.

PACIFIC NORTHWEST
Garden Notebook
BY STEVEN R. LORTON

●

I spend a good part of this month with my nose pressed up against the window, like a little kid at Christmas, waiting for my mail-order plants to arrive. Some of my favorites come from Heirloom Old Garden Roses, 24062 N.E. Riverside Dr., St. Paul, OR 97137; (503) 538-1576. Its catalog ($5) is filled with wonderful old roses, all of them grown on their own roots. Over the years, I've bought dozens of Heirloom's roses, including the big old China rose *R. chinensis*, several rugosas, *R. glauca* (for its leaves and hips), and David Austin English roses.

THAT'S A GOOD QUESTION

Q: How soon after their flowers fade can I cut the foliage off daffodils and paper white narcissus?

A: Don't rush it. The foliage nurtures the bulbs so they will produce big, sturdy, well-formed flowers next year. When the foliage begins to yellow, I push it over and allow other plants to grow up around it. Some fastidious gardeners braid it; others fold it over and tie it in a neat sheath. I just let it languish on the ground until it shrivels up. When the foliage pulls off with a gentle tug, you can remove it and use it for compost.

CHECKLIST
MARCH

Sunset
Western
Garden Book
CLIMATE ZONES

- Mountain (1-2)
- Valley (7-9)
- Inland (14)
- Coastal (15-17)

PLANTING

☐ **PLANT CITRUS.** Zones 7–9, 14–17: Buy young trees in 5-gallon cans; they'll establish faster than trees in larger containers. Try 'Washington' orange, 'Eureka' or 'Improved Meyer' lemon, 'Oroblanco' grapefruit-pummelo hybrid, or 'Moro' blood orange. In zones 15–17, try 'Trovita' orange, which sweetens better than other oranges in cooler temperatures. In zones 7–9, wait until the end of the month to plant.

☐ **PLANT GROUND COVERS.** Zones 7–9, 14–17: If you're fed up with mowing and caring for lawn, consider replacing it with unthirsty ground covers, such as low-growing types of juniper, lantana, manzanita, myoporum, or rosemary.

☐ **PLANT SUMMER BULBS.** Zones 7–9, 14–17: Calla, canna, dahlia, gladiolus, and tigridia bulbs are available at nurseries this month. Plant in well-drained soil or containers (for cannas, use only dwarfs in containers); mix a balanced fertilizer into the soil before planting.

☐ **SET OUT POTATO TUBERS.** Zones 7–9, 14–17: Try potatoes in different colors, such as yellow 'Bintje' or 'Yukon Gold', 'All Red' or 'Red Dale', and 'All Blue' or 'Caribe'. These are among 70 varieties available from Ronniger's Seed Potatoes, Star Route, Moyie Springs, ID 83845 (free catalog).

☐ **TRANSPLANT CONTAINER PLANTS.** Zones 7–9, 14–17: Summer annuals and perennials can go into the ground starting this month. Water them in with a low-nitrogen fertilizer such as fish emulsion. According to university research, vitamin B-1, alone, doesn't prevent transplant shock. Only those products containing low dosages of fertilizers benefit young plants.

MAINTENANCE

☐ **CARE FOR HERBS.** Zones 7–9, 14–17: To rejuvenate perennial herbs such as mint and sage, cut back old or dead growth on established plants, then fertilize and water them to stimulate new growth. Plant new herbs such as mint, parsley, rosemary, sage, and thyme in loose, well-drained soil.

☐ **CHECK DRIP SYSTEMS.** Zones 7–9, 14–17: Flush out sediment from filters and check screens for algae; clean with a toothbrush, if necessary. Turn on water and check to make sure all emitters are dripping water; clean or replace clogged ones (if you can't get an emitter out, install a new one next to it). Check for and repair leaks in lines.

☐ **FEED LAWNS.** Zones 7–9, 14–17: Bent, blue, fescue, and rye grasses begin their spring growth now. Feed them with high-nitrogen fertilizer, such as 20-4-8, following label directions.

☐ **FERTILIZE TREES AND SHRUBS.** Zones 7–9, 14–17: Apply a high-nitrogen fertilizer such as 20-10-10, or use an organic fertilizer. If you use a granular or controlled-release fertilizer on plants watered by drip, apply it in holes drilled into the soil around the plant so it will contact water. Otherwise the fertilizer won't dissolve enough for your plants to benefit from it.

PEST CONTROL

☐ **CHECK FOR INSECTS.** Zones 7–9, 14–17: Check plants for early signs of insect infestations, such as aphids (look for distorted new growth and tiny, often green or black, insects) and spittle bugs (look for white foam on the stems). Blast them off with water from the hose; you can also use insecticidal soap for aphids. Check plants for snails and slugs at night with a flashlight. Handpick and destroy, or use bait.

NORTHERN CALIFORNIA Garden Notebook
BY LAUREN BONAR SWEZEY

After six years of drought, I thought I'd never get tired of rain. But last March was a doozy, and rain tested everyone's patience. Luckily for my plants, the soil around my house drains well, so few of them really suffered from constant moisture (except some newly planted *Coreopsis verticillata* 'Moonbeam', which doesn't seem to like wet feet).

But I realized that my roses could really suffer from diseases such as black spot and rust if I didn't take steps to prevent them (spring rains and mild temperatures always increase the potential for disease). So between deluges, I sprayed the upper and lower leaf surfaces thoroughly with a mixture of 2 teaspoons horticultural oil and 2 teaspoons baking soda (baking soda helps control black spot) per gallon of water. It worked! Despite the wet weather, the leaves had a minimum amount of disease.

•

Last March, I attended Bouquets to Art, an annual floral extravaganza that's always on my "don't-miss" list of spring events. I walked around oohing and ahhing at everything from elegant blossoms arranged simply in the Japanese ikebana style to elaborate floral bouquets fit for a palace, and attended one of the regularly scheduled lectures. For details on this annual show, at the California Palace of the Legion of Honor in San Francisco, call (415) 750-3504.

THAT'S A GOOD QUESTION

Q. "Why add sulfur to the soil? I thought my homemade compost would be all it needs."

A. The most common reason for adding sulfur to the soil is to lower the soil pH, says Lance Walheim, horticultural writer and consultant in Exeter, California. Areas with low rainfall, such as Bakersfield and much of the rest of California, have alkaline soils (high pH). And alkaline soil inhibits iron availability to plants. If many of your plants have yellow leaves with green veins, they're probably chlorotic. Applying sulfur to the soil makes iron more available to plants and helps green up the leaves again. However, the only way to be sure alkaline soil is the problem is to have your soil tested. Your cooperative extension office can recommend a soil-testing lab.

Adding high-quality compost to the soil is always a good idea and should gradually lower the soil pH. If your plants look healthy, there's no need to take action.

PLANTING

☐ **PLANT ANNUALS.** As weather warms, coastal, inland, and low-desert gardeners (zones 22–24, 18–21, and 13, respectively) can replace fading winter-spring annuals with summer flowers. Choices include ageratum, coleus, lobelia, marigolds, petunias, phlox, and verbena. In the high desert (zone 11), set out marigolds, petunias, and zinnias late this month.

☐ **PLANT BULBS, CORMS, TUBERS.** In coastal and inland areas, continue planting caladium, calla, canna, crocosmia, dahlia, gladiolus, gloxinia, nerine, tigridia, tuberose, and tuberous begonia.

☐ **PLANT PERENNIALS.** Fall is the ideal time to plant herbaceous perennials, but nursery selection then is limited. Fortunately, early spring—when nurseries are fully stocked—is also an excellent planting time.

☐ **SOW FLOWER SEED.** Sow seeds of the following annuals in flats, or directly in the garden where you want them to grow: aster, bachelor's button, cleome, cosmos, marigold, nasturtium, nicotiana, statice, sunflower, and zinnia.

MAINTENANCE

☐ **DIVIDE PERENNIALS.** If summer- and fall-blooming perennials (agapanthus, asters, bellflowers, callas, daisies, daylilies, rudbeckia, yarrow) are weak and crowded and last year's blooms were sparse, it's time to divide. Dig each clump so the rootball comes up

Bishop
NEVADA
CALIFORNIA
San Luis Obispo
Bakersfield
Santa Barbara
Tehachapi
Lancaster
Los Angeles
Palm Springs
San Diego
MEXICO

Sunset Western Garden Book
CLIMATE ZONES
1-3 7-9 11 13 14-24

intact. Wash or gently shake off excess soil, then cut into divisions with a sharp knife. Each should have some leaves and plenty of roots. Plant immediately.

☐ **MULCH PLANTS.** Before weeds germinate, add mulch around trees, shrubs, and ground covers. Use a 3-inch-thick layer of bark chips or compost. Keep mulch away from bases of plants.

☐ **THIN FRUIT.** Apricot and peach trees routinely set more fruit than the tree can ripen. Remove extras when fruit is pea- or marble-size. Leave two of the largest and healthiest young fruits on each 12 inches of stem.

☐ **THIN TREES.** To minimize damage from spring winds in the low and high deserts, thin vulnerable trees like acacia, African sumac, carob, and pepper. Stake trees only in windiest areas.

☐ **FERTILIZE PLANTS.** In coastal, inland, and low-desert areas, most bedding plants, citrus, ground covers, shrubs, trees, tropicals, and vines will benefit from feeding this month. Use a complete fertilizer according to package directions. If plants were damaged by frost, hold off until new growth shows.

PEST CONTROL

☐ **CONTROL APHIDS.** Blast aphids off new spring growth with a strong stream from a hose. For further control, use regular applications of insecticidal soap.

☐ **CONTROL POWDERY MILDEW.** The cool nights and mornings and sunny afternoons of early spring encourage powdery mildew. Keep it in check by a weekly foliage spray of baking soda and summer oil (2 teaspoons soda and 2 teaspoons oil per gallon of water), applying an antitranspirant, or treating with a fungicide such as triforine.

☐ **MANAGE SNAILS.** If you find small holes in foliage and slime trails in flower beds or vegetable gardens or on young plants, hunt for snails at night. Handpick, trap by allowing them to collect on the underside of a slightly elevated board, or use commercial snail bait.

Four good reasons to visit the gardens at the J. Paul Getty Museum in Malibu in the near future: 1. The fragrance of the damask rose 'Bifera'. If the lone flower the horticulturist gave me had the power to perfume my entire car, imagine what a heady experience the garden is in spring with all the *Rosa damascena* in full bloom. 2. A peek at the future. Formal gardens are poised for a comeback, predicts San Diego garden writer Pat Welsh. The Peristyle Garden at the Getty, with its perfectly symmetrical design and precisely sheared hedges, is a good example of the return to our Mediterranean roots Welsh sees in her crystal ball. 3. One of the best herb gardens in the West at its peak. 4. The antiquities museum will close to undergo major renovations when the new Getty Museum in Sepulveda Pass opens—the target date is fall 1997. Visit it while you can. But be sure to call for parking reservations (310/458-2003) before you do.

•

My search for the perfect summer annual for cutting has finally ended: 'Yoga' zinnia—which I first tried last March—germinates quickly, produces flowers steadily over a long season, comes in a broad range of cheerful, summery colors, has thick, straight stems

SOUTHERN CALIFORNIA
Garden Notebook
BY SHARON COHOON

like drinking straws that are a breeze to arrange, and lasts more than a week in a vase. Could you ask anything more? 'Yoga' zinnias are available in most nurseries. Or order from Shepherd's Garden Seeds; call (408) 335-6910.

THAT'S A GOOD QUESTION

Q. Tomatoes show up at the nurseries earlier every year. But should I be planting them while the soil is still so cool?

A. That depends on your gardening style. If you like to put your entire crop in at once, it would probably be better to wait until late April. That's what Joyce Smith, chief tomato propagator for the Fullerton Arboretum's Green Scene, does in her own garden. Planting any earlier, she says, just wastes her and the plants' energy. On the other hand, Yvonne Savio, gardening education coordinator of L.A. County Cooperative Extension, plants in succession. She puts in a few plants—especially cherry tomatoes and 'Early Girl'—as soon as tomatoes appear in nurseries, hoping for an early crop. And then, to hedge her bets, she adds new plants every few weeks until early May.

If your space and time are limited, a good compromise would be to plant a cherry tomato now, like 'Sweet 100'—they ripen the quickest—and a full-size variety, like 'Better Boy', next month.

CHECKLIST
MARCH

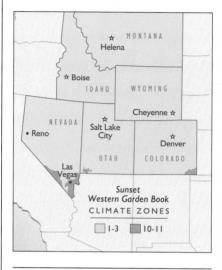

Sunset
Western Garden Book
CLIMATE ZONES

☐ 1-3   ▨ 10-11

PLANTING

☐ **BARE-ROOT PLANTS.** Set out bare-root stock of plants from strawberries and horseradish to fruit and shade trees early this month. Bare-root plants cost less than those sold in containers, and adapt more quickly to native garden soil. It's essential to bring home nursery plants with their bare roots wrapped in damp cloth or sawdust: if roots dry out before planting, the plants die.

☐ **LAWNS.** You can overseed an old lawn or plant a new one this month. By summer, it will be lush and ready for roughhousing. Before overseeding, rough up the soil in the area you want to overseed and sow it with the same kind of grass that was already growing there. Otherwise the texture and color of the new grass will contrast with the old, like mismatched paint on a car. Keep all newly sown areas well watered until the grass is tall enough to mow.

MAINTENANCE

☐ **PREPARE BEDS.** To get beds ready for spring planting, dig in composted manure or garden compost. For bad soil, till 4 to 6 inches of organic matter into the top foot of soil. Rake amended beds, water them, and let them rest for a week before planting. Waiting lets them settle.

☐ **FEED EVERGREENS.** Sprinkle high-nitrogen fertilizer over the plants' root

zones and water it in well.

☐ **FEED SHRUBS.** Do this on a mild day when temperatures are well above freezing. Apply high-nitrogen fertilizer to early-flowering shrubs as soon as they've finished blooming. Feed roses right away.

☐ **FERTILIZE BERRIES.** Blackberries, blueberries, and raspberries can all use a feeding this month with high-nitrogen fertilizer or well-aged manure.

☐ **INSTALL IRRIGATION.** It's easier to put in ooze tubing or drip-irrigation systems now, before root and top growth complicate installation.

☐ **MAKE COMPOST.** As you get the garden in shape for spring and summer planting, use the weeds to start a compost heap. Layer green weeds with dry leaves, straw, or sawdust, then turn the pile weekly and keep it damp; you should have finished compost within a few weeks.

PEST & WEED CONTROL

☐ **BLAST APHIDS.** Vigilance is the best protection against insect pests. Watch tender new growth especially, and when you see a population of aphids develop, blast them off with hose water, or spray with insecticidal soap.

☐ **HOE WEEDS.** Hoe weeds now while they're young and shallow-rooted. If you wait until they form deep taproots, they'll rise—and you'll weed—again. If weeds germinate between the time you prepare a flower bed and when you plant, hoe them off lightly without disturbing more than the top ½ inch of soil. If you weed more deeply or till, you'll just bring up a fresh batch of weed seeds that will sprout in another week or two. Hoe weed seedlings when the soil is dry. Deep-rooted weeds pull out more easily if you water first.

This is the time of year when all my permanent garden plants get their annual performance review. Those that demand more than they put out get the ax. Did my 'Buckley Giant' apple get bitter pit for the fourth season in a row? Fine; I'll swap it for an 'Akane', whose fragrant fruit I will cherish. Have the 'Quinault' strawberries finally been shaded out by my 'Shirotae' cherries? Okay, strawberries are out, sweet woodruff goes in. There are so many productive, trouble-free plants that no garden has to settle for less.

Annual plants are another story: there's more room to experiment with them, since both success and failure are so transitory. I try a few annuals for shade, and learn that of all of them, forget-me-nots seem to go best behind the sweet woodruff that replaced my strawberries. I try a new tomato, and find that its fruit splits in late-summer rainfall, so it's out for the future. With plenty of tried-and-true flowers and vegetables in the mix, I know I'll be satisfied by season's end.

●

The best annual flower gardener I ever knew had a secret: he grew plenty of extras in a back border that was out of sight of the show-quality garden he maintained out front. Whenever the earlier-flowering plants, annual or perennial, died back, he'd cut them back or pull them out and plug the holes with some of the annuals from the

INLAND WESTERN STATES
Garden Notebook
BY JIM McCAUSLAND

back border. If you'd like to try this technique, start growing transplants now to plug in later.

●

Standing ankle-deep in manure this winter, I thought about garden economics. I'd spent $60 on 30 sacks of composted steer manure, which was enough to cover a 4- by 30-foot flower bed 3 inches deep.

It was a deal any investment banker would love. There's no risk, and it pays off for years, improving the yield, strength, and disease resistance of everything that grows in it. Just as important, it's all things to all soils, loosening up heavy earth, helping light soil hold water and nutrients better, and adding fertility.

THAT'S A GOOD QUESTION

Q: On nursery labels, some tomatoes are marked "determinate" and others "indeterminate." What's the difference? Why does it matter?
A: Determinate tomatoes grow to a given height—usually 4 to 5 feet—and stop. Then they put all their energy into producing a crop, after which they die. These grow well in tomato cages, and are favored by people who want a large crop all at once for preserving. Indeterminate tomatoes keep growing and producing fruit until cold or frost cuts them down, so you have to pinch or trellis them to keep them under control. They bear over the longest season.

PLANTING

❑ **ANNUALS.** Set out warm-season flowers, such as blackfoot daisy (*Melampodium leucanthum*), celosia, globe amaranth (*Gomphrena*), lisianthus, Madagascar periwinkle, marigold, portulaca, and salvia. When you take plants out of containers for planting, butterfly the rootball and rough up its edges.

❑ **CITRUS TREES.** In zones 12 and 13, this is a good month to plant Algerian tangerine, Arizona Sweets orange, 'Kinnow' mandarin, or 'Marsh Seedless' grapefruit.

❑ **GROUND COVERS.** Among those to set out this month are aptenia, calylophus, dwarf rosemary, lantana, Mexican evening primrose, verbena, and vinca.

❑ **PERENNIALS.** Aster, autumn sage (*Salvia greggii*), chrysanthemum, coreopsis, feverfew, gerbera, helianthus, hollyhock, penstemon, Shasta daisy, and statice can all go in now.

❑ **SUMMER BULBS.** Set out bearded iris, dahlia, and gladiolus now. Shop for caladium, canna, and crinum this month, but wait until soil warms to 65° before planting.

❑ **VINES.** Good choices include Boston ivy, Carolina jessamine, common trumpet creeper (*Campsis radicans*), Japanese honeysuckle, Lady Banks' rose, silver lace vine, Virginia creeper, and wis-

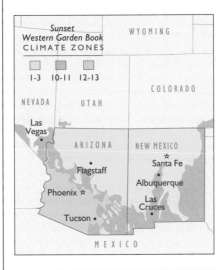

teria. If you want to plant tender vines like bougainvillea, *Mandevilla* 'Alice du Pont', pink trumpet vine, and queen's wreath, wait another month.

❑ **VEGETABLES.** Sow seeds of asparagus beans, black-eyed peas, bush varieties of string beans and limas, cucumbers, melons, soybeans, summer squash, and sweet corn. Set out plants of peppers and tomatoes now, but be ready to cover young plants with cloth

or plastic if frost threatens. Also start sweet potato shoots now for planting next month: just lay a whole sweet potato in a loaf pan and cover halfway with water; shoots will develop along the waterline.

MAINTENANCE

❑ **MULCH PLANTS.** Late in the month, after soil has warmed, spread 3 to 4 inches of organic mulch around roses, shrubs, and trees, and in rows between flowers and cool-season vegetables. Mulch helps hold in moisture and keeps roots cool. Wait a month to mulch around warm-season vegetables.

❑ **MAINTAIN DRIP SYSTEMS.** Now is your last chance to maintain drip systems. Clean out sediment and algae (a solution of bleach and water helps), replace clogged emitters you can't clear, and clean filters.

❑ **PRUNE FROST-DAMAGED PLANTS.** Once new growth begins, you'll clearly see which twigs and branches didn't survive winter frosts. Then you can cut them away. Wait another month, however, before you prune bougainvillea: its new growth appears first at the base of the plant, then moves out the stems.

❑ **TRIM ORNAMENTAL GRASSES.** When new growth appears at the base of the plant, cut back the old grass. If the new and old grow together, the plant will look unkempt.

TEXAS

PLANTING

❑ **HERBS.** Plant all kinds of perennial culinary herbs now. If you don't have room in the garden, grow them in containers.

❑ **SUMMER BULBS.** In South Texas (San Antonio to Rio Grande Valley), Austin, and the Hill Country, buy warm-season bulbs such as caladium, canna, and crinum. Plant when soil warms to at least 65°. Set out bearded iris, dahlia, and gladiolus any time after danger of frost is past.

❑ **VEGETABLES.** In warmer parts of Texas, sow beans, corn, cucumbers, eggplants, melons, peppers, squash, and tomatoes. Nurseries have transplants of most of these: set them out after danger of frost is past where you live. In cooler parts of Texas, start

indoors seed of everything except beans and corn (which are direct-sown after frost), and plant cool-season crops like broccoli, cabbage, carrots, cauliflower, kohlrabi, lettuce, potatoes, radishes, and spinach right away.

MAINTENANCE

❑ **CARE FOR HERBS.** In most of South Texas, cut back perennial herbs like mint and sage—the ones that die back or look ratty in winter—then fertilize and water them. Mint often dies back from the center. Reinvigorate it by stabbing a sharp shovel straight down through the roots several times in a crosshatch pattern.

❑ **DIVIDE PERENNIALS.** In North Texas (Dallas, Fort Worth), dig and divide clumping perennials like bearded iris, chrysanthemum, and daylily.

❑ **MAINTAIN DRIP SYSTEMS.** Before new plant growth covers existing drip systems, test them, looking for even water distribution. Clean algae out of filters with a mild solution of bleach and a toothbrush, and replace clogged emitters. Where alkaline deposits are clogging emitters, try dissolving the deposits with warm vinegar.

FIRST GARDENS

Beginners share the adventures and challenges of installing new gardens and renovating old ones. By Kathleen Norris Brenzel

BEFORE DAN LEHRER AND JOANNE KRUEGER BOUGHT their "falling-down house in Berkeley," neither of them had ever owned a garden. So the prospect of turning a 40- by 70-foot backyard "disaster area" with a battered plywood deck, a small concrete patio, a chain-link fence, a scruffy St. Augustine lawn, and a promising but neglected apple tree into something wonderful puzzled them. What to do with this rangy bit of earth? How? And where to start? ❧ Like most 20- and 30-somethings on tight budgets, they had two choices. Roll up their sleeves and plunge in, shovel first. Or live with the garden for a while, and wait for inspiration. ❧ When we asked our readers to share their first gardening experiences with us, more than 200 new gardeners replied. Their letters spun tales of big dreams and small pocketbooks. Aching backs. Soil-caked fingernails. Schedules so overflowing with first babies, new jobs, and school that gardening time was limited to weekends and evenings. ❧ But Lehrer, Krueger, and other new gardeners persevered. Why? Jean Zeller of San Jose could have been speaking for all of them when she wrote: "If I wanted a garden, there was only one way I was going to get it—sweat equity." ❧ Did their efforts pay off? Absolutely. Zeller's garden brought her "hours of peace, pure joy, and improved mental health." And Lehrer and Krueger? "We improvised, with magic results. Now we're starting a nursery." ❧

JOANNE KRUEGER

BEFORE (above): Construction materials nearly bury scruffy lawn. **AFTER** (right): 'Cl. Cécile Brunner' rose helps awaken the garden with color.

STARTING OVER: A grand adventure into organics

....

DAN LEHRER AND JOANNE KRUEGER, *Berkeley, California*

STARTED WITH: A "disaster area."
CREATED: An old-fashioned organic flower and vegetable garden with herbs and more than 50 old roses. "We call it Flatland Flower Farm," says Lehrer.
HOW: Lehrer and Krueger conquered the garden like pioneers conquering the West—bit by bit. After they tore down the deck, broke up the concrete patio with a sledgehammer, and hauled the pieces off to a concrete recycler, they started at the house and worked their way toward the back fence in 10-foot sections. In each section, they tilled the soil and dug in compost, homemade fertilizer, and rock powder, then planted. The garden took three years to renovate.
BEST FEATURES: "Everything is draped and covered and looks private," says Lehrer of the fences and trellises covered with rambling roses and vines. "The garden is now on autopilot; it just goes. We use no chemicals and make our own compost. It's our way of keeping the soil healthy."
BEST IDEA: Use of recycled materials. The couple built a rose trellis from an old wood ladder (a salvage yard find) and a worm bin from leftover fence posts. "Worm castings are black gold," says Lehrer. "They make great compost. Plants go bonkers for it."
COST: "Cheap. The biggest expense was wood for the deck—about $1,000 worth."

STARTING FROM SCRATCH:
Bare dirt to floral tapestry in less than a year

KAREN AND JEFF INGALLS,
Hollister, California

STARTED WITH: A new house with no landscaping in the backyard. Just "wall-to-wall weeds," says Karen, and "once we rototilled, wall-to-wall soil."

CREATED: A rectangular backyard tapestry of shrubs and flowers laced with paths, and a 20- by 30-foot deck for outdoor living.

HOW: "We made lists of things we liked and wanted," says Karen. "We needed big things to fill the space. On paper, we sketched out our ideas for the deck, a few fruit trees, flower beds, and walkways.

"We completed the work in less than a year. Jeff spent three days working amendments like compost into the soil. During May and June, my brother, who is in construction, built our deck at kinfolk prices. In July, we put in the sprinkler system with help from friends. In August, we built the paths. We planted in September and

October. Our motto for plants? If it works, good. If it doesn't, it gets pulled out."

BEST IDEA: Paths around the deck and leading toward the fruit trees were built of recycled materials. "We started picking up rocks in empty fields and creek beds," says Karen. "We got permission from a local rancher to take down some old redwood fence posts. Rocks and fence posts were set in the clay soil. The finished path took 440 rocks."

COST: About $3,800, including the deck, a toolshed, a sprinkler system, and plants. Labor costs amounted to "a couple of good dinners" for friends

WISTERIA *on a lath trellis spreads a cool, leafy cover over the redwood deck off the back of the house spring through fall; its fragrant lavender blooms dangle in late March and early April. White and lavender sweet alyssum edge the path in the foreground.*

BEFORE *(left): Bare soil from the back of the house to the distant back fence doesn't even hint at the possibilities.*
AFTER *(above): Path of recycled rocks and fencing wanders through profusion of plants, including roses, India hawthorn, California poppies, blue cornflowers, and fruit trees.*

ENGLISH COUNTRY on a rugged California slope

SARAH AND ANDREW SCHWARTZ, *Mill Valley, California*

STARTED WITH: A strip of barren hillside that wrapped the west and south sides of the house.

CREATED: "I wanted lots of flowers all jumbled together, like those country gardens in England, with areas among them for entertaining and for our two young boys to play," says Sarah. "I wanted lots of color—purples, yellows, pinks, reds. I also wanted plants with long stems that would move gracefully—lavender, penstemon, lavatera, and buddleia. And plants that smelled good—jasmine, thyme, mint, pineapple sage, roses. Texture was also important—princess flower and lamb's ears, my son's favorite."

HOW: Sarah hired a landscape contractor to terrace the hillside, bring in topsoil, build steps and a deck, and install a lawn across the bottom of the garden. Then she added the drip tubing, and did all the planting. "I had read that fall is a good time to plant in order to help plants establish strong root systems and ensure a burst of growth in

spring. Early planting and a wonderfully wet winter and spring did just that. I literally watched my garden grow before my eyes," she says. "By May, it was as close to an English garden as one could have in Mill Valley—a sea of color cascading down a winding path of steps." The garden took a year from start to bloom.

BEST IDEA: A sandbox, just 4 by 8 feet, that nestles against the house among flowers. "When the children outgrow it, we'll convert it to a planter box."

COST: About $25,000 (for terracing, retaining walls, fence, gate, deck, and labor), plus another $1,000 for drip tubing. Plants were extra.

GOLDEN COREOPSIS *and pink Mexican evening primrose edge the steps (above) near the house, where bush sweet peas lap at the sandbox. Below, penstemons in shades of red to white are the star performers in spring behind blue ground morning glory.*

RENEE LYNN

GLENN CORMIER

MEDITERRANEAN NATURAL near the Southern California coast

TED WELLS,
Laguna Niguel, California

STARTED WITH: "A challenge! Overgrown, front and back," says Wells. Flat lawns and large trees crowded the 60- by 200-foot lot; ivy completely engulfed the house.

CREATED: "A garden that uses water wisely, that's low maintenance, and has a natural, Mediterranean look."

HOW: Got rid of the lawn, kept the eucalyptus and olive trees, and brought in new topsoil. To add order to the front garden, Wells designed a natural-colored block wall with a glass-

paned French door as an entry gate. A simple arbor adjacent to it supports a bougainvillea. The rear garden is terraced with dry rock walls. Native and drought-resistant plants and scented geraniums fill in around them. Lady Banks' rose (yellow) and bearded iris add seasonal color. "During my yard redo, I gutted and rebuilt the entire house," Wells says. "I'm an architect and a masochist." The garden took four months of weekends to install, then about

four years of constant tinkering to refine. Gardening is a "continual process of editing," says Wells. "The response from my neighbors, in a land of manicured lawns and perfectly sculpted trees, has been overwhelming," he says. "My garden has taught me to respect patience and natural beauty, and it's a perfect antidote for my 70-hour workweek."

BEST IDEA: Instant lighting. "In the evenings, I use propane camp lanterns in trees or along paths to light the yard. This [type of lighting] seems more in keeping with the natural look of the yard."

COST: "Didn't keep track. But I spent a lot every time I went to the nursery."

SIMPLE ARBOR, *inspired by Japanese craftsmen and built of 2-by-2s, supports white bougainvillea 'Mary Palmer's Enchantment'. In rear garden (top), rosemary and lavender billow over the path; white 'Iceberg' rose climbs the eucalyptus tree.*

GREAT IDEAS FROM FIRST-TIME GARDENERS

NEIGHBORLY FENCE

"A PRETTY PIECE OF ART" is what Lisa Murphy and Mark Jensen of Seattle call the free-standing trellis that discreetly marks the property line between their front yard and their neighbors'. Built of pressure-treated wood, it stands about 7 feet tall. To steady it against wind, Jensen set the 4-by-4 side posts 3 feet deep in concrete. The 2-by-6 top rail and 2-by-2 bottom rail were screwed to the posts; 2-by-2 centers were screwed in place between them. A pink-flowered rose, 'Constance Spry', clambers over the trellis and blooms in June.

A ROSE CLIMBS THE LADDER

THIS ROSE TRELLIS had humble beginnings. To make it, Joanne Krueger (page 63) bought an old wood orchard ladder at a salvage yard and separated the two sides. Then, with the two sides facing each other about 30 inches apart, she bolted their tops to two crosspieces of redwood 2-by-4. The trellis supports a 'François Juranville' rose.

MARK DARLEY

THREE SEASONS OF FLORAL GRAPHICS

A SINGLE PYRACANTHA, trained against a trellis, hangs like an ever-changing painting against the garage wall at Eric Holdeman's house in Puyallup, Washington. Creamy white flowers in spring give way to brilliant red-orange berries in fall and winter. The rest of the year, green leaves carry the show. Holdeman built the 7- by 9-foot trellis as a grid of 14 cedar 1-by-2s, mounted it to 1-by-2 spacers against the wall (to allow breathing

MICHAEL SKOTT

room for the plant and to protect the painted surface of the wall), and painted it white to match the house trim. Then he planted the pyracantha (from a gallon can) at the base. It took four years for the plant to cover the trellis. Holdeman shears the plant every year in early spring, then gives it a light shaping once a month during active growth.

RENEE LYNN

Rugged & Natural

THE TRAIL THROUGH Jack and Jacque Burgess's new rear garden in Newark, California, cuts through a small meadow. "We wanted a huge, overgrown, wild look," says Jack. The Burgesses were inspired by a favorite hiking trail in the Desolation Wilderness area of the Sierra Nevada. Their trail looks natural, but it never gets muddy in winter. The Burgesses graded it, then spread landscape fabric atop the compacted, heavy clay soil and covered the fabric with crushed granite. California native plants, and grasses such as creeping red fescue, fill the meadow. Artificial boulders ("cheaper than the real thing") nestle among the grasses.

Recycled Concrete

REMOVING AND REPLACING concrete with a visually softer material was an expensive proposition. So Ted Wells (page 67), with help from a stone specialist, broke up the concrete with a hammer and chisel, rearranged the pieces, and planted ground covers between them. These include dymondia in sunny areas, and baby's tears and Irish moss in shady ones.

GLENN CORMIER

Brick Path Notched with Beds for Greens

THE BRICK PATH surrounding these little rectangular beds keeps Eric Holdeman's feet dry whenever he dashes outdoors to harvest lettuce for a sandwich. The bricks were set in a 4-inch layer of sand atop a 4-inch layer of gravel. Each of the five planting beds is just 3 by 4 feet; they edge the south-facing deck off Holdeman's living room. In spring and summer, they're filled with lettuce. In winter, they serve as holding beds for perennials, or they're planted with cover crops.

5 FIRST-TIMER STUMBLING BLOCKS and what to do about them

COST: How to keep it down?

Design costs can add up fast. But first-timers are finding ways to get help without emptying their bank accounts. "Our most important $250 was spent on a local landscape architect," writes Jill Abere of Wilsonville, Oregon. "She constructed a plan…which allowed us to purchase the plants as our budget permitted." The Aberes did the hands-on work. Eric Holdeman got help from a nursery. "I drew a rough diagram of the site. I contacted a local nursery, and… paid $150 for someone to give me a plant listing and some ideas on paper."

Labor costs can add up, too. But one first-timer asked a girlfriend to bring over her tractor and build some mounds of soil. Another recruited her mother-in-law to dig out fence posts. And friends helped one novice put in a brick patio during a patio-building party.

SAVE THE BEST; DISCARD THE REST. Before you do anything, look around the garden. Ask yourself which features you can keep or reuse, and which ones must go. The more good material you already have, the less you need to buy.

BUY SMALL PLANTS. Plants in gallon cans cost less than those in 5-gallon cans, and they become established just as fast. Start lawns from grass seed instead of sod.

USE RECYCLED MATERIALS. Used wood and paving materials, left over from remodeling projects, are often available at salvage yards. Even plants can be recycled: "We planted everything our wonderful neighbor threw over the fence," writes one gardener.

TACKLE ONE AREA AT A TIME. Breaking the big project into a series of smaller ones is easier on the pocketbook and the psyche. Sara Eaton of Seattle approached her landscaping project in three stages. "First we tore out many overgrown or dead shrubs. Second, we cleaned up and planted the side yard. Third, we planted the front yard."

WEEDS: "They're everywhere"

Hoeing and hand-weeding are effective, but backbreaking in large areas. Many first-timers who wrote us swore by these

two nonchemical methods:

LANDSCAPE FABRIC. Made of woven polypropylene or other synthetic materials, these fabrics screen out weeds (the denser the fabric, the better it suppresses weeds). All allow air, water, and liquid fertilizers to reach the soil. You put them around trees and shrubs to create a barrier against weeds, then cover them with 2 to 3 inches of a weed-free organic mulch such as shredded bark. They're available in various lengths and widths in nurseries.

SOIL SOLARIZATION. You till the soil, moisten it to a depth of 1 foot, spread a sheet of UV-stabilized plastic over the top, then let the sun's heat bake weeds and weed seeds, killing them. This method is most effective when the sun is hot and days are long.

SOIL: Sandpit, or rock-hard

In new housing tracts, construction can strip the topsoil, leaving only infertile subsoil. In sandy soils, the water drains away so fast you can watch it disappear. And heavy soils can be as hard as concrete. Such problem soils need improving before anything will grow in them. To break up hard soils and bind sandy soils, mix in organic matter such as compost. You can buy it in bulk (look in the yellow pages under Landscaping

Supplies) at substantial savings over by-the-bag products from a nursery. Till the entire planting area, then spread a layer of amendment 2 to 3 inches thick over the site, and till the area again. If the area is small enough, use a spading fork.

IRRIGATION: Where to start?

Getting an existing irrigation system working efficiently, or installing a new one, can be the best investment that you make.

To renovate a sprinkler system, first check it out. Look for broken, clogged, and leaking heads and poor spray pat-

terns. Stores that specialize in irrigation equipment sell replacement parts. For more difficult repairs, such as broken

pipes, or to add a new system, it may be necessary to call in a specialist (look in the yellow pages under Sprinklers). For an overview of irrigation options, look in *Sunset Western Garden Book* (1995 edition), under Watering Devices.

PLANTS: Where to put them?

Horror stories abound from first gardeners who discovered—too late—the true character of the plants they'd chosen to grow. One beginner was appalled when a cute little kitten of a salvia she'd bought in a gallon can quickly grew into an elephant and crowded out everything else (even the front door); she had to dig and move it. Paula Doubleday planted lavatera and salvia (unthirsty sun lovers) near rhododendron (a thirstier shade lover) in her Oakland garden. "Not a well-planned area," she admitted.

LEARN ABOUT YOUR FAVORITE PLANTS. One couple took horticulture classes at a

community college so their "first garden wouldn't be entirely random." Another garden maker "made lists, detailing plant height and spread, water needs, disease or bug problems." A third couple went to nurseries. "If we saw something we liked, we checked in the books to see if it would work in the areas we had in mind."

GROW SUITABLE PLANTS. Ones that are best adapted to your climate grow better, and they won't demand as much coddling as plants that don't belong.

BEAT THE BARE-DIRT DOLDRUMS. Annuals, when planted as a temporary cover in a future planting area, can spice the garden with color for a season. One gardener achieved the "overflowing with plants" look she was impatient for by supplementing her first-year perennials with annuals. ■

"OUTCROP" *is made of bricks and concrete. Ground covers and perennials grow out of cracks.*

from jobs, so I decided to do something completely different and fun. In the retaining wall I even used champagne bottles for their color and shape. Now I refer to my raised bed as coming from the Hedonozoic era."

In one corner of the raised bed (shown below left), *Sedum oreganum, Sempervivum arachnoideum,* and *Sesleria caerulea* spill out of the tops of pipes.

In another section (shown at left), an arrangement of peach-colored concrete, pale bricks, rocks, and flagstone looks as if it's been disrupted for years, thanks to the well-established collection of plants. Tucked in and around the outcrop are spiky yellow-flowered sedum 'Blue Spruce',

California geology in miniature

El Cerrito garden takes its inspiration from the creases of earthquake country

W HEN LANDSCAPE designer Jana Olson Drobinsky describes her garden in El Cerrito, California, she begins by explaining the geologic theory of plate tectonics. "California has a folded and faulted landscape. As two plates collide, rocks are tipped up and the earth wrinkles." How does this relate to her garden? "I wanted my backyard to be a joke on California geology, so I created California geology in miniature."

The focus of the garden is a large raised bed surrounded by a quirky mix of "found" objects such as broken concrete and used bricks—all arranged to appear twisted and distorted as if pushed up from the depths below. Plants are tucked into the cracks and crevices.

SHE STARTED WITH
A BLANK SLATE

Olson Drobinsky started with a plot full of mowed weeds—all that was left after

CHAMPAGNE BOTTLES, *clay sewer pipes, and bricks in two colors mimic a newly formed rock outcrop.*

INSPIRED BY WAVING GRASS, *pink and purple fence bends and twists behind foreground of English lavender.*

she removed a Western red cedar hedge.

Since the yard had a substantial slope, a retaining wall was needed to level the upper slope for a patio and vegetable garden. At first Olson Drobinsky was going to construct a wall that was rigid and curved, which would have meant building forms and pouring concrete. "I was planning to do much of the work myself," she explains, "but was feeling lazy on the weekends, since at the time I was working hard as a designer-contractor during the week. I had lots of leftover materials

yellow yarrow, orange monkey flower, orange geum, and mat-forming *Scleranthus biflorus* and *S. uniflorus.*

The lower garden is devoted to a red fescue meadow surrounded by a chaparral planted with English lavender, Santa Cruz Island buckwheat (*Eriogonum arborescens*), sunflowers, tufted hair grass (*Deschampsia caespitosa vivipara*), and *Verbena bonariensis.* Steel manhole covers from a recycled-materials supplier march through the meadow in playful contrast to the natural setting. ∎

By Lauren Bonar Swezey

PETER CHRISTIANSEN

PETER CHAN *has been growing vegetables for 46 of his 66 years.*

Raise a bed of great vegetables

Virtuoso gardener Peter Chan shares his secrets for growing crops in raised beds

WHEN OUR FRIEND PETER CHAN told us he was going to create a new vegetable garden in Northern California, we were eager to watch. Chan is one of the West's best vegetable gardeners, and his gardens are as highly productive as they are beautiful.

We first met him about 15 years ago, when he won a *Sunset* garden contest. He was living in Portland and would soon publish the classic text on Chinese raised-bed vegetable gardening (*Better Vegetable Gardens the Chinese Way,* now out of print). A practical man with an engaging manner, he went on the horticultural lecture circuit, where he's had a major impact on the way Americans garden.

Then, a year ago, Chan moved to the San Francisco Peninsula, where he planned a new garden in his small backyard. He invited us to observe as the garden took shape, and after seeing it flourish, we're happy to report that his techniques work as well in California as they did in Oregon. And they can work in your garden, too.

RAISING THE BEDS

Chan, who once taught at an agricultural college in China, favors raised beds because they get maximum production from minimum space. Soil in such beds warms earlier in spring, drains well, and never gets trod on, so it remains loose and easy for roots, air, and water to penetrate.

In a way, his job was made easier by the native heavy clay soil: it was so bad he didn't even consider planting in it or amending it. Instead, he built the 3½- by 14-foot raised beds. Each is made from recycled redwood 2-by-10s nailed to corner posts of 10-inch 4-by-4s.

The width of the beds was determined by Chan's reach; from the path, he can easily weed the center of each bed (if you have longer arms, make your beds commensurately wider). The length of the beds was determined by the space

A SPRINKLING OF LIME *(left) and a 1-inch layer of blended manures go into the bottom of a bed before it is filled with planting mix. Above, neat rows of 'Tah Choy' Chinese cabbage are replaced with new seedlings as they're harvested.*

available, but Chan advises against anything longer than 20 feet.

The beds are oriented roughly east-west for maximum sun exposure for all plants. Between the beds are 18-inch-wide dirt paths packed down with blows from the back of a spade. In winter, he covers them with straw or bark dust; gravel, brick, or concrete would work as well.

For climbing crops—peas, beans, and cucumbers—he adds an A-frame trellis system (pictured at right) made from galvanized plumbing pipes that were drilled, sprayed with zinc, and bolted together. The A-frames support wire or twine for the vines to climb.

PLANTING MIX IS A SPECIAL BLEND

Before filling the beds with planting mix, Chan dusts the bottom of each with lime, then covers that with an inch of mixed chicken and steer manure or homemade compost. A planting mix composed of 50 percent aged redwood compost, 40 percent topsoil, and 10 percent sand tops off the beds.

The fertilizer is never blended into the planting mix; it stays put on the bottom of each bed to encourage plant roots to grow deep. Keeping the top inch of soil relatively infertile also discourages weed seedlings from getting a fast start.

NOURISHING PLANTS

In China, Chan grew everything from seed. These days, he grows most of his first crop of vegetables from nursery seedlings he buys in mid-March. He favors bok choy and other Chinese vegetables, cabbage, lettuce, spinach, tomatoes, peppers, eggplant, and bitter melon. He grows beans and Chinese pea pods from seed.

After the first nursery-grown

CUCUMBERS CLIMB *twine strung on an 8-foot-tall trellis made of galvanized pipe. Below, tomatoes ripen on the vine before harvest.*

seedlings are in the ground, he starts later crops from seed when warmer air and soil encourage germination. To give seedlings a push, he mixes 1 tablespoon of fish emulsion per gallon of water, then pours it along the sides of growing plants twice each week. He continues this feeding method, called side dressing, all season for leafy vegetables, but fruit-bearing vegetables (like beans, peas, cucumbers, melons, peppers, squash, and tomatoes) get fed only until they flower; then they're on their own.

He also gives fish emulsion to root vegetables like potatoes and radishes through the season, adding a little high-potassium fertilizer if a soil test tells him it's needed.

Watering is done early in the day. Chan irrigates with a watering wand on a hose, dousing the tops of leaf and root crops completely, but keeping water off the fruiting vegetables (he doesn't want to rinse any pollen off the flowers).

ROTATING CROPS

Because his raised beds are used for long-term food production, Chan fights soil-borne diseases by rotating crops. If he plants cabbage family members in a bed this year, he'll put a completely different crop (tomatoes, for example) in that bed next year. Ideally, a bed never grows the same crop more than once in four or five years.

After a crop comes out, Chan freshens the beds by shoveling soil out of the center third of each bed and piling it on the ends. Then he sprinkles lime in the dug-out area, adds another inch of manure or homemade compost, and brings the old soil back. He repeats the process for the ends of the beds, then waters and lets the soil settle before replanting. ■

By Jim McCausland

A KING-SIZE BERRY *forms in each fruit cluster of 'Seascape'; try it dipped in chocolate.*

NORMAN A. PLATE

Until there's a perfect strawberry, try 'Seascape'

This everbearing variety produces big crops of tasty fruit

JUST AS JASON AND THE Argonauts searched for the Golden Fleece, plant breeders have been striving to find the perfect everbearing strawberry—one that produces lots of great-tasting fruit over a long season. While their quest continues, a new variety called 'Seascape' demonstrates how far they've come.

Developed by breeders from the University of California at Davis, 'Seascape' is one of the most productive everbearing varieties yet. In *Sunset*'s test garden, a bed of 'Seascape' yielded good crops of large berries with excellent flavor. Each cluster produces one extra-large berry (called the king berry).

Because 'Seascape' doesn't need much chill to set fruit, it's especially promising for mild-winter parts of the West. In cooler locations, 'Seascape' will probably flower so early that frost will kill its blooms and eliminate the early harvest. Later flowering and harvests won't be affected. If you garden in a cool region with a warm microclimate, however, you'll probably have ripe strawberries before the first California strawberries show up at the supermarket. While 'Seascape' bears over a long season, fruiting is concentrated in late spring.

'Seascape' has good disease resistance but is somewhat susceptible to leaf spot.

PLANTING TIPS

Nurseries and garden centers sell 'Seascape' as bare-root plants. Plant right away in good garden loam. Strawberries don't like salty soil or water; if your native soil is alkaline, plant them in imported topsoil.

If you're tight on space, tuck plants into the sides of strawberry pots, where they'll bear fruit for months. For greater production, set out plants at 16-inch intervals in rows 18 inches apart. Apply complete fertilizer after new growth begins, then again after the first harvest. Spread organic mulch around plants to help keep the soil moist between waterings.

To get maximum berry production, pinch off the first flush of flowers so plants can direct energy into establishing a strong root system. You'll still get fruit the first year—just later. Early disbudding may help eliminate the monkey-faced berries that sometimes show up with the year's earliest crop.

LONG-TERM CARE

Strawberries are notoriously short-lived. Diseases build up in the plants over the years, causing fruit production to drop gradually. That's why commercial growers usually replace everbearing strawberry plants every year or two.

In a home garden, you can keep your strawberry patch going indefinitely by letting the mother plants (the first plants you set out) bear fruit and send out runners for two years. Then pull the older plants out, leaving the daughter plants produced by the runners. If you follow this pattern, you'll never have any plant more than 2 years old in the garden, and you'll always have new, vigorous, disease-free plants starting up. ■

By Jim McCausland

Where rhodies grow for the glory

*See the Northwest's top performers
on Whidbey Island, Washington*

W HAT ARE THE
hottest new rhodo-
dendrons?" mused
a rhododendron
breeder we know. "Ten years
ago I could have told you,
but now there are so many
flooding the market, I can't
keep track. *Nobody* can keep
track, unless it's Meerkerk."

Meerkerk Rhododendron
Gardens, that is. Set in a tranquil 53-acre woodland on
Whidbey Island, Washington,
this garden puts about 50
rhododendrons into a six-year
trial every year, rating each
for flower, form, sun tolerance, and pest resistance.

The flowering season at
Meerkerk starts in earnest
this month, and you're welcome to stop by for a look.
You'll also get the chance to
vote on your favorites, since
much of what makes a great
rhododendron is a matter of
individual taste.

WINNERS FOR
THE NORTHWEST

For many years, the
American Rhododendron
Society has rated rhododen-
drons (these ratings are listed

WHITE 'ALBATROSS'
*rhododendron (left) rises
above 'Peste's Pink to
Yellow'. 'President Roosevelt'
(above right) has red flowers
and variegated leaves.*

in the *Sunset Western Garden
Book*). But this system has
always been flawed: a plant
that shines in Portland may
be a dud in Spokane.

The work at Meerkerk is
of huge benefit to gardeners
in mild parts of the Pacific
Northwest because it shows
which varieties do best in this
climate. Plants for trial are
sent by a wide array of grow-

ers and hybridizers, from
Hachmann's in Germany to
Warren Berg, Bruce Briggs,
Frank Fujioka, Elsie Watson,
and many others in the
United States.

You can see how their
plants perform at Meerkerk.
But remember that all rhododendrons, including those
that prefer shade, are tested
in full sun here, so any plants
you see with sun-bleached
leaves might do far better in
filtered sunlight.

JAMES F. HOUSEL

'MEERKERK MAGIC' *(above) should be on the market next year. 'Golden Genie' (right) is already available at nurseries.*

Since some rhododendrons are ugly ducklings in their youth but mature into exquisite shrubs, only 3-year-old plants are put into the trials. Plants that haven't reached full maturity during the trials but still show promise are transplanted into the gardens among some 3,000 other rhododendrons.

Because Meerkerk is managed with visitors in mind, it sells many of the rhododendrons you see in bloom. Any plants you buy should be set out right away.

STROLL THE GARDENS

After you walk through the test gardens and note your favorites, head over to the Tribute Garden. The best varieties from each previous graduating class of rhododendrons (those that have been through the six-year test cycle) are here in their mature glory.

If you have a taste for species rhododendrons (the wild stock from which present-day hybrids were bred), stop at the Berg Asian Garden. The late Ann Meerkerk, who donated this land to the Seattle Rhododendron Society (SRS) in 1979, had a special fondness for fragrant rhododendrons and azaleas. Some fragrant species include *R. auriculatum, R. decorum, R. fortunei, R. luteum,* and *R. occidentale.* The garden is managed by the SRS according to Ann Meerkerk's vision.

The core of the collection, however, is in the Heritage Garden, where her artistry as a weaver and painter is evident in the textures and colors she used here.

Meerkerk Rhododendron Gardens is open from 9 to 4 daily. Admission costs $2. From State Highway 525 between mileposts 23 and 24, take Resort Road east ⅓ mile to Meerkerk Lane, then turn left and go ⅓ mile.

If you can't visit Meerkerk, you can gain access to the information collected and catalogued here during the past 10 years. It is updated periodically in the *Journal of the American Rhododendron Society.* To find out how Meerkerk rates a particular rhododendron, send a self-addressed, stamped envelope to Kristi O'Donnell, Meerkerk Rhododendron Gardens, Box 154, Greenbank, WA 98253; or send an e-mail request to meerkerk@whidbey.net. ■

By Jim McCausland

GREEK OREGANO *tumbles over the pot's front edges; pineapple sage rises behind. Wheeled platform allows the pot to be moved easily.*

wheeled platform for easy moving.

That pot was the beginning of Morrison's herb-gardening adventure. "I've planted quite a few pots since then," she says. "I love cooking with herbs."

She's tried other shapes and sizes of self-watering pots, too—oblong and hanging ones. They all work well, but the number of plants used has to be adjusted for container size. The pots are widely available at nurseries and home and garden centers.

PLANTING THE HERB POT

Morrison fills the pot with potting mix and adds granular fertilizer to the soil. Then she plants the herbs from 2-inch pots, setting them so they nearly touch ("You can really crowd the plants, and they do great," she says). To ring the edge of the pot, she chooses low growers such as Greek oregano (cascading down the front), variegated lemon thyme, Italian parsley, chives, and 'Tricolor' sage, as well as taller upright rosemary and pineapple sage ("It has the most beautiful red flowers"). Sweet basil, 'Purple Ruffles' basil, and 'Icterina' sage rise in the middle of the pot.

A simpler combination she's tried successfully includes basil, chives, cilantro, garlic chives, oregano, and rosemary.

MAINTAINING THE HERBS

During spring and summer, the reservoir needs refilling once or twice a week, depending on the weather. In winter, rain keeps the pot irrigated, but excess water must be dumped from the reservoir regularly or it turns brackish.

Morrison trims the herbs constantly for cooking and to keep the plants bushy and the foliage looking lush and fresh. She replants annual herbs like basil when necessary. In early spring, she refurbishes the pot by cutting back all of the tired-looking perennial herbs (pineapple sage needs to be hacked more than once during the year) and by adding new annual herbs. At the same time, she gives the plants a boost by adding a liquid fertilizer to the watering trough. ■

By Lauren Bonar Swezey

Easy-care herb pot

Herbs stay watered and fed thanks to this pot's built-in reservoir. All you do is plant

IT DOESN'T TAKE A LARGE PLOT of land or a Master Gardener to grow herbs successfully. That's what Peggy Morrison of Seal Beach, California, discovered when she offered to plant herbs for a friend. "My friend has a brown thumb and is often away from home," she says. "I found a self-watering pot at a warehouse club for about $12 and gave it a try."

The pot she used (above) is plastic and measures 18 inches across and 14 inches deep. Its built-in reservoir gets filled through a horizontal slot in the side of the pot. Since the pot is heavy when filled with soil and water, she set it on a

'VILLE DE LYON' *(left), a hybrid clematis with velvety flowers, blooms profusely in June. C. macropetala (above) blooms in early spring.*

Clematis: A three-season guide to floral beauty

Pick the right kinds for bloom on the vine from early spring through fall

WHEN YOU THINK OF CLEMATIS, you probably think of the big, colorful flowers you see blooming in summer on leafy vines. But summer-blooming clematis represent only one branch of a huge family of flowering vines that flaunt their blossoms over a long period at low elevations of Northern California and the Pacific Northwest.

More than 200 species of clematis are available, as well as scores of hybrids. By choosing the right plants you can have clematis in flower from March all the way to frost.

Many nurseries carry a few varieties of clematis in 1-gallon cans. You can also order plants from mail-order suppliers (see list on facing page). Set plants out immediately.

The following clematis are listed in approximate order of bloom.

MARCH INTO APRIL

Clematis macropetala. This species is prized for its vivid blue 4-inch flowers that bloom in early spring on delicate vines. Named varieties may have double flowers; blooms may be shades of blue, pink, or lavender.

APRIL INTO MAY

C. armandii. This evergreen clematis sends out big, rambunctious shoots filled with red juvenile leaves that turn rich green and leathery. Small (2½-inch) glistening white flowers have pointed petals. *C. a.* 'Apple Blossom', a newly introduced variety, has flowers that resemble large apple blossoms, which open pink and fade to white. This plant will, in time, turn into a thick thatch of tangled branches. Prune it immediately after flowering. It is not hardy in *Sunset Western Garden Book* zones 1, 2, and 3.

C. montana. Commonly called the anemone clematis, it produces masses of pink flowers resembling anemone blossoms. Two varieties are widely available: *C. m.* 'Rubens' (pictured on facing page) and *C. m.* 'Tetrarose'; both have flowers with a stronger pink than the plain species. This vigorous plant develops strong, woody stems; prune hard after flowering to limit growth.

MAY INTO JUNE

C. alpina. This clematis, a gift from the Alps, produces an abundance of blue blooms about 2 inches long. *C. a.* 'Willy' has pale pink flowers that look a bit like fuchsia blossoms.

C. ligusticifolia. This Western native

bears masses of small white blossoms on a vigorous vine. It's one of the best clematis for standing up to dry summers. It's hard to find; check arboretum and plant society sales.

JUNE THROUGH AUGUST

C. lanuginosa. The variety *C. l.* 'Candida' features a burst of yellow stamen in brilliant white flowers that commonly reach 8 inches across. This plant produces flowers on graceful vines of old and new wood; prune it sparingly.

C. viticella. Its buds resemble candles on the vine before opening into purple to rose-purple flowers 2 to 3 inches across with gently ribbed petals that curl back. It's a very hardy, vigorous plant.

C. 'Jackmanii'. Well-known 'Jackmanii' is not a true species but a cultivated variety. It bears big deep purple blossoms. Other selections come in shades of white and red.

Clematis hybrids. There are dozens of them, hybridized for large flowers, rich colors, and a long bloom period. Most put out a flush of bloom in June, then flower sporadically throughout summer. *C.* 'Marie Boisselot' has sparkling white flowers 6 to 8 inches wide. *C.* 'Hagley Hybrid' bears clear pink star-shaped flowers. *C.* 'Nelly Moser' looks like a dish of peppermint candy, with pale pink petals striped with dark rose. *C.* 'Niobe' bears dark red flowers.

C. florida. Little known until recently in the United States, this clematis made a huge splash when *C. florida* 'Sieboldii' hit the market. Its unusual flowers have big creamy white sepals surrounding rich purple and green centers. A new variety, *C. f.* 'Alba Plena', has 3-inch double flowers in pale greenish white. *C. florida* is not hardy in zones 1, 2, and 3.

C. texensis. A Texas native, this species will stand up to dry summers. 'Duchess of Albany', the best-known variety, bears large bell-shaped blossoms of deep rose. The foliage has a bluish tint. In cool, moist summer climates, try planting it in a south-facing location with plenty of air circulation.

SEPTEMBER INTO OCTOBER

C. dioscoreifolia. This clematis produces a cloud of cream-colored inch-wide blossoms in early autumn. When petals drop, the seed heads are feathery tassels that hang on well into winter. To control this aggressive vine, cut it back hard

PINK-FLOWERED *Clematis montana (above) blooms April into May. C. m. 'Rubens' (right) has vines that reach 15 to 25 feet long.*

after flowering or in early spring. (Much confusion exists about this species; it's often sold as *C. paniculata* or as a similar clematis, *C. maximowicziana.*)

SEPTEMBER INTO NOVEMBER

C. tangutica. Small (2- to 4-inch) rich yellow blossoms of this clematis hang like little Chinese lanterns on stiff upright stems. After flowering, fuzzy silver seed pods hang on through winter. It's a tough little vine.

PLANTING AND CULTIVATION

Clematis are relatively undemanding plants, and usually remain free of disease and pests. Most kinds do best when grown in loose, cool, moist soil. There's an old saying about growing clematis that is essential to know: Flowers in the sun, feet in the shade. When grown against a south- or west-facing wall, the plant should come up from behind a shading shrub, planted well enough away that roots don't compete.

To plant, dig a hole 18 inches deep and equally wide. Put a layer of compost or well-rotted manure at the bottom of the hole, and mix generous amounts of the same organic matter into the backfill soil. Most species need plenty of water to flourish.

The vine will need a support system to climb on (a trellis or lattice works well); weave the plant up through the support as it grows, or tie it with twine. You can also train the plant to grow up and through a larger plant.

To keep plants vigorous and floriferous, feed them regularly with a balanced fertilizer. Scatter a dose of 12-12-12 fertilizer around the base of a well-established plant in mid-February, early April, mid- to late May, and early July. Or apply a similar plant food in liquid form monthly throughout the entire growing season.

SOURCES

If you can't find the plants you want at local nurseries, try one of these mail-order sources, which have wide selections of clematis.

D and L Donahue Clematis, 420 S.W. 10th St., Fairbault, MN 55021; (507) 334-8404 (call for price list).

Wayside Gardens, 1 Garden Lane, Hodges, SC 29695; (800) 845-1124 (free catalog). ■

By Steven R. Lorton

Foxglove flower spikes intermingle with white daisies in this Menlo Park, California, garden.
For details on growing foxgloves from seed, see page 86.

APRIL

Garden guide 84

Checklists & garden notebooks 89

The new cutting garden 94

Paradise for plant lovers 102

Shade plants with a sunny look . . . 105

Organic gardening success 106

For the love of lavender 108

Bloom-again bearded irises 110

Backyard poultry 112

Space-saving watermelons 114

'Blue Lake': still the best bean? . . . 115

Tender, tasty bok choy 116

Grow orchids in your trees 117

GARDEN
Guide

Acres of blooming tulips in Oregon

One of the Northwest's most exuberant spring flower shows takes place this month in Woodburn, Oregon, when row upon row of tulips burst into bloom at the Wooden Shoe Bulb Company. This 60-acre bulb farm has been owned and operated by the Iverson

family for more than two decades. During bloom time, the Iversons invite visitors to come and see the flowers, take pictures, make notes, and order bulbs for fall planting. (In 1996, the farm was open from 9 A.M. to dusk daily from March 20 through April 21.)

The farm is just off Interstate 5 between Portland and Salem.

With more than 175 varieties of tulips in flower, it's an ideal time to pick the ones you like. Old-time favorites include rosy pink 'Gander', double yellow 'Monte Carlo', and dark

purple 'Negrita'. New introductions to look for are 'Akela' (ivory flecked with pink), 'Esther' (soft pink with a blue center), and 'Scotch Lassie' (long-lasting deep lavender flowers).

In the gift shop, you'll find decorative pots, handsome vases, and cut flowers for sale.

For more information, or to order a free catalog, call

Pacific Coast irises are undiscovered garden gems

Orchidlike flowers of Iris douglasiana and hybrids come in a variety of colors. Blooms can reach 5 inches across.

NORMAN A. PLATE

The three Pacific Coast states are home to about seven species of indigenous iris, collectively called Pacific Coast irises, all of which grow west of the Cascades–Sierra Nevada mountain ranges.

These species produce tufts of grassy foliage and typical iris blossoms, although the plants are smaller in stature and the flowers aren't as big as those of the more widely grown bearded, Dutch, Siberian, and spuria irises. Yet these native irises are valuable garden plants, albeit somewhat difficult to find.

The most vigorous and easiest to grow is *Iris douglasiana,* found in nature from California's Santa Barbara County north to southern Oregon. It stretches to a height of 12 to 18 inches and has evergreen leaf blades about ¾ inch across. Flowers range from cream to reddish purple. Most common are the pale lavender varieties veined with purple. This species does best in full sun to partial shade.

Oregon native, *I. innominata,* has grassier foliage than *I. douglasiana* but offers a wider range of flower colors—blue, lavender, cream, gold, and copper, both solid colors and veined combinations.

In the garden, *I. innominata* is a woodland or rock garden plant that prefers dappled sunlight or light shade, except in foggy coastal regions.

Hybrids between these two species (and, in some instances, involving one or more of the other species) come in a breathtaking array of colors and patterns. Many boast larger flowers with broader petals than found in their wild ancestors.

Give these irises good, well-drained soil. They tolerate summer drought well; in fact, plants that get frequent summer irrigation tend to bloom less and die out sooner. They naturalize easily: allow seed pods to form, split, and scatter naturally to form colonies of plants. Try tucking them among large stones, edging a path, or carpeting the ground under rhododendrons.

You can sometimes find *I. douglasiana* or *I. innominata* at sales by arboretums and plant societies. More and more retail nurseries are carrying the hybrids in 1-gallon containers. One mail-order source for plants is Siskiyou Rare Plant Nursery, 2825 Cummings Rd., Medford, OR 97501; (541) 772-6846 (catalog $3).

When spider mites bite into conifers

Although generally considered a heat-of-the-summer pest, spider mites also flourish in the mild Northwest climates west of the Cascades. They're experts at sucking the juices right out of coniferous plants like spruces. Affected plants develop a pale, dried-out look, then needles start to drop. Dwarf Alberta spruce seems to get the worst of it.

Although many chemical pesticides can control mites, conifer aficionado Jock Demme of Boring, Oregon, prefers to fight them with water alone. Twice a week during warm weather, Demme drenches his conifers with a strong blast of water from his garden hose. He shoots the water right into the center of the plants, soaking them from top to bottom on all sides.

His persistence pays off: there's no evidence of mites on Demme's plants; they keep their rich color and their needles.

Multicolored morning glories and a great zucchini

Bud Stuckey, coordinator of the test garden at *Sunset*'s headquarters in Menlo Park, California, is always growing new and unusual plants in the 2,000-square-foot plot. And when those plants prove very rewarding to grow—for their productivity, stamina, beauty, or extraordinary flavor—he's eager to share his finds. Last summer, two of these plants stood out as clear winners.

Multicolored morning glories.
Summer-flowering morning glories (*Ipomoea tricolor*)

Morning glory flowers are at peak perfection early in the day. By afternoon, they fade, but others soon open.

NORMAN A. PLATE

are well loved for their sky blue flowers that open in the morning and fade by afternoon. Less familiar but equally handsome are other morning glories in shades of brown, crimson, lavender, maroon, pink, purple, red, and white.

Last spring, Bud bought seed packets of four kinds of morning glories at the nursery—'Crimson Rambler' and 'Giant Mixed' (from Ferry-Morse Seeds), and 'Early Call' and 'Scarlet O'Hara' (from Lake Valley Seed)—and mixed them together before planting them on a trellis. The results, as

shown in the photograph above, were stunning.

By early summer the vines had reached the top of the 8-foot-tall trellis and were producing a rainbow of colors each morning. The dominant vines were the 'Giant Mixed', which grow to 10 feet tall and bloom in shades of blue, crimson, pink, and white.

To speed germination, Bud soaked the seeds in warm water for 2 hours right before planting. Then he sowed the seeds in place, following the seed packet directions for spacing distances. Lake Valley seeds are

sold only through nurseries. Ferry-Morse seeds are now available by mail; write to Box 488, Fulton, KY 42041, or call the company at (800) 283-3400 (catalog is free).

A round zucchini. 'Ronde de Nice' is even rounder and nicer than Bud had hoped. He knew this French heirloom zucchini would produce cute little squash. That's why he tried it. But he didn't expect the same adjectives to apply to the plant itself.

Most zucchini bushes are big, sprawling things. This one is compact and neat, confining itself to a mound of foliage. It's attractive enough to plant in a flower bed, making it a good choice for small gardens. The squashes it produced turned out to be as tasty as they were attractive; with a firm, creamy texture and lots of vegetable sweetness, it's good both raw and cooked.

Although the plants are relatively compact, do give them a little elbowroom. Bud didn't do this with his first crop, and the plants were too crowded. With his second crop, he followed the 3- to 4-foot spacing recommended on the seed packets, and he found 'Ronde de Nice' to be as prodigiously productive as any other zucchini.

Seeds are available from Shepherd's Garden Seeds, (408) 335-6910; or from The Cook's Garden, (802) 824-3400.

Golden blossoms unfurl on 'Ronde de Nice' zucchini.

Rotate your vegetable crops

Diseases and soil-dwelling pests (such as root-knot nematodes) tend to build up fastest where closely related plants are grown in the same ground year after year. The best way to stay ahead of such problems is to rotate your crops.

Keep in mind that vegetables fall into just a few basic family groups. If you avoid putting plants from the same group into the same ground any more than once every four or five years, you'll minimize disease buildup.

Here are the six main vegetable groups:

Alliums. These include chives, garlic, leeks, and onions.

Brassicas (also called cole crops). Familiar ones are broccoli, brussels sprouts, cabbage, cauliflower, kale, kohlrabi, and radish.

Chenopodiaceous vegetables. More simply referred to as "chenopodes," these include beets, chard, and spinach.

Cucurbits. In this group fall cucumbers, melons, pumpkins, and squashes.

Legumes. Here are all kinds of beans and peas.

Solanaceous vegetables. These include widely-grown eggplants, peppers, potatoes, and tomatoes.

Some well-known edibles—including basil, carrots, corn, lettuce, and okra—don't belong to any of these six main groups, so you can rotate them in any time. But it's still best not to grow any one of these plants in the same ground in consecutive years.

By Sharon Cohoon, Steven R. Lorton, Jim McCausland, Lauren Bonar Swezey

PLANTING

BARE-ROOT STOCK. In zones 1–3, hurry to plant bare-root cane berries, fruit trees, ornamental trees, and perennial vegetables such as asparagus. Keep bare roots moist until you can get plants into the ground.

BERRIES. Throughout the Northwest, blackberries, blueberries, raspberries, and strawberries can be planted this month.

SUMMER-BLOOMING BULBS. In zones 4–7, nurseries offer acidanthera, calla, crocosmia, dahlia, gladiolus, ranunculus, tigridia, and others for immediate planting.

VEGETABLES. Throughout the Northwest, plant cabbage, carrots, lettuce, parsnips, peas, potatoes, radishes, spinach, and Swiss chard.

MAINTENANCE

ADD TO COMPOST. Prunings (cut into small pieces), spent flowers, grass clippings, and weeds all go onto the compost pile. Accelerate decomposition by mixing new material into old compost. Keep the pile as moist as a wrung-out sponge.

AMEND SOIL. Whenever the ground is dry enough to dig in, you can add organic matter. Spade in generous amounts of compost, peat moss, or well-aged manure. Let the amended soil settle for a week, then plant.

DEADHEAD FLOWERS. Removing faded flowers makes plants look better

PACIFIC NORTHWEST
CHECKLIST
APRIL

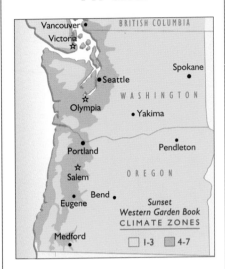

Sunset
Western Garden Book
CLIMATE ZONES

☐ 1-3   ☐ 4-7

and also channels the plant's energy into producing new growth now and robust bloom next year. You can snap off most defunct rhododendron blossoms with your fingers. Be careful not to take off the new growth buds that appear just below the old bloom heads.

DIVIDE PERENNIALS. Summer bloomers like daylilies, phlox, and Shasta daisies can still be divided without diminishing summer bloom. Divide clumps with a spade or sharp knife, then replant. You can also dig and divide spring bloomers whose flowers have already faded.

FEED CONIFERS. Dormant plants wake up hungry this month. Scatter high-nitrogen fertilizer around the plants. But don't feed pines; they don't like a rich diet.

FEED FLOWERING SHRUBS. As soon as blooms fade, apply a high-nitrogen fertilizer to promote strong new growth.

MOVE OUT TENDER PLANTS. In zones 4–7, cymbidiums can go outdoors early in the month. Begonias, fuchsias, and geraniums can go out from midmonth on (they tolerate a chill but not a freeze). Now is a good time to take these plants out of their pots, prune their roots, and repot them with fresh soil mix. Water plants well after repotting, and begin fertilizing.

MOW LAWNS. If the grass is dry enough to cut, mow it.

PRUNE. Cut back flowering trees and shrubs after bloom has faded. Get rid of suckers.

PEST & WEED CONTROL

SLUGS. If you don't want to use bait, investigate commercial slug traps. Many of them use beer to lure, then drown, slugs. Or lay a plastic bottle on its side in a trench deep enough for the neck and opening of the bottle to align with the soil surface. Pour in enough beer so there's a puddle of it in the bottle. The slugs can crawl into this "tavern," but they can't get out.

WEEDS. Hoe them or pull them before seeds form.

When April arrives, all my gardening friends start gushing over flower color. "Oh, the azaleas and rhodies!" "Oh, the perennials and bulbs!" Sure, those plants produce a wide spectrum of flower colors. But the truth is, my favorite spring color is green. As the plants leaf out in my garden, I'm delighted to see the diversity of greens—emerald, lime, sea green—and a slew of hues in between.

Last year, I spotted yet another spring green belonging to a new form of Japanese larch (*Larix kaempferi* 'Diana'), a deciduous conifer. Its soft needles start out with a slight bluish cast halfway between a rich moss green and celadon, then as summer progresses, the needles turn a deeper green. Finally in autumn, they turn a bright golden orange before dropping. In winter, its bare reddish brown branches form a handsome filigree. The twigs are contorted, almost like an ornamental filbert. The needles are slightly twisted, too, giving the branches a feathery look that is even more pronounced than that of other larches. In my garden, the tree grows in a sunny spot where it will have plenty of room (it eventually reaches 60 feet tall).

•

PACIFIC NORTHWEST
Garden Notebook
BY STEVEN R. LORTON

A couple of years ago, I looked at all the big trees around the edges of my garden in the Skagit Valley and thought, "I want to see flowering vines scrambling up those trees, tumbling out of the branches, stretching for the sun!" Up the north side of an old cedar went *Clematis montana* 'Rubens'. I tied it to the trunk straight up for the first 10 feet, then let it head through the branches. The results were spectacular. I planted *C. dioscoreifolia* among a cluster of alders and encouraged it to grow up into the trees on twine strung from a stake in the soil to the lower branches. It produces masses of bloom with intense fragrance in September, and clouds of fuzzy, silver seed pods in winter.

THAT'S A GOOD QUESTION

Q: What do you use to get a vine or climbing rose to grow up a wall?
A: Eye screws and twine work well. Put the eye screw into the wood or masonry (using a masonry bit to predrill a hole), then tie the stem in place with two thicknesses of twine. About the time the twine rots away, the plant stalk has either thickened enough that the twine needs to be replaced, or it is stout enough that it's self-supporting.

PLANTING

☐ **PLANT SUMMER FLOWERS.** Zones 7–9, 14–17: All warm-season flowering annuals can be planted now. If you need instant color, use 4-inch plants. Try ageratum, dwarf dahlias, globe amaranth, impatiens, lobelia, Madagascar periwinkle, marigold, petunia, phlox, portulaca, salvia, statice, sunflower, sweet alyssum, verbena, and zinnia.

☐ **PLANT VEGETABLES AND HERBS.** Zones 7–9, 14–17: Sow seeds of beans, corn, cucumbers, squash, most root crops, and greens (chard, lettuce, mustard, spinach). Leave space for another planting—two to three weeks later—of bush beans and root crops. Set out seedlings of eggplant, peppers, and tomatoes. Nurseries should have a good selection of herbs this month.

☐ **SHOP FOR TENDER PLANTS.** Zones 7–9, 14–17: Set out tender plants now so they have the growing season to get established. Plant them in protected sites, such as against a south-facing wall or under an overhang, or grow them in containers and move the containers to a protected area in winter. Try bougainvillea, hibiscus, jacaranda, mandevilla, Mexican lime, pandorea, and plumeria. However, keep in mind that such plants are risky to grow in Northern California, since severe freezes can damage or kill them.

☐ **SOW HARDY VEGETABLES.** Zones 1 and 2: As soon as soil can be worked,

Sunset
Western
Garden Book
CLIMATE ZONES

☐ Mountain (1-2)
☐ Valley (7-9)
☐ Inland (14)
☐ Coastal (15-17)

• Eureka
Redding
CALIFORNIA
NEVADA
• Mendocino
• Sacramento
Santa Rosa
San Francisco
San Jose
Fresno •
Monterey

sow seeds of beets, broccoli, cabbage, carrot, cauliflower, endive, kohlrabi, lettuce, onions, parsley, parsnips, peas, potatoes, radishes, spinach, Swiss chard, and turnips.

MAINTENANCE

☐ **DIG OR HOE WEEDS.** Zones 7–9, 14–17: Dig out deep-rooted weeds, such as dandelion, with a hand weeder or trowel (water first to loosen soil). To make sure you get the entire root, slip the tool into the soil and pry up the tap-

root. You can hoe out all types of weeds when they're small by cutting just below the soil surface with a sharp hoe or cultivator. To prevent them from surviving on nighttime dew, hoe in the morning so the sun bakes the weeds.

☐ **FEED ACID LOVERS.** Zones 7–9, 14–17: After azaleas, camellias, and rhododendrons finish blooming, feed them with an acid fertilizer.

☐ **GROOM AND FEED SPRING BULBS.** Remove spent flowers where the stems rise from the base. Leave on foliage to manufacture nutrients for next year's show, and feed with a bulb fertilizer. When the leaves start to yellow, cut back on water.

☐ **PRUNE.** Zones 7–9, 14–17: After new growth appears, prune out frost-damaged wood on tender plants, such as bougainvillea and citrus. Also, prune to shape spring-flowering shrubs (after bloom) and overgrown hedges. Zones 1 and 2: Finish pruning deciduous fruit and ornamental trees before new growth emerges. Prune flowering vines, grapes, and roses. Wait until after bloom to prune spring-flowering shrubs.

PEST CONTROL

☐ **CONTROL ANTS.** Zones 7–9, 14–17: To keep ants off trees and shrubs, wrap their trunks with 1- to 2-inch-wide strips of masking tape, and coat with a sticky barrier. Reapply when the barrier gets dirty.

Not long ago I visited Sonny Garcia and Tom Valva's wild, wonderful garden in San Francisco. These avid plantsmen should win an award for fitting the greatest number of plants into one small space (a 30- by 60-foot garden).

The garden is filled with an amazing assortment of unusual foliage and flowering plants, from *Cantua buxifolia*, a tall, gangly shrub with magnificent red flowers, and golden-leafed *Carex phyllocephala* 'Sparkler' to a number of interesting fuchsias.

One fuchsia that really struck my fancy was 'Island Sunset'. It's not grown for its flowers (which are purple), but for the foliage, which is beautifully variegated with cream and pink (plants are wholesaled by Monrovia Nursery Co., of Azusa, California). One drawback: it seems to get fuchsia mite in some areas. If mites are a problem where you live, pinch off distorted foliage at first sign of infestation. Oil sprays provide some control, but miticides are more effective. Also growing in their garden is *Fuchsia thymifolia*, a 3- to 9-foot-tall, small-leafed species with tiny pink flowers; this one is mite resistant.

•

One of my favorite chores in April is harvesting sweet peas that I planted in fall. I call it a chore only because sweet peas (like all peas)

NORTHERN CALIFORNIA
Garden Notebook
BY LAUREN BONAR SWEZEY

must be picked constantly if you want them to keep producing. If the flowers are allowed to form seeds, the plant's energy goes into seed production, and blooming stops.

THAT'S A GOOD QUESTION

Q: I am building a raised vegetable garden. Is it safe to use pressure-treated wood where food will be grown?
A: Pressure-treated wood is used where wood is exposed to rot and insect attack. The topic was reviewed recently in *Priorities for Long Life and Good Health* (Vol. 7, No. 3, 1995), a magazine published by the American Council on Science and Health (ACSH), a consumer education consortium. Researchers Craig E. Shuler and Patrick J. Pellicane of Colorado State University concluded "that when properly processed and appropriately used, chromated copper arsenate (CCA)–treated wood is harmless to humans, plants, and nontargeted animals." ACSH explains that "CCA-treated wood is not classified as hazardous (by the Environmental Protection Agency) because CCA 'fixes' to the wood in a way that makes the chemical highly insoluble and leach resistant." The report concludes, "No problems have ever been reported that indicate that these preservatives migrate into plants and cause any health effects."

CHECKLIST
APRIL

PLANTING

❏ **PLANT SUMMER VEGETABLES.** If you live within sight of the ocean, you can continue planting cool-season crops such as broccoli, cabbage, cauliflower, leaf lettuce, and spinach. Inland (*Sunset* climate zones 18–21), shift attention to warm-season crops: beans, corn, cucumbers, eggplant, pumpkins, squash, and tomatoes. In the high desert (zone 11), gardeners should delay planting for two to four weeks; until midmonth, frost is still a possibility.

❏ **START ANNUALS.** Start summer flowers such as ageratum, celosia, coleus, cosmos, lobelia, marigolds, nicotiana, petunias, portulaca, sanvitalia, verbena, and zinnias. In the high desert, you still have time to plant pansies, snapdragons, stock, sweet alyssum, and violas. To save water, mulch after planting.

❏ **BUY AND PLANT BULBS.** In coastal and inland areas (zones 22–24 and 18–21, respectively), cannas and dahlias are available, and tuberoses can also be planted now. In low desert zone 13, buy gladiolus corms, but refrigerate them until August planting time. For continuous summer bloom in the high desert, plant gladiolus at two- to three-week intervals.

MAINTENANCE

❏ **PREPARE GARDEN BEDS.** Amend the soil before planting your summer flow-

Bishop

NEVADA

CALIFORNIA

San Luis Obispo

Bakersfield

Tehachapi

Santa Barbara

Lancaster

Los Angeles

Palm Springs

San Diego

MEXICO

Sunset Western Garden Book CLIMATE ZONES

1-3 7-9 11 13 14-24

ers, herbs, and vegetables. Spread compost 2 to 3 inches deep over planting area, sprinkle fertilizer at label rates. Cultivate both deeply into the soil.

❏ **DIVIDE CYMBIDIUMS.** In Southern California's coastal and inland areas, it's time to refresh plants if pots are packed with bulbs, some brown and leafless. Knock the root mass out of the pot, and separate as many clumps as you can by hand or with pruning shears. Keep at least three healthy bulbs with foliage in each division. To discourage rot, dust cuts with sulfur.

❏ **FERTILIZE PLANTS.** Most plants benefit from a feeding of all-purpose fertilizer such as 10-10-10. Apply it with a light touch; overfeeding now will result in softer, thirstier growth. On the other hand, plants struggling for nutrients use water less efficiently.

❏ **TREAT PLANTS FOR IRON DEFICIENCY.** In coastal, inland, and low-desert areas, if bottlebrush, camellias, citrus, gardenias, geranium (*Pelargonium*), hibiscus, pyracantha, roses, or other plants have yellowing leaves with green veins, feed them with a fertilizer containing chelated iron.

PEST AND WEED CONTROL

❏ **CONTROL WEEDS.** Dig out deep-rooted weeds such as dandelion with a hand weeder (water first to loosen soil). Slip weeder into soil, and pry against taproot to make sure you get its entire length. Use a sharp hoe to scrape out other weeds when they're small, cutting just below the soil surface.

❏ **MANAGE PESTS.** April and aphids are practically synonymous. To control them, blast foliage and flowers with strong streams of water, or apply insecticidal soap. Treat severe caterpillar damage with *Bacillus thuringiensis* (BT), sold as a liquid or powder. Look for Safer and Green Light brands. Trap snails and slugs under raised boards, handpick, or use bait.

"**Y**ou chose well," said the woman behind the cut-flower sales table at the Orange County Rose Society Show last year. And, looking at the bouquet in my hand, I knew I had.

'Pristine', 'Bewitched', 'Bride's Dream', 'Fragrant Memory', and 'Royal Highness' were my selections, each a hybrid tea and each a pale pink. Yet each soon revealed its own personality. Some ripened and shattered quickly. Others took their time to unfold. 'Royal Highness'—the deepest, fattest, most regal-looking rosebud imaginable—held out the longest, taking a full week to reveal her charms.

I practically wore a groove in my floor circling the vase that held these beauties, trying, and failing, to pick a favorite. Some nights I even dreamed about them. At a mere dollar a stem, I'd say that's remarkable entertainment value.

Gorgeous garden roses at moderate prices are reason enough to visit a rose show this month or next. Virtually all rose societies defray the cost of staging shows by selling members' surplus blooms. You won't find roses of this quality anywhere else, and if you appreciate cut flowers, take advantage of this opportunity.

Another good reason to visit a rose show is to talk to rosarians. Unlike, say, lawyers or computer technicians, these people don't

SOUTHERN CALIFORNIA
Garden Notebook
BY SHARON COHOON

resent giving free advice. When it comes to discussing roses, they have no off-hours, so don't be shy about approaching club members.

•

Daylily and iris fans might want to add this number to their files: (310) 984-8409. This handy recorded hotline, courtesy of the Orange County Iris & Daylily Club, tells the status of blooms at iris and daylily specialty nurseries in Southern California, along with hours and locations as well as dates and places of garden club shows, meetings, and other events.

THAT'S A GOOD QUESTION

Q: "What are those fat, ugly, white, wormlike things in my compost?" And what should I do about them?"

A: These are larvae of *Cotinus mutabilis*, commonly known as the fig beetle. They are nasty looking, but if you leave them alone to feed on decomposing matter in your compost, they'll grow up to be gorgeous, metallic green insects that look like Egyptian scarabs; you might have seen some buzzing lazily around your garden last summer. Since the adult beetles primarily feed on fruit that's bird damaged or overly ripe, most gardeners consider them amusements rather than pests. If the larvae really offend you, though, toss them to the birds.

CHECKLIST
APRIL

PLANTING

❑ **BARE-ROOT STOCK.** Depending on where you live, you may still be able to set out bare-root small fruits, fruit and ornamental trees, asparagus, and rhubarb this month. Bare-root stock is less expensive than containerized, and it adapts to garden soil more easily. Just don't let roots dry out before you plant.

❑ **HARDY VEGETABLES.** Early in the month, plant bare-root asparagus, horseradish, and rhubarb. As soon as you can work the soil, sow beet, carrot, chard, endive, kohlrabi, lettuce, onion, parsley, parsnip, pea, radish, spinach, Swiss chard, and turnip. Set out transplants of broccoli, brussels sprouts, cabbage, cauliflower, and green onions; plant seed potatoes. Floating row covers will protect seedlings, take the edge off cold nights, and get plants off to a fast start.

MAINTENANCE

❑ **FERTILIZE LAWNS.** Apply 1 to 2 pounds of high-nitrogen fertilizer per 1,000 square feet of turf (more on heavily used lawns and those growing in poor soil), and water it in well.

❑ **MULCH.** A 2- to 3-inch layer of organic mulch, such as compost or

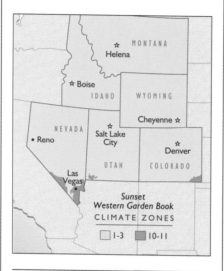

Sunset Western Garden Book
CLIMATE ZONES
❑ 1-3   ❑ 10-11

straw, suppresses weeds, holds in moisture, and keeps roots cool when the weather heats up. Spread it around annuals, perennials, trees, and shrubs, especially if summers are hot and dry where you live. Keep mulch a few inches back from warm-season vegetables, such as peppers and tomatoes, since

their roots need the warmest soil they can get until hot weather sets in.

❑ **PRUNE.** Early in the month, before new growth emerges, finish pruning deciduous fruit and ornamental trees, as well as vines, grapes, and roses. You can wait until after flowering to prune forsythia, Japanese apricot, spiraea, and other trees and shrubs that bloom in early spring. Or prune them lightly after buds swell, and put the cuttings in vases indoors: they'll flower for you there.

PEST & WEED CONTROL

❑ **APPLY DORMANT SPRAY.** After pruning, spray fruit trees with a mixture of oil and lime sulfur or oil and copper. If rain washes it off within 48 hours, reapply. If you use oil and copper, keep spray off walls, fences, and walks that might be stained.

❑ **DIG OR HOE WEEDS.** When weeds are small, wait until soil is dry, then hoe early in the day. Sun and dryness will kill tiny roots by day's end. For larger weeds, water thoroughly, then pop weeds out with a hand weeder, roots and all. Let whole weeds dry in the sun before you compost them; otherwise they'll retain enough life to flower and disperse seeds.

I love the soft, spongy feeling of grass turf under bare feet, but I have too much of it. Every year, I take out a few dozen square feet of lawn to extend my flower beds or make more room for growing shrubs or trees. This spring, I have a new perennial bed in the works, and in a frenzy to get it done, I tore up the turf with a rear-tined tiller, then covered the bed with a thick layer of manure. I let the manure sit for a month to smother the chopped-up grass below, then I dug it in and planted.

If you're pinched for time, try this speedy method: Just strip the top 1 to 2 inches of turf off the bed with a spade (I take it off in 9- by 24-inch strips) and stack the strips nearby. Then dig out the bed to a depth of 10 to 12 inches and line the bottom of the bed with the strips laid upside down.

Put the amended backfill on top, soak the bed, and plant the next day, after the soil has had the night to settle and dry out a little.

•

Whenever I try to make a rectangular flower bed without first outlining the edges, I always wind up with something that looks like an uneven parallelogram. I finally solved that problem by going to a

INLAND WESTERN STATES
Garden Notebook
BY JIM McCAUSLAND

mountaineering supply store and paying $6 for a half-dozen aluminum tent stakes with holes in the top. I hammer them in at 6-foot intervals and run twine through them, outlining my beds perfectly before I dig or till them.

•

I hate "crack" weeds—broad-leafed ones that grow up through cracks in the sidewalk or driveway—but I've found a neat way to control them: heat up the teakettle and pour boiling water on them. You may have to do this more than once for weeds that come back from deep roots, but eventually you'll win.

THAT'S A GOOD QUESTION

Q: I've heard that it's a bad idea to spread lime and fertilizer on my lawn at the same time. Why can't I do it all at once?

A: Assuming that the soil under your lawn needs lime in the first place (and only lawns with a pH of less than 6 do), you should apply lime first, water it in well, then fertilize a couple of months later. When lime and nitrogen mix, the nitrogen tends to revert to gas and dissipates into the air before grass roots can use it.

PLANTING

☐ **ANNUALS.** Try ageratum, calliopsis, celosia, cosmos, four o'clock, globe amaranth, gloriosa daisy, kochia, lisianthus, marigold, Mexican sunflower, portulaca, strawflower, vinca rosea, and zinnia.

☐ **PERENNIALS.** Start chrysanthemum, columbine, coreopsis, gaillardia, gazania, geranium, gerbera, hollyhock, Michaelmas daisy, salvia, or Shasta daisy.

☐ **SUMMER BULBS.** After the danger of frost has passed, plant caladium, canna, crinum, dahlia, daylily, gladiolus, iris, and montbretia. You can also buy container-grown agapanthus, society garlic (*Tulbaghia*), and zephyranthes.

☐ **VEGETABLES.** In the low desert (zone 13), sow beans and cucumbers by mid-April; set out eggplant, okra, peanut, squash, and sweet potato any time this month. In the intermediate desert (zone 12), sow cucumber, melon, okra, pumpkin, soybean, squash, and watermelon, as well as seedlings of eggplant, pepper, sweet potato, and tomato. Also plant Jerusalem artichoke tubers.

☐ **CITRUS.** In zones 12 and 13, plant 5- to 7-gallon citrus in full sun, each tree in a hole that's as deep as the rootball but two to three times as wide. Water two or three times per week at first; by summer's end you'll need to water only

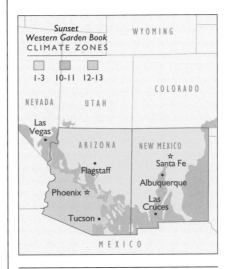

every five to seven days. To prevent sunburn, wrap trunks in white cloth or paint with white latex.

☐ **LAWNS.** When average night temperatures top 70°, plant hybrid Bermuda grass.

MAINTENANCE

☐ **FEED GARDEN PLANTS.** Almost every plant can use a dose of complete fertilizer now, during the most active growing time of the year. Apply about 1 pound of 10-10-10 fertilizer per 100 square feet. Water the day before you spread the fertilizer, and water again immediately after you apply it.

☐ **FERTILIZE LAWNS.** To give Bermuda grass a push for the summer, apply 3 to 4 pounds of high-nitrogen fertilizer per 1,000 square feet of turf about two weeks after the grass greens up. Water the fertilizer in thoroughly.

☐ **FINISH PRUNING.** Check plants damaged by freeze. New growth makes damaged older growth apparent, giving you easy targets as you move in and prune out the dead and damaged wood.

☐ **MULCH SOIL.** Spread a 2- to 3-inch layer of organic mulch around plants to suppress weeds, hold in moisture, and keep roots cool. Put mulch around annuals, perennials, vegetables, trees, and shrubs, especially where summers are hot and dry.

PEST & WEED CONTROL

☐ **DIG OR HOE WEEDS.** When weeds are small, wait until the soil is dry, then hoe early in the day. Sun will kill rootlets by day's end. For larger weeds, water thoroughly, then pop weeds out with a hand weeder, roots and all. Let weeds dry and die before you compost them, or they still might flower and disperse seeds.

TEXAS

PLANTING

☐ **ANNUALS.** Now is the time to set out ageratum, calliopsis, celosia, coleus, cosmos, four o'clock, globe amaranth, gloriosa daisy, kochia, lisianthus, marigold, Mexican sunflower, portulaca, strawflower, vinca rosea, and zinnia.

☐ **COOL-SEASON CROPS.** If you act right away in North Texas (Dallas and Fort Worth) and the Panhandle, you can still set out such cool-season crops as cabbage, chard, lettuce, and root vegetables.

☐ **WARM-SEASON CROPS.** In South Texas (San Antonio to the Rio Grande Valley), sow your last beans and okra, and set out well-developed nursery seedlings. In Central Texas (Austin and the Hill Country), plant seeds of beans, black-eyed peas, corn, eggplant, melons, and peppers; sweet potato slips;

and tomato transplants. In North and West Texas (El Paso and Midland), sow beans, cucumber, pepper, pumpkin, a last crop of radish, squash, and tomato. Later in April plant black-eyed peas, corn, eggplant, melon, pepper, and sweet potato slips. In the Panhandle, wait until at least a week after last frost to plant beans, cucumber, okra, pepper, pumpkin, radish, squash, and tomato. Plant black-eyed peas, corn, eggplant, melon, okra, pepper, and sweet potato late in the month.

☐ **SUMMER BULBS.** As soon as the danger of frost has passed, plant summer-flowering bulbs such as caladium, canna, crinum, dahlia, daylily, gladiolus, and iris.

☐ **CITRUS.** In South Texas, set out citrus plants from 5- or 7-gallon cans.

☐ **LAWNS.** As soon as danger of frost has passed, you can start a new lawn or repair an old one by planting plugs or seeds of warm-season grasses.

MAINTENANCE

☐ **MULCH SOIL.** Spread organic mulch around almost all plants to suppress weeds and hold in moisture.

THE NEW CUTTING

It has everything a bouquet maker needs any day of the year...flowers, foliage, grasses. Here's how to plan and plant your own cutting garden

BY LAUREN BONAR SWEZEY WITH SHARON COHOON

LIKE FLOWER FACTORIES, traditional cutting gardens have one function: to keep pumping out long-stemmed annuals, perennials, and bulbs for bouquets. For this reason, they are often confined to a specified border or even an out-of-the-way part of the garden where the ravages of constant cutting aren't so visible. ♦ But contemporary floral designers are changing all that. By expanding the concept of floral arrangements, they're helping to change the way gardeners plant and use cutting gardens. Arrangements of flowers emerging in perfect symmetry from low silver bowls have given way to free-flowing works of art that combine many materials, from foliage to twigs to berries. Cutting garden

RENEE LYNN

boundaries have disappeared, too: entire gardens are yielding material for bouquets. ♦ These days, just about any attractive garden plants that last a reasonable length of time in water can be used in arrangements: delicate annuals mixed with floppy-flowered perennials and grasses, or colorful trusses from large flowering shrubs with bulky berry-festooned branches. By taking from the entire garden, you'll always have plenty to snip and plenty left to enjoy. ♦ The three gardens pictured on the following seven pages were designed especially to yield material for bouquets. You don't have to start from scratch to create such a garden. If your garden already contains trees and shrubs, you'll likely find that at least some of them offer good cut foliage and flowers for arrangements.

DARIEL ALEXANDER

GARDEN

THIS NONSTOP BLOOMING border in Dariel Alexander's garden combines flowering perennials and roses, with a feverfew "hedge" along its edge. "I try to arrange plants in the border so that when one stops

Bouquet in a Border
LAFAYETTE, CALIFORNIA

blooming, something else is there to take its place," she says. Flowers are at their peak in summer with blue salvia, campanula, dahlias,

gloriosa daisies, heliopsis, lavatera, lythrum hybrids, monarda, montbretia, penstemon, phlox, and yarrow. Shrubs and trees form the

Planning a Garden for Cutting

THE PERFECT GARDEN FOR CUTTING is a handsome landscape that also happens to yield great material for bouquets. It can be any size and shape you want, but good planning and design are important. It can incorporate the entire garden or just the front or back of the house. When you plan it, keep these things in mind.

FLOWER CARE TAKES TIME. Consider how much time you want to spend tending the garden. A cutting garden doesn't have to require high maintenance, especially if it's filled with trees and shrubs. But the more annuals, bulbs, and perennials you add, the more time you'll need to allow for planting and maintenance.

KEEP IN MIND THAT MANY CUTTING FLOWERS PREFER FULL SUN (6 hours at midday). When a good portion of the garden is devoted to cutting, you're more likely to have plenty of planting areas where flowers will thrive. Though a shady garden can be planted for cutting, the flower choices will be more limited.

START WITH BACKBONE PLANTS. These are the trees and large shrubs that yield great material for bouquets. Deciduous trees with good fall color (liquidambar, redtwig dogwood) and shrubs with berries (cotoneaster, toyon) are real bonuses. Flowering shrubs, such as hydrangea and lilacs, are mainstays. Consider the plant's height, the exposure it needs (sun or shade), its foliage color and texture, and how it fits into the landscape (screening, etc.).

FILL IN WITH FLOWERS, GRASSES, AND FOLIAGE. Set out smaller shrubs that provide foliage or flowers (such as spiraea and roses), and ornamental grasses. Then fill in with flowers of all kinds—annuals, biennials, perennials, and bulbs. You can have one main display bed, as in Dariel Alexander's garden bordering a lawn (page 95), or scatter flowers throughout the garden.

PLAN FOR A SUCCESSION OF BLOOM AS WELL AS FOR YEAR-ROUND COLOR. During spring and summer, it's easy to have plenty of cutting choices. Fall can be floriferous, too, especially in milder climates, but it takes a little more planning. Fortunately, much of the West is mild enough to offer plenty of choices. For a succession of bloom, choose plants that blossom in different seasons, so as one is going out of bloom another will replace it.

TRY EXISTING PLANTS. If you're not sure whether existing plants in your garden are good for cutting and they're not listed on pages 99 through 101, try them out. Cut a couple of stems and place them in deep water. Use them in an arrangement, or let them stand alone in a container. If the foliage or flowers drop off within a day or so, they're probably not a good choice for cutting.

Three Tiers for Cutting

PASADENA, CALIFORNIA

"THERE ARE TWO SCHOOLS OF THOUGHT about cutting from your garden," says gardener Joan Banning. "Some people are afraid to cut anything because they think it will denude the garden. But, actually, it works out just the opposite. The more you cut, the more things seem to grow."

In Banning's cutting border, flowering shrubs such as roses, camellias, and viburnum are foundation plants. Herbaceous perennials provide the middle tier. Annuals and bulbs add the final touch. All plants in the border were chosen as much for vase appeal as for garden charm. Banning's favorite cutting materials include Iceland poppies, David Austin English roses, 'Really Green' annual nicotiana, and the New Zealand tea tree, red-flowering currant, pink alstroemeria, and bright red anemones shown in the bucket at right.

JOHN HUMBLE

Northwest Classic

SEAVIEW, WASHINGTON

FLOWERS, SHRUBS, AND GRASSES make handsome garden and cutting companions in Dale Brous's garden. The garden is shown in full bloom with campanulas, roses, Shasta daisies, and leather leaf sedge. Bloom starts in January with early bulbs, forsythia, hellebores, and witch hazel. The show lasts until November and December, when asters, ornamental grasses, rose hips, holly berries, and Japanese anemones are at their peak. Below are Austrian black pine, 'Bloodgood' Japanese maple, foxglove, and Japanese iris. Feverfew, foxglove, 'Pink Pearl' rhododendron, and 'Sally Holmes' rose bloom below the window, above.

ALLAN MANDELL

RENEE LYNN

■ PERENNIALS

ARTEMISIA. Perennials or shrubs. Full sun. All zones. Grows 1 to 4 feet or more. Silvery gray foliage. Lasts at least a week. Cut early or late in day. Slit stem bases, recut, and dip in boiling water. Remove leaves below the waterline.

ASPARAGUS DENSIFLORUS. Full sun or partial shade. Zones 12–24. Upright ('Myers') or arching ('Sprengeri') fluffy branches. Lasts a week. Cut when stalks are fully developed. Condition in deep water.

GRASSES. Many kinds, including *Carex, Miscanthus, Muhlenbergia, Pennisetum,* and *Stipa.* Full sun to partial shade. Zones vary. Harvest leaves or flower heads. Dip stem ends in vinegar for a few minutes.

HEUCHERA MAXIMA. Perennial. Partial shade. Zones 15–24. Grows 1 to 2 feet. Heart-shaped dark green leaves. Pink, red, and white flowers can also be cut. Lasts about a week.

LADY'S-MANTLE (*Alchemilla mollis*). Perennial. Partial or full shade. Zones 2–9, 14–24. Pale green leaves look silvery. Grows to 2 feet. Lasts up to two weeks. Yellow flowers can also be cut.

LAMB'S EARS (*Stachys byzantina*). Perennial. Full sun or light shade. All zones. White woolly foliage. Lasts about a week. Cut fresh leaves.

RUE (*Ruta graveolens*). Perennial herb 1½ to 3 feet. Full sun. All zones. Blue-green finely divided foliage. Lasts at least a week. Split stem ends.

Foliage bouquet contains breath of heaven, camellia, Eucalyptus cinerea, leptospermum, nandina, pittosporum, and spiraea.

■ WOODY TREES & SHRUBS

Cut fresh foliage. Scrape and split 2 inches of woody stem ends, or smash with a hammer. Remove foliage below waterline; stand stems in deep water.

ABELIA
BREATH OF HEAVEN (*Coleonema, Diosma*)
CALIFORNIA BAY (*Umbellularia californica*)
CAMELLIA
CORKSCREW WILLOW (*Salix babylonica* 'Crispa')
DOGWOOD (*Cornus*)
EUCALYPTUS
EUONYMUS JAPONICA **'SILVER QUEEN'**
HOLLY (*Ilex*)
LEPTOSPERMUM
LILAC (*Syringa*)
LOQUAT (*Eriobotrya japonica*)
MAGNOLIA
MAPLE (*Acer*)
MOCK ORANGE (*Philadelphus*)
NANDINA
PITTOSPORUM **'MARJORIE CHANNON'**
PODOCARPUS
PRUNUS (evergreen)
PUSSY WILLOW (*Salix discolor*)
PYRACANTHA
RHAMNUS ALTERNATUS **'AUREO VARIEGATA'**
SPIRAEA
SWEET BAY (*Laurus nobilis*)
VARIEGATED WEIGELA
VIBURNUM
WAX-LEAF PRIVET (*Ligustrum japonicum*)

FLOWERS FOR CUTTING

■ SPRING

ALSTROEMERIA. Perennial. Full sun. Zones 5–9, 14–24. Grows 2 to 5 feet tall. Many soft to intense colors. Lasts one to two weeks. Cut when flowers begin to open. Change water often.

BACHELOR'S BUTTON (*Centaurea cyanus*). Annual. Full sun. All zones. Grows 1 to 2½ feet. Colors include blue, pink, rose, red, and white. Lasts four to seven days. Cut when open.

DELPHINIUM. Perennial. Full sun. Zones vary. Stalks up to 6 feet with blooms of blue, lavender, pink, purple, and red. Lasts five to eight days. Cut when half the flowers are open. Change vase water daily.

DIANTHUS. Annuals, biennials, and perennials. Full sun to light afternoon shade. All zones. Plants reach from 6 inches to 2½ feet or more. Many colors. Lasts 5 to 10 days. Cut when flowers have begun to open.

DUTCH IRIS. Bulb. Full sun. All zones. Grows to 2 feet. Colors include blue, brown, mauve, orange, purple, white, and yellow. Lasts three to six days. Cut when buds show color. Split stem bases.

FREESIA. Corm. Full sun or partial shade. Zones 8, 9, 12–24. Flowers in rainbow colors on 1- to 1½-foot stems. Lasts 5 to 12 days. Cut when first flowers are open. Keep cool (45° to 50°) until ready to use.

Spring flower bouquet contains alstroemeria, delphinium, dianthus, freesia, godetia, larkspur, scabiosa, and tulip, plus feather grass and nandina foliage as filler.

GODETIA (*Clarkia amoena*). Annual. Full sun. All zones. Colors include lavender, lilac, pink, red, rose, salmon, and white. Grows 10 inches to 3 feet. Lasts 5 to 10 days. Cut when first flowers open. Briefly dip stem ends in boiling water. Strip off lower leaves.

LARKSPUR (*Consolida ambigua*). Annual. Full sun. All zones. Stalks up to 5 feet. Colors include blue, lilac, pink, rose, and salmon. Lasts five to eight days. Cut when a third of flowers have opened. Condition in a mixture of ½ teaspoon alcohol to 2 quarts of water.

NARCISSUS. Bulb. Full sun. All zones. Grows 6 inches to 2 feet. Colors include cream, salmon pink, white, and yellow. Lasts four to seven days. Cut when tip of bud shows color. Split stem, and stand in deep, cool water (with sugar).

PINCUSHION FLOWER (*Scabiosa*). Annual, biennial, or perennial. Full sun. Zones vary. Grows 1½ to 2½ feet. Colors include lavender blue, pink, rose, salmon pink, white. Lasts four to eight days. Cut when open.

Strip lower leaves, split stem ends, stand in cold water.

POPPIES (*Papaver*). Annuals and perennials. Zones vary. Grow 1 to 5 feet. Many colors. Last three to five days. Cut when buds are tight. Sear stem ends in flame. Stand in cold water in dark place.

POPPY-FLOWERED ANEMONE (*A. coronaria*). Tuberous-rooted perennial. Partial shade. All zones. Grows 6 to 18 inches. Tones of red, blue, and white. Lasts four to seven days. Cut when flowers begin to open. Use a few drops of bleach in the conditioning water.

RANUNCULUS. Tuber. Full sun. All zones. Grows to about 1½ feet. Colors include cream, orange, pink, red, white, and yellow. Lasts five to seven days. Cut when ¾ open. Split stem ends, and dip in boiling water.

SNAPDRAGON (*Antirrhinum majus*). Perennial grown as annual. Full sun. All zones. Many colors. Heights vary; tall ones are best for cutting. Lasts up to a week. Cut when lower flowers open. Plunge stems into hot water, allow to cool.

STOCK (*Matthiola*). Biennial or perennial grown as annual. Full sun to light shade. All zones. Grows 1 to 3 feet. Colors include cream, lavender, pink, purple, red, and white. Lasts six

to eight days. Cut when half the flowers are open. Slit stems, stand in deep, very cold water. Change water daily.

SWEET PEA (*Lathyrus odoratus*). Annual. Full sun. All zones. Bushy or tall vines. Many colors. Lasts four to seven days. Cut when flowers open. Stand in a cool mixture of eight drops alcohol per quart of water.

TULIP (*Tulipa*). Bulb. Full sun. All zones. Grows to 6 inches to 2½ feet. Many colors. Lasts about a week. Cut when buds begin to show color. Stand in cool water (adding a little gin helps firm the flowers and stems).

■ SUMMER

ASTER. Perennial. Full sun. All zones. Grows up to 3 feet. Colors include blue, lavender, pink, purple, red, and white. Lasts up to a week. Cut when flowers begin to open. Split stems, and stand in deep water with sugar.

BABY'S BREATH (*Gypsophila paniculata*). Perennial. Full sun.

Summer flower bouquet is filled with baby's breath, celosia, China aster, coreopsis, dahlia, kangaroo paw, lily, statice, strawflower, sunflower, and yarrow, along with purple fountain grass plumes and podocarpus foliage as filler.

RENEE LYNN

Zones vary. Grows 1½ to 3 feet or more. Colors include carmine, pink, and white. Lasts about a week. Cut when half of flowers on stem are open.

CHINA ASTER (*Callistephus chinensis*). Annual. Full sun. All zones. Grows 1 to 3 feet. Colors include lavender, pink, purple, and red. Lasts as long as two weeks. Cut when partially open. Remove foliage.

COCKSCOMB (*Celosia;* plume type). Annual. Full sun. All zones. Grows 1 to 3 feet. Brilliant shades of crimson, gold, orange-red, and pink. Lasts at least a week. Cut when ¾ to fully developed. Dip ends in boiling water, then stand stems in water.

COREOPSIS. Annuals and perennials. Full sun. Zones vary. Grows to 3 feet. Colors include maroon, orange, pink, and yellow. Lasts about five days. Cut when open.

DAHLIA. Tuberous-rooted perennial. Full sun to light shade. All zones. Grows 15 inches to 6 feet. Many colors. Lasts up to a week. Cut when open. Dip end in boiling water, then stand stem in deep water.

FALSE SUNFLOWER (*Heliopsis helianthoides*). Perennial. Full sun to partial shade. All zones. Grows 2 to 4 feet. Colors are yellow to orange-yellow. Cut when flowers open.

GERBERA JAMESONII. Perennial. Full sun, partial shade. Zones 8, 9, 12–24. Grows to 1½ feet.

Colors vary. Lasts two weeks. Pick when center disk has ring of pollen. Split stem ends, dip in boiling water, and stand in deep water with sugar.

HYDRANGEA. Shrub. Partial shade. Zones vary. Grows to 12 feet. Colors include blue, pink, purple, red, and white. Lasts a week or more fresh. Can be dried. Cut when flowers have colored or in fall when faded.

KANGAROO PAW (*Anigozanthos*). Evergreen perennial. Full sun. Zones 12, 13, 15–24. Grows 3 to 6 feet. Colors include green, purple, red, and yellow. Lasts about a week. Cut when developed. Stand in deep water.

LILY (*Lilium*). Full sun. All zones. Grows 1 to 6 feet. Many colors. Lasts a week or more. Cut

Fall flower bouquet contains chrysanthemum, echium, gaillardia, gerbera, gloriosa daisy, Japanese anemone, lion's tail, Mexican sunflower, purple coneflower, tuberose, and 'Edward Goucher' glossy abelia. Leptospermum provides flowers and foliage, with cotoneaster and pyracantha for foliage and berries.

when buds show color or when partially open. To prevent staining from pollen, remove anthers. Split stem ends.

NICOTIANA. Annual. All zones. Grows 18 inches to 3 feet. Colors include green, pink, purple, red, and white. Lasts about a week. Cut when several flowers are open, slit stems, stand in tepid water.

ROSE (*Rosa*). Shrub. All zones. Grows to 8 feet or more. Many colors. Lasts three to seven days. Cut when buds start opening. Slit stem ends.

STATICE (*Limonium*). Annuals and perennials. Full sun. Zones vary. Grows 2 to 3 feet. Many colors. Lasts indefinitely. Cut when flowers show color.

STRAWFLOWER (*Helichrysum bracteatum*). Annual. Full sun. All zones. Grows 2 to 3 feet. Colors are yellow to red and white. Dries well. Cut before central disk shows pollen.

SUNFLOWER (*Helianthus*). Annuals and perennials. Full sun. All zones. Grows up to 10 feet. Colors include brown, cream, maroon, orange, and yellow. Lasts about a week.

TUBEROSE (*Polianthes tuberosa*).

Tuberous-rooted perennial. Full or partial sun. Zones 15–17, 22–24. Grows to 3 feet. White. Cut when first buds are opening. Stand in deep water.

YARROW (*Achillea*). Perennial. Full sun. All zones. Grows to 3 feet or more. Lavender, pink, red, white, and yellow. Foliage also used. Flowers last about a week. Cut before pollen shows. Slit stem ends, condition in deep, cool water.

■ FALL

ASTER (see summer).

CHRYSANTHEMUM. Annuals and perennials. All zones. Height varies. Many colors. Lasts one to two weeks. Cut when flowers open, slit stems, stand in deep water.

COREOPSIS (see summer).

GAILLARDIA. Annuals and perennials. Full sun. All zones. Grows to 4 feet. Colors include bronze, gold, red, and yellow. Lasts up to a week. Cut flowers with tight centers. Slit stems. Stand in deep water with sugar.

GERBERA JAMESONII (see summer).

JAPANESE ANEMONE (*Anemone hybrida*). Perennial. Partial shade. All zones. Grows to 4 feet. Rose, silvery pink, and white. Lasts four to seven days. Cut when flowers begin to open. Stand in cold, deep water with bleach (1 teaspoon per quart).

LION'S TAIL (*Leonotis leonurus*). Shrub. Full sun. Zones 8–24. Grows to 6 feet. Orange flowers. Lasts as long as a week. Cut when flowers open. Stand in deep water.

MEXICAN SUNFLOWER (*Tithonia rotundifolia*). Perennial grown as an annual. Full sun. All zones. Grows to 6 feet. Orange-scarlet flowers.

PURPLE CONEFLOWER (*Echinacea purpurea*). Perennial. All zones. Grows 2 to 5 feet. Colors include purple, rosy pink, and white. Lasts as long as a week. Cut when flowers are open, slit stem, condition in cool water.

RUDBECKIA. Biennials and perennials. Full sun. All zones. Grows 10 inches to 7 feet. Colors include mahogany and yellow. Lasts up to two weeks. Cut when flowers have tight centers. Stand in water with sugar. ■

HARVESTING & CONDITIONING FLOWERS

EVERY FLOWER has an optimum stage at which it should be harvested for longest vase life. Flowers can be harvested later than indicated, but they won't last as long. For best results, snip the blooms during the cooler morning or evening hours.

Strip off lower leaves on stems, so they don't sit in water. To make sure stems absorb water after harvest, it's best to recut them under water (keep a small bowl next to you) before conditioning.

Conditioning flowers also improves their vase life (methods differ depending on the flower type). It isn't necessary, but definitely prolongs the vase life of some kinds. Commercial floral preservatives also help lengthen vase life.

Except where noted, immerse stems in deep water up to the bases of the flower heads or the leaves. Let stand for several hours or overnight. Sugar helps feed the flowers; where it's indicated, add 1 teaspoon per quart of water.

Paradise for plant lovers

In California's Sonoma County, specialty nurseries sell everything from Japanese maples to perennials and roses. Visit a few in a day, or make it a nursery-crawling weekend

IF THERE'S A PARADISE FOR horticulturists and gardening enthusiasts, it's surely Sonoma County. Aside from scenic rolling hills and quiet pastoral valleys lined with row after row of grapevines, it's home to some of the best plant shopping in California. The area's temperate climate, available land, and wonderful views have attracted growers of everything from Japanese maples to bug-eating plants.

People like Bruce Shanks of Cottage Garden Growers of Petaluma, for instance. For years, Shanks dreamed of owning his own nursery, but the high cost of land in the Bay Area kept him from realizing his dream there, so he moved north. "About five years ago, I realized the popularity of perennials," he says. "I decided to forget about oleander and photinia and just grow interesting things." Shanks took the remnants of an old culinary herb farm on the side of a hill and began building terraces where he could grow and sell perennials. Now he and his wife, Daria, run the 1-acre nursery.

Another grower, Marca Dickie, lives 2,000 feet up in the pine forests above Sonoma, where it actually snows occasionally. Dickie found her niche with Japanese maples. She's been collecting varieties for 15 years. At her mountain retreat, she offers 150 kinds, ranging in size from 1-gallon cans to 36-inch boxes.

Visiting these and the other nurseries listed here—all of which have great collections of plants—is a perfect way to spend a spring day. All are only a few hours' drive from the greater Bay Area (call the nurseries you wish to visit for directions; area code is 707). If you enjoy plants of all kinds, or you have a lot of landscaping to do, plan a nursery-hopping weekend and rent a trailer to carry the plants home.

EIGHT NURSERIES TO VISIT

PETALUMA
• *Cottage Garden Growers,* 4049 Petaluma Blvd. N.; 778-8025. Open 9 to 5 daily. Retail only.

This nursery offers every kind of perennial (about 400) you can imagine, as well as David Austin English roses and 40 varieties of clematis. To help you choose, signs by each plant give information including where to grow it and what conditions it needs. Some signs include photographs of the flowers. Prices are reasonable, since everything is grown on the premises. Owners Bruce and Daria Shanks are always here to offer growing advice.

• *Garden Valley Ranch,* 498 Pepper Rd.; 795-0919. Open 10 to 4 Wednesdays through Saturdays, 11 to 4 Sundays. Mail-order roses available in January only.

If you love roses, don't miss Garden Valley Ranch. About 14 years ago, Rey Reddell planted thousands of rose bushes on 9½ acres for his cut-flower business (you see these bushes when you first enter the nursery; they're usually in full bloom by Mother's Day weekend). "People accused me of being a sadist—tempting them with blooms but not selling the plants," says Reddell. So six years ago, Reddell opened a nursery for roses and companion plants. It includes a garden gift store and demonstration gardens featuring fragrant plants, rose arches, a koi pond, and heritage roses. And it also contains the only All-America Rose Selections garden in Northern California (of 25 in the country). All of the AARS picks since 1931 are displayed here.

SEBASTOPOL
• *Bamboo Sourcery,* 666 Wagnon Rd.; 823-5866. By appointment only; catalog $2.

Gerald Bol began collecting bamboo about 16 years ago. What started as a hobby turned into a passion. He has scoured bamboo-growing parts of the world, including Chile, to find new varieties to introduce back home. His 5-acre nursery—landscaped with more than 300 kinds—is on a hillside in damp coastal woodlands about 4 miles west of Sebastopol. Bol sells 160 varieties (about

SALES AREA *at Western Hills Nursery offers a wide range of flowering plants such as clematis, salvia, and yarrow. Just a few yards away, in the display garden, visitors can see full-grown specimens. At Marca Dickie nursery (right), a path winds through display gardens planted with 'Sango Kaku' Japanese maple and 'Robert Youngi' bamboo. Maples in nursery cans are scattered throughout the gardens.*

CHAS McGRATH

BOARDWALK *at Sonoma Horticultural Nursery leads visitors through a birch forest. Rhododendrons and foxgloves thrive in the dappled shade.*

a third of these are clumpers that do not run) ranging from dwarf ground covers to giant timber varieties 50 feet tall.

• *Sonoma Horticultural Nursery,* 3970 Azalea Ave.; 823-6832. Open 9 to 5 daily March through May, Thursdays through Mondays the rest of the year.

Some 800 kinds of rhododendrons and 400 azaleas grow in nursery cans throughout this 7-acre nursery; you'll also find many other flowering trees and shrubs. In spring, the floral extravaganza takes your breath away: rhododendrons, azaleas, and wisteria are in full bloom around the pond, the laburnum arching over a path is dripping with yellow flowers, and the birch woodland is full of flowering foxglove.

Polo de Lorenzo and Warren Smith have spent 18 years developing the nursery. It could take hours to see the many plants and walk the paths.

OCCIDENTAL
• *Western Hills Nursery,* 16250 Coleman Valley Rd.; 874-3731. Open 10 to 5 Thursdays through Sundays March through October; call for winter hours.

A granddaddy of nurseries in Northern California, Western Hills has been the model for other nurseries. Nestled among redwoods in the Coast Range, it began in the late '50s as the 3-acre gardens around the country home of Marshall Obrich and Lester Hawkins—two forward-thinking plantsmen who introduced generations of gardeners to unusual trees, shrubs, vines, and perennials from South Africa, Chile, and the Mediterranean. The nursery evolved in the early '70s and has been a destination for gardeners ever since.

A few years ago, Obrich willed the nursery to longtime friend Maggie Wych, who sells 800 to 900 kinds of plants. Most of these plants can be seen in mature form in the garden.

SANTA ROSA AND POINTS NORTH
• *California Carnivores,* 7020 Trenton-Healdsburg Rd., Forestville; 838-1630. Open 10 to 4 daily. Retail and mail order.

Peter D'Amato and Marilee Maertz started this nursery as a wholesale business selling Venus flytraps from a garage. Now they sell 100 to 200 kinds of carnivorous plants out of a greenhouse on the grounds of the Mark West Winery.

Their display includes 500 kinds; all are labeled for self-guided tours. D'Amato has been growing these plants since he was 10 years old (he'll even show you a photo of himself at age 14, with a carnivorous plant, taken at the county fair). "They're the easiest plants to grow. You can't overwater them, and you don't have to fertilize," he says. Visitors can BYOB (bring your own bug) to feed a plant.

• *California Flora Nursery,* 2990 Somers St. at D St., Fulton; 528-8813. Open 9 to 5 weekdays, 10 to 4 Saturdays.

In 1981, Philip Van Soelen and Sherrie Althouse started California Flora as a native plant nursery in the flatlands near Santa Rosa. But natives weren't driving the business, so the two began growing perennials and other non-native plants. Their timing was impeccable. The perennial boom was close at hand, followed quickly by a resurgence in the popularity of natives. Now the nursery offers about a third native and two-thirds non-native plants, including perennials, shrubs for shade (especially dry shade), and plants resistant to deer. It carries a good selection of perennials, many with golden or variegated foliage, in 4-inch containers. The rest are in 1-gallon cans.

SONOMA AREA
• *Marca Dickie Nursery,* Box 1270, Boyes Hot Springs; 996-0364. By appointment only. Will ship 1-gallon plants in midwinter.

It's a long (4.3-mile), narrow, winding road off State Highway 12 north of Sonoma to this nursery, but the drive is worth it for the sweeping valley views from the road. Japanese maples for every taste and situation fill the nursery—maples that weep, dwarf maples, maples that need full shade, maples that turn almost every color of the rainbow in fall, and maples whose buds and foliage change color several times during the growing season.

Dickie learned to graft maples onto older rootstocks in 1-gallon containers (most maples are grafted onto very small plants). So her plants grow faster and she can offer large trees sooner.

The ¾-acre nursery also has a handsome display garden of maples in containers; they are mixed with irises and arranged around a water garden and a patio. When the sun filters through the maple leaves, few plants in the world are more striking. ■

By Lauren Bonar Swezey

GLOWING FOLIAGE *of variegated Japanese sedge, bamboo, dead nettle, and hosta contrasts with cool greens of calla lily, impatiens, and deer fern. Design: Michael Barclay.*

Shade plants with a sunny look

Use them for their bright foliage

BRIGHTENING GLOOMY areas with year-round color, variegated foliage plants are a sorcerer's solution for shady garden beds. Their mottled or striped leaves can play tricks of light, giving dark areas the look of dappled sun. They can alter perspective, their bold punch making a recessive corner seem more prominent. Played off against dark green foliage, they can give the illusion of depth to a narrow border.

IN SHADY BORDER, *flowering maple, holly-leaf osmanthus, lily-of-the-valley shrub, and Japanese aucuba mix with bulbs.*

Filling a border with repeating groups of these plants maximizes their impact while providing continuity. The bed shown above combines varieties with white and yellow markings, playing their colors off against green foliage.

Used sparingly, variegated plants can highlight a border or entry garden. For changing seasonal color, interplant with flowering perennials or bulbs, as shown below left.

The shade lovers listed here need little maintenance. They're commonly sold in 1-gallon cans; shrubs also come in larger sizes.

PERENNIALS

Bamboo (*Pleioblastus viridistriatus* or *Arundinaria auricoma*). Bright yellow- and green-striped leaves; to 2½ feet.

Bethlehem sage (*Pulmonaria saccharata*). Silvery spotted leaves on 1½-foot plants. Takes dense shade.

Dead nettle (*Lamium ma-*

culatum). Trailing, mounding form to 12 inches. Green leaves with silvery centers.

Gladwin iris (*I. foetidissima* 'Variegata'). White-striped, stiff grasslike leaves to 2 feet. Takes dry soil and dense shade.

Hosta (*H. decorata*). Heart-shaped green leaves have silvery white markings, mound to 2 feet. Resists snails more than other hostas.

Houttuynia (*H. cordata* 'Variegata'). Deciduous ground cover to 10 inches. Heart-shaped leaves, cream and red markings.

Lily turf (*Liriope muscari* 'Variegata'). Grassy foliage, striped cream and green, mounds to 12 inches.

Variegated Japanese sedge (*Carex morrowii* 'Aurea-variegata'). Forms 1-foot mound of grasslike leaves striped green and gold.

SHRUBS

Flowering maple (*Abutilon pictum* 'Thompsonii'). Rangy shrub to 10 feet. Leaves mottled with creamy yellow. Prune to shape. Frost tender.

Golden elaeagnus (*E. pungens* 'Maculata'). To 10 feet. Gold-centered leaves. Tolerates wide range of conditions.

Holly-leaf osmanthus (*O. heterophyllus* 'Variegatus'). Slow-growing to 5 feet. Hollylike leaves edged in creamy white.

Japanese aralia (*Fatsia japonica* 'Variegata'). Reaches 8 feet. Tropical, fan-like leaves edged with golden yellow to creamy white.

Japanese aucuba (*A. japonica* 'Picturata'). To 6 feet. Leaves have yellow centers, dark green edges with yellow dots. Takes dense shade.

Lily-of-the-valley shrub (*Pieris japonica* 'Variegata'). To 5 feet. Leaves edged creamy white, tinged with pink in spring. ■

By Emely Lincowski

INTERPLANTING annual and perennial flowers among vegetable crops (left) helps to attract beneficial insects. Below, beets, beans, and other crops are grown organically from start to finish.

beneficial life. Many organic gardeners observe that as soil health improves, plant disease problems decline.

For instant results in rocky or otherwise unusable native soil, build raised beds. McCombs and Newton filled theirs with topsoil enriched with organic fertilizer (3-2-1). To further enrich the soil after the growing season ended in fall, they sowed a cover crop of annual ryegrass and topped off the beds with a 3-inch layer of manure. In spring, they dug the cover crop into the soil before planting.

You could follow the same routine to improve native soil, digging 3 inches of manure into the top 10 to 12 inches of each bed before planting, then sowing fall cover crops of crimson clover, rye, buckwheat, or hairy vetch, all to be tilled under before spring planting.

3. KILL THE COMPETITION. If you're gardening in soil that's laced with weed seeds (any native soil, for example), do this: after beds are prepared, water every couple of days for two weeks. Your goal is to germinate as many weed seedlings as possible. Hoe them off lightly as they appear (if you disturb the soil deeper than 2 inches, you'll just bring more weed seeds to the surface). Then plant.

The keys to organic gardening success

Seven techniques can help your garden grow better naturally

S UCCESSFUL ORGANIC GARDENERS have to be some of the best gardeners around, since they must battle infertile soil and pests with only natural weapons.

We asked several organic gardeners to share their most important techniques. Among these experts were Kelly McCombs and Saint Elmo Newton, who practice these techniques in the Seattle garden pictured here.

1. PICK A GARDEN-FRIENDLY SITE. That means a location in full sun and sheltered from constant winds, which stunt plants. McCombs and Newton planted their garden on an unused sunny lot.

2. BUILD OR BRING IN GOOD SOIL. Ideal soil is deep, loose, and fertile, and contains plenty of organic matter, which in turn holds water, nutrients, and plenty of

You can also mulch to keep more weeds from germinating. McCombs and Newton layered each of their raised beds with 3 inches of straw after vegetable seedlings were established, and had no weed problems.

If weeds do appear in your garden, pull or hoe them well before they flower and reproduce. Be especially vigilant for grasses, since they're among the most difficult weeds to control and the fastest to spread.

4. PLANT THE RIGHT VARIETIES AT THE RIGHT TIME. Choose varieties with disease resistance bred in, and with successful track records in your area. County extension offices often have lists of recommended varieties and suggested planting dates. McCombs and Newton used mostly varieties from Territorial Seed Company, whose seeds are selected to do especially well in the coastal Northwest. Plant seedlings close enough together so that as they mature, they'll shade out any weeds that emerge beneath them.

5. INTERPLANT FLOWERS AND VEGETABLES. Harmful insects usually prefer environments in which only one type of plant is grown. Beneficial insects like diversity. McCombs and Newton include annual flowers, perennials, roses, and strawberries in their planting scheme to provide cover, food, and water for beneficial insects. And they keep honeybees in the garden to promote pollination. However, some crops, such as corn, have to be planted alone to ensure pollination and also to avoid cross-pollination from other corn varieties.

6. KEEP THINGS GROWING. There's nothing like vigorous growth to help plants overcome insects and diseases, and to guarantee abundant harvests. When growth is checked by drought, poor soil, or insect infestation, it's difficult to get plants back to full vigor. McCombs and Newton never let plants dry out completely before watering, and they give plants a monthly boost with side dressings of 3-2-1 fertilizer throughout the season.

7. BE THERE. McCombs and Newton walk through their garden every morning and evening, partly for the pure pleasure of it, but also so they can spot plant problems before they get out of hand. ■

By Jim McCausland

SPREADING *a thick mulch of straw around plants in raised beds cuts down on weeds and conserves soil moisture.*

For the love of lavender

If English lavender's got your heart but won't stick around, try one of these varieties. They're better for Southern California gardens

AUDREY HEPBURN AND well-known garden writers like Rosemary Verey are to blame. They introduced us to British gardens full of misty drifts of lavenders through books and videos, and they led us to covet these subtly beautiful perennials. If a plant has both English and lavender in its title, we want it.

Unfortunately, our admiration for *Lavandula angustifolia* is not mutual. English

lavenders hate Southern California. They abhor our clay soil; loose gravel is more to their liking. Our alkaline water isn't to their taste, either; they prefer a twist of lime. And, thanks just the same, but they'd rather live with London's chill than L.A.'s mild, rainy winters, which make them prone to fungal attacks.

Even the best gardeners have trouble keeping English lavender going more than a

few years here, and no one succeeds in keeping plants from looking like wet mops in the winter. If you grow lavender to harvest, you forgive all that. But if you want a handsome, pleasantly aromatic, and relatively long-lasting landscape plant, try one of the following lavenders (listed from easiest to most challenging) instead.

L. heterophylla. If it's a gauzy, gray look you're after, sweet lavender is your best

bet. It is similar to English lavender in many respects: same height (2 to 3 feet tall), same needlelike leaves, same tall violet-purple flower spikes (1 to 2 feet). But this plant has more of a pewter than silver gray cast, and it blooms virtually year-round; English lavender blooms just once a year. Most important, sweet lavender takes to life in clay soil with perfect aplomb. It's the easiest lavender to grow in our climate.

L. dentata. For good reason, French lavender has been a long-standing landscape staple in Southern California. Its rough-toothed leaves, stocky flower spikes, and gnarled stems make it look very provençal. It's a natural

NORMAN A. PLATE

CHAD SLATTERY

PAHO MARSH

BLUE-PURPLE FLOWER SPIKES *of Canary Island lavender (left) make a stunning show against a Tuscan-red wall in a Santa Monica garden designed by Tina Beebe. French lavender (above) provides an aromatic welcome in a Pasadena garden designed by Rick Fisher of Toyon Design.*

companion to rosemary, oleander, olive trees, and other Mediterranean plants common in our gardens. Growers say that gray-leafed *L. dentata candicans* is easier to grow than the green. Both kinds grow to 3 feet tall and wide. They bloom nonstop.

L. canariensis. Canary Island lavender and its nearly identical cousins, *L. multifida* and *L. pinnata buchii*, aren't the least bit English. There's nothing understated about this trio. All sport feathery dark green foliage and 3- to 4-foot-tall flower stalks terminating in a trident of deep purple spiked flowers. In bloom, they're showstoppers. And as with sweet lavender and French lavender, that's for

most of the year. This lavender, however, is only for frost-free areas (*Sunset Western Garden Book* climate zone 24), because it won't tolerate temperatures below 28° without damage.

L. stoechas. Another attention grabber, Spanish lavender is a compact shrub. It's a great choice for smaller gardens, topping out at 2 feet. Its narrow, needlelike gray leaves give it the look of dainty rosemary. (Its resinous fragrance is rosemary-like, too.) This lavender's flowers look like little purple, square-sided pineapples crowned with darker bracts that mimic rabbit ears. It usually blooms only once a year, in early summer. Repeat bloom occurs, but not reliably.

L. 'Goodwin Creek Grey'. The parentage of this newcomer is uncertain. Its woolly leaves suggest the little-known *L. lanata,* its ever-

FLOWERS VARY: *Spanish lavender (right) and Canary Island lavender (far right).*

blooming tendency *L. dentata,* and its tolerance for clay soil *L. heterophylla.* But whatever it is, this lavender selection from Goodwin Creek Gardens in Oregon is a winner. It forms a 2- to 3-foot-tall, neat mound, has a beautiful silvery presence in the garden, and blooms virtually year-round.

L. intermedia. This hybrid is more of a challenge than the others listed here. In Southern California's mild winters, it is prone to black spot and what one grower calls "the woody blues." But it does have the gray

foliage and the fragrance we so admire in *L. angustifolia.* 'Provence' is the most widely grown and one of the best. 'Grosso' is shorter and more compact. Both plants have tall stems (about 1½ ft.) and lavender-blue flower spikes.

CARE AND MAINTENANCE

Though none of these lavenders is as demanding as English lavender, all need good drainage. Add plenty of compost to heavy soils, and plant on a mound in an area that gets full sun. Water established plants deeply but infrequently, and give them little or no fertilizer. Shear them regularly to keep them tidy; to promote new bloom, cut off flowers when the majority are past bloom. Lavenders that grow much larger than 3 feet or so need to be periodically cut back by as much as half to keep them from turning woody. (Start this hard pruning no later than the second year, in early fall.) ■

By Sharon Cohoon

'MOTHER EARTH' IRIS *has the subtle shading and strong sculpted shape so admired in modern bearded irises. But this hybrid comes with a bonus: it blooms twice a year.*

Bloom-again bearded irises

New varieties are bred for repeat bloom— at least twice a year

U NDER SUNNY APRIL SKIES, a clear blue bearded iris is a grand sight. But there's nothing unexpected about it. On the other hand, a clear blue iris blooming under a leaden November cloud cover is a serendipitous delight.

"The bright, clear colors of bearded iris are a wonderful surprise on a gray winter day," says Bill Maryott of Maryott's Iris Gardens in San Jose. "The contrast with the dull sky makes the colors appear even more intense than they do in spring."

Why the surprise? Unlike the best-known bearded irises, which bloom only once a year—in spring—reblooming

'CINDERELLA'S COACH' *has a rounded shape and ruffled petals as yellow-orange as a pumpkin.*

irises bloom at least twice a year.

Irises that come back are not new. Their existence was recorded in the 16th century: John Gerard mentions an iris that "flowereth againe" in fall in his *Herball,* published in 1597. But it wasn't until the 1920s that hybridizers began actively breeding for repeat bloom. And it has been only since the mid-'80s that hybridizers have created rebloomers with the ruffled petals of award-winning once-bloomers. More than 2,000 reblooming varieties are now available. And today, reblooming irises are just as likely to garner medals.

Herb Holk of Cal-Dixie Iris Gardens in Riverside, California, predicts: "The same thing will happen with iris that did with roses. Who will settle for a solo performance when there are flowers just as great that bloom two, three, four, even five times? You'd be crazy not to take advantage of them."

Reblooming irises come in every color from white to chocolate brown, including plicatas (darker stippling on a white ground), bicolors (lighter upper petals with darker contrasting lower petals), and amoenas (white upper petals and colored lower petals). Every size from miniature dwarf (shorter than 8 inches) to tall bearded iris (27 to 42 inches) is represented, too. Though some varieties will rebloom reliably only in mild coastal climates, the majority tolerate temperatures as low as -20°.

Rebloomers will change forever the way gardeners look at bearded irises, predict Holk and Maryott. Instead of being of interest only to collectors, they'll move into landscaping along with other valuable repeat bloomers like roses and daylilies. "Plant a reblooming bearded iris near a nighttime light source like a streetlamp or porch light," suggests Maryott, "and prepare yourself for a colorful change in your winter landscape scheme."

BLOOM PATTERNS VARY BY REGION

Depending on the variety and your climate, reblooming irises follow different bloom patterns. Repeat irises bloom in early spring and then once more, shortly thereafter, from the same rhizome. Continuous rebloomers flower only once per rhizome but develop new rhizomes so quickly that in mild climates they are rarely without flower spikes. Fall rebloomers take a break after spring bloom and come back with a second show in autumn.

If your garden is designed around a carefully controlled color scheme, you can take advantage of bloom patterns. A blue-toned iris that blooms in spring and again in fall—'Solstice', for instance—would complement your cool-season pastels but would not dilute a hot-colored, warm-season border. A more kaleidoscopic gardening style, on the other hand, could take full advantage of a nearly continuous bloomer such as deep purple 'Rosalie Figge'.

Climate can influence bloom patterns. If you buy rhizomes of repeat bloomers from a grower in a colder climate than yours, for instance, it may take several years for the rhizomes to adjust. The irises may not rebloom at all the first year (30 to 40 percent of once-bloomers also withhold blooms the first year after planting). But any iris that reblooms in a colder climate will rebloom eventually in the West's milder climates.

The nearer to home a rhizome is grown, the quicker it will settle into its bloom pattern. Buying locally has another advantage: you can visit growers' fields, see plants in bloom, study colors

THE CAYENNE AND CHILI POWDER *hues of 'Paprika Fono's' warm up the garden in spring and fall.*

and forms, ask questions, and later place a well-informed order.

HOW TO GROW AND CARE FOR REBLOOMERS

Bearded irises are undemanding. All they need is a half-day of full sun, average soil, and adequate drainage. Ensure the latter by planting each rhizome on a small mound. Plant so that rhizomes are barely covered with soil. Unlike once-blooming irises, rebloomers need summer water for best bloom. (If rebloomers dry out in the summer, they become semidormant and stop flowering.) Water regularly—about once a week—from early spring through fall. To encourage rebloom, fertilize with a low-nitrogen formula such as 5-10-5 or 6-8-4 after each bloom cycle. ∎

WHERE TO BUY REBLOOMING IRISES

If reblooming irises are so wonderful, why aren't they advertised more? Large growers were initially reluctant to promote rebloomers because they are difficult to harvest. But all that is changing.

Eight Western sources are listed below. Reliable reblooming varieties to look for include 'Baby Blessed', 'Blessed Again', 'Champagne Elegance', 'Clarence', 'Double Up', 'I Bless', 'Leprechaun's Delight', 'Low Ho Silver', 'Matrix', 'Mother Earth', 'Pink Attraction', and 'Ultra Echo'.

Aitken's Salmon Creek Garden, 608 N.W. 119th St., Vancouver, WA 98685; (360) 573-4472. Catalog $2.

Buena Creek Gardens, 418 Buena Creek Rd., San Marcos, CA 92069; (619) 744-2810. Retail.

Cal-Dixie Iris Gardens, 14115 Pear St., Riverside, CA 92508; (909) 780-0335. Catalog $1.

Greenwood Iris + Daylilies, 5595 E. Seventh St., Box 490, Long Beach, CA 90804; (310) 494-8944.

Maryott's Iris Gardens, 1073 Bird Ave., San Jose, CA 95125; (408) 971-0444. Retail and mail order.

Shepard Iris Garden, 3342 W. Orangewood Ave., Phoenix, AZ 85051; (602) 841-1231. Retail and mail order; catalog $1.

Superstition Iris Gardens, 2536 Old Highway, Cathey's Valley, CA 95306; (209) 966-6277. Catalog $1.50.

Sutton's Green Thumber, 16592 Rd. 208, Porterville, CA 93257; (209) 784-9011. Catalog $1. ∎

By Sharon Cohoon

DOMINIQUE VORILLON

Backyard poultry

A few chickens will keep you in eggs, compost,
and dinner-party conversation

IT SEEMS I HAVE become famous for my chickens. Recently I was at a neighbor's party. "Where's your farm?" a woman asked. I gave her a blank look. "You know, where do you keep your chickens?"

When I told her that I lived in the suburban house just around the corner, she was astonished. "You mean you have chickens right in your own backyard?"

Absolutely.

I have kept laying hens for the past two years, enjoying a bountiful supply of fresh, tasty eggs laid only a few steps from my back door.

Anyone who has a little dirt out back, the right zoning ordinances, and tolerant neighbors can keep enough chickens to provide eggs for the family—and manure for the compost pile—with minimal labor and expense. Chickens are hardy, easily managed, and fun to watch— a great learning experience for my 4- and 6-year-old sons, who helped build a coop and who have taken over managing egg sales and recording and spending the proceeds.

Of course, like any other animals, our four hens must be fed, watered, and cleaned up after, all of which takes about 10 minutes a day and an hour or so four times a year when we clean out their pen and line it with fresh straw. When we go on vacation, our neighbors pitch in to feed and water the chickens. In return they get to keep the eggs.

EGGS & COMPOST

Why bother with chickens? For one thing, there is a natural connection between the henhouse behind my garage and my vegetable plot. Garden cuttings—broccoli stems, lettuce and cabbage leaves, pea vines, and leafy green carrot tops—go to the chickens, which also eat weeds, worms, and all kinds of table scraps. Sometimes I even let my chickens wander around the yard to keep the slug population in check (although the chickens are fond of my lettuce patch, too). When I clean out their pen, I shovel the manure into the compost pile, where it degrades and eventually gets spread over the garden to feed next year's crop.

I enjoy being part of this earthy cycle almost as much as I enjoy opening my back window and hearing the musical *cluck, cluck, cluck* of four happy hens.

Then there are the eggs. Really fresh eggs, plucked from the nest still warm, have dark golden yolks that stand up high in the frying pan. The albumen, or white of the egg, holds together in a firm circle instead of running all over the pan. In contrast, the flavor of an egg that has spent days getting from farm to supermarket pales compared with the intense taste of an egg laid a few hours before being eaten. And with eggs selling for $1.50 to $2 a carton, we pretty much break even on our chickens, which eat about 50 pounds of commercially produced laying mash each month, costing me about $9. Feed is also available in pellets.

GETTING STARTED

When I decided to begin the grand chicken experiment in the spring of 1994, I first checked with my municipal code–enforcement officer. I found that in my city, Monrovia, California, I could keep as many as 10 hens but no roosters. No problem there, since hens produce lovely eggs without ever laying eyes on a rooster.

I also explained to my neighbors what I planned to do and got their approval. My husband was the one who needed the most persuading, but he agreed to go along with the experiment as long as we both understood that he would not be shoveling manure anytime soon.

I started with 2-day-old female chicks, which I picked up at a nearby feed store for $2 each (sounds obvious, but make sure you're buying female chicks). Hens can also be purchased as young pullets—18- to 22-week-old adolescents just about ready to begin laying eggs—for about $12 each. It is easier to skip the baby stage, but despite the work entailed in raising chicks, it seems a shame to miss out on the adorable downy peepers.

We brought our fluffy yellow babies home in a paper bag and put them in a newspaper-lined box with a lightbulb suspended inside to keep things warm.

After about six weeks, when their downy fluff had been completely replaced by feathers, they were ready to live without the artificial heat of the lightbulb. By that time, I had penned off a 6- by 13-foot area behind the garage, sinking chicken wire into a 6-inch-deep concrete curb and stapling it to wooden posts about 6 feet tall. I put the now-gawky teenage pullets into their enclosure, where they had everything they needed to stay healthy: food and a feeder, an automatic waterer, a roost, plenty of dirt in which to scratch, peck, and take dust baths, and a coop built about 3 feet off the ground to keep them safe from predators at night. In time, we put a cat carrier (a plastic box enclosed except for a small door in front) into the pen to serve as a communal nesting box for the hens.

Through the years, I have increased my flock. The most important thing I have learned is that chickens must be kept safe from the suburban raccoons, opossums, and neighborhood dogs that would love to make a nice meal out of a plump hen. I lost my original pair of white Leghorn chickens to marauding raccoons one tragic night because I had forgotten to latch the coop door. I decided to strengthen the pen and cover it with mesh after I spotted an owl lurking in my backyard one evening not long after.

A few hens in the backyard is certainly not a way to turn a profit. But buying cold eggs at the grocery store is no match for gathering warm ones each morning and marveling at the freshness and perfection of nature.

PULLET POINTERS

■ COST. The biggest initial expense is the pen, which consists of an enclosed area for the chickens to walk around in by day (they need exercise), and a coop for them to sleep in at night. A Leghorn coop should have at least 2 square feet of floor space and $1\frac{1}{2}$ feet of headroom per bird, as well as space for a nest. Larger birds need more room. You can make the coop as elaborate as you want, or put it together cheaply using salvaged lumber. Don't skimp on the chicken wire, though. Make sure it is heavy gauge.

■ VARIETIES. Around Easter, feed stores have a good selection of chicks. White Leghorns are the most popular commercial breed because they lay 250 to 300 white eggs annually during their prime laying years. For the home poultry keeper, however, the heavier red, brown, and black hens are probably better choices. I have had

THE AUTHOR'S SON *Matthew holds a morning's haul from his backyard chicken ranch. At far left, Araucanas—a South American breed known as Easter egg chickens—occupy a neighbor's coop.*

good results with so-called sex-linked chickens, hybrids that are a little larger than Leghorns and lay 180 to 240 brown eggs a year. Araucanas lay colorful eggs (ours are blue-green) that never fail to raise eyebrows when you sell them or give them as gifts.

■ SUNLIGHT. Egg production is related to the length of day, so the pen should be in a sunny spot, although it should also be shaded during summer. Some backyard-poultry enthusiasts put lights in their coops to increase production. If you do not use lights, your hens will slow or

stop laying for a few weeks or more between November and February.

■ LIFE EXPECTANCY. Hens mature at 5 to 6 months, depending on the breed, and then start laying eggs. They will lay at their best rate for one or two years, and at a reduced rate into their third, fourth, and fifth years. If you decide to let them live out their days in your yard, they could survive for 10 years. Many poultry keepers, however, put their nonproductive hens into the stew pot.

■ TO LEARN MORE. *The Chicken Book,* by Page Smith

and Charles Daniel, is a wonderful guide, with everything from tips on how to raise chickens to chicken lore and history. I've found it in several libraries.

Eggs and Chickens, by John Vivian (Storey Communications, Pownal, VT; $2.95 plus shipping; 800/441-5700), is a 32-page booklet that shows you how to build a basic coop and offers practical information on basics such as diet. Storey publishes other books on chickens, too. When you call, ask for a catalog. ■

By Karen E. Klein

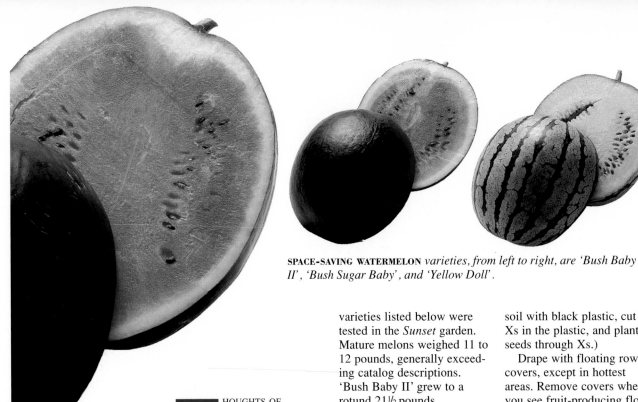

SPACE-SAVING WATERMELON *varieties, from left to right, are 'Bush Baby II', 'Bush Sugar Baby', and 'Yellow Doll'.*

Space-saving watermelons

Bush types take only half the space of standard melons

HOW DO YOU KNOW *when it's ripe? Pick when the tendril next to the stem has withered and the spot on the underside of the melon has turned from whitish to creamy yellow.*

THOUGHTS OF growing your own crunchy, sweet watermelons in the backyard vegetable garden are enticing—until you discover that most vines grow 6 to 9 feet long. One plant can devour an entire small-space vegetable garden.

Fortunately for watermelon lovers, a few varieties aren't space hogs. Bush watermelons take up only about half the area of standard kinds (most grow about 3 to 4 feet long). And they still deliver the flavor that you expect from a home-grown melon. Keep in mind, though, that even bush watermelons aren't small plants. Make sure you give them plenty of space to grow, so they don't take over your bush beans, carrots, or other small prey.

Watermelons should be planted as soon as possible. Order seeds right away.

CHOOSE FROM THREE REDS AND A YELLOW

Bush watermelons are considered icebox types—depending on the variety, they weigh 5 to 12 pounds, and are small enough to fit in the refrigerator. The four varieties listed below were tested in the *Sunset* garden. Mature melons weighed 11 to 12 pounds, generally exceeding catalog descriptions. 'Bush Baby II' grew to a rotund 21½ pounds.

Each vine generally produces only a couple of melons; 'Yellow Doll', which grows on semicompact vines, produces more fruit.

'Bush Baby II' (80 days). Shiny, dark green 10-pound fruit, bright red flesh. Very sweet, and much larger than 10 pounds in our test.

'Bush Sugar Baby' (80 days). Dark green 12-pound fruit, orangy red flesh. Not as sweet as others in our test.

'Garden Baby' (70 to 76 days). Round, dark green 6- to 8-pound fruit, red flesh. The sweetest red in our test.

'Yellow Doll' (65 to 76 days). Light green 5- to 8-pound fruit with dark green stripes, yellow flesh. Vines 4 to 5 feet long. Very sweet and succulent in our test.

PLANT IN A WARM, SUNNY LOCATION

Choose the sunniest location in the garden. Add some compost or other organic matter to the soil. Plant seeds 18 to 24 inches apart in rows 3 feet apart, or plant in mounds spaced 3 feet apart. (In coastal or cooler climates, plant where vines will get reflected heat from a wall or fence. Cover the soil with black plastic, cut Xs in the plastic, and plant seeds through Xs.)

Drape with floating row covers, except in hottest areas. Remove covers when you see fruit-producing flowers—they have bulbous stem ends. (If your soil is below 70° now, start seeds indoors and transplant seedlings when the soil warms.)

Water regularly (don't let plants wilt or they may develop hollow heart—a hollow center), and fertilize with fish emulsion or other fertilizer. Cut back somewhat on watering when melons form, so flavor concentrates.

ORDER SEEDS BY MAIL

The watermelons described here are available through these mail-order sources. Catalogs are free.

W. Atlee Burpee & Co., 300 Park Ave., Warminster, PA 18991; (800) 888-1447. Sells 'Bush Sugar Baby'.

Park Seed Co., Cokesbury Rd., Greenwood, SC 29647; (800) 845-3369. Sells 'Bush Baby II'.

Territorial Seed Company, Box 157, Cottage Grove, OR 97424; (503) 942-9547. Sells 'Garden Baby' and 'Yellow Doll'.

Vermont Bean Seed Co., Garden Lane, Fair Haven, VT 05743; (802) 273-3400. Sells 'Garden Baby' and 'Yellow Doll'. ∎

By Lauren Bonar Swezey

DARROW M. WATT

NORMAN A. PLATE

PLUMP, 6-INCH-LONG *'Blue Lake' beans develop in clusters on the vine.*

Is 'Blue Lake' still the best bean?

Yes. But the perennial winner now has competition

FOR YEARS, 'BLUE LAKE' HAS been considered the standard-setting pole bean. Although it has rather humble origins as a canning bean, many gardeners and growers now consider it a gourmet bean. Its succulent crunch and mild bean flavor are tough to beat. Fine grocery stores and produce markets usually identify it by name (instead of selling it as a generic green bean), particularly when it's harvested at the immature stage and sold as baby 'Blue Lake'.

But with all of the new bean varieties now available through mail-order catalogs, does 'Blue Lake' still rate at the top of the pack for flavor? Last season we grew and tasted a dozen different varieties of green pole beans. Five of our six tasters still considered 'Blue Lake' the best.

HOW THE CANNING BEAN
TURNED GOURMET

In the early part of this century, 'Blue Lake' was *the* bean grown for canning in the Blue Lake District near Ukiah, California. In 1923, this variety arrived in Oregon, where much of the bean research has since been done. By 1952,

western Oregon grew 10,000 acres of the beans, according to James Baggett, retired horticulture professor at Oregon State University in Corvallis.

Early on, 'Blue Lake' beans were stringy, and some strains had colored seeds. But seed companies improved the bean and released new strains, and by the '50s, the only beans grown were stringless, white-seeded strains resistant to common bean mosaic. The current 'Blue Lake' is descended from developments by Ferry-Morse Seed Company.

WHAT MAKES IT THE BEST?

'Blue Lake' beans are dark green, round in cross section, stringless, firm, and straight. Our tasters described their flavor as mild and sweet and the texture as tender-crisp. Tasters reported that other beans, such as 'Romano', tasted

beanier (which some people prefer) and less sweet, and had a mealier texture.

In our test garden, 'Blue Lake' was extremely productive. Vines grew taller than 8 feet and produced for a long period (about two months).

RUNNERS-UP

'Kentucky Blue', a cross between 'Bush Blue Lake' and 'Kentucky Wonder', has a flavor much like that of 'Blue Lake' and came in a close second in our tasting. "Fresh, bright, and sweet," one taster called it. When raw, it's particularly juicy. It's very tender, but Baggett warns that it gets stringy as it develops on the vine.

Tied for third place were 'Cascade Giant', a sweet, round stringless bean developed by Baggett; and 'Kwintus', a flat-podded bean bred in Europe that's very productive over a long period, and flavorful and tender whether small or very large.

We also grew 'Bush Blue Lake' to see how it compared with the pole variety. We found the bush variety less flavorful. Flavor can vary among 'Bush Blue Lake' beans; hybridization has brought out the characteristics of some non–'Blue Lake' parents.

WHERE TO BUY SEEDS

'Blue Lake' pole beans are available on seed racks everywhere (plant seeds as soon as soil is warm). You can also order 'Blue Lake', 'Kentucky Blue', and 'Cascade Giant' from Territorial Seed Company (541/942-9547). 'Kwintus' is available from The Cook's Garden (802/824-3400). Catalogs are free. ■
By Lauren Bonar Swezey

'Kentucky Blue'

'Bush Blue Lake'

'Cascade Giant'

'Blue Lake'

'Kwintus'

115

FRESH FROM THE GARDEN, *from left, white-stalked Chinese bok choy and green-stemmed 'Mei Qing' and 'Shanghai' await stir-frying. Bok choy flowers (center) are also edible.*

NORMAN A. PLATE

Bok choy: The tender, tasty green

It's like health food from the garden. And it's easy to grow

BROCCOLI, CABBAGE, AND cauliflower are all excellent choices for a healthy diet. But when it comes to the garden, and especially a small one, bok choy (also spelled pak choi) is a better brassica. Why? Let us count the ways:

Space savings. Compared with the girth of a cabbage, bok choy is as slim-hipped as supermodel Kate Moss. Because its growth is mostly upright—like the Swiss chard it resembles—it can be planted closely: 8 inches apart (versus the 14-inch minimum required for cabbage) if you want mature heads, or as close as 2 inches if you harvest some of the young seedlings. And, since it doesn't need much root space either, you can grow it in a container.

Time savings. It's barely a blink from germination to dinner plate. Fully developed heads can be picked 40 to 50 days after sowing. Immature heads can be harvested a month after sowing. Cabbage, by comparison, takes two to four months to mature.

Versatility. Because bok choy can be harvested at different stages, it can be used many ways. Young leaves are good raw in salads. Whole heads of baby bok choy can be braised in butter and/or

broth or gently stir-fried for an elegant presentation. The mature crop is good chopped in stir-fries. And when the plants bolt, you can sprinkle the tasty flowering stalks and their pretty yellow flowers into salads.

Though the divisions blur, especially in the hybrids, there are four types of bok choy. What you're used to seeing in supermarkets is the Chinese white-stalked type. Its thick, white stalks contrast with its dark green leaves. 'Chinese Pak Choi', which grows to 12 inches tall, is the standard; 'Joi Choi' is a choice hybrid of this mild-tasting variety.

Green-stemmed varieties have pale green stalks, dark green leaves, and a hint of mustard in their taste, and they are shorter (8 to 10 inches tall) than their white-stemmed cousins. This is the type often harvested early as baby bok choy. 'Shanghai' is an old variety, 'Mei Qing' a newer hybrid. (Incidentally, these two took second and first place, respectively, in our test garden tastings.)

Two other categories include taller (18-inch), thinner types like 'Tah Tsai', with leaves shaped like Chinese soup spoons, and very short (4- to 6-inch) types like 'Canton Dwarf'. But seeds for these are harder to find.

TIPS FOR A GOOD CROP

Bok choy presents two challenges. One is pests: Slugs and snails love these succulent plants, so be prepared to hand-pick or sacrifice outside leaves when you harvest. Cabbage worms, a lesser problem, can be combated with the caterpillar-destroying bacteria *Bacillus thuringiensis,* alone or with row covers.

The other obstacle is premature bolting. Bok choy sets seed at the first sign of trouble—too cold, too hot, too much temperature variation (especially in spring), or too much stress (from lack of water or fertilizer). The best preventive for stress is growing the plants fast. Feed early and often with a weak solution of fish emulsion. Add compost or manure to the planting area before sowing seed, and side-dress young plants. Keep soil consistently moist.

The question of when to plant is trickier. The surest route is to sow seed at the same time you would for cabbage or broccoli. But since some types of bok choy are heat or cold tolerant, or both, and all types have such a short growing period, most gardeners push the calendar.

April is a great time to start seed of bok choy in the Northwest and mountain areas, as well as in coastal California (gardeners here can plant in succession right through summer). In hotter inland areas such as the Central Valley, sowing seed now is worth a try (grow heat-tolerant green-stemmed or Canton varieties). In all these areas, you can sow another crop in early fall (late July in the Northwest, late August through early October elsewhere; November's not too late for coastal Southern California). In the desert, wait until fall to grow bok choy.

Experiment. Sow small crops often and try different varieties. You really can't lose. What other vegetable gives you feathers or flowers?

WHERE TO FIND SEED

Get seed at a nursery or order it by mail from one of these sources: Nichols Garden Nursery, 1190 N. Pacific Highway, Albany, OR 97321, (541) 928-9280; DeGiorgi Seed Company, 6011 N St., Omaha, NE 68117, (402) 731-3901. ∎

By Sharon Cohoon

A ROOTBOUND CATTLEYA *orchid will probably do better tied to a tree than it would have in a container.*

JOHN HUMBLE

No space? Grow orchids in your trees

Brad Carter has a mini–rain forest in his Costa Mesa garden

THE CASE OF THE shrinking garden has a simple solution: just look up. That's what Brad Carter did when he moved into his condominium in Costa Mesa. Friends thought Carter's small (22 by 44 feet), shadowy courtyard garden had little potential. But Carter, who's the assistant director of the UC Irvine Arboretum, saw a mini–rain forest waiting to happen. It didn't take much to create a glamorous showplace for his collection of exotic epiphytes.

By taking advantage of his vertical space, Carter was able to squeeze more plants into his small garden than if he had stayed at ground level. "Epiphytes are perfect for gardeners short on space," he says. "They don't even need soil—epiphytes get their nutrients from the air and water. All they need is something for the roots to attach to."

In Carter's garden, the trunks and lower limbs of jacaranda trees supply that support. The trees' lacy foliage above provides a junglelike canopy, with giant bird of paradise, variegated ginger, and bamboo making up the understory. Clivia, ligularia, and other shade lovers create the illusion of a forest floor.

Two epiphytic bromeliads—*Neoregelia* and *Tillandsia ionantha*—are suitable for a treetop garden and are often sold in small containers as house plants. Both do fine without soil. Four kinds of orchids—*Cattleya, Encyclia, Oncidium,* and *Laelia anceps*—will also work. Many nurseries carry both types of bromeliads, and *Cattleya* orchids, too. For more choices, search out nurseries specializing in orchids or tropicals.

To plant—or perhaps it's "unplant"—any of the plants mentioned, follow these simple steps: Remove the epiphyte from its pot, and knock off the dirt. Place the plant where desired on the chosen support. Lash it securely in place with several wraps of monofilament fishing line. Shroud the plant's roots in a piece of sphagnum moss (for moisture retention), and tie the moss in place with more line.

Within 6 to 12 months, the epiphyte will have put out enough fresh roots to secure itself to its new home. At that point you can—and with a living host, should—snip away the monofilament.

And that's that—which is another reason Carter loves these plants. Though he has the horticultural knowledge and skill to grow more demanding plants, like most gardeners today he's as short on time as he is on space.

"The neat thing about epiphytes is all the work is upfront," he says. "After that, they're a breeze." Just mist regularly and fertilize periodically with a water-soluble product. "I rarely get around to fertilizing," admits Carter, "but they bloom anyway."

So if you're cramped for both time and space, don't despair. "Look up," urges Carter. And you can take that advice literally. ∎

By Sharon Cohoon

Azaleas, rhododendrons, and a dogwood (at far left) burst with color along a path in Bellevue, Washington. For tips on growing these May bloomers, see page 122.

MAY

Garden guide......................120

Checklists & garden notebooks...125

Window box renaissance..........130

New perennials fast—for free.....134

Bellflowers: Six great choices.....136

Easy-to-live-with palms...........138

Lingonberries for ground cover..140

Lusher-looking impatiens.........141

Growing pawpaw trees...........142

Wander among wildflowers........143

GARDEN
Guide

Pretty, private, and deerproof in Carmel Valley

When Elaine and Mark Schlegel bought their house in Carmel Valley, California, the front yard was a parking lot. "People used to drive their cars right up to the front porch!" Elaine says. The Schlegels replaced the parking lot with a haphazard collection of plants, mostly vegetables.

"As landscape designers, we were always creating beautiful gardens for our clients. Then we'd come home to a mishmash," says Elaine. So the Schlegels began transforming the mishmash into the private entry garden pictured at right. Now it's filled with flowers and fragrance, and has room for entertaining.

The first step was enclosing the garden. "I had to have a formal rose garden," Elaine says. But for roses to survive, they had to be protected from marauding deer. An existing rock wall—an 1880 landmark that divided two ranchos of Carmel and Carmel Valley—created part of the enclosure; a redwood fence with double entry gates completed it.

To design the garden beds, the Schlegels plunged sticks into the soil to mark the boundaries. Then they edged the beds with rocks.

The planting beds reflect a combination of wildness and order. Roses form their backbone. These include 'Buff Beauty', apricot 'Crépuscule', light pink David Austin English rose 'Belle Story', light pink

White sweet alyssum, cosmos, and roses—with a few poppies between them—edge a wide river of gravel.

'Kathleen', light yellow 'Mermaid', and light pink 'Penelope'.

Sweet alyssum, catmint, and Santa Barbara daisy ramble beneath the roses. California poppies, cosmos, hollyhocks, lamb's ears, and Mexican evening primrose fill other beds.

Like classic early-California gardens, this one has

Colorful coleus that love the sun

When you think of plants that can take Texas's summer sun and the heat that goes with it, mesquite might come to mind, but coleus? You'd think not, at least until you talked with horticulturists at Texas A & M. After running summer trials on 70 coleus varieties at various sites around Texas, they've selected two—'Burgundy Sun' and 'Plum Parfait'—that can handle full sun all summer anywhere in Texas. These two varieties also did quite well in shade.

'Burgundy Sun' has solid wine-colored leaves throughout the season. It looks best massed at a distance, where the block of color really stands out.

'Plum Parfait' has leaves that start out entirely plum-colored, but as the summer heats up, their ruffled edges become pink. Plant this one close to walking and sitting areas so you can appreciate its leaves' detailed beauty.

Because heat- and drought-resistance don't always go hand in hand, give these varieties plenty of water when the weather gets hot. They won't tolerate wet feet, however, so plant them in soil that has good drainage. These coleus normally grow to about 3 feet, but if you shear them back by about a fourth in midsummer, they'll remain thick, lush, and compact.

Though both these coleus were introduced just last year, they should be widely available throughout the Southwest in nurseries and garden centers this year.

STEVEN W. GEORGE

'Plum Parfait' coleus has lance-shaped leaves with ruffled edges.

no lawn to irrigate; adobe pavers form the front walk, and a layer of gray gravel covers the soil between the flower beds.

NORMAN A. PLATE

How much mulch should you buy?

Not all of us are good at math. That's why it's always nice when someone else does calculations for us.

Gardening experts (and *Sunset*) recommend spreading a 2- to 4-inch-deep layer of mulch around plants to help maintain soil moisture, keep the soil cool, and control weed growth (use the deeper amount around larger plants).

Bulk quantities of mulch are sold by the cubic yard. How do you translate a 2- or 4-inch layer into cubic yards? Once you know how many square feet you want to cover (simply multiply the area's length by its width to get square feet), consult the list at left to determine the approximate amount of mulch you need in cubic yards.

Spread the mulch over the soil around your plants, but do not pile it against trunks or stems.

HOW MUCH MULCH TO USE			
TO COVER THIS AREA	2 INCHES DEEP	3 INCHES DEEP	4 INCHES DEEP
100 sq. ft.	⅔ cu. yd.	1 cu. yd.	1⅓ cu. yd.
250	1⅔	2½	3⅓
500	3⅓	5	6⅔
1,000	6⅔	10	13⅓

A living classroom for gardeners in Salem

The Martha Springer Botanical Garden, filling a slice of fertile land at Willamette University in Salem, Oregon, is named for a professor of biology who dreamed of an arboretum-like area and outdoor classroom on campus.

The late Professor Springer's dream came true when the garden opened in 1987. Today it offers visitors a host of lessons in landscape design and plant husbandry.

The garden is divided into 12 parts, and plants are well marked. Four sections are devoted to natives; you'll see how to use plants ranging from bear grass and manzanita to bigleaf maples, and you'll observe the beginnings of a native oak savanna and a wildflower meadow. You'll also get good ideas for using plant colors, textures, and scents as well as for attracting birds and butterflies.

The garden is open from dawn to dusk daily. From Interstate 5, take State Highway 22 (exit 253) west. Follow the highway for 1½ miles; you'll start to head up an overpass. At the top of the overpass, take the right-hand exit (there's a sign for the university). Keep to the left as the exit divides. The main parking lot is on the right about 200 feet past the green Willamette University sign. The garden is just north of the parking lot.

Flowering shrubs go color crazy in May

So many plants that normally pose in subdued tones explode into bloom this month that it seems as if nature has suddenly swung from a sedate minuet to a throbbing samba beat. In the photo on page 118, you see May color madness at its wildest in the garden of Dr. Ned Brockenbrough of Bellevue, Washington.

Along the path is a mix of evergreen rhododendrons and deciduous azaleas with flowers in shades of cream, yellow, pink, red, and purple. To the left of the path, an Eastern dogwood (*Cornus florida*) adds a big puff of pink. Once this gaudy flower show is over, though, the woodland landscape once again becomes a subtle tapestry of foliage.

Since Dr. Brockenbrough is a rhododendron hybridizer, many of the plants he grows are not available on the market. But you can buy similar plants in bloom this month at nurseries throughout the Pacific Northwest. If you buy one in flower, you may want to let its blooms enliven a patio before you plant it in the ground. For tips on getting rhododendrons off to a good start, see Planting Opportunities on the facing page.

One of the best times to prune established flowering shrubs is while they're in bloom. Remove branches that have grown erratically, and lightly cut back top and side growth so plants stay compact. Save the flowers you remove for indoor display.

On a sunny May day, visitors walk among raised beds at Willamette's Martha Springer Botanical Garden.

A perfect marriage: Roses and perennials

Susie Hubbard's rose garden in Tehachapi, California, isn't your typical rose garden. Its colorful jumble of tough, free-blooming roses and carefree perennials looks more like an old-fashioned cottage garden. And it won the Grand Prize in the All-America Rose Selections' 1994 Landscape with Roses Contest.

The secret to Hubbard's success? She doesn't plant just *any* rose in her garden. She chooses ones that bloom over a long season and, since she shuns chemical sprays, ones that resist disease. She also favors varieties with single blooms, because they seem to produce more flowers overall.

Her favorites include floribundas such as 'Iceberg' (white), 'Lady of the Dawn' (light pink), and 'Playboy' (red with gold eye); climbers such as 'Altissimo' (red) and 'Dortmund' (red with white eye); and shrub roses such as 'Ballerina' (pink with a white eye), 'Graham Thomas' (yellow), 'Linda Campbell' (red), 'Red Coat' (red), and 'Sally Holmes' (white). She also has some old standbys like the grandiflora 'Queen Elizabeth' (pink) and the hybrid tea 'Dainty Bess' (rose pink).

For companion plants, Hubbard selects perennials

JOHN HUMBLE

Roses in shades of red and pink make a big splash among more demure white Shasta daisies and feverfew, and gold calendulas.

that also bloom over a long season, including artemisia, catmint, centranthus, coral bells, cranesbill, dusty miller, dwarf bush german-der, lavender, *Salvia superba* 'East Friesland', and veronica.

Blooming roses and perennials such as catmint are available in containers at nurseries this month. Choose plants for flower colors that look pleasing together.

PLANTING OPPORTUNITIES

Getting rhodies off to a good start

Nowhere in the world do rhododendrons grow better than they do west of the Cascades—in *Sunset Western Garden Book* climate zones 4 through 7. And, nursery owners will tell you, more rhododendrons are sold this month than at any other time. Why? May is a good planting month, the blooming plants are irresistible, and they make great gifts for Mother's Day.

If you buy one, consider these planting tips.

Rhododendrons do best in loose, rich, acid soil that's moist but provides good drainage. Pick a planting site that gets partial sun (preferably in the morning) or one that provides some shade, such as the sun-dappled area beneath a large deciduous tree.

If your soil isn't the good acid loam that covers much of the Northwest, dig out the planting hole to a depth of at least 2 feet and backfill it with an enriched soil mixture. Try blending equal parts of native soil and organic matter (compost, peat moss, or leaf mold), or mix 3 parts new topsoil to 1 part organic matter.

Let the soil settle for a week or so before planting. Then set the rhododendron in the hole so that the soil line of the container plant is even with or slightly above the surrounding soil level.

PLANTING OPPORTUNITIES

Painted daisies for spring color

Covered with flowers in vivid shades of pink, white, or red, *Chrysanthemum coccineum* richly earns its common name—painted daisy. But unlike its fall-flowering cousins in the chrysanthemum family, the painted daisy's striking

Painted daisies unfurl like parasols on 2- to 3-foot stems.

blooms appear in May or June, often at the same time as those of the iris.

This bushy perennial grows to 2 or 3 feet tall and bears long-stemmed single or double flowers that rise above finely divided, bright green leaves. Painted daisies will grow almost anywhere, but they tend to do best in hot-summer climates. In mild-winter climates, blooms may start in April. They make excellent cut flowers.

You can start plants by sowing seed now or setting out plants from nursery containers. Although plants in nursery cans may not have very many blooms, once painted daisies become

established in the garden, they'll be strong enough to produce a flower show worthy of their name.

After spring bloom, cut back established plants; sometimes they'll flower again in late summer or fall. Divide clumps of daisies every three or four years; fall is the best time to do this.

THE NATURAL WAY

Beneficial insects help control giant whitefly

Giant whitefly first appeared in 1992, on hibiscus in coastal San Diego. Since then, this tenacious new pest (*Aleurodicus dugesii*) has spread inland and is beginning to encroach upon Orange County.

It likes many plants, including avocados, bananas, begonias, citrus, and palms. Though infestations are alarmingly ugly—the whitefly deposits so much waxy honeydew on

host plants that leaves look as if they've sprouted stringy white beards—their appearance doesn't spell doom for plants.

Two natural enemies, released in the fall of 1995 in San Diego, show great promise. They were tested in separate projects by the Biological Control Program of the California Department of Food and Agriculture and the San Diego County Agricultural Department. The predaceous ladybird beetle (*Delphastus catalinae*) is reproducing, a good sign that it is feeding on whitefly nymphs, according to Charles Pickett, bio-

THE NATURAL WAY

Fish fertilizer goes dry

Liquid fish emulsion is one of the most popular natural fertilizers around.

Now you can buy pelletized fish fertilizer. Just scatter the pellets over plant

roots, work into the soil, and water.

The new product, called Alaska Dry Fish Fertilizer, is available in various formulations, including those for general-purpose feeding (7-7-2) and flowering plants (5-7-3). You should be able to find it in local nurseries and garden centers.

logical control specialist at CDFA. And the nonstinging parasitic wasp (*Entedononecremnus*), collected by Mike Rose of Texas A & M University, is parasitizing whitefly nymphs. More releases of both beneficial insects are planned.

Until the beneficials multiply enough to bring down the whitefly population, David Kellum, San Diego County entomologist, advises combating giant whitefly infestations with frequent applications of strong streams of water and/or insecticidal soap. (Whiteflies develop an immunity to pesticides.)

NEW PRODUCT REVIEW

An easy liner for hanging baskets

Do you love the look of wire hanging baskets but hate the job of lining them? Well, so did Ted and Rick Mayeda of M & M Nursery. Hanging baskets are a specialty at their retail nursery in Orange County, California, and every year they put together thousands.

That daunting task led them to create the labor-saving E-Z Liner, a polyester drop-in pouch that eliminates the mess of sphagnum moss.

The plastic inner layer

Plastic liner fits neatly into a wire basket.

also helps keep the soil moist. Simply pop the durable green liner into a wire basket and fill it with

soil, and you're ready for the fun part of the job—planting. (To insert plants on the side, use scissors to cut slits in the pouch.)

E-Z Liners are available by mail from M & M in 12- to 24-inch round and 14- to 18-inch shallow sizes, and in 14- and 16-inch wall pockets. Prices range from $6.49 for a 12-inch round liner to $16.99 for a 24-inch round liner, plus shipping and handling. Liners and wire baskets are also sold together as sets. To order, call (800) 644-8042.

By Sharon Cohoon, Steven R. Lorton, Jim McCausland, Lauren Bonar Swezey, Lance Walheim

CHECKLIST

MAY

Vancouver
Victoria
BRITISH COLUMBIA
Spokane
Seattle
WASHINGTON
Olympia
Yakima
Portland
Pendleton
Salem
OREGON
Bend
Eugene
Sunset Western Garden Book CLIMATE ZONES
Medford
☐ 1-3 ☐ 4-7

PLANTING

☐ **ANNUALS.** From the beginning of the month in zones 4 through 7 and after the last hard frost in zones 1 through 3, you can set out plants of lobelia, petunia, snapdragon, and other summer annuals in beds and containers. Direct-sow seeds of bachelor's button, calendula, clarkia, cosmos, impatiens, marigold, nasturtium, nicotiana, pansy, salvia, and sunflower.

☐ **BEGONIAS, FUCHSIAS, GERANIUMS.** In zones 4 through 7, you can put these plants in the ground and into containers early this month. In zones 1 through 3, wait until late in the month, when the threat of frost has passed.

☐ **PERENNIALS.** Nurseries will be well stocked with plants in all sizes. Buy now and plant immediately.

☐ **VEGETABLES.** As soon as the soil is warm, set out seedlings of cucumbers, eggplants, peppers, and tomatoes; sow seeds of melons, squash, and pumpkins. Beans, corn, and New Zealand spinach can also go into the ground.

MAINTENANCE

☐ **BATTLE SLUGS.** Whether you hand-pick, bait, or use traps, keep the war going. If you use bait, be careful to keep it away from pets and children.

☐ **DIVIDE PERENNIALS.** Throughout the Northwest, you can divide plants that have just finished blooming and plants that bloom in late summer and fall without interrupting the flower cycle. Gingerly dig a circle around a plant with a spade or shovel, and pop it out of the ground. A clump the size of a dinner plate will divide neatly into four pieces. Replant and water well.

☐ **FERTILIZE ANNUALS.** Feed annual flowers in beds and pots early in the month and again at midmonth. A liquid plant food such as fish emulsion works well, since the dissolved nutrients go directly to the plants' roots.

☐ **FEED FLOWERING SHRUBS.** Apply a balanced or high-nitrogen fertilizer on flowering shrubs this month. Scatter granular fertilizer around the bases of plants to encourage strong growth and good bud sets.

☐ **FEED LAWNS.** Throughout the Northwest, mid-May is the perfect time to give lawns a generous feeding. Apply ½ to 1 pound of actual nitrogen per 1,000 square feet of turf to keep grass green and vigorous.

☐ **PRUNE LILACS AND RHODIES.** As you cut flowers to take indoors, do some light pruning. Cut judiciously, with an eye to the plant's form. When blossoms fade, prune more heavily.

☐ **REMOVE FADED BLOOMS.** There are two main reasons for deadheading: to stop flowers from forming seed and to make plants look better. If you spend a few minutes each day on deadheading, you'll be surprised at how much you can accomplish in a week, and delighted by the appearance of your plants.

☐ **TEND COMPOST.** Spent flowers, grass clippings, and prunings should all be turned into the compost pile. You can compost most weeds, too, if they do not have viable seeds. Put noxious weeds like morning glory, deadly nightshade, and horsetail in the trash.

PACIFIC NORTHWEST Garden Notebook

BY STEVEN R. LORTON

I once visited Brazil in springtime hoping that I'd see more flowers blooming there in the Southern Hemisphere than I'd ever seen anywhere else. Didn't happen. I could have stayed home—in the Pacific Northwest. Nothing compares to the flower show that nature puts on here this month, and there's no better way to enrich your horticultural love affair with our region than to observe some of the fabulous gardens all around us. I plan to spend time walking through Seattle's old neighborhoods, like Queen Anne Hill, Washington Park, and Capitol Hill. And I hope to head to Portland for a stroll through the southwest hills, the Japanese Garden, and Bishop's Close at Elk Rock.

•

Whenever I visit great gardens, I invariably get the itch to grow the plants I'm admiring. Last year, Himalaya honeysuckle (*Leycesteria formosa*) tickled my fancy. I thought its 6-foot green canes, handsome leaves, and dangling flower spikes would look splendid in my Skagit Valley garden. I managed to find a plant in a 5-gallon can, but while planting it, I accidentally broke off a big stem. Ouch! I decided to perform emergency surgery: I cut the broken stem into three 8-inch lengths and put them in a vase of water. They rooted in a flash, and by midsummer, not one but *four* Himalaya honeysuckle plants were growing around my garden pond.

•

My family will be planting a pumpkin patch this month in our vegetable garden. Last year, we sowed a patch of 'Ghost Rider', a round variety with dark orange skin and yellow-orange flesh, available from W. Atlee Burpee & Co. (300 Park Ave., Warminster, PA 18991; 800/888-1447; free catalog). In autumn, we harvested hundreds of pumpkins. We carved some, gave others to friends, and stored many in a cool basement, where they stayed in perfect shape through February. All winter long, we turned those pumpkins into pies and breads, casseroles and side dishes, gobbling them up until they were all gone.

THAT'S A GOOD QUESTION

Q: When can you move rhododendrons?

A: Rhodies are generally good-natured about being relocated. The only times not to move them, really, are just prior to and during bloom—or you may lose the flower show. Prepare the new planting hole first (see Planting Opportunities, page 123), dig a generous hole around the rootball (rhodies have surprisingly shallow roots), and transplant. Once in place, water plants well now and throughout the first two summers after transplanting. Don't fertilize plants during the first summer in their new home.

PLANTING

☐ **BUY TOMATO SEEDLINGS.** It's late to start plants from seed, so look for seedlings at nurseries. Young tomato plants should be stocky, not leggy, with rich green leaves. Pull off the lowest leaves and plant up to the next leaf set; roots will form along the stem.

☐ **HARDEN OFF SEEDLINGS.** Zones 1 and 2: Move warm-season flower and vegetable seedlings to a coldframe or other protected spot. Gradually expose them to longer periods of stronger sunlight and cooler nights.

☐ **PLANT DAHLIAS AND BEGONIAS.** Both plants provide a long season of bloom into fall. Dahlia choices include dwarf kinds or ones that grow 6 feet tall and have plate-size flowers. Tuberous begonias come as hanging types for baskets, or upright ones for planting beds, in vibrant or soft flower colors.

☐ **PLANT FOR PERMANENCE.** Now is a good time to plant almost any perennial, shrub, tree, or vine (in zones 1 and 2, wait until after last frost to set out tender plants). But wait until fall to plant *Fremontodendron*; summer water can cause root rot.

☐ **PLANT VEGETABLES.** May is prime time to plant heat-loving vegetables such as beans, corn, eggplants, melons, okra, peppers, pumpkins, squash, and tomatoes. In cool-summer areas or mountain regions, use short-season varieties, plant through black plastic, and protect from late-spring frosts.

Covering vegetables with fabric row covers gives them an added boost.

☐ **SET OUT HERBS.** Fresh-picked herbs add a special zest to recipes. Now is a good time to plant basil, chives, cilantro, oregano, parsley, rosemary, sage, and thyme. To keep woody types such as oregano and rosemary producing fresh green growth, prune regularly once plants are established.

MAINTENANCE

☐ **BEGIN COMPOSTING.** You can add these items to the compost pile: annual weeds that have not gone to seed, coffee grounds, eggshells, conifer needles, fruit and vegetable peels, grass clippings, leaves, prunings, sawdust, small wood chips, and tea leaves. Never add animal or fish residue, fats (such as oil and butter), cheese, peanut butter, or pet manure. Keep the pile as moist as a wrung-out sponge, and occasionally add a handful of nitrogen fertilizer. Turn frequently with a spading fork. When the compost turns a soil-like earthy brown, use as a soil amendment.

☐ **CHECK DRIP SYSTEMS.** Before the weather turns hot, check your drip-irrigation system to make sure it's operating properly. Clean filters, check emitters and spray heads to see that they're working (replace ones that aren't), and inspect lines for leaks. Adjust the timer for warmer weather. After making any repairs, open end caps and flush lines before running the system.

☐ **PINCH MUMS.** To encourage bushiness, pinch off growing tips regularly until midsummer.

PEST CONTROL

☐ **COMBAT PESTS.** Knock aphids off with a strong stream of water from the hose, or spray with insecticidal soap. Trap, handpick, or bait for snails, slugs, and earwigs. Spittle bugs (look for their foam) are harmless in small numbers; knock them off with a blast of water. For large numbers, spray with insecticidal soap; add cooking oil or a lightweight summer oil as a spreader-sticker.

"**A** garden is never finished. It's always in transition," goes the old saying. I always recall these words around midspring when I'm out carefully scrutinizing my garden's plant combinations and overall effect. By now, plants have had a good stint of mild, sunny weather. Spring-blooming ones are usually in their full glory, and other plants have a healthy crop of new leaves. Of course, I'm never satisfied by what I see.

Leather leaf sedge (*Carex buchananii*), 'Homestead Purple' verbena, 'Maori Chief' New Zealand flax, and salmon *Salvia greggii* all look great. 'Black Knight' buddleia always outdoes itself in growth and blue flowers. But some sections of my fence look absolutely naked. So this season, I'll plant some fast-growing colorful vines. One of the best for winter and early-spring color is *Hardenbergia violacea*. I like the pink-flowered 'Rosea'. And for nonstop bloom in sun or partial shade, violet trumpet vine (*Clytostoma callistegioides*) is a winner, though it quickly grows big and needs pruning to stay tidy.

NORTHERN CALIFORNIA
Garden Notebook
BY LAUREN BONAR SWEZEY

THAT'S A GOOD QUESTION

Q: Why aren't my acidanthera (*Gladiolus callianthus*) blooming? About four years ago, a friend gave me some bulbs. The first year, I had lots of flowers. In subsequent years, I've had wonderful foliage but no flowers. Is there anything I can do to get the plants to bloom?

A: All glads, including acidanthera, require full sun. If bulbs are planted in too much shade, they produce foliage but no flowers. Another problem might be that the bulbs aren't getting the nutrients they need right after blossoming, when next year's flowers are forming. Choose a site that gets full midday sun, and mix a bulb food into the hole at planting time. In subsequent years, top-dress with bulb food in spring, or dig bulbs after foliage dies and store in a cool, dark place until planting time next February or March, then replant with bulb food.

CHECKLIST
MAY

PLANTING

☐ **PLANT EXOTIC FRUIT TREES.** This is the best time of year to plant avocado, banana, cherimoya, citrus, guava, macadamia, mango, sapote, and other tropical and subtropical fruit trees. (Tropicals require a frost-free location.)

☐ **PLANT SUMMER ANNUALS.** Heat-loving annuals, abundant at nurseries now, will add welcome color to the garden well into fall. Choices include ageratum, annual salvia, celosia, cosmos, creeping zinnia, dwarf dahlia, gomphrena, marigold, periwinkle, petunia, phlox, portulaca, sunflower, verbena, and zinnia. In shade, plant caladium, forget-me-nots, impatiens, mimulus, and semperflorens begonias.

☐ **PLANT SUMMER VEGETABLES.** Continue planting warm-season crops. Coastal, inland, and high-desert gardeners (*Sunset Western Garden Book* zones 22–24, 18–21, and 11, respectively) can sow seeds of beans, chayote, corn, cucumber, melon, okra, pumpkin, and summer and winter squash. Set out eggplant, tomato, and pepper seedlings. Sow seed or plant seedlings of basil, cilantro, and dill. In the low desert (zone 13), plant Jerusalem artichokes, okra, peppers, and sweet potatoes.

☐ **PLANT TENDER ORNAMENTALS.** Subtropical ornamentals such as bougainvillea and hibiscus can go into the ground this month.

Sunset *Western Garden Book*
CLIMATE ZONES

1-3 7-9 11 13 14-24

☐ **SHOP FOR LATE-BLOOMING PERENNIALS.** For the most show for your dollars, look for kinds that will bloom through summer and beyond. These include coreopsis, daylily, gaillardia, gayfeather (*Liatris*), lion's tail (*Leonotis*), nicotiana, penstemon, salvia, tulbaghia, and yarrow (*Achillea*).

MAINTENANCE

☐ **FEED AZALEAS AND CAMELLIAS.** To support strong growth and a heavy set of flower buds for next year in coastal and inland gardens, feed azaleas and camellias after they finish blooming. Use at half-strength an acid-type fertilizer formulated for these plants. Feed camellias two or three more times at six- to eight-week intervals during this growth period. Feed azaleas once more in late September.

☐ **FERTILIZE SUBTROPICALS.** The first flush of new growth on banana, bougainvillea, citrus, gardenia, hibiscus, lantana, and Natal plum indicates this is the right time to give these plants a dose of high nitrogen. Continue feeding regularly through summer.

☐ **THIN FRUIT.** On such trees as apple and peach, twist off fruits growing closer than 6 inches apart.

☐ **WATER THOUGHTFULLY.** Young plants may need daily watering. Irrigate just-planted container-grown trees and shrubs slowly to soak the original rootball and reduce runoff. Water established plants deeply to encourage deep root growth. Use a soil probe to test for moisture content, and water only when necessary.

☐ **CONTROL WEEDS.** Spread a 3- to 6-inch layer of mulch around trees, shrubs, perennials, and annuals. To prevent diseases, leave clear areas around the bases of trunks and stems. Around newly planted trees, maintain mulch for at least three years. Mulch also helps conserve moisture.

SOUTHERN CALIFORNIA
Garden Notebook
BY SHARON COHOON

A friend whose business is propagating scented geraniums sees my garden as an insurance policy. Whenever she adds a new variety to her line, she urges another plant on me. That way if her mother plants get clipped to the bone, she can turn to my plants for cuttings. This state of affairs doesn't always please me. "How did I end up with so many homely plants that all look alike?" I grumble, looking out at my growing collection in midwinter.

But then the weather heats up, and the geraniums leaf out. And when I run my fingers through them to slough off yellowing leaves the way she taught me, my hands are perfumed with lemon, rose, and nutmeg scents. Which makes me groom them some more, which compels me to examine the aromatic leaves more closely—and leads me to conclude that scented geraniums don't really look anything alike, except that they are all charming.

●

Chickweed is a "tasty and highly nutritious gift from nature," writes Ed Mitchell of Los Angeles. And not, he says, a useless weed, as most people think. Mitchell's appetite for natural flora came from following Christopher Nyerges into the Los Angeles foothills on wild-food outings, and from reading Nyerges's book, *In the Footsteps of Our Ancestors: Guide to Wild Foods.*

Some of the guide's more fascinating claims: Dandelion leaves have more beta-carotene than carrots, dock leaves more vitamin C than oranges, and lamb's quarters more vitamins and minerals than any supermarket green.

If the idea of foraging intrigues you, order Nyerges's book ($16.24) from the School of Self-Reliance at (213) 255-9502, or write to Box 41834, Eagle Rock, CA 90041. If you're serious about sampling, you might want to sign up for an educational tour as well. Some wild plants—hemlock, for instance—can kill you.

THAT'S A GOOD QUESTION

Q: *Bacillus thuringiensis* is not stopping geranium budworms from devouring my zonal geraniums. What can I do?

A: BT works if you can catch the caterpillar before it burrows into the safety of the flower bud. But unfortunately, many of us miss this window of opportunity. You could aim your attack at the budworm eggs instead by releasing trichogramma wasps every few weeks now until fall. They parasitize a wide range of caterpillar eggs, including those of budworms. A few nurseries stock these wasp eggs. Otherwise order from an insectary such as Buena Biosystems; call (805) 525-2525.

CHECKLIST
MAY

PLANTING

❑ **FLOWERS.** Nurseries are filled with annuals and perennials this month. Shop early to get the best selection. On cold nights, protect annual seedlings against frost by using row covers; take the covers off when the danger of frost is past.

❑ **VEGETABLES.** Plant cool-season crops from nursery seedlings, or sow warm-season crops (corn, cucumbers, eggplants, melons, peppers, squash, tomatoes) indoors right away for transplanting into the garden after danger of frost has passed. If frost is over where you live, you can sow these, and beans, directly into prepared garden soil right away.

❑ **PERMANENT PLANTS.** You can plant almost anything—including trees, shrubs, vines, and ground covers—from containers this month.

❑ **LAWNS.** Sow bluegrass, fescue, ryegrass, or (better) a combination of the three. New plantings should go into tilled, raked, fertilized, relatively rock-free soil. To overseed bare spots in an old lawn, rough up soil surface with a steel bow rake, scatter seed, cover with compost, and keep soil surface damp until grass is tall enough to mow.

MAINTENANCE

❑ **CARE FOR TOMATOES.** Indeterminate varieties, which keep growing all season, need to be staked or caged early. To minimize blossom-end rot, keep soil moisture even (mulch helps).

❑ **FERTILIZE.** Dig in 1 to 2 pounds of complete fertilizer per 100 square feet

MONTANA
Helena
☆ Boise
IDAHO
WYOMING
Cheyenne ☆
NEVADA
Salt Lake City
• Reno
Denver ☆
Las Vegas
UTAH
COLORADO

Sunset
Western Garden Book
CLIMATE ZONES
☐ 1-3   ☐ 10-11

of soil before planting vegetables or flowers. Feed flowering shrubs after they bloom, and start a monthly fertilizing program for long-blooming perennials, annuals, and container plants.

❑ **HARDEN OFF TRANSPLANTS.** Take seedlings to a lath house, patio, or partly shaded cold frame to expose them gradually to more sun and nighttime cold. After 7 to 10 days, they'll be tough enough to be transplanted.

❑ **MAINTAIN INDOOR PLANTS.** After last frost, move house plants to a shady place outside for the summer. Prune them for shape, fertilize, and water well. The extra light will help them fill out and grow strong before you bring them back in next fall.

❑ **MAKE COMPOST.** Alternate 4-inch-thick layers of grass clippings and weeds with layers of dead leaves and straw, watering the pile between layers. Turn the pile weekly, and you'll have compost within two months.

❑ **MULCH PLANTS.** Mulch with ground bark, compost, grass clippings, rotted leaves, or even sawdust to keep down weeds and hold in moisture.

❑ **PROTECT COOL-SEASON CROPS.** Suspend laths or row covers above vegetables such as broccoli, cauliflower, lettuce, and spinach to keep them from bolting (going to seed) when the weather warms up. Bolted leaf vegetables often become bitter.

❑ **PINCH AND PRUNE.** Encourage branching and compact growth by pinching or tip-pruning plants such as azaleas, fuchsias, geraniums, marigolds, verbena, and zinnias. Prune spring-flowering plants such as lilac, mock orange, and spiraea after bloom ends.

❑ **REMOVE SUCKERS.** Fast-growing vertical shoots that grow up from the roots of roses, fruit trees, and grafted ornamentals are suckers. Cut them off flush with the root system. Also cut out vertical sprouts (water sprouts) along horizontal fruit tree limbs.

❑ **WEED.** Hoe or pull weeds before they go to seed.

Computers taught me the value of gardening. After passing countless midnights debugging databases, learning programming languages, and generally shortchanging my family, I had an epiphany: almost everything I learned about computers was obsolete within five years; but almost everything I learned about my garden was good for life.

Beyond that, gardening pays. Plant 100 seeds, add work, and you get 10,000 seeds back three or four months later. It's a wonder farmers aren't the richest people in the world. (Note to farmers and computer programmers: don't send hate mail—I know your work isn't that simple!) With all that in mind, go out and plant, harvest, learn, and feed your families. You are engaged in truly the oldest and most honorable endeavor in the world.

•

Spring isn't just spring for plants; it's spring for all kinds of pests, too. Insects, snails, and slugs love to munch on all that tender new growth, and weeds pop up everywhere. Unable to keep up with it all, I finally established a penny fund. I give my kids a penny per dandelion (with root), slug, or snail.

INLAND WESTERN STATES
Garden Notebook
BY JIM McCAUSLAND

•

As new seedlings emerge in rows, I find that anything but the gentlest watering can wash them away. For some row crops, I water in furrows. To keep the hose from hydraulically excavating the garden, I stick the end into a coffee can that has rocks in the bottom and holes in the sides. Water flows into the furrow gently.

THAT'S A GOOD QUESTION

Q: A week after spraying herbicide over a weedy patch along my driveway, I noticed that some nearby shrubs started flagging. Looks like herbicide damage to me, but I didn't spray them. What happened?

A: When you adjust the nozzle on a tank sprayer (even on some hand-held sprayers) to produce a fine mist, that mist can drift, in even light breezes, enough to injure or kill sensitive plants that it touches. The solution is to spray only when the air is perfectly still (mornings are usually best) and to use a coarser spray so that what comes out of the nozzle is more in droplet form. Heavier than mist, droplets don't blow as far.

SOUTHWEST
CHECKLISTS
MAY

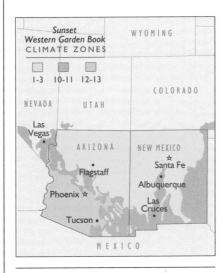

PLANTING

☐ **FLOWERS FOR SUN.** As early in the month as possible, set out ageratum, celosia, coreopsis, cosmos, firebush (*Hamelia patens*), four o'clock, gaillardia, globe amaranth, gloriosa daisy, kochia, lantana, lisianthus, nicotiana, portulaca, salvia, strawflower, tithonia, *Vinca rosea* (*Catharanthus roseus*), and zinnia.

☐ **PLANTS FOR SHADE.** Some good choices include begonia, caladium, chocolate plant (*Pseuderanthemum alatum*), coleus, gerbera, impatiens, lobelia, oxalis, pentas (*P. lanceolata*), and spider plant.

☐ **LAWNS.** Plant Bermuda or improved buffalo grass when nighttime temperatures rise above 70°.

☐ **SUMMER BULBS.** Plant acidanthera, caladium, canna, crinum, dahlia, daylily, gladiolus, iris, and montbretia. You can also purchase container-grown agapanthus, society garlic (*Tulbaghia*), and zephyranthes.

☐ **VEGETABLES.** Heat-loving crops, including eggplants, Jerusalem artichokes, okra, peanuts, peppers, soybeans, summer squash, and sweet potatoes, go in this month.

MAINTENANCE

☐ **CARE FOR CITRUS.** Fertilize trees whose leaves aren't dark green, spreading 1 cup of ammonium sulfate per inch

of trunk diameter. Water it in well. Give mature trees a 2- to 3-hour sprinkler soaking every two to three weeks thereafter (more in sandy soil, less in clay). Soak young trees 1 to 2 hours every 5 to 10 days.

☐ **CARE FOR ROSES.** When heat starts to take its toll on May's flush of rose bloom, water plants deeply, mulch, and fertilize. In the Phoenix area, give plants afternoon shade.

☐ **CARE FOR TOMATOES.** If you've had problems with sunburned tomatoes in the past, protect this year's plants with row covers.

☐ **INCREASE WATERING.** When the first 100° days come, check plants—especially new growth—at least twice a day for wilting. Everything needs extra water, even cactus and succulents.

☐ **MAKE COMPOST.** Build a compost pile with weeds and grass clippings. Water it regularly to keep the pile as moist as a wrung-out sponge.

☐ **MULCH PLANTS.** Mulch everything in the garden to improve soil, cool roots, keep weeds down, and hold in soil moisture. Any organic mulch will work well and look good.

☐ **REMOVE SUCKERS.** Suckers are fast-growing vertical shoots that spring up from the roots of roses, fruit trees, and grafted ornamentals. Cut them off flush with the root system.

PEST CONTROL

☐ **FIGHT INSECT PROBLEMS.** Blast aphids and whiteflies off plants with a jet of water from the hose, then spray affected plants with insecticidal soap.

☐ **TREAT GRAPE LEAF SKELETONIZER.** Spray with *Bacillus thuringiensis* (BT) in the evening, hitting the undersides of the leaves. BT kills caterpillars within a few days.

TEXAS

PLANTING

☐ **SUMMER BULBS.** Plant caladium, canna, crinum, dahlia, daylily, gladiolus, iris, montbretia, and other summer-flowering bulbs.

☐ **WARM-SEASON CROPS.** In Central Texas, sow the last beans, okra, Southern peas, and sweet potatoes, and set out well-developed seedlings of whatever crops remain in nurseries. In North and West Texas and the Panhandle, plant beans, corn, cucumber, eggplant, Jerusalem artichoke, melons, okra, pepper, pumpkin, radish, Southern peas, squash, sweet potato, and tomato. Most should go in as early in the month as possible, but you can put in okra, Southern peas, and sweet potato through midmonth.

☐ **LAWNS.** In the northern half of

Texas, use plugs or seeds of warm-season grasses to start new lawns or to repair old ones. If you still need to do it in the southern half of the state, act early in the month. Water the plot daily until new grass is tall enough to mow.

MAINTENANCE

☐ **CARE FOR TOMATOES.** Use row covers to minimize sunburn on leaves and fruit.

☐ **FERTILIZE.** Feed flowering shrubs after they bloom, and start monthly feedings of long-blooming perennials, annuals, and container plants.

☐ **MULCH PLANTS.** Lay down a 2- to 4-inch layer of organic matter to hold in water and keep roots cool.

☐ **MAKE COMPOST.** Start a pile by mixing nonmeat kitchen leftovers with garden waste. Water the pile weekly and turn it periodically with a spading fork.

PEST CONTROL

☐ **APHIDS, WHITEFLIES.** Keep an eye on plants, especially tender new growth, and blast insect colonies off with a jet of water before their populations explode. Follow up with a spray of insecticidal soap.

Rich blooms
of schizanthus, or poor
man's orchid, billow from
these window boxes in the
Italian Garden at The
Butchart Gardens near
Victoria, British Columbia.
These plants get plenty of
light, some even direct sun.
Preparation starts in April,
when greenhouse-grown
plants are put into boxes
of fresh soil, watered, and
fertilized with a complete
liquid plant food. Plants are
pinched back lightly until
the last week in April.
Then, in May, they explode
into bloom and keep on
performing through June,
when they are replaced
with summer annuals. In
cool coastal climates,
schizanthus will continue
to flower if plants are
protected from sun and
heat, and watered and
fertilized generously.

THE BUTCHART GARDENS

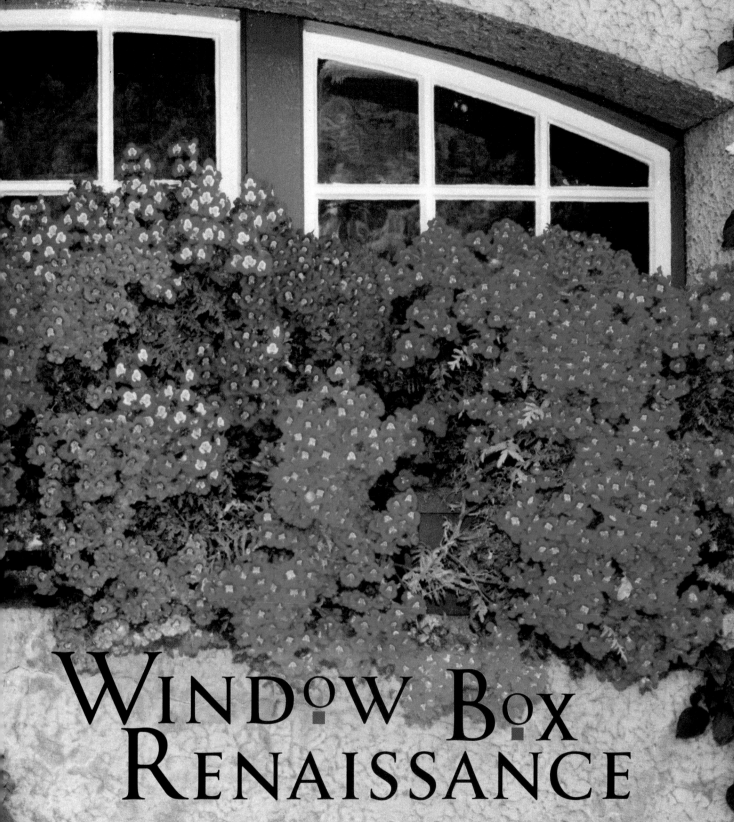

WINDOW BOX RENAISSANCE

BY STEVEN R. LORTON

When asked his opinion of window boxes, the late, great landscape architect Thomas Church reportedly offered this terse verdict: "Remove them." Though Church evidently considered window boxes déclassé, these days many Western gardeners obviously disagree. In fact,

a window-box renaissance is blooming. We've been watching this growing phenomenon, and for nearly a year we've been collecting evidence submitted by home gardeners and professional horticulturists from around the West. Scores of *Sunset* readers—from Alaska

A cheeky cherub tiptoes under the watchful eyes of two crocodiles in this whimsical box inspired by a Victorian design from Wales. It adorns the house of Brian Coleman and Howard Cohen in Seattle. For this fall-winter display, designers Glenn Withey and Charles Price used variegated ivies, assorted hybrid pansies, and the berry-bearing shrubs *Callicarpa* 'Profusion' and *Pyracantha* 'Mohave' planted from 1-gallon cans. When the box is emptied in spring, the shrubs go into permanent planting beds.

BRIAN COLEMAN

to Arizona—have shared their secrets of success and sent us photos of their boxes. On these pages, we're pleased to pass along some of their collective window-box wisdom.

THE BOX

Window boxes are simply containers, albeit longer and skinnier than most. Remember that the bigger the box, the heavier it is, but also the more room it provides for roots to spread.

Most garden and home supply stores stock ready-made boxes in a variety of shapes and sizes.

Good materials for building your own box include cedar, redwood, and pressure-treated lumber; painting or staining the wood will prolong its life. You can plant directly in the box or use plastic or metal liners. Plastic liners are sold commercially, and metal liners can be custom-fabricated inexpensively by many metal shops. All boxes (and liners) need drain holes: a ½- to ¾-inch hole for each foot of box will suffice.

Window boxes should be supported from the bottom. Decorative wooden braces, sturdy metal shelf braces, large angle irons screwed into the wall, and custom-made steel or iron brackets all work well as supports.

The box should also be securely

NORMAN A. PLATE

Rustically elegant redwood box rests below a leaded-glass window on the seaside cottage of Ben and Barbara Booth in Fort Bragg, California. In the box, tall viscaria is underplanted with plump clumps of schizanthus. Petunias, lobelia, white alyssum, and jasmine spill down. The box, designed by Peggy Quaid, is 47 inches long, 8 inches high and wide. Each spring, the box is refilled with fresh planting mix topped with controlled-release fertilizer. From mid-summer into fall, the plants get an extra dose of nutrients from twice-monthly applications of liquid 15-30-15 fertilizer diluted to half-strength.

anchored to the wall behind it so that it won't lean forward and topple off the supports. But do not attach the box directly to a wooden wall or you'll encourage the siding to rot. Instead, cut a pressure-treated 2-by-2 or 2-by-4 into a piece slightly shorter than the length of the box, and bolt it horizontally to the wall. Then screw the back of the box to the horizontal runner. This allows plenty of clearance for drainage and air circulation between the box and the wall.

THE SOIL MIX

Commercial potting soil mixes work best. Most of these are lightweight but retain moisture well. Some gardeners like to mix well-aged manure into potting soil (a good recipe is 1 part manure to 3 parts potting mix, although it can be mixed 1 to 1).

To be sure plants get the nutrients they need, you can work a controlled-release fertilizer into the soil mix at planting time or make monthly applications of a complete liquid fertilizer (12-12-12, for example).

In most cases, soil needs to be replaced only once a year. If your box is empty in the winter, remove the soil and give the wood a chance to dry out. Many gardeners fill empty boxes with cut evergreens for winter display.

THE PLANTS

In May, nurseries and garden centers are well stocked with candidate plants in sixpacks and 4-inch pots. Begonias, fuchsias, geraniums, impatiens, lobelia, marigolds, petunias, and dusty miller are among the classic summer choices for window boxes.

A typical window-box planting consists of three parts: *background* (tall plants such as geraniums), *foreground* (low-growing plants like dwarf marigolds), and *trailers* to spill out of the box (verbena and various ivies).

If you live in one of the West's mild coastal climates, you may want to change plantings three times a year: annuals for summer; cyclamen, pansies, and ornamental cabbages and kales for winter; and primroses or bulbs for spring.

Since window boxes are often exposed to full sun, drying winds, and the reflected heat of the house, it's crucial to water at least daily, and perhaps even twice a day in the hottest weather (drip-irrigation tubing can save you a lot of effort). Pinching off faded blooms helps keep flowers coming. ∎

A leafy cascade

of variegated *Vinca major* and trailing pink verbena pours down from the second-story window of Ann Dare's house in Vancouver, Washington. White African daisies, pink geraniums, and trailing lobelia are used as fillers. This box keeps its lush looks from May to frost with only regular watering, fertilizing, and pinching of faded blossoms.

New perennials fast—for free

Many root easily from stem cuttings. Start them now, and they'll be garden-ready in as little as a month

EVER PLANT ALL YOUR PERENNIALS, then notice that you still have spaces to fill? If so, there's a good chance you'll find a source of additional plants right in your own garden—or that of a friend.

Many perennials are easy to propagate from stem cuttings. Typically, these are nonclumping plants—ones that develop shoots and stems you can snip and root; the box on page 135 lists 14 examples. When placed in a growing mix, cuttings generally root quickly (often within a week or two) and produce plants identical to the ones from which they were taken. In a month or two, you'll have your favorite perennials rooted and ready to set into the ground.

COLLECT THE CUTTINGS

Spring and early summer, when plant growth is soft and fleshy (not woody), is the best time to take cuttings, although many nonclumping perennials can be rooted from stem cuttings taken almost any time the growth is still soft. It's best not to take cuttings from blooming plants, because the plants' energy is going into the bloom, so the cuttings may not root as well.

Take cuttings only from healthy plants, and choose vigorous young shoots or side shoots.

Collect the cuttings early in the day, when the air is cool. Use sharp pruning shears, a knife, or a razor blade to snip 5- to 6-inch-long pieces from the plant. Cut just above a node, the swelling where leaves emerge.

Inspect the cuttings carefully to make sure they're free of insects and diseases. Pinch off any flowers or buds. Then trim the bottom of each shoot to just below a node, so the remaining cutting is about 3 inches long. Pinch or cut off leaves from the lower half of the stem, leaving two to four leaves. As you remove the leaves, take care not to strip off any skin from the stem.

Plant within an hour or so. Until you're ready to plant, seal the cuttings in moistened plastic bags and keep them in a shady place.

Fresh stem cuttings of buddleia, dusty miller, lion's tail, and Salvia greggii are dipped in liquid rooting hormone, then planted in growing medium. To avoid damaging cuttings, poke holes in medium before planting.

CREATE THE RIGHT ENVIRONMENT FOR ROOTING

Softwood cuttings root fastest in a warm, well-drained growing mix and humid air. A good mix is 1 part sphagnum moss and 1 part perlite or sand packaged as a soil amendment. But any high-quality, well-drained commercial potting mix also works well.

Use almost any containers that have drainage, such as 4-inch pots; plant four to six cuttings per pot.

Heating cables or a heating mat will warm the soil to encourage faster rooting. But they're not really necessary; if the soil is cool, rooting just takes longer.

To encourage rooting, it's also a good idea to dip cut ends into a rooting hormone (liquid Dip 'N Grow is easier to use than powdered).

What's the optimal environment for rooting stem cuttings? In tests we performed last spring at *Sunset,* perennials were rooted with and without heating cables, with and without hormone, and with and without plastic covers. The covered plants rooted the fastest, regardless of whether they were dipped in hormone or given heat. When hormone was added, rooting was consistent and quick. (The weather was warm when we conducted our tests, so heating cables didn't make the difference they would have made in cool weather.)

Within just eight weeks, the cuttings grow into bushy seedlings ready for planting out in the garden. To give the roots room to grow, rooted cuttings were transplanted from flats into these 4-inch pots two to three weeks after planting.

PLANT THE CUTTINGS

Fill the containers with the growing mix, and water thoroughly.

Insert the cuttings into the growing mix. With a pencil or a chopstick, make a 1- to 1½-inch-deep hole in the growing mix. Dip ¼ inch of the stem end into rooting hormone (if you're using it), and insert the stem into the hole; the stem should sit in the bottom of the hole. Tamp the planting mix around the stem to leave no air pockets. Label each group of cuttings with plant name and date.

---

14 EASY PLANTS TO PROPAGATE FROM CUTTINGS

Artemisia

Aster

Buddleia

Catmint (*Nepeta*)

Dead nettle (*Lamium maculatum*)

Dianthus

Dusty miller (*Senecio cineraria*)

Geranium (*Pelargonium*)

Germander (*Teucrium*)

Lavatera

Lavender

Lion's tail (*Leonotis leonurus*)

Penstemon

Salvia

Set the containers in a bright spot out of direct sun. Keep the soil moist. To provide humidity, cover containers with a clear plastic tent. Place small pots in plastic bags, blow air into the bags, and tie them closed (open the bags every few days for air circulation). For larger containers, make a minigreenhouse by draping plastic over wire or wood supports stuck into the soil. Tuck the ends of the plastic under the containers.

Cuttings should root in one to five weeks. Watch for new growth to appear (you can also tug on the plants to see whether cuttings are rooted enough to offer resistance, but be gentle or you may injure them). Transplant rooted cuttings into individual 4-inch containers; when they're well rooted and growing new leaves, they're ready to go in the ground. ■

By Lauren Bonar Swezey

Tall flower heads of clustered bellflower brighten a shady border.

Bellflowers that will brighten any garden

Here are six great choices in a range of colors and forms

TALL OR SHORT, SPREADING OR compact—for variety of form in a flowering plant, it's hard to surpass the bellflower (*Campanula*). Blooms range from powder blue to purple to white and usually have the shape of a bell, but some are upward-facing saucers and others are star-shaped.

Landscape uses are as varied as the plants. Upright forms are striking additions to flower borders or woodland gardens. Low growers work well as ground covers or tucked into rock gardens.

This month, nurseries stock many varieties in 1-gallon containers ($5 to $7). Near the coast, plant in a sunny spot; in hot-summer areas, provide filtered shade.

Bellflowers like neutral to slightly alkaline, fast-draining, fertile soils. Amend sandy or heavy soils with plenty of organic material. Most bellflowers should be watered when the top inch of soil is barely damp; two types, however, are drought tolerant.

In early spring, apply a complete low-nitrogen fertilizer—too much nitrogen causes tall types to become lanky. To encourage repeat bloom, remove spent flowers. You can expect few problems besides snails and slugs.

Every three or four years, divide clumps in the fall. Plants can also be propagated by stem cuttings or seeds.

The following six perennials are reliable growers in the West. Except as noted, they're widely available.

Tussock bellflower (*C. carpatica*). The dense, spreading clump of leafy stems grows 8 to 12 inches tall; dwarf types reach about 6 inches. Saucer-shaped flowers, in white and various shades of blue, bloom late spring through summer, especially if old flowers are cut back. Fine for rock gardens, the front of flower borders, and containers.

Clustered bellflower (*C. glomerata*). Erect stalks, crowned with dense flower clusters in June and July, reach 1 to 3 feet tall. In moist, shady locations, plants spread rapidly by underground rhizomes. Flowers range from white to blue to intense violet-blue. A good choice for flower borders and woodland gardens.

Peach-leafed bluebell (*C. persicifolia*). Stems reach 2 to 3 feet tall, with loose clusters of blue, pink, or white flowers in summer. 'Telham Beauty' is popular for its large powder blue flowers. Plants usually need staking. Good for flower borders and as cut flowers.

Dalmatian bellflower (*C. portenschlagiana*). It spreads to form a 6-inch-tall mat with purplish blue flowers in late spring through summer, often reblooming in the fall. Plants take some drought. Use as a ground cover, in rock gardens, or in containers.

Serbian bellflower (*C. poscharskyana*). Spreading plant mounds 18 inches high, with starry lavender-blue flowers spring through summer. It takes drought and shade. A vigorous ground cover for small areas; also good for rock gardens or trailing over walls.

C. punctata. Mounding plants with arching stems reach 2½ feet tall and just as wide. Nodding elongated bells in white, lilac, or pink—spotted inside with red or purple—tend to be somewhat hidden by foliage. *C.p.* 'Nana Alba', a 10-inch-tall plant with full-size white flowers, makes a good ground cover; you can order it from Lamb Nurseries, Route 1, Box 460B, Long Beach, WA 98631 (catalog $1.50). Full-size varieties, available in specialty nurseries, work well in flower borders or woodland gardens. ∎

By Emely Lincowski

Less common white form of Serbian bellflower (above) and variegated ajuga drape over rock.

Glowing blue of peach-leafed bluebell contrasts handsomely with pink bells of rambunctious C. punctata.

Upward-facing cups of tussock bellflower measure 1 to 2 inches across.

Carpet of purplish blue Dalmatian bellflower (right) can take some drought.

A graceful stand of queen palms sets off this house in Capistrano Beach, California. Most of these trees are about 15 years old. The queen is called "self-cleaning" because its arching fronds drop when they die; all you do is pick them up off the ground.

Palms that won't grow up to be headaches

MILES OF MEXICAN FAN PALMS and Canary Island date palms line the streets of California cities, accumulating dead fronds until an arborist must

King palm has a smooth green sheath between its fronds and flowers. With a smaller head than a queen palm, the king can fit into closer quarters.

go up and prune them out. It's no wonder home gardeners avoid planting these messy giants in their gardens. Mexican fan palms can reach a height of 100 feet, and date palms can have a spread of 50 feet. Fortunately for gardeners who appreciate palms' lush, tropical look, a flock of smaller candidates fit more easily into home landscapes and won't cause maintenance headaches.

Palms grow as single-trunked trees or in clumps; either kind may be topped with feather- or fan-shaped leaves. Their growth habit may seem obvious when you shop for them, but you can be fooled: palm clumps are so popular that sometimes nurseries grow several single-trunked

palms in the same container. You can buy and plant palms any time of year. In the Southwest deserts, May and June are ideal months to plant palms.

Palms can lose a large proportion of their root systems and still be successfully transplanted. For that reason, a fairly large palm may be sold with a remarkably small rootball, making it easier to transport and plant. You don't have to worry about planting a palm deeper in the ground than it was originally grown, since roots can grow out of the trunks.

SINGLE-TRUNK PALMS
Climate zones are from the *Sunset Western Garden Book*.

Pindo palm (*Butia capitata;* zones 7, 8, 9, and 12 through 24) reaches 15 feet tall, with arching, feathery leaves that shelter huge, grapelike clusters of apricot-colored fruit in summer. When the sweet fruit is ripe, it falls onto the grass, where you can gather it to eat.

Queen and king palms are two other feather palms with single trunks. Since each can grow quickly to 50 feet, it's fortunate that they're self-cleaning; that is, as their fronds die, they tend to fall away freely, so you don't have to send an arborist up after them.

The tougher of the two is queen palm (*Syagrus romanzoffianum;* zones 12, 13, 15, 16, 17, and 19 through 24), with 10- to 15-foot fronds. King palm (*Archontophoenix cunninghamiana;* zones 21 through 24) is a stunner in the mild coastal range in which it thrives. Its 8- to 10-foot feathers rise over a smooth, red-green sheath. Below the sheath, creamy flowers and darker fruit resemble a bouquet hanging on a lamppost.

Mexican blue palm (*Brahea armata;* zones 10, 12 through 17, and 19 through 24) has fan-shaped leaves that are silvery blue-green. It grows slowly to 40 feet, and shows remarkable tolerance of both heat and cold.

The hardiest single-trunk fan palm is Chinese windmill palm (*Trachycarpus fortunei;* zones 4 through 24), which grows to 30 feet. You can identify this one in a heartbeat because its brown trunk seems to be covered with hair and eventually grows thicker at the top.

CLUMPING PALMS

These four work especially well in the garden.

The smallest is needle palm (*Rhapidophyllum hystrix;* zones 7, 8, 9, and 12 through 24), which does well except in California's high desert. It grows only about 5 feet tall, with 3- to 4-foot-long, fan-shaped green leaves that are silver below and armed with black spines. It makes an impenetrable hedge.

One of the most elegant clumping kinds is slender lady palm (*Rhapis humilis;* zones 16, 17, and 20 through 24). This palm, a native of south China, forms bamboolike stems to about 18 feet tall. It likes light shade.

For a hardy, medium-size clumping palm, try Mediterranean fan palm (*Chamaerops humilis;* zones 4 through 24). It tops out at about 20 feet with green to bluish green fans.

If you live in one of Southern California's mild coastal zones (23 or 24) and you'd rather have a feather palm, Senegal date palm (*Phoenix reclinata*) may be for you. It grows fairly quickly to 20 to 30 feet, with graceful 9-foot fans. But if just one really hard freeze comes, it's firewood. ■

By Jim McCausland

Senegal date palm, a native of tropical Africa, forms large clumps of shoots with feather-shaped leaves.

Harvest crops of glossy red fruit twice a year from an established lingonberry plant.

Grow lingonberries for evergreen ground cover or tart fruit

Plants bear flowers and berries twice a year

IT HAS FLOWERS LIKE HEATHER, LEAVES like boxwood, fruit like cranberry, and the hardiness of a malamute. It's lingonberry, an evergreen shrub whose tart red berries are prized in northern Europe. Scandinavians collect the fruit from wild plants for jams and sauces, but they grow the cultivated plants mostly for ornament. You'll probably start out growing them as ornamentals, too, but don't be surprised if you develop a taste for lingonberry jam on your pancakes.

Lingonberry plants grow in *Sunset Western Garden Book* climate zones 2 through 7 and 14 through 17. Because lingonberry breeding is still in its infancy, only a few varieties are available, and most are only a generation removed from the wild.

Dwarf lingonberry (*Vaccinium vitis-idaea minus*) is the most ornamental of the lingonberries. These plants reach 6 inches tall. They do not bear a lot of fruit, but in May, when they are covered with pink flowers, they rival heather as a flow-ering ground cover. Blueberry-size fruit follows in July. Then there's another round of flowers in August, followed by a last crop of fruit in late October.

Standard lingonberry (*V. vitis-idaea*),

Young lingonberry plant in a 4-inch pot is already bearing fruit.

also called foxberry or cowberry, is a taller plant (to 1 foot) that yields abundant fruit. It, too, produces flowers and berries twice a year, bearing heavy crops of pea-size red fruit, but its blossoms aren't as showy. Look for the common species or for named varieties such as 'Koralle' (the standard European variety), 'Ammerland' (larger, darker foliage and less fruit), 'Erntekrone' (heavy crops in both summer and fall), and 'Red Pearl' (upright plant, with $1/3$- to $1/2$-inch fruits, the largest of the lingonberries).

After harvest, store lingonberries by freezing them as you would blueberries.

Nurseries sell lingonberry plants in containers. You can transplant them anytime into acid soil amended with a 50-50 mix of sand and peat moss. These plants of the northern forests thrive in filtered sunlight. Commercial lingonberries, however, are grown in full sun.

Water plants regularly the first year; after that, they get by on remarkably little extra summer water. If it gets especially cold or dry where you live, spread a mulch of peat or pine needles around plants.

Feed plants after each flowering with quarter- to half-strength acid fertilizer (rhododendron food, for example). Scratch the fertilizer into the soil, and water it in well.

Root weevils sometimes munch on lingonberries' leaves and roots. No chemical is registered for root weevil control on lingonberries, but if weevils become a serious problem, you can pick them off the leaves at night.

SOURCES

If you can't find lingonberries at a nursery, you can order plants now for May delivery from Raintree Nursery, 391 Butts Rd., Morton, WA 98356; (360) 496-6400. ■

By Jim McCausland

Hanging baskets of New Guinea impatiens from the Spectra series bear flowers in shades of red, rose, and pink, with leaves ranging from maroon-green to variegated green and cream. Below, red-hot blooms sizzle in a shady spot.

NORMAN A. PLATE

Lusher-looking impatiens

New Guinea impatiens flaunt flowers and foliage in more vivid shades. Tuck these show-offs into beds or baskets

WHEN THEY FIRST APPEARED in garden centers more than 20 years ago, New Guinea impatiens had plenty of promise and many problems. Although the early plants had larger, more exotic flowers than standard impatiens, they bloomed sparsely and sporadically, and their leaves were variegated—great if you liked cream on green, but not the right look for every garden.

Over the years, breeders have been working to civilize these plants, which were brought to the United States in 1970 by botanists who had been exploring the remote terrain of New Guinea. The new hybrid plants bloom consistently over a long season, bearing larger flowers in much more vivid shades. The leaves of the dense, well-branched plants come in solid hues of green, bronze, and maroon, as well as variegated.

FILL A BED OR HANG THEM UP

This month, you'll find New Guinea impatiens in nurseries all over the West. They're sold mostly as bedding plants in 4-inch pots or 1-gallon containers, and are showing up more as hanging-basket plants. You can also start them from seed; look for Spectra and Rainforest, which are related lines in many colors, and the award-winning orange 'Tango'.

Some good choices in the full-size series (as tall as 30 inches) include Celebration, Danzinger, Lasting Impressions,

and Pure Beauty. Flower colors include white, orange, red, magenta, and purple; fuchsia and lavender shades are becoming especially popular. Blooms are typically 2 to 2½ inches in diameter, and come as doubles and the more popular, elegant singles.

For hanging baskets, midsize varieties (9 to 18 inches tall) are most manageable. Try the Paradise series (individual varieties are named after tropical islands) and the Celebrette series, new this year.

For small pot plants, look for the Mini Gini and Pot of Gold series (also new this year). Their flowers tend to be smaller but profuse. The plants grow 4 to 6 inches tall.

CARING FOR PLANTS

When you plant, keep in mind that these hybrids are the offspring of plants that were found growing along streams. New Guinea impatiens love water. Mulch well around plants, and don't let them dry out completely or they'll collapse into a wilted mass (if that happens, water again and they'll usually spring back to life).

Give them about a half-day's sun (filtered shade during the hottest part of the day). The harsher your summer climate, the more shade they need; too much sun will result in smaller flowers and greater leaf variegation. Plants are averse to drying wind, frost, and extreme heat (flowering stops when temperatures regularly top 85°).

New Guinea impatiens' ability to cover ground helps offset their relatively high price—$2 to $3 per 4-inch pot, compared with $1.20 to $1.60 for standard impatiens. Set bedding plants 15 to 18 inches apart; space them farther apart where the climate is mild, closer together where summers are hot and dry.

For best performance, feed plants monthly with a complete fertilizer. Since these are tender tropical plants, expect to enjoy them for a single season, until the first hard frost hits. ■

By Jim McCausland

Just-ripe fruit is yellowish green and soft like a peach. Creamy flesh has the texture of custard and a banana-mango flavor. Large seeds fill two rows, but they're easy to scoop out.

Scoop out a little pawpaw fruit

Cold-hardy trees produce these creamy-fleshed "tropicals"

"IF YOU LOVE TROPICAL FRUIT, you'll love pawpaws," says Ray Jones, an avid fan of these exotic, slightly curved fruits. Jones, who grows pawpaw trees in his Santa Clara, California, garden, calls pawpaws love-hate fruits. "They're creamy, custardy, floral, and perfumy all in one. But you have to like sweet-tasting fruit." Other pawpaw aficionados describe the flavor as somewhere between mango and piña colada or banana.

Although its fruit tastes and looks tropical, the pawpaw tree (*Asimina triloba*) is native to the eastern United States. The pyramid-shaped tree grows slowly to about 15 to 20 feet tall, and withstands temperatures down to −15°. Its dark green, glossy leaves—about 8 to 12 inches long and 3 to 5 inches across—turn a beautiful yellow in fall. Musky, dark maroon flowers appear in spring on the previous year's wood.

The fruits have never caught on in markets, primarily because their soft skin makes them too perishable to ship and store. But that's not a problem for home gardeners.

Also, ½- to 1-inch-long, dark brown seeds stud the flesh. To make sure you cut between the seed rows when slicing a pawpaw, follow Jones's advice. Turn the concave side of the fruit up, and slice the pawpaw in half lengthwise. Then scoop out the flesh; the seeds normally separate easily.

The fruit contains high levels of amino acids, vitamins A and C, and other nutrients. Compounds in the bark, leaves, and twigs are toxic to mammals, but the bark and leaves taste so bad that even deer shun them.

YOUNG TREES NEED PARTIAL SHADE

For a year or so after planting, until trees are about 3 feet tall, they can't tolerate strong doses of ultraviolet light. But after that they prefer to get full sun.

Fortunately, home gardeners have an easy way to shade young trees. Plant them in 2-foot-tall, biodegradable tubes such as Tubex Treeshelters (see source below). Remove the tubes when foliage starts to shade the trunks, or leave them on until they disintegrate in 3 to 5 years. Or make a cage about 2 feet in diameter around the tree (similar to a tomato cage, but smaller). Bend a 2- to 3-foot-tall piece of 6-inch-mesh concrete-reinforcing wire around the tree's trunk, and cover it with shadecloth.

Trees don't need much pruning, except to control their height and keep them shapely, and they are resistant to insects and diseases.

Fruits usually ripen from mid-August to mid-October. You'll know they're ripe and ready to eat when they start falling from the tree (ripe pawpaws are best eaten immediately). Jones catches his fruit in midair by suspending ½-inch bird netting from stakes placed under the branches.

WHERE TO BUY TREES

Eight grafted varieties are now available from Western mail-order sources. 'Prolific' and 'Taylor' are Jones's favorites for flavor. Seedlings are also sold through catalogs, but their fruits can vary greatly in flavor. At its worst, seedling fruit tastes like turpentine.

Trees are most productive when two different varieties grow side by side and cross-pollinate. Pawpaws become established faster if planted in spring when buds are breaking and the ground is still cool; avoid disturbing the roots.

Northwoods Nursery, 27635 S. Oglesby Rd., Canby, OR 97013; (503) 266-5432. Eight varieties, plus tree shelters.

Raintree Nursery, 391 Butts Rd., Morton, WA 98356; (360) 496-6400. Four varieties. ∎

By Lauren Bonar Swezey

Visitors to Mount Pisgah Arboretum stroll under lichen-laced Oregon white oaks that rise among blue camas and other wildflowers.

Wander among wildflowers

Mount Pisgah Arboretum near Eugene is full of native plants

BEFORE EXOTIC PLANTS SUCH AS Scotch broom invaded Oregon's Willamette Valley, the landscape looked much different from the way it does today. One place where you can still get a vivid sense of the historic landscape is at Mount Pisgah Arboretum, just off Interstate 5 near Eugene.

This month, spring wildflowers speckle the landscape. Trilliums and giant fawn lilies bloom in the dappled shade of Douglas and grand firs and white oak, while white, yellow, and purple Pacific Coast native irises pop up in grassy meadows. Forest glades turn blue with larkspur, and giant cow parsnips are unmistakable in moist areas.

Mount Pisgah shines as a wildflower sanctuary partly because the staff ruthlessly eliminates exotic plants that might compete with natives and partly because the place has many habitats. Lying along the Coast Fork of the Willamette River, the arboretum takes in a mosaic of fields, swamps, woodlands, and slopes. The 200-acre arboretum is laced with 7 miles of well-maintained trails, many accessible to wheelchairs. Other trails lead into Lane County Parks's 2,300-acre Howard Buford Recreation Area, where Mount Pisgah tops out at 1,520 feet.

Wildflowers bloom in colonies all over both arboretum and park. You can just wander through and look for them, or stop at the visitor center any weekend between 10 and 4 for a plant list and directions to the day's best blooms. Wildflower season usually peaks in late April and early May.

In recent years, the arboretum has put on a wildflower show and festival in May. Volunteers gather and label hundreds of wildflowers to display in one place. Other highlights include guided walks, a plant sale, food, music, and edu-cational activities for children. A donation of $2 per person or $5 per family is requested.

If you're even remotely interested in birds, bring binoculars; this place is rife with songbirds, hawks, and more. Pick up a bird checklist at the visitor center or at the information kiosk before you start your hike.

Mount Pisgah Arboretum is open daily from dawn to dusk. Admission is free, but if you feed the donation box, you'll help this privately funded organization continue its good work.

To get there from Eugene-Springfield, take I-5 south to the Lane Community College/30th Avenue exit (189). Cross to the east side of the freeway and jog north onto Seavey Loop Road. Follow it about 2 miles to the arboretum's entrance. For more information, call the arboretum office weekdays at (541) 747-3817. ∎

By Jim McCausland

A pavilion of tree stakes festonned with morning glory vines, nestles among sunflowers, white roses, and Queen Anne's lace in this San Marcos, California garden. For details, see page 150.

BOB WIGAND

JUNE

Garden guide........................146

Garden notebooks 151

Garden checklists..................153

Beautiful pots 158

Terra-cotta to treasure 162

The right potting mix.............165

Thyme to plant, thyme to spare ..167

SUNSET'S
GARDEN
Guide

A cool and calming garden of white flowers

"I want to be surrounded by something cool and calming" is how interior designer Bill Overholt describes the use of whites in his Seattle townhouse garden, designed by landscape architect Robert Chittock. "I need to arrive home, shut the gate behind me, and enter a restful world."

For his summer whites, Overholt depends on geraniums ('Ice Queen' is his favorite), 'White Cascade' petunias, and impatiens. Billowy masses of geraniums and petunias in containers fill sunny spots. White impatiens form icy sheets in shady spots. The white flowers and furniture, gray columns and pavers, and dense green background of boxwood and clipped English holly give the garden a cool, pristine look on even the sultriest days.

Overholt's garden also makes good use of other seasonal white flowers. In spring, primroses, tulips, hyacinths, daffodils (such as 'Mount Hood', 'Petrel', and 'Thalia'), and 'Snowstorm' crocus frost the garden. Later on, the blossoms of 'Mount Fuji' cherries hover over the garden like big cumulus clouds. Then come blooms of 'Mount Everest' azaleas, mock orange (*Philadelphus lewisii*), *Rhododendron loderi* 'King George', English hawthorn (*Crataegus laevigata* 'Double White'), Eastern dogwood (*Cornus florida* and *C.* 'Eddie's White Wonder'), Chinese dogwood (*C. kousa chinensis*), Chinese wisteria (*W. sinensis* 'Alba'), *Styrax japonicus,* climbing hydrangea (*H. anomala*), and *Magnolia grandiflora.*

To keep his garden looking crisp, Overholt takes a daily stroll to pinch off faded flowers. To keep plants lush and floriferous, he feeds them about every three weeks using a liquid 15-30-15 fertilizer.

Puffs of white geraniums and petunias give a cool look to this Seattle garden.

Garden tools made for kids to handle

A good way to teach children about gardening is to have them help with chores such as planting, raking, and weeding. But adult-size tools just don't work for small children.

Now scaled-down garden tools—hoes, two kinds of rakes, and a long-handled shovel—are available in different sizes and materials from Ames Lawn & Garden Tools. (A D-handle shovel is available in a smaller size only.)

The small-size tools, with 32-inch-long handles (except the D-handle shovel, which has a 26-inch-long handle), fit ages 2 through 6 and are made of sturdy, colorful plastic. Tools cost $7 to $9 each; a set of three costs $25 to $27.

The larger-size tools, which are made for ages 7 and up, have metal heads and wood handles 42 to 44½ inches long. The shovel head is of tempered carbon steel, and the hoe head is welded steel. Cost is $9 to $11 per tool, or $30 to $32 for a set of three.

The tools are available at many garden and home improvement stores. If you can't find them locally, call Ames's dealer-locator number: (800) 725-9500.

The "American Gothic" pitchfork has given way to tools like these spades and rakes designed for child gardeners.

Super-size blueberries

About 15 years ago, 'Darrow' blueberry came on the market. It was one of the first super-size blueberries that was also flavorful, with a sweet-tart taste. In the past five years, two more large-fruited varieties have come out, and both are winners.

'Sierra', whose parentage includes a berry native to the Sierra Nevada, is for gardeners who want the whole crop to ripen in a one- to two-week period—for freezing or preserving, for example. Its sweet berries come on a shrub that grows quickly to about 6 feet throughout most of the non-desert West; it has even survived -25°

'Toro' blueberry bears clusters of plump fruits among glossy leaves.

weather in Michigan. Fruit ripens in early midseason.

'Toro' is a strong, stocky 4-foot plant named for its vigor and large leaf size. This is a beautiful landscape shrub, with 14- to 16-inch clusters of fruit hanging among huge, dark green leaves that turn bright red in fall. 'Toro' grows well in all except the very coldest Western climates but isn't suited to deserts. Fruit comes over a two-week period in midseason.

On the horizon is a super blueberry called 'Chandler'; it's expected to hit the market in 1997. It produces huge, great-tasting berries.

Blueberry plants are self-fruitful (they don't require a pollenizer), and they grow best in a well-draining soil containing plenty of peat moss. Buy and plant them anytime from containers.

NEW PLANT REPORT

A perennial nemesia that's almost everblooming

Specialty nurseries usually offer a few little-known gems. *Nemesia fruticans* is one of them. Both the plant and its small lavender and pink flowers with yellow centers look somewhat delicate, but the plant blooms prolifically. In mild climates (*Sunset Western Garden Book* zones 16 through 24), it blooms practically nonstop. A cold snap is just about the only thing that will stop the bloom.

Native to South Africa, *N. fruticans* arrived in California from England, and Western Hills Nursery in Occidental helped to popularize it.

Flowers of *Nemesia fruticans* have distinctive yellow spots near their centers. The plant has shiny, deep green leaves.

Nemisia fruticans reaches about a foot tall with a slightly larger spread. It prefers moderate water and full sun, although it will take light afternoon shade. Group plants at the front of a border, or intersperse them between other low-growing perennials. This little gem also makes a fine container plant, and can live quite happily in the same pot for years.

Cut this nemesia back twice a year (in summer and winter) to keep it compact. Stems can break easily, so be careful when planting it or grooming plants around it. (*N. capensis,* a similar plant, has pink flowers.)

If you can't find *N. fruticans,* have your nursery order it from a wholesale supplier, such as Emerisa Gardens in Santa Rosa or Rosendale Nursery in Watsonville.

THE NATURAL WAY

Does baking-soda spray hurt roses?

In the past year, we reported how researchers at Cornell University control powdery mildew on roses with a spray of 2 teaspoons baking soda and 2 teaspoons SunSpray Ultra-Fine Year-Round Pesticidal Oil dissolved in 1 gallon of water. (Many hopeful *Sunset* readers have tried this on black spot, and confirm that while it's great for mildew, it does nothing against black spot.)

This spring, we learned of two university studies (one at Auburn, Alabama, and one at Oregon State) that link the use of baking soda and SunSpray oil

TIPS, TRICKS & SECRETS

Pinching pines

Pines grow from the branch tips, which elongate into "candles" in spring, then fatten into mature, needle-covered branches. To minimize pine growth, just pinch off the ends of the candles. You can take off half of each

CARING FOR PLANTS

How to feed and divide Siberian irises

Siberian irises are much loved for their leaves as well as for their masses of flowers that appear in early June. They form handsome clumps of sword-like leaves 1½ to 3 feet tall. Each flower stalk can stretch as high as 4 feet and bear two to five blooms. The flowers come in shades of blue, lavender, purple, wine, pink, yellow, and white.

As Siberian irisclumps age, they die out in the middle, so you're left with a ring of foliage. You can deal with this in a couple of ways: fertilize the center of each clump to keep it growing, or dig and

Siberian iris blooms rise above dense clumps.

to leaf damage and reduced flowering in roses. In both studies, researchers used double the recommended rate of soda, and more than quadruple the rate of oil recommended by Cornell. "I'm not surprised that such high rates caused problems," said Ken Horst at Cornell. "The lower rates [listed at left] have been tested, and they work well."

There's more to tell, however. In the trials at Oregon State, researchers Molly Hoffer and Jay Pscheidt found that a mix of only oil and water gave nearly the same protection against mildew as the oil-soda-water mix, and resulted in virtually no leaf damage. They used 1 percent SunSpray oil, or about 2½ tablespoons per gallon of water. A higher percentage of oil would likely cause leaf damage.

with no harm to the tree, but don't pinch out the leader (the top candle on the tree). Most gardeners candle pines a few weeks after growth starts in spring.

If you pinch too early, before needles have formed on the lower half of the candle, the candle can die. By June, candles are usually stretched out and well enough clad with needles that candling doesn't cause any problems.

divide plants to start new clumps.

As with most other perennials, it's a good idea to fertilize this iris during the growing season. One good system is to apply a granular 20-20-20 fertilizer in mid-February, followed by doses of granular 12-12-12 fertilizer in early April, again in mid- to late May, and again in early July. In addition, for established plants it's best to scatter a light application of granular 12-12-12 in the center of the clump immediately after bloom and water it well.

If you choose to divide plants, autumn is the traditional time to do it. However, if you have a tired old clump of Siberian iris, you can dig it out and divide it immediately after bloom. Replant the divisions and water them well throughout the summer, but do not fertilize until early next spring.

Floral tapestry holds a garden slope

Acolorful patchwork of perennials tames a slope in Lyn Ballard's garden in Occidental, California. The slope used to be bare. And because it dropped 8 feet to the house, it was a disaster waiting to happen if heavy rains were to fall. Ballard turned to Sebastopol landscape designer Maile Arnold for help.

Arnold's design called for a 3-foot-high stone retaining wall along the bottom of the slope to hold the bank, which gently slopes up to an existing driveway. The soil was topped with newspaper and compost, and a user-friendly path of steppingstones was built down to the house (it traverses the slope rather than steeply descending it).

Ballard wanted "a pretty garden that's soft and feminine," says Arnold. Plants also had to be deer resistant. So Arnold selected and set out soft-looking, textural perennials such as artemisia, catmint, Mexican bush sage, *Origanum laevigatum* 'Hopley's', Russian sage, Santa Barbara daisy, society garlic, and *Verbena tenuisecta*. To balance the bold lines of the surrounding redwood trees, Arnold developed a strong horizontal pattern with flower colors. Among them, "golden touches"—plants like gold-foliaged feverfew (shown at the border's far end in the photo at right)—

CHAS McGRATH

Perennials, including Russian sage and blue-flowered catmint (foreground), cloak this slope between driveway and house.

are as eye-catching as a car's headlights. To go between the steppingstones, she selected several kinds of thyme, including variegated and lemon thymes. Ballard did all the planting.

The slope needs very little mainte-

nance. It's watered automatically every other day during the warm season. Then, in winter, Ballard cuts back the perennials to clean them up and rejuvenate them. At the same time, she applies a new 2-inch layer of mulch.

Plant collars cut from nursery cans

Many trees and shrubs are sold in 5-gallon plastic containers. After you've removed the plants, one way to reuse the containers is to use them as collars around plants, especially ones surrounded by lawn. The collars protect tender young trunks against errant lawnmowers, weed and grass trimmers, pets, and children. The collars can serve as funnels to channel water and fertilizer down to the plants' roots, and they also encourage roots to grow deeply.

To make a collar, use pruning shears to cut the bottom out of the container. Then slip the collar over the plant and push it into the soil 8 inches or so, leaving 3 to 4 inches of plastic above ground.

NORMAN A. PLATE

A bottomless nursery can forms a protective collar and watering basin around a newly planted shrub.

In about two years, when the plant is well established, lift the collar off and store it for use on another fledgling plant. If the plant is too large to allow the collar to slip off easily, slit the side of the collar and pull it out of the ground.

Watering young trees

In a normal or even moderately dry summer, established trees should be able to take some drought without irrigation. However, young trees planted earlier this year will need summer water this year and for the next two summers as well. Normally, 15 gallons of water a week is ample, though trees growing in exceptionally sandy soils may require more.

Jerry Clark, Seattle's city arborist, suggests that each young tree be given 5 gallons of water three times a week. Form a shallow basin in the soil around the trunk, and slowly run water into the basin so that it soaks into the developing root mass. If rain doesn't fall, water the young trees faithfully until they go into dormancy.

Streisand Center is now open to visitors

Anyone who has ever read and loved fairy tales has surely entertained the fancy of living in a secret castle deep in the woods. Well, Barbra Streisand must have loved fairy tales, because she turned that dream into a reality. In 1974 Streisand bought 8 wooded acres in a secluded Malibu canyon and created a whimsically rustic house, which she called The Barn, to live in. Then she deepened her woods wherever she could, right up to the edges of the wilderness, adding 16 more acres. In the process she acquired three more castles, each distinct. Then, in 1993, Streisand gave it all away.

The Santa Monica Mountains Conservancy, a state agency mandated to acquire parkland, was the lucky and logical recipient. The stream-fed, shade-canopied property now houses the Streisand Center for Conservancy Studies. Though primarily an environmental think tank, the center shares its fairytale setting with the public. In April it began giving reservation-only group garden tours. The tours—currently limited to two weekdays a month—include an hour-long, docent-led walk through the oak-studded grounds, followed by an hour of free time to savor the setting. (Fancy a solo in the Meadow, where the

CHAD SLATTERY

Art deco doors of The Barn open onto Streisand's patio and garden.

1986 *One Voice* fund-raising concert was held?)

Tours for 12 to 20 people cost $30 per person. The cost is tax-deductible, and the money is used to maintain the gardens. For details and reservations, call (310) 589-2850, ext. 105.

A garden for wildlife and people in Oceanside

Doug and Stephanie Platt's backyard garden in Oceanside is a flower-filled haven for birds and butterflies.

Plants such as agapanthus, golden coreopsis, white and pink cosmos, foxglove, and roses, whose nectar attracts butterflies, bloom in delightful profusion in an area bordered by a picket fence. Flagstone pavers cut a small path through the flower beds to a garden bench where the Platts sit on sparkling days.

GLENN CORMIER

Flowers provide nectar for butterflies.

"We wanted our garden to be a retreat for us and for birds, bees, butterflies," says Stephanie.

On a bank opposite the butterfly garden, acacia, eucalyptus, hibiscus, India hawthorn, lantana, Mexican evening primrose, and oleander play host to a variety of birds that come to sip nectar, to eat berries or seeds, or just to hang out and chatter.

The Platts created this lush haven from bare soil in just a year (the house was new when they bought it).

Other plants that attract adult butterflies—available in many nurseries this month—include asters, erigeron, penstemons, and Shasta and gloriosa daisies.

Leafy pavilion for summer dining, alfresco

Judy Wigand created a morning glory–festooned pavilion in her backyard nursery as a summer playhouse for her granddaughters Rachel and Nicole. But adults like it just as much.

Everyone, it seems, is drawn to its morning glory walls and roof and its sunflower columns (see photo on page 144). Visitors to Judy's Perennials—Wigand's nursery in San Marcos, California—frequently use it as a backdrop for photos. Guests eat lunch in it. "The little house seems to bring back everyone's childhood fantasies," says Wigand.

The pavilion was built by Wigand's husband, Bob, from a dozen tree stakes, each 2 inches thick and 6 feet long, assembled into a freestanding cube. Four stakes form the base, four the sides, and four the crossbeams. The stakes are deeply notched about 2 inches from the ends, and they lock together like children's Lincoln Logs. Wood glue and a heavy jute twine securely hold the connections.

The 'Heavenly Blue' morning glory vines climb around bamboo poles, positioned between the stakes, to create see-through flowering "walls," then continue across crisscrossed jute twine on the "roof."

Outside the pavilion, Wigand planted white roses ('Gourmet Popcorn'), cosmos ('Purity'), Queen Anne's lace, golden gloriosa daisies, and red dahlias to add splashes of color.

In March, Wigand begins the planting process. First she soaks the morning glory seeds overnight, then starts them and the sunflower seeds in flats or 4-inch pots. She transfers the seedlings to the garden when they have developed their second set of leaves. Flowers begin appearing in early summer and blooming continues until mid-October.

The pavilion is now in its fourth summer. "It's been a real treat for everyone," says Wigand. "I can't imagine summer without it."

By Sharon Cohoon,
Steven R. Lorton, Jim McCausland,
Lauren Bonar Swezey

PACIFIC NORTHWEST
Garden Notebook

BY STEVEN R. LORTON

When I was growing up in Ohio, my family's house was filled all summer with great bouquets of zinnias. Dad grew them. Mother put them in vases. And Grandmother, in what we called her van Gogh period, painted them. I carry on the family tradition by growing zinnias in my Skagit Valley garden. But in the cool, moist summers of the Pacific Northwest, these heat-loving flowers can be a bit tricky to grow. I have to be content with a shorter bloom season, from late summer to autumn.

Although I've tried planting seedlings from sixpacks, 4-inch pots, and 1-gallon cans, I find I have the most success with seeds. Transplanted seedlings sit and sulk in the ground before taking off. Seeds germinate, sprout, and shoot up in the heat of summer, quickly outpacing transplants. But timing is everything: zinnias require warm soil and weather to germinate and grow well. They also need rich soil with perfect drainage, and lots of water applied around the base (overhead watering promotes mildew).

About June 1, I sow a 60-foot row of zinnia seeds into manure-enriched soil along the west side of my vegetable patch. I plant all kinds of zinnias—from dwarfs to giants. About three weeks after they germinate, I thin the row. The plants, boosted with feedings of granular rose food (6-10-4) in July, August, and September, produce zillions of zinnias until the first hard frost.

•

A few years ago, as more gardeners discovered balloon flower (*Platycodon grandiflorus*), the popularity of this perennial began to inflate. First came a blue-flowered variety, followed by white, then pink and violet. The plant gets its name from the balloonlike buds the size of large marbles that open into star-shaped flowers about 2 inches across. Plants grow 2 to 3 1/2 feet tall.

Balloon flower is hardy enough to grow in all Northwest climate zones. It takes full sun in the cool-summer climates west of the Cascades and light shade in areas that get intense summer sun. It grows best in loose, quick-draining soil enriched with plenty of organic matter. This month, nurseries will be selling plants with buds or blooms, in 1-gallon cans ready to set out immediately. Plants bloom from June into, if not through, August.

THAT'S A GOOD QUESTION

Q: Is the litter that my big cedar tree drops good for the soil or bad? Do I rake it up or leave it?
A: Fallen leaves and needles are one way nature keeps a new supply of topsoil coming. However, this litter can smother small plants growing below the tree. Also, as the plant material decomposes, it extracts some nitrogen from the soil. If you have a wild or native garden, let the litter lie as a natural mulch. But if the litter falls on beds of annuals or perennials, rake it up, put it on the compost pile, let it rot, and use it to amend soil next year. Composted cedar needles make a rich acid additive.

NORTHERN CALIFORNIA
Garden Notebook

BY LAUREN BONAR SWEZEY

One practice that makes me cringe is planting flowers right against the base of an old native oak tree. I've seen such plantings on my walks around Palo Alto. These old oaks that matured on only natural rainfall don't like water near their root crowns (at the bases of their trunks) during the normal dry season. It makes them much more prone to diseases such as crown rot.

Even the most caring gardeners are guilty of putting the wrong plants under old, existing oaks. Recently, at our headquarters in Menlo Park, we lost huge branches from several majestic oaks—a sign of tree decline. Over the years, the trees were underplanted with begonias and other flowers that needed regular watering. Now we know better.

To keep an old oak healthy, remove all plants within 10 feet of the trunk and do not water there. Apply mulch such as bark chips over the bare soil, taking care to keep it away from the trunk. From the edge of the mulch to well outside the drip line, plant only drought-tolerant plants, such as artemisia, blue-eyed grass, catmint, ceanothus, native currant (*Ribes*), Pacific Coast iris, purple needle grass, rockrose, salvia, and Santa Barbara daisy. For a stunning spring tapestry of bloom beneath an oak, in fall plant *Geranium endressii* 'Wargrave Pink', Santa Barbara daisy, and blue forget-me-not, and let them ramble together.

•

Every time *Bob's Honest-to-Goodness Newsletter* (Box 1841, Santa Rosa, CA 95402; $20 per year for four issues) comes across my desk, I find something in it to chuckle about. Robert Kourik's style is entertaining. But the information is serious and useful; the winter newsletter, for example, carried an article about subsurface lawn irrigation and "What the EPA Doesn't Tell You About the Lead in Your Drinking Water." Last fall, Kourik expounded on "How Tree Roots *Really* Grow!" I appreciate Kourik's sense of humor, and the fact that he's not afraid to tell the truth or admit when he's wrong. If you're ready for entertaining journalism that covers important gardening subjects in depth, give the newsletter a try and enjoy a laugh every now and then.

THAT'S A GOOD QUESTION

Q: Some time ago, I read an article about a pepper spray that would repel deer. Can you tell me about it?
A: One product containing capsaicin (which gives pepper its heat) has been marketed for a number of years on the East Coast but has just been registered in California as Deer Away Deer and Rabbit Repellent. This repellent is completely natural. It contains common food ingredients such as mustard oil and extract of lemon. You can buy it at nurseries and by mail from W. Atlee Burpee & Co. (800/888-1447).

SOUTHERN CALIFORNIA
Garden Notebook
BY SHARON COHOON

Daylilies (*Hemerocallis*) get no respect, grumbles John Schoustra of Greenwood Irises + Daylilies. Though daylilies produce wave after wave of sunny summer trumpets—even when planted in poor soil and treated indifferently—they're rarely applauded for their efforts. Gardeners take this summer show so much for granted they don't even bother to learn the performers' proper names.

I've been guilty myself. But I'm making up for it. I bought a new *Hemerocallis* with a name so perfectly suited to its appearance I'm not likely to ever forget it. 'Dixieland Band' is as sassy as it sounds: its bright red, medium-size trumpet has a crisp white stripe down the center of each petal and a brassy green throat—"like the white-piped, brass-buttoned red uniforms of the band," Schoustra prompts. It blooms later than most daylilies—just in time for the Fourth of July—then parades through again in late fall.

•

Many gardeners—myself included—don't need much of an excuse to return to Buena Creek Gardens. This San Marcos nursery has an outstanding plant collection, and the memory of the plants we didn't buy but wish we had is usually all it takes to draw us back. But the nursery isn't counting on that. It's offering additional inducements: a demonstration garden to give us planting ideas, and a series of Saturday morning garden lectures to lead us further into temptation. The nursery is at 418 Buena Creek Road. For a lecture schedule and directions, call (619) 744-2810.

•

Shatter-Proof is a great find for the dried-flower hobbyist, says Jeanne Dunn of Herban Garden in Rainbow. "In our heat, my dried flowers would disintegrate without it." This spray-on preservative forms an acrylic film that holds flower petals together. It's not yet widely available; order it from the manufacturer at (800) 678-7377. It costs $14.95 a quart in concentrate, $7.95 ready-to-use, plus shipping.

THAT'S A GOOD QUESTION

Q: Why did my 'Meyer' lemon tree drop tons of immature fruit last year?
A: Citrus trees drop fruit in reaction to many kinds of stress. Last year's heavy winter rain and an unusually cool spring, possibly compounded by poorly draining soil, are the likely culprits in this case, says Bill Nelson, owner of Pacific Tree Farms in Chula Vista. To determine how well your soil drains, dig a 12-inch-diameter hole about 2 feet deep 3 to 4 feet from the tree. Fill it with water and allow to drain. Repeat. The hole should drain within 12 hours of the second filling. If it doesn't, tree roots are probably running into heavy clay or impenetrable hardpan, both of which hold water the way a porcelain sink does. If the tree is small, move it to a better-draining location. Or dig down into your testing hole until you reach soil with good drainage, then fill up the hole with pea gravel to maintain drainage. For details on drainage correction for citrus, send a self-addressed, stamped envelope to Pacific Tree Farms, 4301 Lynwood Dr., Chula Vista, CA 91910, or call (619) 422-2400.

INLAND WESTERN STATES
Garden Notebook
BY JIM McCAUSLAND

While I'm working in the garden, I keep two eyes on pest populations: one eye on the short-term situation, the other on long-term trends.

For example, if I see tent caterpillars building up on birches, I remember what has happened before: as caterpillars increase, so do the creatures that eat them. I watch a Steller's jay pick caterpillars out of a web-walled colony, and see ichneumon wasps gingerly probing the webs with their ovipositors, hoping to inject an egg into a caterpillar that wanders too close to the perimeter. Tachinid flies also see caterpillars as food for their offspring: looking closely, I see many caterpillars with white eggs glued to their backs. Some thrash wildly as larvae from the hatched eggs eat the caterpillars alive from the inside.

Taking the long view of this grisly business, it's clear that things aren't really out of control: insect populations explode and crash, with the predator populations always lagging just a year behind the prey. After two horrendous years of tent caterpillars, they have virtually disappeared from my landscape, regrouping slowly for another assault sometime hence.

Be patient, I've learned, and most problems take care of themselves.

•

During a recent interview with Molly Hoffer, an Oregon State University grad student doing pest-control work on roses, I learned that she has studied the effectiveness of controlling aphid colonies with jets of hose water. It turns out that when you hose down a rose bush, you blast off aphid predators along with the aphids. With that in mind, it makes the most sense to spray only aphid colonies, which usually concentrate on new growth, and leave the rest of the bush alone.

•

June is a grow-for-broke month in the garden, and with woody plant growth at its peak, lots of unwanted new growth also appears. There are suckers (sprouts that grow up from beneath the graft on roses and fruit and nut trees) and watersprouts (the vertical sprouts that shoot up from horizontal deciduous fruit tree limbs). I remove them now while their wood is soft and easy to snap off with a pinch of my thumb or a swipe of my knife. At the same time, I prune out other growth I don't want, such as white-flowered branches on pink-flowered plants, or all-green leaves on a variegated plant.

THAT'S A GOOD QUESTION

Q: My apple tree drops many of its young apples every June. What's wrong?
A: Nothing. "June drop" is the apple tree's way of removing little apples that weren't pollinated during spring, and apples that are too crowded to develop. After June drop, continue thinning excess fruit so those that remain will be larger.

PLANTING

❏ **ANNUALS.** If you haven't done so already, you can set out annuals in all Northwest climate zones. Begin fertilizing plants as soon as you plant them.

❏ **PERENNIALS.** All over the Northwest, nurseries will be offering perennials in bloom in 1-gallon cans. You can slip them into a decorative pot to enjoy on a patio table, or plant them immediately. Soak plants well the night before you plant so that roots take up as much water as possible. Remove plants from their cans, gently massage the rootball with your hands to loosen the roots, set them into the planting hole, fill in with soil, and water again. Don't fertilize until blooms have faded and you've picked them off.

❏ **DAHLIAS.** There's still time to get dahlia tubers into the ground for bloom in late summer and early fall. As you plant the tubers, put stakes in place to support the plants as they grow.

MAINTENANCE

❏ **CLIP HEDGES.** The base of a clipped hedge should be wider than the top so that sunlight and rain reach the entire surface. If you are a twice-a-season hedge trimmer, do it early this month and again in late summer or early autumn. If you are a once-a-season trimmer, clip in late June or early July.

❏ **CUT ROSES.** Before you cut a flower,

Vancouver
Victoria
BRITISH COLUMBIA
Spokane
Seattle
WASHINGTON
Olympia
Yakima
Portland
Pendleton
Salem
OREGON
Bend
Eugene
Medford

Sunset
Western Garden Book
CLIMATE ZONES

☐ 1-3   ▨ 4-7

look carefully at the leaves. The leaves closest to the blossoms have three leaflets each. The leaves farther down have five leaflets. Cut the stem just above a group of five leaflets. New growth will start just below your cut. If you cut above a group of three leaflets, you'll get a stub and no new growth.

❏ **DEADHEAD RHODIES.** Snapping off spent blossoms makes plants look neater and helps them channel their

energy into new growth rather than seed production. With thumb and forefinger, break off defunct blooms at their bases, being careful not to take the new buds with them. Be careful, too, that no bees are in the blossoms.

❏ **DIVIDE PERENNIALS.** As soon as flowers fade on early-blooming plants, you can divide them. Cut back flower stalks, and slice around the plant with a spade or shovel. Pop the clump out of the ground. A clump 12 inches across will divide nicely into four equal parts. Set divisions into the planting hole and water them well. Don't fertilize until early next spring.

PEST & WEED CONTROL

❏ **HELP THE SNAKE PATROL.** In the cool climates west of the Cascades, garter snakes are great friends to the gardener. They're docile and nonpoisonous, and gobble slugs and other annoying critters. One way to encourage snakes to hang out in your garden is to give them a warm, dark, damp place to hide. A 4- by 8-foot piece of plywood flat on the ground in full sun next to the vegetable garden works well. In a couple of weeks, you'll likely have six to eight snakes curled up under it.

❏ **WEED.** Pull weeds before seeds form and scatter. Shake dirt from weed roots, let them wither, and toss them onto the compost pile.

CHECKLIST
JUNE

PLANTING

❑ **PLANT SUMMER BLOOMERS.** Annuals available this month include garden verbena, gentian sage, globe amaranth, Madagascar periwinkle (*Vinca rosea*), portulaca, scarlet sage, sunflower, 'Victoria' mealy-cup sage, and zinnias. Perennials to look for include coreopsis, gaillardia, 'Homestead Purple' verbena, penstemon, rudbeckia, Russian sage, salvia, statice, and summer phlox.

❑ **PLANT VEGETABLES.** June is prime planting time for warm-season vegetables. Sow seeds of beans (both bush and pole types) and corn (try one of the supersweet or sugar-enhanced varieties, which stay sweeter longer after harvest). Use transplants for cucumbers, eggplant, melons, okra, peppers, pumpkins, squash, and tomatoes.

❑ **SOW HERBS.** To make sure you have plenty of basil and cilantro for cooking through the summer and fall, plant seeds every six to eight weeks for successive crops. For basil, try 'Anise', lemon, 'Red Rubin' purple, or one of the Italian types, such as 'Genova Profumatissima'. Grow a slow-bolt variety of cilantro. (All are available from Shepherd's Garden Seeds, 408/335-6910.)

MAINTENANCE

❑ **CARE FOR ROSES.** To encourage growth and additional blooms on repeat bloomers, remove faded flowers. Feed plants with a complete fertilizer and, if necessary, iron chelate; then water. For deep watering with a hose, build a basin around the plant. For drip irrigating, place two emitters on opposite sides of

Sunset
CLIMATE ZONES

❑ Mountain (1-2)
❑ Valley (7-9)
❑ Inland (14)
❑ Coastal (15-17)

the plant. Mulch to conserve soil moisture and keep roots cool.

❑ **CHECK SPRINKLERS.** Inspect your sprinkler system to see that it's working properly and has no broken, malfunctioning, or misaligned heads. Turn the system on and inspect each head; replace broken ones. If a head bubbles or squirts irregularly, it may be clogged. Check slits for dirt or small pebbles. If you can't unclog it, replace it. To readjust a misaligned head, turn it until it's spraying in the right direction.

❑ **HARVEST VEGETABLES.** Zones 7–9 and 14–17: For early-planted crops of

beans, short-season corn, cucumbers, or squash, harvest should be starting. Pick in the early morning, when the air is cool, and harvest vegetables at their peak maturity—firm, fully colored, and full flavored, but not too large. Pick lemon cucumbers before they're yellow, and beans before seeds swell. Zucchini and pattypan squash can be harvested when they're just a few inches long. Check corn about four days after the silk turns brown (gently pull down husk and nick a kernel with your fingernail; cloudy milk should spurt out).

❑ **SHAPE PLANTS.** On young or fast-growing trees, shrubs, and vines, pinch or prune poorly placed growth and stems growing at awkward angles. Cut back vigorous shoots to give the plant the shape and size you want, but don't shear plants into unattractive balls or gumdrops.

❑ **TEND CONTAINER PLANTS.** To keep plants from drying out as quickly (so you can reduce water use), mulch the top of the soil, group containers together so they shade one another, and protect plants from wind. For new plantings, use large, thick containers that insulate from heat.

PEST CONTROL

❑ **CHECK ROSES FOR RUST.** Cool, moist days promote rust—a fungus that causes rust-colored pustules on the undersides of leaves. Handpick and dispose of diseased leaves. Spray plants with a sulfur-based fungicide. To prevent rust, water early in the morning and avoid wetting foliage.

CHECKLIST
JUNE

Sunset Western Garden Book CLIMATE ZONES

1-3 7-9 11 13 14-24

PLANTING

❏ **PLANT FOR FRAGRANCE.** Sweet-smelling flowers were made for long summer evenings. Double your sun-down pleasure by adding one of the following fragrant plants to your garden: gardenia, heliotrope, night jessamine (*Cestrum nocturnum*), sweet olive (*Osmanthus fragrans*), or tuberose. Near the coast (zones 23 and 24), you can also plant Madagascar jasmine (*Stephanotis floribunda*).

❏ **PLANT SUBTROPICALS.** Exotics you can plant now include banana, floss silk tree (*Chorisia*), fig, gold medallion tree (*Cassia leptophylla*), and orchid tree. Subtropical shrubs to plant now include bird of paradise, gardenia, hibiscus, and philodendron.

❏ **PLANT VINES.** Summer-blooming vines add vibrant color to the land-scape. Nurseries are well stocked now with the following choices: bougainvil-lea, with magenta or red bracts; Cape honeysuckle, red-orange flowers; man-devilla, hot pink flowers; *Thunbergia grandiflora,* true-blue flowers; and trumpet vine (*Distictis*), purple, red, or violet flowers.

❏ **PLANT VEGETABLES.** In coastal and inland areas (zones 22–24 and 18–21, respectively), set out seedlings of cucumbers, eggplant, peppers, squash, and tomatoes. Sow seeds of beans, beets, carrots, corn, cucumbers, pump-kins, and summer squash in vegetable beds. In coastal gardens, you can still plant lettuce seeds and seedlings. In high-desert gardens (zone 11), sow seeds of corn, cucumbers, muskmelon, okra, squash, and watermelon.

MAINTENANCE

❏ **DIVIDE BEARDED IRISES.** Late June is a good time for inland and coastal gardeners to divide bearded irises (a good rule of thumb: after bloom peri-od, rhizomes need four to six weeks to mature before being divided). Each division should have one fan of leaves, a section of young rhizome, and devel-oped roots. Discard woody centers, rotted or diseased portions, and rhi-zomes without leaves. Shorten leaves, using scissors, to compensate for root loss. Let divisions dry in the sun for a few hours. Replant with rhizome just below soil level and leafy end pointed in the direction you want growth. In high and low deserts (zones 11 and 13), wait until October to divide irises.

❏ **PAMPER CITRUS.** In coastal, inland, and low-desert gardens, feed plants with high-nitrogen fertilizer as directed on the label, then water thoroughly. To protect newly planted trees from sun-burn, wrap trunks with burlap, cloth, or commercial tree wrap, or paint with white latex tree paint. To keep ants out of trees, apply a sticky ant barrier such as Tanglefoot to trunks.

❏ **STOP WATERING NATIVES.** Many natives, including ceanothus, flannel bush, and oaks, are disease-prone in warm, wet soils. If young plants are not yet established and still need watering, let water drip slowly over the rootball, away from leaves and trunk. Water at night or during cool weather.

❏ **PINCH AND SHAPE FUCHSIAS.** If fuchsias are growing leggy, pinch off branch tips just above a set of leaves to force growth into side branches. Pick flowers as they fade.

PEST CONTROL

❏ **CONTROL CATERPILLARS.** Petunias, geraniums, and nicotiana are favorites of the geranium budworm (alias tobac-co budworm). At first signs of the green larvae, spray with *Bacillus thuringiensis*.

❏ **WATCH FOR PESTS.** Keep spider mites, thrips, and whiteflies in check by spraying foliage with a strong stream of water and/or insecticidal soap.

CHECKLIST
JUNE

PLANTING

❑ **FLOWERS. Sow annuals:** Scatter seeds of cosmos, marigold, portulaca, sunflower, and zinnia. **Sow perennials:** Plant seeds of aster, basket-of-gold, campanula, columbine, coral bells, delphinium, erigeron, gaillardia, gilia, penstemon, perennial sweet pea, potentilla, and purple coneflower in a bed that won't be disturbed all summer, then transplant seedlings into permanent positions in late summer. **Set out nursery plants:** African daisy, bachelor's button, calendula, clarkia, coreopsis, forget-me-not, gaillardia, globe amaranth, lobelia, pansy, penstemon, salvia, snapdragon, sweet alyssum, sweet William, and viola can go into the ground now. After last frost, set out coleus, dwarf dahlia, geranium, impatiens, Madagascar periwinkle, marigold, nasturtium, and petunia.

❑ **SUMMER BULBS.** For late-summer color (except in highest elevations), plant canna, dahlia, gladiolus, montbretia, tigridia (tiger flower), and tuberous begonia.

❑ **STRAWBERRIES.** Set out plants from nursery sixpacks or pots.

❑ **VEGETABLES.** Sow cucumbers and squash, as well as successive crops of beets, bush beans, carrots, chard, kohlrabi, lettuce, onions, parsnips, peas, radishes, spinach, Swiss chard, and turnips. If the season is long and warm enough in your area, sow corn, pumpkin, and watermelon, and plant seedlings of eggplants, peppers, and tomatoes.

❑ **LANDSCAPE PLANTS.** At lower elevations, transplant container plants. At the highest elevations, plant either balled-and-burlapped or container-grown shrubs and trees. Plant ground

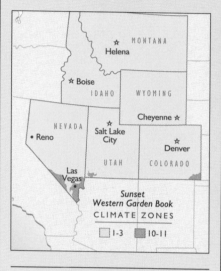

MONTANA
Helena

☆ Boise
IDAHO | WYOMING
Cheyenne ☆
NEVADA | ☆ Salt Lake City
• Reno | Denver ☆
UTAH | COLORADO
Las Vegas
•

Sunset Western Garden Book CLIMATE ZONES

☐ 1-3   ▨ 10-11

covers from flats or cans.

❑ **NATIVE GRASSES.** At month's end, sow blue grama, buffalo grass, and crested wheatgrass. For a quicker cover, plant from plugs or sod.

MAINTENANCE

❑ **LAWNS.** Feed lawns now with nitrogen fertilizer; repeat in four to six weeks. Mow lawns to about 2 inches for bluegrass, fescue, and ryegrass.

❑ **ROSES.** Cut off faded flowers, and fertilize plants. Build soil basins around plants to channel water to the roots.

❑ **FERTILIZE.** If you haven't done so already, apply fertilizer to flower beds and vegetable gardens; water it in thoroughly.

❑ **INDOOR PLANTS.** Fertilize them at least monthly until winter, and pinch

back tip growth to force compactness.

❑ **MULCH.** Spread a 2- to 4-inch-thick layer of organic mulch such as compost, ground bark, leaves, or pine needles around plants. For vegetable plants, use black plastic sheets for the first month to increase warmth around heat-loving crops such as peppers and tomatoes.

❑ **FLOWERING SHRUBS.** After blooms fade from flowering quince, forsythia, lilac, spiraea, and weigela, remove dead and deformed branches, and cut out about a third of the old growth.

❑ **STAKE PLANTS.** Dahlias, delphiniums, gladiolus, tomatoes, and other tall plants should be staked now before they become top-heavy.

❑ **TEND FRUITS.** In all but coldest areas, thin apples, apricots, pears, and plums. Space apricots and most plums 4 to 5 inches apart, apples and pears 6 to 8 inches apart. Cover strawberries with row covers and ripening cherries with bird netting until fruit is ready to pick.

❑ **WATER.** Focus your watering on seedbeds, new plantings, and container plants. Soak established ground covers, shrubs, and trees between rains.

PEST & WEED CONTROL

❑ **CONIFER PESTS.** If mountain pine beetle or Western spruce budworm infests your area, spray pines and spruces with carbaryl. If trees are too tall for you to spray, call in an arborist.

❑ **SOD WEBWORMS.** If brown spots appear in lawns and grass blades pull out easily, check for webworms (look at night with a flashlight). If you find them, spray the infested area and the perimeter with carbaryl on a dry evening.

❑ **WEEDS.** Remove weeds before they go to seed.

SOUTHWEST
CHECKLISTS
JUNE

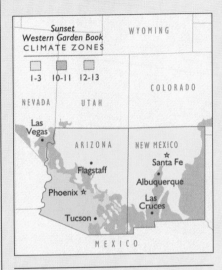

PLANTING & HARVEST

❏ **SUMMER COLOR.** Plant cockscomb, firebush, globe amaranth, Madagascar periwinkle, portulaca, purslane, salvia, starflower, and zinnia early in the month in a place that gets filtered sun in the hottest part of the day.

❏ **PALMS.** Plant or transplant a palm in a hole that's the same depth as the rootball and twice as wide. Tie the fronds up over the bud to protect it. After new growth begins, cut the twine.

❏ **VEGETABLES.** In intermediate and low deserts (zones 12 and 13), you can still plant black-eyed peas, corn, melons, okra, peanuts, sweet potatoes, and yard-long beans. In the high desert (zones 10 and 11), plant corn during the first days of the month, and cucumbers, melons, and summer squash by midmonth.

❏ **HARVEST SUMMER CROPS.** Pick cantaloupe when the skin is well netted and the fruit slips from the vine with little pressure, corn after tassels turn brown and milk comes from popped kernels, eggplant when the skin turns glossy, peppers after they turn color, watermelon when the tendrils closest to the fruit begin to turn brown, new potatoes just after plants flower, and full-size spuds when tops start to die.

❏ **SOW FALL CROPS.** In zones 10 and 11, sow brussels sprouts, cabbage, and carrots anytime this month. Wait until midmonth to sow broccoli and cauliflower. In zones 12 and 13, sow tomato seeds indoors now for transplanting outdoors in late July. Some good varieties include 'Champion', 'Early Girl', 'Heatwave', 'Solar Set', and 'Sunmaster'.

MAINTENANCE

❏ **MOW LAWNS.** Mow Bermuda, St. Augustine, and zoysia 1 to 1½ inches high. Keep hybrid Bermuda grass at about 1 inch.

❏ **MULCH.** Spread a 2- to 4-inch organic or gravel mulch over the root zones of trees, shrubs, vines, flowers, and vegetables.

❏ **TREAT CHLOROSIS.** Plants suffering iron deficiency (chlorosis) develop yellow leaves while veins remain bright green. Correct the condition with iron chelate.

❏ **WATER.** Deep-water plants by flooding or drip irrigation; if you use drip, flood-irrigate monthly to flush salts out of the root zones.

PEST & WEED CONTROL

❏ **BEET LEAFHOPPERS.** These greenish yellow inch-long insects spread curly top virus to cucumber, melon, and tomato plants. Protect crops by covering them with shadecloth. Remove infested plants.

❏ **SPIDER MITES.** If you see mottled leaves and fine webs, blast mites off with a strong jet from the hose, or treat with a miticide.

❏ **SQUASH BORERS.** Look for tiny eggs on squash vines. Rub them off before borers hatch, drill into the vine, and weaken the plant.

❏ **WEEDS.** Hoe or pull young weeds before they go to seed.

TEXAS

PLANTING & HARVEST

❏ **PLANT VEGETABLES.** In North Texas, you can still plant okra through the first few days of June, and cantaloupe, eggplant, pumpkins, and watermelons through midmonth.

❏ **HARVEST HERBS.** For best flavor, pick herbs before flower buds open, and harvest in the morning just after the dew has dried.

❏ **PICK SUMMER CROPS.** Follow the guidelines listed under "Harvest Summer Crops" in the Southwest checklist (above).

MAINTENANCE

❏ **CARE FOR ROSES.** Cut off faded flowers and fertilize plants. Build a soil basin around plants to channel water to the root zone. Then wet the soil, apply fertilizer, and immediately water again.

❏ **PRUNE HEDGES.** Clip a hedge so that its bottom is wider than its top. If you don't, the shade cast by top foliage will make lower growth sparse.

❏ **TREAT CHLOROSIS.** Iron deficiency in plants (called chlorosis) is common in areas with alkaline soil. Affected plants show yellow leaves while veins remain bright green. Treat the problem with iron chelate.

❏ **WATER.** Concentrate your watering on new plantings, annual flowers and vegetables, and container plants. Deep-water your permanent landscape plants regularly.

PEST CONTROL

❏ **SPIDER MITES.** Fine webs and yellow-stippled leaves are signs of spider mites. Blast them off plants with a jet of hose water. Treat serious infestations with insecticidal soap or a miticide.

❏ **SQUASH BUGS.** These sucking insects do the most damage to pumpkins and winter squash. Put a wooden shingle under plants, let bugs gather under it during the heat of the day, then lift up the shingle and destroy the bugs.

At right, light pink, double-flowered 'Jupiter' Hiemalis begonias with upright pink-and-white 'Nancy Lowe' fuchsia and large-leafed 'Silver Queen' Rex begonia create a shimmering arrangement that fills a 24-inch-wide cobalt blue pot. At left, maidenhair fern, lacecap hydrangea, pink polka dot plant, and snow bush (Breynia nivosa) spill out of a 13-inch-wide Italian pot.

Beautiful pots

Pair a great pot with the right plants, and the results will delight you all summer. Here are eight pages of ideas: great plant combinations, handcrafted pots, and potting soil secrets

"I'M THE QUEEN OF STUFFING," SAYS Jean Manocchio of Belli Fiori in Redwood City, California. "You'd be surprised how many plants I can get into a pot."

Manocchio makes a living creating instant gardens in pots. "You can do a lot more with large containers, be much more dramatic than with small pots," she says. "You have a greater variety of plants to choose from—plants with large foliage, shrubs, and trees—plus you can do multilayered plantings."

Manocchio finds that plant-filled big containers are perfect solutions for paved-over areas where plants otherwise wouldn't be able to grow, such as beside a front door, along a broad expanse of paving, or where pavement meets a house or garage wall.

"But the best thing about large containers," says Manocchio, "is that you can change plants and change the look and experiment whenever you want."

Manocchio created the designs shown on these pages. The plants she used, and many other summer show-offs, are available at nurseries now. June is prime time to shop for them, and to create your own garden in a pot in just an hour or two.

CHOOSE YOUR CONTAINER, THEN YOUR COLOR SCHEME

Manocchio suggests choosing the container first, because its shape and size will help determine the kinds of plants you'll choose. "I'm a container nut," says Manocchio. "If I see a pot with a wonderful shape, fabulous glaze, or great feel, I have to have it." She's even lugged huge pots home from overseas trips.

Manocchio considers where the pot will go, and the style of the backdrop. If the house's interior and garden are Asian, she might choose an Asian pot. For a Spanish-style house, she might use one of her favorite containers from Tlaquepaque, Mexico. "Of course, you can always break the rules and choose something avant-garde," she says.

You should decide whether you want to emphasize the plant or the pot, or both. "If the pot is strong in character, you may want to fill it with a simpler plant, such as a camellia or other evergreen." But if the pot is simple, the plants it holds can dominate, with colorful and bold-leafed varieties to carry the show. "Or you can have a little fun and put brightly colored plants in a colorful pot," as shown below. "Those are my Liberace pots," says Manocchio. "Too much is never enough."

With so many plants to choose from, it's tough to know where to start. Manocchio advises choosing a color scheme first. "Sometimes I work off fabric sam-

This arrangement combines nagami kumquat with gold-flowered Becky Mix dwarf gloriosa daisy and Scaevola aemula 'New Blue Wonder' in a 22-inch square concrete container. Below left, hot-colored "Liberace" arrangement contains princess flower, coreopsis, and red-orange dahlias in a 20-inch-wide raku-fired pot.

ples from interior drapery, fabric-covered chairs, and accent pillows. But some of my clients just prefer certain color schemes."

Manocchio avoids the "Barnum & Bailey look"—using too many colors in one pot. She pairs blue with gray because gray makes blue pop out. One of her favorite combinations is gray *Plecostachys serpyllifolia* with lavender-flowered *Limonium perezii* and blue trailing lobelia—"like a silver cloud with blue stars." Other handsome choices in this color range are blue hibiscus, salvias, scaevola, and artemisia.

She also likes combining shades of pink, which she often accents with white or gray. For a pot in the shade, that might mean planting pink fuchsias, begonias, and impatiens with pink polka dot

plant and 'White Nancy' lamium.

Manocchio describes her "neon" look as "less serious and more playful." Plantings combine bold colors, such as orange, purple, red, yellow, and lime green. For example, she combines yellow begonias, bright orange 'Gartenmeister Bonstedt' fuchsia, and orange-red impatiens.

"There are no hard-and-fast rules" when combining colors, Manocchio says. "You can set the mood and create what you feel."

THE PLANTS, AND THE PLANTING

"Large pots always get lots of attention, so you want them to look presentable year-round, even if there's not much flower color," she says. So she first selects a foundation plant—one with foliage that always looks good. Some of her favorites are citrus, flax, *Limonium perezii,* maple, princess flower, and sago palm. But she's always willing to break the rules for a special plant, such as fuchsia, even if it has some downtime. And she avoids plants whose roots take over the pot quickly, such as laurel and Myers asparagus.

Once you have a foliage plant, choose plants whose flowers pick up its colors. Manocchio spends time walking through nurseries and looking for plants. She even hunts for plants in the house plant section. "I carry around leaves and other parts of plants so I can match colors or choose complementary textures." For instance, "there are many shades of green, and not all greens go together. And [New Zealand] flax comes in different shades of pink and salmon."

One word of caution when choosing plants: never mix plants with different water requirements.

Before you plant, put your pot, the plants, and bags of potting soil where you want to display the container permanently (once planted, a big pot is heavy, and difficult to move). For air circulation, Manocchio sets the pot in place, then raises it on clay feet. If she's using drip

'Maori Maiden' New Zealand flax, 'Barbara Karst' bougainvillea, and purple heliotrope in a 20-inch-wide Italian urn. Below, warm colors for shade include yellow abutilon, crotons, and yellow and orange Hiemalis begonias—clustered in an oval 29-inch-long Italian pot.

irrigation, she runs ¼-inch laser tubing up through the hole in the bottom of the pot and allows enough slack so she can run it around the soil surface a couple of times when she's finished planting.

Manocchio partially fills the pot with a mixture of potting soil and well-composted chicken manure, adding just enough of the mixture so that the top of the rootball rests about 2 inches below the pot rim. Then she loosens or scores the foundation plant's roots and sets the plant in the pot, putting its best side forward. She finishes filling the pot with planting mix (only up to the top of the biggest rootball) and fills in the gaps with smaller flowering and foliage plants. Finally, she incorporates a controlled-release fertilizer and gives the planting a thorough watering.

What do you do after a few years, when the foundation plant and some of the fillers have spread out and there's no room for flowers? Manocchio suggests root-pruning the plants and replanting them with new soil, dividing them (which is possible with New Zealand flax and other clumping plants), or starting over.

By Lauren Bonar Swezey

In rear pot above, blue hibiscus rises above Brachycome 'Billabong Sunburst' and variegated agapanthus in an 18-inch-wide Italian pot. In front pot, miniature yellow roses are ringed with catmint in a 17½-inch-wide Italian pot.

Terra-cotta to treasure

Handmade or hand-finished and inspired by ancient designs, these clay pots are shapely and stylish, and they complement plants beautifully

A REBIRTH OF FINELY CRAFTED terra-cotta pottery is changing the look of plant containers. Modern potters, taking their cue from the beautiful hand-hewn pots that were made of terra-cotta (baked earth) thousands of years ago by Etruscan craftsmen and later sculpted of fine Italian clay by Renaissance artists such as Andrea Della Robbia, are turning out pots that are distinctive and durable works of art.

Many of these new pots still come from small villages in Italy, but nurseries and garden shops also sell pieces from craftsmen in England, Greece, Spain, and California.

Unlike mass-produced, utilitarian clay pots, or the low-fired Mexican clay pots that flake apart within a couple of years, these hand-hewn or hand-finished pots are fired at high temperatures and last for years. They come in a range of shapes, from urns to deep bowls.

"Italian terra-cotta from Impruneta [Tuscany] is made by highly skilled artisans whose families have been in the business for generations," says Lenore Rice of Seibert & Rice Fine Italian Terra Cotta. "You can tell they're handmade. Each pot is slightly different, and you can even see fingerprints on some of them."

Depending on where they come from, the pots tend to have signature styles that make them stand out from knockoffs often made in China and Thailand. Pinkish white clay and fine detail are typical of the Impruneta pots. When embellished with flower garlands, fruit clusters, or lions' heads, these pots are especially formal. Classic olive jar shapes, rough-textured finishes, and pale clay are typical of pots from Crete. English terra-cotta pots are usually fairly plain.

The sound and feel of the clay identify a pot's quality. High-fired clay has a ring to it when you tap it with your knuckles, and touching it doesn't leave terra-cotta

Clay pots from around the world include (from top left) Italian circular lemon pot, 7¹/₂ inches tall by 17¹/₂ inches wide; Italian fluted flower pot, 15 inches tall by 20 inches wide; Cretan pot, 10 inches tall by 15 inches wide; California rope pedestal pot, 22¹/₂ inches tall by 16¹/₂ inches wide; Italian urn with glazed interior, 16 inches tall by 20 inches wide; and Cretan urn, 23¹/₂ inches tall by 11¹/₂ inches wide.

ED CAREY

powder on your fingertips. A low-fired pot makes a dull thud when you tap it, and its surface can be easily scratched.

WHY TERRA-COTTA MAKES THE BEST POTS

Unlike plastic or glazed containers, terra-cotta breathes. And roots develop best when they get plenty of oxygen. Soil in a pot that breathes won't stay overly soggy after watering, because the clay absorbs any excess water, which then evaporates.

And since clay is porous, it helps prevent harmful salt buildup around plant roots. Water and fertilizer, which can cause salts to accumulate in the soil around potted plants, migrate out through the container walls.

The terra-cotta containers on this page show a sampling of the many high-quality pots now available. Depending on where you live, you may find other styles and shapes of equal quality.

Italy. Rustic, handmade pot from Impruneta has non-uniform shape. Thick walls are extremely durable and frost resistant. Pot is 14 inches long by 8 inches wide. The Gardener, Berkeley; $46.50.

Crete. Firing in outdoor kilns that burn grape seed (a 4,000-year-old method) gives clay its uneven coloring. Pot is 14 inches tall by 15½ inches wide. Smith & Hawken; $59.

Spain. Pale terra-cotta pots are made in Basque villages; every family makes a different style. Pot is 9 inches tall by 8 inches wide. Smith & Hawken; about $25.

Italy. Formal pot is handmade in Impruneta by an ancient process. Pot is 7 inches tall

ED CAREY

by 10 inches wide. From Seibert & Rice Fine Italian Terra Cotta; $65.

England. Rustic, hand-thrown pot is made from local clay by a potter in Herefordshire. Pot is 7½ inches tall by 7 inches wide. From Kinsman Company; $14.95.

NORMAN A. PLATE

California. Steve Jahnke of Architectural and Fine Art Sculpture in Vallejo, California (wholesale only), incorporates a variety of methods, including a potter's wheel for hand-finishing. His pots are available in nurseries; prices vary.

CHOOSING AND USING THESE NEW POTS

Let the setting inspire your plant choices. Or experiment with different plantings. "Look at the containers and plants with a fresh eye, and accept any combination that's beautiful," says Oakland landscape designer Bob Clark. In a client's formal Italian containers, Clark planted dwarf Alberta spruce trained in upright spirals,

FRED MERTZ

and then he added *Fuchsia procumbens* to drape over the edges. "If you have a gorgeous pot, you don't want the plants to cover it completely."

Use these pots to display favorite plants, or cluster them around the garden. Anne Roth, designer for Roger's Gardens in Corona del Mar, California, suggests putting an empty urn in a rose garden, then planting ground covers at its base. "We also use large containers on either side of a gravel or stone path to define an entry into a garden. If it's a formal entry, we might plant a boxwood hedge beside them."

When Roth clusters pots, she combines ones with different shapes, styles, and sizes, such as pots in 24-inch, 18-inch, and 14-inch widths. It's okay for the pots to be different, but for the best overall effect, they must look good together, says Roth. She likes to cluster pots that fit a theme. In a kitchen garden, for instance, a 24-inch pot might contain a large rosemary with trailing thyme around it; an 18-inch container might show off assorted lettuces; and a 14-inch pot might contain herbs such as parsley, cilantro, and basil.

WHERE TO BUY CLAY POTS BY MAIL
High-quality terra-cotta pots are available at many nurseries and at garden stores and pottery specialists. You can also order them by mail from any of the following sources.

Kinsman Company, Box 357, Point Pleasant, PA 18950; (800) 733-4146. Sells English pots.

Seibert & Rice Fine Italian Terra Cotta, Box 365, Short Hills, NJ 07078; (201) 467-8266. Prices range from $44 to $1,000, plus shipping; catalog $2.

Smith & Hawken; call (800) 776-3336 for a catalog or the name of the store nearest you. Sells pots from Crete by mail, Spanish pots in stores.

By Lauren Bonar Swezey

Potter Steve Jahnke of Vallejo, California, finishes the still-moist edge of a low, ribbed terra-cotta container.

How to shop for the right potting mix
Not all are created equal. Here's a guide to the differences

POTTING MIXES, WIDELY SOLD BY the bag at nurseries and home improvement centers, may seem pretty much the same, whatever the brand. But they're not all alike. Some brands are lightweight and dry out too quickly. Others are overly heavy with sand and tend to compact.

On the bag labels, manufacturers are required to list only the ingredients that make up the bulk of the potting mix but not all of the ingredients or the exact amount of each. They "can put almost anything in a bag, slap a label on it, and call it potting soil," says Peggy Campbell of Molbak's Nursery in Woodinville, Washington.

Products in a mix may or may not be well defined on the label; they're generally listed in descending order according to quantity. These might include Canadian sphagnum peat moss or something called "peat," compost, fir bark or "forest products," sand, perlite, pumice, dolomite limestone, and a wetting agent.

How do you know what you're getting in a bag of potting mix? You don't.

How do you know what combination of ingredients is good for your plants? If you learn how to read the label, you can glean some information from the limited details it provides. Ultimately, though, finding the right mix is largely a matter of trial and error.

WHY NOT USE GARDEN SOIL?
Besides nutrients, plants need air and water to grow. The soil also has to drain well. When plants grow in the ground, gravity pulls water down through the soil to drain away (assuming other factors, such as hardpan, aren't limiting the soil's drainage). Containers are too shallow for gravity to affect drainage, so you have to create good drainage by combining ingredients of the right particle size—the kinds that exist in good potting mixes.

PEAT MOSS AND GROUND BARK
Canadian sphagnum peat moss and fir or redwood bark are widely used in potting mixes. (If the label says just "peat moss," be wary; the bag could contain Michigan or Delta peat, neither of which has good air-holding capacity.) Which is better, bark or sphagnum peat moss?

Sphagnum peat moss "is consistent, so you know what to expect," says Virginia Walter, horticulture professor at Cal Poly San Luis Obispo. She prefers it to forest products such as ground bark. "It's durable (doesn't break down as fast as forest products), and it has a high water-holding capacity plus very good aeration." That means that even if the planting medium is wet, air is still available to roots. On the downside, it's more expensive and, if it dries out, difficult to rewet.

Forest products are less expensive, so the potting mix they're in will be less expensive. But because these wood products break down faster than peat moss, the mix eventually compacts, limiting aeration. That's why mixes should also contain perlite or pumice.

The best bark for potting mixes is composted. If the product is too fresh, it could be high in tannins (toxic substances). And since wood products use up nitrogen as they break down, this element will be depleted from the mix. Some manufacturers try to compensate for the poorly composted wood product by adding too much nitrogen, but the excess nitrogen results in a high salt content, which can burn roots of sensitive plants.

COMPOST
Many labels do not list the kind of compost the bags contain. The compost could be made from almost anything. Other labels do spell out the kind of compost, such as "composted fir bark and sawdust," for example. But the kind of compost used may not be the best. Mushroom compost, for example, is often high in soluble salts and can be potentially harmful to sensitive plants.

PUMICE, PERLITE, AND SAND
These ingredients add airspace and improve drainage in potting mixes. Perlite and pumice are lightweight materials derived from volcanic glass. Both hold water and, unlike sand, are sterile. Perlite is more expensive than pumice or sand.

The best mixes contain 10 to 15 percent perlite or pumice.

Sand is widely used in some mixes, mainly because it's cheap. It doesn't hold water, it's heavy, and, if it's rounded and too fine-grained (like table salt or fine sugar), it can clog airspace and hinder drainage. Mined sand, which is coarser and sharper-edged, is preferable.

LIMESTONE, PH, AND FERTILIZER

Potting mixes that contain peat moss are acidic, usually with a pH of 4 (the optimum range for potting mixes is 5.5 to 6.5), so manufacturers add limestone (dolomite is preferable) to the soil to raise the pH. Some bags list this ingredient; others don't. Salt content and pH can vary.

Most manufacturers don't list nutrient analyses on labels because doing so would bring them under fertilizer label laws. Some do, but nutrient amounts may be insignificant.

MISCELLANEOUS ADDITIVES

Organic potting soils sometimes include earthworm castings, which add nutrients to the mix. When combined with ingredients such as peat moss, they're beneficial. But too many castings can turn a mix into something resembling a block of concrete when water is added.

Because soil mixes containing peat moss can be very difficult to moisten, especially if they dry out, some manufacturers add wetting agents to help the peat moss absorb moisture. If a wetting agent is listed on the label, that's a good sign.

Soil polymers (water-absorbing gels that supply water to plant roots) are sometimes added. For people who water spottily, they can be a bonus.

Some products contain sewage sludge, sometimes called biosolids, which can be tainted with heavy metals. Avoid using them when growing vegetables.

WHAT TO LOOK FOR

Choose a mix whose label specifically identifies the products inside. If the bag says just "peat," "forest products," or "compost," you may want to avoid it.

Be wary of inexpensive brands. Labels may promise sphagnum peat moss, for example, but contain only minuscule amounts.

HOW TO USE SOIL MIX

Take these steps to make your mix the best possible medium for your plants.

1. Flush the soil with water once or twice before planting. Nitrogen and salt levels may be high, and this practice minimizes the chances of the mix burning your plants, according to Gregg Kitagawa of Soil and Plant Laboratory in Santa Clara, California.

2. Follow the label's recommendation for fertilizing (if there is one). Some labels recommend that you add no fertilizer for a certain length of time. Check out your plants (lush, green, healthy foliage generally means plants have plenty of nutrients), and fertilize when necessary.

3. Keep unused mix moist. Store the bag closed. If mix dries out and is difficult to wet, add a drop or two of mild dishwashing soap to a gallon of water, and soak mix thoroughly. The soap breaks the surface tension and helps rewet the mix. ∎

By Lauren Bonar Swezey

Sampling of potting mixes available by the bag includes **1.** *Black Magic Potting Soil: forest products, perlite.* **2.** *Sunshine All-Purpose Potting Mix: Canadian sphagnum peat moss, perlite, composted bark, dolomitic limestone, wetting agent.* **3.** *Supersoil Potting Mix: forest products, including fir bark and redwood, Canadian sphagnum peat moss, pure sand.* **4.** *VitaHume Potting Soil: forest products, compost, sand, perlite.* **5.** *GreenAll Organic Potting Soil: fir bark, Canadian sphagnum peat moss, and other organic materials, including earthworm castings.*

Thymes in this large pot include (clockwise from top left) lemon, orange balsam, caraway-scented, and oregano.

Thyme to plant, thyme to spare

They're favorite herbs for cooking. Grow one, or grow a bunch

GOOD COOKS NEVER WIND UP with too much thyme on their hands. Subtle, versatile, and nearly impossible to misuse, thyme is the most frequently snipped herb in the garden. And now, more varieties are available to snip, including such off-beat varieties as caraway-scented and orange balsam. "Use it a little, use it a lot, use it on everything," urges Kate Jayne of Sandy Mush Herb Nursery. "You won't use it wrong. I can't think of a solitary reason not to have a half-dozen varieties."

Neither can we—especially since the small-leafed, compact plants are as adaptable in the garden as in the kitchen. Upright types (6 to 12 inches tall) make splendid edging plants. Creeping forms (2 to 3 inches tall) are wonderful between paving stones, where the pressure of footsteps releases their herbal scents. And all varieties look handsome in containers.

Here are some of the favorite thymes of kitchen gardeners.

THE CLASSICS
Common thyme (*Thymus vulgaris*), sometimes sold as English thyme, is the basic culinary thyme—the one you reach for to spice a soup, stew, or pot roast. The French form has a similar flavor, but its leaves are narrower and grayer and the plant doesn't grow as wide. "French is more complex and perfumy," says Rose Marie Nichols McGee of Nichols Garden Nursery. "But English is a more robust grower, so I like to have it on hand as a backup."

Silver thyme (*T. v.* 'Argenteus') is similar to common thyme in flavor, but gray foliage with cream edges gives it a silvery appearance.

THE CITRUS-FLAVORED
Lemon thyme (*T. citriodorus*) is favored for its lemon-scented leaves. Many varieties are available, including golden and silver-edged types and upright and creeping habits. Use it to enhance lemon juice or as a lemon substitute. Good with meat, chicken, fish, eggs, vegetables, green and fruit salads, and salad dressings.

Orange balsam thyme (*T. vulgaris* 'Orange Balsam') is an upright grower (to 6 inches) with tiny gray-green leaves. Sweeter than most thymes, with a slightly smoky overtone, it's good with fish or pork, and particularly well suited to fruit salads. "Wonderful with sliced oranges and red onions," suggests food and garden writer Carole Saville. "Try it with mango, pineapple, guava—anything tropical," says Sylvia Thompson, another food and garden writer, "or in a cold fruit soup, like cantaloupe."

THE ROBUST
Caraway-scented thyme (*T. herbabarona*) forms a low mat about 4 inches tall with shiny dark green leaves on reddish stems; pink flowers bloom in spring. It's the traditional seasoning for roast beef, but is also good with any meat dish, says McGee. She recommends wrapping stems around shish kebab before grilling. Because it's also good with root vegetables and cabbage, Saville suggests trying it on slaws. "Good in beet or cabbage soup, too," says Thompson. "Or on cottage cheese."

Oregano thyme (*T. pulegioides* 'Oregano-scented') is a vigorous, mounding plant that grows 12 to 18 inches tall. Large, oval, dark green leaves have the distinct aroma and flavor of oregano, making this herb a natural flavoring for tomato-based pasta sauces and sliced fresh tomatoes, and for rice, bulgur, and other starches. "Try it with chopped parsley and butter over cooked potatoes," says Jayne.

HOW TO GROW THYME
Few herbs are easier to grow than thyme. All it needs is average garden soil—preferably amended with compost—and occasional irrigation. Shear plants back once a year after flowering to keep them from getting woody in the center.

The essential oils that give thyme leaves their flavor will be more concentrated if you never allow your plants to flower. But if there are gardeners steel-hearted enough to lop off those sweet lavender blossoms so beloved by bees, Thompson doesn't want to meet them. "That's cutting off your nose to spite your face," she says. "Just harvest more leaves." And allow yourself a little more thyme.

WHERE TO BUY THYME
These sources offer thymes by mail.

Cherub Farms, 6382 Cooper St., Felton, CA 95018; (408) 335-7090; 12 culinary varieties of thyme. Catalog $2 (refundable with first order).

Nichols Garden Nursery, 1190 N. Pacific Highway, Albany, OR 97321; (541) 928-9280; 8 culinary varieties. Catalog free.

Sandy Mush Herb Nursery, 316 Surrett Cove Rd., Leicester, NC 28748; (704) 683-2014; 16 culinary varieties. Catalog $4. ■

By Sharon Cohoon

Zinnias, cosmos, black-eyed Susans, purple coneflowers, red geraniums, and cut sunflowers pack a garden nook near Tillamook, Oregon. For details on this colorful entry garden, see page 172.

ALLAN MANDELL

168

JULY

Garden guide.........................170

Garden notebooks....................175

Garden checklists....................177

Fresh-flower wreaths 182

A garden for the senses.............186

Stewartias crown the garden........188

Landscaping, South African-style ..189

Terrorists in your tomato patch 190

A nectar bar for butterflies 191

Mendocino's little-known jewel

Northern California's Mendocino coast may be better known for its beautiful views, gorgeous beaches, and wonderful hotels (such as historic Little River Inn) than for its plants. But for gardeners, this splendid stretch of coast offers one more good reason to visit: the Mendocino Coast Botanical Garden.

Located at the southern end of Fort Bragg (18220 N. Highway 1), the 47-acre botanical garden is a plant lover's jewel set among native coastal woodlands and coastal bluffs, all against a backdrop of incredible views.

The garden was founded in 1961 by a retired nurseryman. In 1992, the Mendocino Coast Recreation and Park District bought the property, which is now supported with the help of volunteers.

The front half of the botanical garden contains 20 plant collections, including a heritage rose garden filled with old-fashioned roses adapted to coastal conditions, a perennial and dwarf conifer collection, a camellia and lily collection, ornamental grasses, fuchsias, and hundreds of rhododendrons. The heather collection is in peak bloom in July.

As you walk west along the trails, the plant collections fade into a cool, shady pine forest underplanted with ferns, rhododendrons, azaleas, and native ground covers. The soothing sound of

NORMAN A. PLATE

Deep blue agapanthus edges the path near the garden's conifer section.

running water from two creeks is always close at hand. The trails eventually deposit visitors onto a coastal bluff where they can view wildflowers and, on clear days, the Fort Bragg coastline.

The two main trails are wheelchair-accessible. Picnickers are welcome. Summer hours are 9 to 5 daily. Admission costs $5, $4 for seniors, $1 for ages 6 through 12. Call (707) 964-4352.

A border that matches the bridal bouquet

Oakland, California–based landscape designer Bob Clark, whose specialty is garden color, knew exactly what was needed for a backdrop when he took on the challenge of readying Colleen and Julian Willke's garden for a September wedding: annuals and perennials that put on their best show in late summer and fall.

The flower colors had to be compatible with the soft pink 'Bonica' roses the bride planned to carry in the wedding. Clark settled on a border of pastel blues, corals, pinks, and purples. He also wanted the border to be massive, so he chose some tall plants for the back.

Salvia guaranitica 'Purple Majesty', which reaches 5 feet, grows in the rear. In front, Clark planted coral *S. coccinea* 'Brenthurst', blue-flowered *S. patens,* and cleome in shades of pink. At their feet, he added pink and white petunias and white sweet alyssum.

The plants were set out in early sum-

DAVID DUNCAN LIVINGSTON

Cleome in pink and white rises behind coral *Salvia coccinea* 'Brenthurst'; white sweet alyssum edges the border.

mer in well-drained and well-amended soil. Clark planted most of them from containers, but the cleome reseeded itself from previous year's planting. All of the plants were watered often and fertilized every two weeks to get them established. By late summer, watering was cut back to once a week. The border bloomed from midsummer through October.

A bluer agapanthus is storming the West

Lily-of-the-Nile (*Agapanthus orientalis*) is nearly perfect, producing big, showy clusters of sky blue flowers summer through fall. And it does so whether given a full day's sun or just a few hours, fluffy loam or heavy clay soil, lots of water or (once established) virtually none. About the only way to improve this plant would be to find a way to make its flowers a shade or two darker. Saratoga Horticultural Research Foundation has been working on that, and 'Storm Cloud' is the result.

JAMIE HADLEY

'Storm Cloud' agapanthus has showy, deep blue clusters.

'Storm Cloud'—a vigorous cross between deciduous 'Mood Indigo' and an evergreen agapanthus—produces flowers in a beautiful new shade of deep violet-blue. Otherwise, the hybrid has all the virtues of its paler blue parent, 'Mood Indigo'. 'Storm Cloud' should be available at nurseries this month. If you can't find it, ask your nursery to order it for you. (One wholesale supplier is Monterey Bay Nursery.)

Saratoga Horticultural Research Foundation, a nonprofit organization, depends on private contributions to fund its research. If you'd like to help support its efforts, call (408) 779-3303 or write to the foundation at 15185 Murphy Ave., San Martin, CA 95046.

High times in the backyard "pond-erosa"

John Jung spent many happy hours dipping into ponds looking for pollywogs when he was a boy. He hasn't changed much since then, taking every opportunity he gets to check out some body of water. Opportunity for that has just moved closer. Now all Jung has to do is walk outside his back door in Downey California, and 20,000 gallons of pond water greet him. Ponds of all sorts—above and below ground level—now take up much of his backyard. He has just enough dry land left to walk between them. Shirley, Jung's wife, calls the watery expanse that used to be their back lawn the "pond-erosa."

A single water lily, a present from Shirley 28 years ago, was the impetus for the first pond. More plants and ponds soon followed.

"Water gardening is the most fascinating hobby," says Jung. "It's intriguing, relaxing, and, best of all, easy." Jung now grows hundreds of water lilies, both hardy and tropical, day- and night-blooming, in a wide range of colors.

There is more to water gardening than flora, though, says Jung. The fauna associated with it has its appeal, too. Goldfish add color and movement to the ponds, and gobble up mosquito larvae. Bullfrogs provide summer serenades. ("How often do you hear those in the city?" Jung asks.) Even aquatic snails, dragonflies, and whirligigs have their own charm.

GREY CRAWFORD

Knee-deep in pond water, John Jung of Downey inspects his water lilies.

Ponds are especially cooling to look at during summer. Even if you don't have enough space for a "pond-erosa" in your backyard, a small pond with a few water plants can have much the same effect. Just about anything can hold water and pond plants—even a large ceramic pot without a drain hole.

"Add a pond to a garden," says Jung, "and you add life."

An entry garden, brimming with blooms

When guests arrive at Linda Terhark and Jerry Miesen's house near Tillamook, Oregon, they're welcomed into an entry garden filled to the brim with blooms (see photo on page 166). The couple's garden demonstrates the diversity of summer-flowering plants it's possible to pack into a relatively small space: in this case, a 15- by 25-foot area.

The owners started by removing the rocky native soil and replacing it with a load of rich topsoil, aged manure, and compost. They built a handsome shingled wall, not only for privacy but also to shield plants from the stiff wind that blows in off the ocean. After laying a stone path, they began to plant perennials.

To pack in as much color as possible, the couple chose plants with a long bloom season and beautiful foliage, including delphinium, eryngium, lychnis, monarda, phlox, rudbeckia, salvia, and verbena. They placed the plants according to height, with tall ones at the back near the walls, shorter plants in the middle, and low-growing ones near the path.

With the perennials in place, the own-

ers filled in the gaps with annuals, including African daisies, cosmos, impatiens, marigolds, snapdragons, sunflowers, and zinnias. The mix of annual and perennial flowers ensures a steady procession of colorful blooms starting in early spring and continuing well into autumn.

Terhark and Miesen devote a couple of hours a week to maintaining their densely planted garden. They use a watering wand for ground-level irrigation; by keeping water off the foliage, they reduce the threat of powdery mildew. They scatter a complete granular fertilizer around the plants once a month from April to October, and they snip off blooms as they fade.

Spend quality time with spring bloomers

If you want spring-flowering shrubs to bloom their best next year, now is the time to give azaleas, rhododendrons, camellias, pieris, and lilacs a little extra attention. If you didn't prune while plants were in bloom, shape them now. Prune from the bottom up, from the inside out, and *when in doubt, don't.* Weed around the shrubs. Water them well, then scatter a complete granular fertilizer around the base of the plants and water it in thoroughly. Then spread a layer of organic mulch over the root zones of plants.

Protect potted plants while you're on vacation

Outdoor container plants dry out fast in warm summer weather, especially when the containers are made from clay. When you go on vacation, you can help your potted plants retain moisture by sinking the containers into soil up to their rims. This also keeps them from blowing over. Put them in a shady spot, but still tell your stand-in irrigator to give them special attention—thirsty roots can pull all the available water out of a small amount of soil in very little time. A mulch over the potting soil also helps hold in moisture.

Flexible plant stakes

Among many types of plant stakes now available for tall perennials are Y-Stakes. Designed in England, they're made of brown coated aluminum tubing with two galvanized wire arms emerging from the tops. The arms can be bent into various positions—a single arm to embrace a flopping gladiolus stem, for instance, or the arms of two stakes placed on opposite sides of a bush to encircle and support it.

Y-Stakes are available in 1-, 2-, 3-, and 4-foot heights from Garden Works, 1551 127th Place N.E., Bellevue, WA 98005; (206) 455-0568. Cost ranges from $2.70 for a 1-foot stake to $5.40 for a 4-foot stake, plus shipping.

Santolina flaunts silver leaves, golden blooms

With its mounds of sterling silver foliage, santolina (*S. chamaecyparissus*) can really brighten up a garden. This month, the silver mounds will be plated with gold as hundreds of bright yellow buttonlike flower heads cover santolina. This plant forms a mound up to 2 feet tall with an equal spread. *S. c.* 'Nana', a smaller cultivated variety, seldom exceeds a foot in height but sprawls out 2 to 3 feet.

Santolina takes any soil and full sun. It can be grown in all Western climate zones. In the coldest-winter areas (*Sunset* climate zones 1, 2, and 3), plants may die back to the ground, but the roots will live on to resume growth in the spring. In the landscape, santolina can be used as a ground cover or as an accent plant to edge garden paths.

Look for blooming plants in 1-gallon cans this month. You can put them in the ground immediately. Water them well through the summer. Once plants are established, they are quite drought tolerant.

After the blooms turn brown with age, shear the plant lightly, removing the spent flower buttons and nipping back the foliage. The plant will soon send out new growth. In mild-winter areas, where foliage stays on all year, cut plants back hard in early spring to rejuvenate them.

Like artemisia and lavender, santolina is not long-lived and it gets woody with age. When plants start looking ratty, pull and replace them.

MICHAEL S. THOMPSON

Like shiny gold buttons, the flower heads of *Santolina chamaecyparissus* glow above silver foliage.

Cauliflower goes green

Mark Twain once wrote that "cauliflower is nothing but cabbage with a college education." Indeed, cabbage, cauliflower, broccoli, and brussels sprouts are closely related. Moreover, new breeds of cauliflower are turning broccoli green with envy.

Here are two kinds of green cauliflower you can plant this summer for fall harvest.

'Alverda' is a bright green cauliflower that's mild-flavored and tender. It goes from seed to harvest in about 80 days.

'Brocoverde' is a sweet cauliflower that resists bolting in warm weather. The heads average about 14 ounces each and reach full maturity about 70 days after being transplanted into the ground.

Some nurseries sell plants of green cauliflower, but it may be easier to find seed from mail-order suppliers. 'Alverda' is available from Harris Seeds (800/514-4441) and Territorial Seed Co. (541/942-9547). 'Brocoverde' is available from J. W. Jung Seed Co. (800/247-5864) and Otis S. Twilley Seed Co. (800/622-7333).

ELECTRONIC GARDENING
Virtual Garden news

Already the most heavily used garden site on the Internet, The Virtual Garden (*http://vg.com*) has a new look and even more information this month. Produced by Time Warner, The Virtual Garden will allow users to electronically test-drive the *Sunset Western Garden Book,* as well as connect to *Sunset*'s new, searchable *Problem Solver,* a guide to help answer questions about plant diseases, pests, and other horticultural problems.

The Virtual Garden also includes links to *Sunset* and *Southern Living* magazines. You can read on-line versions of garden articles from these publications.

IRRIGATION TIP

An oscillating sprinkler with adjustable coverage

Hose-end sprinklers are cheap and easy alternatives to built-in sprinkler systems. But until now, you were lucky if you could find a sprinkler whose watering pattern matched the shape of the area you needed to water.

A new oscillating sprinkler from L. R. Nelson lets you adjust the coverage area, from a rectangle to an almost square plot of land.

The sprinkler doesn't allow water to puddle at the ends of each cycle, so you get even distribution. And some models come with built-in timers that shut off the sprinkler after it has dispensed a preset volume of water.

You can find these sprinklers at garden centers for $20 to $35 each. To find a retailer near you, call (800) 635-7668.

Dial near hose end sets sprinkling time.

NORMAN A. PLATE

GARDEN STRUCTURES
A raised bed with all the options

Raised-bed gardening can solve many problems, as Kelman and Kirsten Acres found when they designed and built this big wooden box next to the patio, where the Acreses sometimes dine on summer days. "It's great for growing flowers and vegetables." And since the box is raised, "it keeps our puppy out of the plants," says Kirsten.

The rectangular box, measuring 5 feet wide by 10 feet long by 2 feet tall, is made of cedar, which will age to gray to match the gray flagstone patio. On the side nearest the patio, a 12-inch by 10-foot plank nailed to the box's top edge doubles as a garden bench and a place to display small pots. On the opposite side, two lattice panels mounted to a frame of cedar 4-by-4s form a privacy screen that turns leafy as crops such as pole beans and snow peas scramble over it.

JOHN RIZZO

A bench, a place for growing vegetables, and a privacy screen—this raised bed has it all.

Summer crops, which the Acreses grow mostly from seed, include carrots, green peppers, radishes, romaine lettuce, spinach, and tomatoes, with a few colorful annuals such as marigolds and calendulas.

SUMMER READING
Do you know where a really big tree grows?

Native trees identified with particular Western states seem to have the curious habit of growing even bigger on "foreign" soil. Arizona, for example, has the biggest New Mexico locust. New Mexico has the biggest Arizona sycamore. And Texas, as you might expect, has the biggest Mexican plum.

These are some of the surprising entries you'll find in the *1996–97 National Register of Big Trees* (American Forests, Washington, DC, 1996; $7.95), which lists the largest tree of every species in the United States. Although the focus of the publication is on natives, the register includes naturalized trees as well.

The list changes every day as former champs die off and new candidates are nominated by the public. In the last two years, 198 new champs made the list.

Colorado has its champion ash, cottonwood, and pines; Idaho its hawthorns, maples, and willows; Montana its larch; Utah its conifers; and Nevada the biggest turbinella oak. There are several species without champions: Coulter pine, Western honey mesquite, Siberian elm, and a whole slew of willows.

The *1996–97 National Register of Big Trees* is also part of the winter issue of *American Forests* magazine, which comes with a $30 membership in American Forests, a tree conservation group. You can get a single copy and a brochure telling how to nominate big trees by sending $7.95 to American Forests, Box 2000, Washington, DC 20013.

By Sharon Cohoon, Steven R. Lorton,Jim McCausland, Lauren Bonar Swezey

PACIFIC NORTHWEST
Garden Notebook

BY STEVEN R. LORTON

Put on the Pavarotti. Uncork the Chianti. It's garlic harvest time. I plant garlic in my Skagit Valley garden in November, let it grow through winter and spring, and harvest the bulbs in July. I learned a good trick from Ron Engeland, who grows garlic organically in the Okanogan Valley: don't wait to harvest until the leaves have totally yellowed—pull the garlic when 60 percent of the leaves are still green. This preserves the tissuelike protective wrappers around the cloves. After pulling the garlic bulbs, gently knock off as much soil as possible, then hang clumps of 5 to 10 bulbs by their leaves out of direct sunlight and where air can circulate around them. In about a month, trim the leaves off the bulbs and use the garlic immediately. Ron has written an excellent book, *Growing Great Garlic*. For a copy, send $14.95 to Filaree Farm, 182 Conconully Highway, Okanogan, WA 98840. For a catalog that lists more than 100 varieties of garlic, send an additional $2.

•

I like to hang potted plants on my porch. Unfortunately, hanging plants dry out quickly, and since my family and I travel often, we're not always able to water them every day. So we keep a nearby plastic garbage can filled with water. One by one, we suspend each plant over the can by a long chain hung on an S-hook, completely submerging the soil. We let the plant hang in the water for a couple of hours, sometimes overnight. Because the soil is soaking wet when the plant emerges, we let the runoff water drip back into the garbage can. When the plant stops dripping, we re-hang it on the porch. This deep drenching keeps the soil moist for a few days, and we haven't lost a hanging plant yet.

•

Want to locate a source for hard-to-find native plants, or need some guidance to navigate through horticultural cyberspace? Check out the 1996 addendum to *The Northwest Gardeners' Resource Directory*, an indispensable reference compiled by Stephanie Feeney. To order the directory and the addendum, send $28.25 to Cedarcroft Press, 59 Strawberry Point, Bellingham, WA 98226; (360) 733-4461.

THAT'S A GOOD QUESTION

Q: With greater demands on our water supply, how do you keep a lawn green all summer?

A: I don't even try. I've come to think of summer as the dormant season for grass, so I stop watering it and let it go brown. Since I live on the moist west side of the Cascades, my grass seldom gets fried to a crisp, and when the autumn rains come, it greens up almost overnight. If you live east of the Cascades, where heat and sun can be relentless for the next three months, you may want to irrigate your lawn once a week, if local water-use ordinances permit. Do it in the evening so the water has all night to soak into the soil.

NORTHERN CALIFORNIA
Garden Notebook

BY LAUREN BONAR SWEZEY

I heard some surprising news the other day about mushroom compost, which is sometimes found in potting mixes. This widely used soil amendment has its limitations, which probably explains why the plants in my newly renovated front yard had such difficulty getting established a couple of years ago. In a word: salts.

Mushroom compost doesn't actually contain mushrooms. Composed of horse manure, chicken manure, straw, sphagnum peat moss, and cottonseed meal, it was formulated as a growing medium for mushrooms.

Gregg Kitagawa of the Soil and Plant Laboratory in Santa Clara, California, explains the saltiness this way: animal manure in mushroom compost is a good source of nitrogen and potassium, but the material is considered "hot." When applied at typical rates, the salts from the high levels of nitrogen and potassium can burn leaf edges and shut down root growth, which can stunt plants.

Kitagawa suggests adding only 10 to 15 percent by volume—or 1 part mushroom compost to 9 parts soil—to the soil instead of the typical 1 to 2 ratio (1 part amendment to 2 parts soil) recommended for other amendments, such as redwood soil conditioner and peat moss. Kitagawa recommends using something like redwood or peat at a ratio of 1 to 3 if you need additional amendments.

•

Monterey Bay gardeners take note: there's a new book out just for you called *The Gardener's Resource Guide for the Monterey Bay*, by Steve McGuirk and Richard Merrill (Two Bays Horticultural Communications, Soquel, CA, 1995; $9.95, plus shipping; call 408/462-9981). The book, available at Monterey-area bookstores and garden centers, is chock-full of information about the area's climate, planting calendar, public gardens, tours, shows, and retail garden stores. It also lists mail-order suppliers around the country.

THAT'S A GOOD QUESTION

Q: For the past two years our plants have been beleaguered by whiteflies. We do a thorough winter cleanup and spray dormant oil, and then use malathion and/or a systemic insecticide on the insects. Any suggesstion that will help us better control these pests?

A: Whiteflies can be difficult to control because they quickly build up resistance to most insecticides. At the same time, the insecticides kill the whiteflies' natural enemies. Also, whiteflies spend most of their time on the undersides of leaves, so they can be difficult to reach with sprays. To keep their numbers in check, try a balanced approach. First, hose off the infested plants, hitting both sides of all leaves to wash off and destroy immature crawlers (nymphs). Do this every few days. Second, spray insecticidal soap, making sure to completely cover the leaves, including undersides. Insecticidal soap is less harmful to the whiteflies' natural enemies than conventional insecticides. Third, install yellow sticky traps around the garden to attract and trap the adult whiteflies. Use one trap for every two large plants. You can either buy the traps at a nursery or make them by cutting 1/4-inch plywood into 6- by 6-inch pieces, painting them yellow, and mounting them on pointed wooden stakes. Cover the boards with a sticky substance such as Tanglefoot, and place each trap so the sticky side faces the plant (but is out of direct sun). Clean the traps regularly. Avoid spraying toxic chemicals. Finally, clean up garden debris around the plants in fall and apply a dormant spray to plants in winter.

SOUTHERN CALIFORNIA
Garden Notebook

BY SHARON COHOON

This is the story of Murray, Moody Mary, and Clyde. The three praying mantids hatched out of an egg case at Heard's Country Gardens in Westminster last spring, liked what they saw, and decided to stay. Murray, the boldest, chose the top of a clump of feverfew as his hangout. Moody Mary hid out under the blossoms of a Shasta daisy. And constant Clyde stuck to the scabiosa. Life was good. Nursery staff took them for pleasure cruises on their shoulders and hand-fed them cabbage moths and other fine things. A great place for youngsters, the trio decided, and left lots of egg cases in shrubs and vines before they departed.

Now, praying mantids may not be the best choice for pest control. Their appetites are delicate compared to those of ladybug beetles, and they dine on good as well as bad bugs. But having met Heard's mascot mantids, I can fully understand why you'd give these amusing creatures names and treat them like pets. They eat some insect pests, and keeping the mantids looks like fun. Their size—up to 5 inches long—and their territorial ways make them easy to spot and track, says Mary Lou Heard. "Watching them grow up is great entertainment."

Summer gardens have an ample supply of insects to feed praying mantids. Nurseries often stock egg cases. You can also order them from Unique Insect Control at (916) 961-7945. Thread a string through the top of the case and hang it from the branch of a shrub several feet off the ground. The emerging mantids will crawl up the string, spread through the shrub, and disperse through the garden.

•

Speaking of insects, if you have mystery critters in your yard and want a good identification manual, take a look at *Insects of the Los Angeles Basin*. With excellent color photos and black-and-white illustrations, and a clear but comprehensive text, it's a surprisingly entertaining read. Published by the Natural History Museum of Los Angeles County, the book is available at the museum bookstore for $27.95. Call (213) 744-3434 to order by mail. There will be a shipping charge.

THAT'S A GOOD QUESTION

Q: "Why do nepeta [catmint] and achillea [yarrow] split in the middle, and what should I do about it?"

A: Many Mediterranean perennials share this habit. In the wild, side branches that were fanning out would root when they touched the ground, forming new plants that would live on independently when the older parent plant died. To discourage splitting, says Los Angeles garden designer Cheryl Lerner, shear plants back sharply after bloom to lessen branch weight and encourage fresh center growth. Cut nepeta back to 4 inches at least three times a year. "Pick it up the way you would a ponytail and just lop it off," Lerner says. Shear yarrow back to 6 inches after bloom.

INLAND WESTERN STATES
Garden Notebook

BY JIM McCAUSLAND

The dog days of summer are named for Sirius the Dog Star, which chases the sun across the southern sky during the hottest days of summer. But when I think of dog days, I think of our family dog, Stormy, who lies panting in the shade of a big pine tree. Pruned high, the pine casts dappled shade that not only soothes the dog's fevered brow but also shelters a patch of lettuce, slowing its tendency to bolt (go to seed) until I can harvest the last of the leaves.

•

Because plants grow so fast in July, anything wrapped around them can restrict their growth and act as a tourniquet. I go around checking plant tags and stakes, and loosening them when necessary. As tomato vines thicken up, for example, they can strangle themselves on the twist-ties connecting them to name tags and stakes. It's better to have things a little too loose than too tight.

•

When I first started gardening, I saw my lawn as an ocean and my flower beds as islands. I was well on my way to making a whole archipelago (I liked the idea of having less grass to mow) when I realized that every island has its shoreline, and every shoreline needs edging. My new islands cost me more time in edging than I'd previously spent mowing. So I altered my landscaping to create more continents and fewer islands, giving me less to mow *and* less to edge. It makes for a less demanding gardening world.

•

Sold on the idea of raised-bed gardening, but without a square foot of empty ground to her name, *Sunset* reader Maya Conn asked whether she could build a raised bed on a brick patio.

Building a raised bed atop a solid surface like bricks or concrete is certainly possible, but I've found there is a far simpler, less messy solution. I bought four half-barrels and filled them with potting mix. I planted potatoes in one, tomatoes in another, zucchini in the third, and lettuce, carrots, and radishes in the last one.

It helps to put the barrels on casters so you can roll them where you want them. And it makes the most sense to use determinate tomatoes, since their growth is limited, and bush-type zucchini that grow well in a confined space.

I've also succeeded in growing lettuce in a window box that I made from a 6-foot section of rain gutter from a hardware store. I just filled it with potting mix, planted the seedlings, and fertilized and watered until I got a salad crop.

THAT'S A GOOD QUESTION

Q: Should I harvest my bell peppers when they're green, or should I wait until they turn color?

A: Like many vegetables, most kinds of peppers change color as they ripen. You can, of course, pick and eat them green, but they're a little sweeter and usually more attractive when they color up. Depending on variety, bell peppers can turn yellow, orange, red, purple, or a combination of colors (including green) when they mature.

PLANTING

❏ **ANNUALS.** There's still time to get summer annuals into beds and containers for a long run of seasonal bloom. Buy plants in sixpacks or 4-inch pots and set them out immediately.

❏ **CROPS.** You can still direct-sow seeds of beets, broccoli, bush beans, carrots, chard, Chinese cabbage, kohlrabi, lettuce, peas, radishes, scallions, spinach, and turnips.

❏ **SHRUBS.** Because of summer heat and drought, July and August are probably the worst times to plant shrubs. But if you find a plant you just have to have, it's probably safer in the ground than it is in a nursery container. Dig a planting hole, enrich it with organic matter, fill the hole several times with water, and let it soak in. Plant the shrub and water again. Then spread organic mulch around the root zone of the plant, but don't pile it against the trunk.

❏ **SHOP FOR BULBS.** Catalogs offering spring-blooming bulbs for fall planting will start arriving soon. Order early for the best selection.

MAINTENANCE

❏ **CARE FOR GROUND COVERS.** After they bloom, shear plants back to keep them compact. Scatter a complete granular fertilizer over the beds and water it in well.

❏ **FEED CHRYSANTHEMUMS.** To ensure a bumper crop of flowers this autumn, fertilize chrysanthemums every three weeks until the buds begin

Sunset
CLIMATE ZONES
❏ 1-3 ▨ 4-7

to show color. Once bloom starts, feed plants weekly.

❏ **GROOM STRAWBERRIES.** Clean out dead leaves and stems. Fertilize and water plants thoroughly.

❏ **MANAGE THE COMPOST PILE.** In hot weather, the compost is more active than ever. Keep piling on the organic matter, turn the pile, and if it's dry, add water to keep it moist.

❏ **MULCH SHRUBS.** One good way to conserve water is to mulch heavily. Spread a 3- to 4-inch layer of organic mulch over shrubs, especially flowering

shrubs that love cool weather, such as azaleas, rhododendrons, and camellias.

❏ **TEND FUCHSIAS.** To keep flowers coming, snip off faded blossoms before seed heads form. Feed plants monthly with a solution of complete liquid plant food like 5-10-10.

❏ **TEND ROSES.** To be certain hybrid teas send out new bloom shoots when you cut flowers, snip just above a leaf with five leaflets. Water plants well (at the ground to lessen chances of mildew) and fertilize regularly.

❏ **WATER HANGING BASKETS.** If they dry out completely, you've done long-term, if not permanent, damage. Water daily, or twice daily in hottest weather.

❏ **IRRIGATE WISELY.** Water in the early morning. You'll reduce the amount of water lost to evaporation, but still give leaves and stems time to dry out during the day, reducing the chances of mildew.

PEST & WEED CONTROL

❏ **BATTLE SLUGS.** No matter what your weapon of choice (bait, traps, handpicking), keep fighting slugs. If you don't control them, they will decimate newly emerging shoots and leaf crops. If you set out poison bait for slugs, keep pets and children away from it.

❏ **CONTROL THISTLES.** Put on a pair of sturdy gloves and a long-sleeved shirt, and cut thistle blossoms to the ground before seed ripens and scatters. You'll notice a big reduction in the thistle population next summer.

CHECKLIST
JULY

PLANTING

❏ **MAKE A POND.** Preformed ponds or flexible liners make it easy to do. Or use a large glazed urn that has no drainage hole. Fill the pond with water plants, such as Japanese water iris (*Iris ensata*), parrot's feather (*Myriophyllum aquaticum*), water lilies, and water poppy (*Hydrocleys nymphoides*). Add mosquito fish, goldfish, or koi.

❏ **SET OUT MUMS.** To add bright color to the fall garden, plant garden chrysanthemums now. If plants haven't formed flower buds yet, pinch growing tips to keep plants compact.

❏ **START PERENNIALS.** To get ready for fall planting, take cuttings of dianthus, geraniums, scabiosa, Shasta daisies, verbena, and other herbaceous perennials. Dip them in rooting hormone and then plant them in a mixture of 1 part perlite and 1 part peat moss. Sow seeds of campanula, columbine, coreopsis, delphinium, forget-me-not, foxglove, rudbeckia, and purple coneflower in the same growing medium.

MAINTENANCE

❏ **ADJUST AUTOMATIC CONTROLLER.** Depending on where you live, the weather can be hot or cool and foggy this month. If you water with an automatic controller, make sure it is set to run often enough that plants get plenty of water, but not so often that the soil stays overly wet. As a test, check soil moisture just before the system is due to come on by digging down with a trowel or using a soil probe. If the soil

Sunset
CLIMATE ZONES

☐ Mountain (1-2)
☐ Valley (7-9)
☐ Inland (14)
☐ Coastal (15-17)

seems too dry or too moist, adjust the controller.

❏ **CARE FOR FRUIT TREES.** To prevent breakage, support limbs of apple, peach, pear, and plum trees that are overladen and sagging with fruit.

❏ **CUT BACK CANE BERRIES.** After harvesting blackberries, raspberries, and boysenberries from June-bearing plants, cut spent canes back to the ground and tie up new canes.

❏ **DEADHEAD FLOWERS.** Pick off old flowers as soon as they fade, to promote additional flower production. Make sure to remove the entire flower (including the ovary where seeds form), not just the petals; otherwise, seed production will continue and sap energy from the plant.

❏ **DEEP-WATER TREES.** By midsummer, the soil has long since dried out from the last spring rains. If you haven't watered your mature fruiting, flowering, or shade trees, they may be suffering from drought stress. Deep-water fruit, citrus, and flowering trees once every week or two (use the higher frequency in hot climates). Water drought-tolerant trees about once a month. (Young trees need to be watered more often.)

❏ **FERTILIZE ANNUALS AND VEGETABLES.** Feed annuals and vegetables with high-nitrogen fertilizer. Apply water-soluble types through a hose-end sprayer. Spread dry fertilizers over the soil or apply in trenches next to rows of plants; water thoroughly afterward.

❏ **STAKE FLOPPY PLANTS.** If you haven't already done so, stake beans, delphiniums, gladiolus, peonies, and tomatoes, especially in windy areas. Drive stakes at least 1 foot into the ground; tie plants securely. (For details on new stakes, see item on page 173.)

PEST CONTROL

❏ **CONTROL SPIDER MITES.** Mottled leaves and fine webs indicate the presence of spider mites. Spray the undersides of leaves thoroughly with insecticidal soap, lightweight summer (horticultural) oil, or a stronger miticide. To discourage mites, keep foliage clean by rinsing both sides with water.

CHECKLIST
JULY

PLANTING

❑ **PLANT SUMMER ANNUALS.** Coastal (zones 22–24), inland (zones 18–21), and high-desert (zone 11) gardeners can fill empty spots in the garden with heat-loving annuals such as celosia, globe amaranth, marigolds, portulaca, salvia, sanvitalia, verbena, vinca rosea, and zinnia.

❑ **PLANT VEGETABLES.** If prepared to water diligently, coastal and inland gardeners can plant for a late harvest of summer vegetables. Plant seeds of beans, beets, carrots, corn, cucumbers, and summer squash. Transplant cucumber, eggplant, pepper, pumpkin, squash, and tomato seedlings.

❑ **START BIENNIALS.** For blooms next spring, sow seeds of foxglove, Canterbury bells, hollyhocks, and verbascum in flats now. Transplant the seedlings into the garden in fall when they are 4 to 5 inches tall.

MAINTENANCE

❑ **MOW LAWNS.** Cool-season grasses are slowing down now. To keep their roots shaded and to conserve soil moisture, leave these grasses tall—1½ to 2 inches for ryegrass, 2 inches or more for tall fescues. Warm-season grasses such as Bermuda, St. Augustine, and zoysia, meanwhile, are growing rapidly. Mow frequently, keeping shorter than 1 inch, to lessen thatch buildup.

❑ **CARE FOR CYMBIDIUMS.** Next year's flower spikes are developing now. To ensure proper development, water weekly and feed plants with a

Sunset
CLIMATE ZONES

1-3 7-9 11 13 14-24

high-nitrogen fertilizer this month and next. Follow label directions.

❑ **HARVEST VEGETABLES AND FLOWERS.** For a longer harvest and more attractive plants, pick heat-loving vegetables such as beans, cucumbers, eggplant, peppers, and squash frequently. Some fast-growers, like summer squash, should be checked daily. To encourage more flowers, cut off developing seed heads of cosmos, dahlias, marigolds, rudbeckias, and zinnias.

❑ **FERTILIZE SELECTIVELY.** Summer annuals should be fed monthly. Many vegetables will benefit from the same

treatment. (Not tomatoes, though, or you'll get a lot of leaves and not much fruit.) Also feed warm-season lawns and subtropicals such as bird of paradise and hibiscus. Give camellias and azaleas their last feeding of the year. Water plants thoroughly a day or two before feeding and immediately afterward.

❑ **WATER CITRUS.** Shallow-rooted citrus trees need to be watered more frequently than other fruit trees. To prevent fruit drop, irrigate thoroughly at regular intervals—two to three weeks apart, depending on soil conditions. Avoid wetting the bark, however, as citrus are susceptible to brown rot gummosis, a fungus that can infect trunks.

❑ **MOVE HOUSE PLANTS OUTDOORS.** Give them a summer vacation. Many grow faster and look healthier if they spend all or part of the summer outdoors. Protect them from strong winds and bright light. Spray foliage with water occasionally to wash off dust.

PEST CONTROL

❑ **CONTROL CATERPILLARS.** Petunias, geraniums, and nicotiana are favorites of geranium budworm (alias tobacco budworm). At first signs of the green larvae, spray with *Bacillus thuringiensis.* Inspect tomato plants for tomato hornworms. Treat small worms with *Bacillus thuringiensis;* pick off the larger ones.

❑ **WATCH FOR PESTS.** Keep aphid, spider mite, thrip, and whitefly populations in check by spraying affected foliage with a strong stream of water and/or spraying with insecticidal soap.

CHECKLIST
JULY

PLANTING

❑ **PLANT IRISES.** Dig up overcrowded clumps three weeks after flowers fade. Discard dried-out or mushy rhizomes; cut apart healthy ones, trim leaves back to 6 inches, and replant in fast-draining soil in full sun. Plant new rhizomes the same way.

❑ **PLANT FALL CROPS.** In all but the highest elevations, plant beets, broccoli, bush beans, cabbage, carrots, cauliflower, green onions, peas, spinach, and turnips. Below 5,000 feet, plant winter squash among spinach; it will cover when you harvest the spinach. Above 7,000 feet, plant warm-season vegetables in large pots. If temperatures below 60° are predicted, move the pots under cover.

MAINTENANCE

❑ **CARE FOR BULBS.** In the coldest climates, pluck faded flowers and seed heads from daffodils, tulips, and other spring-flowering bulbs. Let leaves remain until they brown. When bloom is finished, feed with high-phosphorus fertilizer.

❑ **CARE FOR CONTAINER PLANTS.** To encourage bloom, feed plants with a water-soluble fertilizer and pick off spent flowers.

❑ **COMPOST.** Add leafy garden debris, grass clippings, and annual weeds to the compost pile. Turn and water the pile regularly to keep it working.

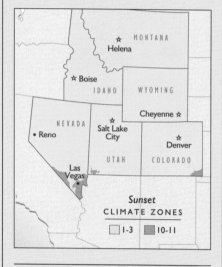

Sunset
CLIMATE ZONES

❑ 1-3   ❑ 10-11

❑ **FERTILIZE.** Feed annuals and vegetables with high-nitrogen fertilizer, and water it in well.

❑ **MULCH.** To conserve moisture and reduce weeds, spread organic mulch around and under plants. Substitute black sheet plastic around heat-loving vegetables like eggplant, peppers, and tomatoes.

❑ **POLLINATE MELONS, SQUASH.** In hot-summer areas, high temperatures inhibit fruit set on melons and squash. You can improve matters by dabbing pollen-bearing male flowers with a small artist's brush, then painting the pollen onto female flowers (they have swollen bases).

❑ **PRUNE CANE BERRIES.** After harvest, remove old raspberry canes as they begin to die. This helps prevent mildew by encouraging air circulation. In coldest climates, wait until August.

❑ **STAKE TALL PLANTS.** If you haven't done so already, stake beans, delphiniums, peas, peonies, and tomatoes against high winds. Drive stakes at least 1 foot into the ground, and tie plants securely.

❑ **TEND FRUIT TREES.** On trees with heavy fruit set, thin apples, nectarines, and peaches no closer than 4 inches apart, and plums 2 inches apart.

❑ **WATER.** Continue a regular deep-watering program for ground covers, lawns, shrubs, and trees. For big trees, a deep-root irrigator can help you direct the water down into the ground.

PEST & WEED CONTROL

❑ **CONTROL SPIDER MITES.** Yellow-stippled leaves and fine webs indicate the presence of spider mites. Blast them off with hose water, and follow up by spraying with insecticidal soap or a stronger miticide.

❑ **WEED.** In highest elevations, where weeds are just emerging, get rid of them now or they will steal food, water, and space from desirable plants.

PLANTING & HARVEST

❏ **PLANT VEGETABLES.** In all but the highest elevations of New Mexico (zone 10) and the low desert of Arizona (zone 13), plant beets, broccoli, cabbage, carrots, cauliflower, green onions, leaf lettuce, peas, spinach, and turnips for fall harvest. Plant winter squash among the spinach: as you harvest spinach, the squash will fill in.

❏ **HARVEST CROPS.** As vegetables mature, pick them often to keep new ones coming and to keep ripe ones from becoming overmature (cucumbers, zucchini) or downright rotten (tomatoes).

❏ **HARVEST FLOWERS.** To encourage continued bloom, pick flowers or shear them off before they go to seed.

MAINTENANCE

❏ **CARE FOR ROSES.** After each bloom cycle, remove faded flowers, cutting them off just above a leaf node with five leaflets (nodes closest to the flower have three leaflets). Then fertilize and water deeply to encourage the next round of bloom.

❏ **MULCH.** Spread a 3-inch layer of organic mulch around permanent plants to keep the soil moist, hold down weeds, and give plants a cool root run. You can mulch with leaves, shredded

SOUTHWEST
CHECKLISTS
JULY

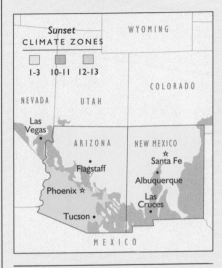

garden waste, or lawn clippings—even tree limbs that have gone through a grinder.

❏ **PRUNE CANE BERRIES.** In all but the coldest parts of the Southwest, cut out old raspberry canes after the harvest (they'll turn brown and stiff). Cut off blackberry canes that have borne fruit, and tie new canes to the trellis. In coldest areas, wait until August to do this.

❏ **TEND CYMBIDIUMS.** To help build buds for next year's bloom, apply a quarter-strength dose of liquid fertilizer every time you water.

❏ **TIP-PRUNE.** Pinch off the tips of chrysanthemums, fuchsias, and recently planted marguerites for thick, compact growth.

❏ **WATER.** Irrigate annual vegetables and flowers only after the top inch of soil has dried out. Basins and furrows help direct water to the roots. Deep-rooted permanent plants can be watered less often, but when you irrigate, water them deeply.

PEST CONTROL

❏ **APHIDS, SPIDER MITES.** You can cut down the number of leaf-sucking creatures like aphids and spider mites by hosing off leaves from time to time.

❏ **BUDWORMS.** Voracious budworms eat through the buds of geraniums, nicotiana, and petunias, preventing flowering. To control budworms, spray these plants every 7 to 10 days with *Bacillus thuringiensis* (BT).

❏ **TOMATO HORNWORMS.** If you see chewed tomato leaves spotted with black droppings, hornworms should be your chief suspects. When they're small, you can control them by spraying BT. They can eventually reach cigar size.

TEXAS

PLANTING & HARVEST

❏ **PLANT VEGETABLES.** In North and West Texas and the Panhandle, plant Southern peas any time, plus all kinds of peppers, tomatoes, and winter squash. At midmonth, plant cantaloupe, eggplant, okra, pumpkin, and watermelon. Plant potatoes at month's end.

❏ **HARVEST CROPS.** As vegetables mature, pick them often to keep new ones coming and to keep ripe ones from becoming overmature (cucumbers, zucchini) or downright rotten (tomatoes).

MAINTENANCE

❏ **CARE FOR ROSES.** After each bloom cycle, remove faded flowers, cutting them off just above a leaf node with five leaflets (nodes closest to the flower have three leaflets). Then fertilize and water deeply to stimulate the next round of bloom.

❏ **MULCH.** Spread a 3-inch layer of organic mulch around permanent plants to keep soil moist, hold down weeds, and give plants a cool root run. You can use leaves, shredded garden waste, lawn clippings, even tree limbs that have gone through a grinder (city

forestry departments often supply wood chips for free or a nominal fee).

❏ **TEND CYMBIDIUMS.** To help build buds for next year's bloom, apply a quarter-strength dose of liquid fertilizer every time you water.

❏ **WATER.** Irrigate annual vegetables and flowers only after the top inch of soil has dried out. Basins and furrows help direct water to the roots. Deep-rooted permanent plants can be watered less often, but when you do irrigate, water them deeply.

PEST & WEED CONTROL

❏ **APHIDS, SPIDER MITES.** You can reduce the numbers of leaf-sucking creatures like aphids and spider mites by hosing off leaves from time to time.

❏ **SOLARIZE SOIL.** To clean weeds out of a planting bed, cultivate and water the soil, then cover the bed with a sheet of clear plastic for one month. When weed seedlings emerge, the trapped solar heat will quickly kill them.

Elegant purple-and-pink wreath features pink China aster, white baby's breath, and purple Limonium perezii, with pink-and-white 'Stargazer' lily as the accent flower. Background is made up of nandina and lily-of-the-valley foliage.

CELEBRATE SUMMER WITH

fresh~
flower
wreaths

USE YOUR GARDEN'S

ABUNDANT BLOOMS AND

A GRAPEVINE BASE TO

CREATE A WREATH IN

LESS THAN TWO HOURS

By Lauren Bonar Swezey

Fresh flowers make every event more special. And hanging a fresh floral wreath on a garden gate or front door is a delightful way to welcome guests to a summer garden party. These quick and easy wreaths make use of grapevine bases and little bouquets of flowers in water-filled tubes. Bud Stuckey, *Sunset*'s test garden coordinator, was inspired to make them after seeing garden catalog photographs of wreaths made from brightly colored freeze-dried flowers. Fresh flowers may not last as long as freeze-dried ones, but if you choose fragrant flowers such as 'Stargazer' or 'Casablanca' Oriental hybrid lilies, they can perfume the air around them for days.

make your own wreath in four steps

Start with the foliage, then add the flowers

1 COLLECT MATERIALS AND TOOLS TO GET STARTED

At a craft or floral supply store, buy:

- 17-inch to 19-inch grapevine wreath base (tightly woven)
- 10 to 15 water picks (green plastic water tubes with snap-on rubber tops and pointed bottoms)
- Large (3½-inch) clear water tube
- Floral wire
- Wreath hanger (optional)
- Pruning shears

2 CHOOSE A COLOR SCHEME

Flower colors that complement each other—whether pastels, hot summer colors, or even pure whites—are key to an attractive wreath. "Choose flowers as you would if arranging them in a vase," says Stuckey. He usually picks his largest flower—the wreath's dominant element—first, then builds a color scheme around it. (Lilies, roses, and large sunflowers make good accents.) Then he collects 16 to 20 other long-lasting flowers and 20 to 24 snippets of foliage, from either the garden or the store. ✦ The flowers and foliage will last longer if they're conditioned in deep water overnight. Strip off lower leaves on stems, recut stems underwater, and immerse in deep water up to the bases of the flower heads or the leaves.

3 MAKE A FRAMEWORK OF FOLIAGE

Prop the wreath base against a wall in an upright position (unless you're building a wreath to be displayed on a table; then keep it flat). Select one type of foliage, such as variegated pittosporum, for the background and stuff two or three stems in each of 7 to 10 water-filled water picks (depending on how full you want the wreath to be); push each pick into the wreath base so it lies almost flat against the base. For color contrast, combine pittosporum with colored foliage, such as gray-green *Eucalyptus cinerea* shown in the in-progress wreath at right, or use the eucalyptus separately and alternate it with the pittosporum. Cover about a third of the wreath with foliage.

4 BUILD MINIBOUQUETS

Select about three flowers and insert the stems into a water-filled pick. Stuckey varies the mix of flowers in each minibouquet so the wreath doesn't look symmetrical—for example, using *Zinnia haageana* Old Mexico, coreopsis, and German statice (*Limonium tartaricum*) in one bouquet, strawflowers and gloriosa daisies in another, and sunflowers and German statice in a third. Save a spot for the accent flower; insert the stem in the large water tube and set it in the wreath. ✦ Finally, fill in the wreath with more foliage to hide bare spots or water picks.

Sunny yellow wreath combines 'Sunrich Lemon' sunflower (top) with golden rudbeckia, copper-colored dahlias, and burgundy-ringed Zinnia haageana Old Mexico. Variegated pittosporum and silvery gray Eucalyptus cinerea form the background; sprays of silver-lavender German statice accent the top.

MAINTENANCE

These wreaths will last a couple of days—long enough for a garden party or special event. But if you want them to last as long as a week or so, refill the water picks regularly. Check them the day after constructing the wreath and again every couple of days. Some flowers drink up water fast. If necessary, slide the picks out from the wreath and dunk them in a bucket of water. Bend plant stems a bit to allow water to seep through the hole in the rubber top. Always transport the wreath in the same position in which it was built (usually upright) so water doesn't flow out of the picks. Display it out of direct sunlight.

A garden for the senses

Plants, water, art, and whimsy come together magically in this California garden

Bob Clark (right) and Raul Zumba pause beside a mirror- and marble-encrusted concrete bench. Below, colorful stacked pots show off small succulents.

PLAYFUL, IMAGINATIVE, AND FUN. Bob Clark and Raul Zumba's garden in Oakland, California, is all of this and more. It's a garden to get lost in. A browser's delight. A maze of paths, embellished here and there with artful surprises, winds through it. Nothing is linear in this magical garden. "The garden is designed to make people forget the outside world for a moment," Clark says.

At each turn in the path is a new vista. Turn one corner and you come upon a spouting fountain. Turn another corner and there's a mini-amphitheater flanked with raised perennial beds and concrete benches. Roses and salvias are just around another corner. Everywhere you look, a surprisingly beautiful scene asserts itself, even underfoot—stepping-stones flanked by lime green moss, for instance.

Clark and Zumba, both masters of the unexpected, enjoy combining "kitschy things with fine art"—a beautiful sculpture displayed against a brick wall that's accented with pot fragments, for example. Even objects as mundane as rubber gardening boots are prominently displayed. Clark describes the garden as "thought-provoking" and one that "makes people stop and look." But, he emphasizes, nothing in it is to be taken too seriously.

The garden is a living laboratory where Clark and Zumba experiment with plants and with design concepts that Clark hopes to use in his clients' gardens. He tests plants such as chartreuse feverfew and *Helichrysum petiolare* 'Limelight' by tucking in one or two plants here and there. If they're successful, he masses them in other gardens.

"We also purposely leave holes between permanent plantings, where we can use seasonal color and play with new plants," says Zumba.

Clark and Zumba also experiment with color. "I like to try different combinations—to use playful colors such as

Concrete pavers edged with moss trail between garden beds.

yellow," says Clark. "If they work, my clients eventually get them, too."

FIVE YEARS IN THE MAKING

The garden didn't go in overnight but evolved over five years (and is still evolving). First, the sloping hillsides in the front

and back were terraced into level planting areas. In the back, a brick retaining wall decorated with marbles and random objects supports the upper terrace. Clark and Zumba brought in more than 300 cubic yards of soil. Then the paths went in,

and initial planting started.

Clark prefers informality close to the house, formality farther away. Next to the house, his plants are purposely lush and tangled; clematis and passion vines intertwine, and ferns mingle with shrubs. A 25-foot-tall tree stump left when a dying tree was cut down will soon be covered with vines.

Farther out in the garden, low boxwood hedges surround planting beds where Clark and Zumba test new annuals and perennials.

When the perennials go dormant in

A tapestry of foliage and flowers nearly engulfs a garden bench just off a main pathway. Geraniums, grasses, and other plants in various shades of green edge the lower patio. At left, tiny sedum grows around a piece of terra-cotta, set on its side into the soil.

winter, the garden's structure reasserts itself. Paths and walls become more visible again, as do dwarf and slow-growing conifers. Trunks and branches of deciduous trees stand out. Clark and Zumba don't mind the quietness—it's their time to take a break too. ∎

By Lauren Bonar Swezey

Korean stewartia bears 3-inch flowers in June and July.

MICHAEL S. THOMPSON

Stewartias crown the garden with regal form, summer flowers

I

F THERE WERE A REGISTRY OF THE plant world's great royal families, the genus *Stewartia* would rank high on the list. These delicately scaled deciduous trees bring an understated majesty to the garden throughout the entire year.

In summer, they're crowned with creamy white flowers that resemble single camellias. Their leaves deepen from a delicate lime shade in spring to dark green in summer, then turn brilliant shades of red and orange in fall. Come winter, they display their statuesque form—with a strong, upright branching habit—and their handsome bark.

Despite all their pleasing attributes, stewartias aren't commonly planted in home landscapes. Why? For one thing,

they grow very slowly. For another, they can be hard to find. The four species listed here are the ones you're most likely to find in the Pacific Northwest. All of them are native to either Asia or North Ameri-

ca. In the Northwest, they grow only in the mild coastal climates—*Sunset Western Garden Book* zones 4, 5, and 6. They do best in moist, acid soil with plenty of organic matter, and they prefer partial shade (try growing them near large evergreens). You can set plants from nursery cans in the ground this month.

Japanese stewartia (*S. pseudocamellia*) is the tallest of the stewartias, growing to a height of 40 feet and sometimes reaching even 60 feet. Fall foliage is dark purple-red.

Korean stewartia (*S. koreana*) seldom exceeds a height of 20 to 25 feet. Flowers measure 3 inches across. Dark green, 4-inch-long, heavily veined leaves become brilliant orange or orange-red in fall. The flaky bark is silvery gray splotched with muted tones of cream, brown, orange, and green.

Mountain stewartia (*S. ovata*), which is native to the southeastern United States, grows 15 feet tall (its lower branches need pruning to assume tree form). Of all the stewartias, it has the largest flowers, often more than 3 inches across. Fall foliage is deep orange to scarlet.

Tall stewartia (*S. monadelpha*) eventually reaches 25 feet in height. It has the most open, spreading form of any of the species. Both flowers and leaves are about half the size of those of *S. koreana*. Fall foliage is smoky yellow, red-orange, or sometimes purple. Mature trees have bright cinnamon-orange bark that glows in the low winter light.

Look for stewartias in specialty nurseries and at arboretum and plant society sales. One mail-order source that sells all the species listed is Gossler Farms Nursery, 1200 Weaver Rd., Springfield, OR 97478; (541) 746-3922. Plants in 1-gallon cans range in price from $10 to $50 each. Water newly planted stewartias well and often during the first two summers, until they are well established. ■

By Steven R. Lorton

DAVID McDONALD

Japanese stewartia bears 2½-inch flowers in July and August. This tree commonly grows 40 feet tall and may eventually reach 60 feet.

Red proteas rise above sweeps of orange Ursinia speciosa and yellow Ursinia abrotanifolia. Blue Felicia heterophylla blooms at far left in this bed at Kirstenbosch botanical garden in Cape Town.

Landscaping, South African–style

Familiar plants and fresh ideas for California gardens

WHERE WOULD WESTERN gardens be without calla lily, agapanthus, clivia, bird of paradise, a host of heaths and flower bulbs, cycads, Transvaal daisy (gerbera), ice plants? All are native to South Africa, and all are common in Western landscapes.

On a recent trip to South Africa, I learned how gardeners there—especially those in Western Cape Province, which has a Mediterranean climate similar to that of California—use their horticultural treasures.

Western Cape Province, at Africa's southern tip, gets much of its garden style from the natural landscape, which is covered with *fynbos*—a plant community that looks (and periodically burns) very much like Southern California's chaparral. Fynbos plants are familiar: many kinds of heaths (*Erica*) predominate, with pelargoniums, geraniums, and proteas popping up all over—especially in recently burned areas. Wildflowers make fabulous displays in open country, and many of them are bulbous plants such as *Babiana, Ixia, Ornithogalum,* and *Sparaxis* that also do well in mild-winter parts of the West.

Borrowing from nature, South African gardeners blend heaths, proteas, and evergreen perennials such as birds of paradise and felicias in large islands of mixed shrubs.

In the West, this planting scheme would work well with many of the heaths, which adapt well to our often alkaline soil, and proteas. Proteas are useful plants in *Sunset* climate zones 16, 17, and 21 through 24, if you grow them in fast-draining soil.

DAISIES EN MASSE

The landscape of Western Cape Province is loaded with daisies, and dozens of kinds find their way into every part of the gardens there. The list of choices seems to go on forever: *Arctotis, Dimorphotheca, Euryops, Felicia, Gazania, Gerbera,* and *Osteospermum* are woven into shrub and perennial beds, splashed over bare spaces in the border, and allowed to spill out of containers.

For much larger annual beds, gardeners use grand sweeps of annual daisies such as *Ursinia speciosa* in the same way that California poppies are used here.

All the daisies named here are tender or half-hardy perennials.

A BLEND OF FORMAL AND INFORMAL DESIGN

South Africa's garden design shows a strong European influence, particularly English. You see these influences in statuary and brick courtyards that offer wonderful jumbles of herbs and vegetables.

Exotic Leucospermum cordifolium can be grown in mild parts of California.

Queen's wreath (Petrea volubilis) covers a trellis in a garden near Pietermaritzburg. This vine grows in Southern California's mildest coastal areas.

Carefully pruned fruit trees have roses or potato vines rambling through the branches, and symmetrical flower beds are often interwoven with masses of herbaceous perennials. That blend of formality and informality works well there—and here.

GARDEN TOURING

If you'd like to visit South Africa on a garden tour, remember that when it's late spring in the West, it's late autumn there. September and October are ideal months to visit. Cape Town, in Western Cape Province, is the home of Kirstenbosch, South Africa's national botanical garden.

For garden tour information, call the South African Tourism Board at (800) 782-9772; John E. Bryan Horticultural Consultants at (415) 331-7848; or National Wildflower Research Center at (512) 292-4200. ■

Plump green tobacco hornworm feasts on the leaves. It'll eat the fruit, too.

Terrorists in your tomato patch

You may love your vine-ripened tomatoes, but so do insect pests and diseases. Here are the worst ones and what to do about them

JUST ABOUT EVERYONE WHO gardens grows at least one tomato plant, because the flavor of vine-ripened tomatoes is tough to beat. But even though the plants are fairly easy to grow, they're not pest-free. Insects and diseases can and do damage them.

Four of the most common tomato problems are listed here, along with guidelines for controlling them.

TWO PESKY INSECTS

Tobacco hornworms devour foliage, often stripping stems bare, and nibble on fruit. Telltale signs include black droppings peppering the leaves. If you search through the foliage, you'll find 1/2- to 5-inch-long green larvae with diagonal white stripes and a single red horn on their rear.

Control: Handpick and destroy them. To control young larvae, carefully spray with *Bacillus thuringiensis* (BT), a bacteria that's nontoxic to mammals and other wildlife. Or use a more toxic pesticide such as carbaryl, pyrethrin, or rotenone.

Whiteflies, the white, 1/12-inch-long insects that flutter around the plant when it's jostled, suck sap from the undersides of leaves. The pinhead-size larvae, covered with waxy white filaments, also suck sap. When whitefly numbers are large, leaves become spotted and yellow, and the plant can be severely weakened.

Control: Place a yellow sticky trap next to each plant (either buy the traps or make them with yellow cards and a sticky substance such as Tanglefoot). Face the sticky side toward the plant. Whiteflies quickly build up resistance to toxic chemicals (which also kill their natural enemies); avoid these chemicals if possible. Instead, use insecticidal soap and thoroughly cover the leaves.

TWO SERIOUS DISEASES

Fusarium wilt causes plant parts to yellow, curl up, and wilt, usually starting with the oldest leaves and then moving upward, often on only one side of the plant. When the plant's stem is sliced open lengthwise, dark brown streaks may be evident. The fungus lives in the soil and enters the plant through the roots. It's most prevalent in warm-weather regions.

Control: Remove and destroy infected plants. To avoid the disease, don't plant tomatoes in that spot for several years, and choose resistant varieties (usually identified on the plant label with the letter *F*).

Verticillium wilt causes plant parts to gradually wilt, turn yellow and brown, and then drop off the plant. The outer or lower leaves are infected first. Fruit is stunted or fails to develop. When sliced open lengthwise, stems may appear brown or yellow inside. The plant often dies.

The fungus lives in the soil and enters the plant through wounds or cuts. It's most prevalent in cool, moist soils, although it may not show up until warm weather arrives.

Control: Remove and destroy infected plants. To avoid the disease, change planting locations each year—the fungus survives in the soil for many years—and choose resistant varieties (usually identified on the plant label with the letter *V*).

LEARN MORE ON CD-ROM

Insects, diseases, and horticultural problems afflict many garden plants other than tomatoes. But identifying the culprit is not always easy. A new CD-ROM called *Sunset Garden Problem Solver* can help you solve more than 400 garden problems.

Its Plant Doctor feature presents photos of plant damage. Once you find the troublemaker, you can call up more photos of it in the Rogues' Gallery of pests and diseases, and you can read descriptions of the culprit. Controls are also given. A Garden Calendar can be customized to your climate and garden, allowing you to identify monthly pest-control tasks and print out the calendar each month.

The CD-ROM is available through home and garden centers and some software dealers, or by calling (800) 829-0113. It costs $39.95. ∎

By Lauren Bonar Swezey

Buddleia flowers come in a range of colors— most are lightly fragrant.

RENEE LYNN

A nectar bar for butterflies

Plant a buddleia and its colorful flowers will beckon the winged beauties to your garden

BUTTERFLIES AREN'T AS PLENTIFUL as they used to be, complain naturalists and observant gardeners. Squeezed from their habitats by urban sprawl, winged beauties such as red admirals and West Coast ladies don't show up in gardens every summer the way they once did. Neither do sulphurs or blues, monarchs or metalmarks, skippers or swallowtails. We need an irresistible attraction, a seductive allurement, a plant they simply adore before they'll favor our gardens with a visit. We need, in a word, butterfly bush.

Buddleia isn't called butterfly bush for nothing. When it blooms, squadrons of butterflies are never far away. Just a hint of the nectar-rich blossoms seems to set them fluttering. Ask anyone who grows this shrub—Ray Prag of Forestfarm in Williams, Oregon, for instance. Last summer, Prag, who propagates nearly two dozen varieties, pulled a 1-gallon 'Lochinch' buddleia out of the greenhouse and set it outside his office door. The plant bloomed slightly ahead of the other plants. "There it was, all by itself, with nothing else around it in bloom," says Prag. "And yet the minute it flowered, there were butterflies all over it. Buddleias are really amazing that way. They're like magnets for butterflies."

If that isn't reason enough to plant this reliable, summer-blooming shrub, consider this litany of virtues. Buddleia is one of the least demanding shrubs. It adapts to any well-drained soil, needs little or no fertilizer, has virtually no pest or disease problems, takes full sun or partial shade, and is reasonably drought tolerant. It grows in all *Sunset* climate zones. (In areas with cold winters, it may die back to the ground, but because its roots are hardy, it comes back unharmed the following spring.) Showy flower clusters are reminiscent of lilac blooms.

Another appeal of buddleia is its exuberance. A plant that shoots out 6 feet or more of new growth in a single season adds excitement to any garden. But the vigor comes with a price. If left unpruned, buddleias can resemble brush piles in a few seasons. That's why many gardeners cut back the entire plant annually to about 3 feet. Doing so maintains a buddleia's willowy grace and fountainlike form. And, since most varieties bloom on new wood, no flowers are sacrificed. (Cut back after fall flowering in zones 4 through 9 and 12 through 24; after spring flowering in zones 1, 2, 3, 10, and 11.) To encourage a strong second show, cut the shrub back by a third after the first bloom.

WHERE TO BUY BUDDLEIAS

The following mail-order sources sell most of the varieties mentioned here: Forestfarm, 990 Tetherow Rd., Williams, OR 97544; (541) 846-7269 (catalog $3). Heronswood Nursery, 7530 N.E. 288th St., Kingston, WA 98346 (catalog $4). ∎

By Sharon Cohoon

CHOICE BUDDLEIAS

Buddleia davidii, the best-known buddleia species, is deciduous in colder climates, evergreen where winters are mild. Its height (8 to 15 feet), coarse texture, and open habit make it well suited for the back of a border. Long, narrow, dark green leaves have silvery undersides. Small flowers are loosely clustered in plumes at branch ends. *B. davidii* comes in many varieties, including 'Black Knight' (very dark purple flowers); 'Royal Red' (bright reddish purple flowers);

'Pink Delight' (clear hot pink, very large flowers); 'Pink Charming' (rose pink flowers); 'White Bouquet' (pure white, exceptionally fragrant flowers); and 'Harlequin' (reddish purple and white flowers and olive green leaves with cream edges).

A dwarf form of *B. davidii* that grows 4 to 6 feet tall and wide has smaller leaves and flower clusters and needs considerably less pruning. It's available in two flower colors: 'Nanho Blue' (also sold as 'Nanho Indigo')

and 'Nanho Purple' (also sold as 'Nanho Plum').

B. fallowiana 'Alba' has beautiful silver foliage and fragrant white flowers. It's similar in height and habit to *B. davidii.*

B. 'Lochinch' (a cross between *B. davidii* and *B. fallowiana*) has silvery gray foliage and lavender blue flowers.

B. weyeriana is a cross between *B. davidii* and *B. globosa.* 'Sungold' has yelloworange flowers in ball-shaped clusters.

Delicate trailing verbena, petunias, and purple heliotrope spill from a well-camouflaged pot. Learn more about this colorful container planting on page 196.

AUGUST

Garden guide.......................194

Garden notebooks 197

Garden checklists..................199

Unforgettable garden fragrances .204

A passion for heathers............210

Bananas!..........................213

GARDEN
Guide

A shady forest glen in Vancouver, B.C.

Baby's tears (*Soleirolia soleirolii*) and mosses fill the cracks along a stone path lined with ferns, hostas, and other shade-loving plants.

August has a bad reputation as a planting month: the sun and heat are rough on both plants and gardeners. But there is a happy exception—the shade garden. Just how creative can you be with shade plants? Take a look at the garden above. Landscape architect Ron Rule of Vancouver, British Columbia, created an enchanting glen out of a boring mass of dry shade cast by huge old conifers and London plane trees.

Rule started by cultivating the soil to a depth of about 18 inches, dodging the conifers' big roots as he went, and tilling in 4 inches of commercial compost. Then he laid down a stone walk and began to plant.

To give the landscape a lush look, he used a variety of ferns, including native sword fern (*Polystichum munitum*), Japanese shield fern (*Dryopteris erythrosora*), and Tasmanian tree fern (*Dicksonia antarctica*), which is proving to be a hardier plant in the coastal Northwest than gardeners first thought.

As a contrast to the ferns' foliage, he set out hostas and Siberian irises. Although the irises bloom sparingly in this heavy shade, their spiky foliage provides more than six months of greenery. Rule also planted ground covers, including *Epimedium grandiflorum*, *Vancouveria hexandra*, and *V. chrysantha*. Rising along the edges of the garden, rhododendrons and vine maples give the plot a pleasant sense of enclosure.

Once a week during the hottest months, the owner turns on the sprinkler system in early morning and lets it run for about an hour. This sprinkling keeps the organically rich soil moist for the rest of the week.

Arcadia's best-known jungle has a new look

The green lagoon swims with water lilies under a canopy of palm fronds and leathery ficus leaves. On the forest floor beside it, flowering cannas and clerodendrum compete with ferns for space. Orchids, bromeliads, and slithering vines vie for footholds in the trees. No doubt about it: the Tropical Forest at the Arboretum of Los Angeles County looks like the real thing. The tropics have come to Arcadia.

Apparently, Hollywood thinks so, too. Columbia Pictures shot the concluding scenes of its upcoming movie *Anaconda*, which stars a 35-foot-long mechanical snake, at this location. But stand at the lagoon's edge on a still August day and danger fades. The "Amazon" becomes tranquil, like television's old *Fantasy Island*—you can almost imagine Ricardo Montalban in his crisp whites waiting to receive his guests with a lei, a kiss, and a cool tropical drink.

The Tropical Forest, a new attraction adjacent to Baldwin Lake near Queen Anne Cottage, replaces the jungle that grew in this location. The high water table that occurs here naturally is a magnet for invasive plants such as arundo grass and bamboo, which had overtaken the area and created a fire hazard.

"It took a 10-man, machete-wielding crew a full year to hack down all the vegetation," says Tim Lindsay, the arboretum's assistant superintendent. But the effort unveiled a few surprises.

Palm and ficus trees spread a lush, cooling canopy over the arboretum's lagoon.

Three Mexican fan palms—accustomed to the thick cover of vegetation—grew more horizontally than vertically, their trunks twisting and turning along the ground before finally straightening up and heading for the sun. These "snake palms" were too amusing not to keep. And, unlike *Anaconda,* they're more likely to elicit laughs than nightmares.

Signs throughout the garden explain the roles of the many plants in their native environments, as well as their usefulness to humans. Interesting features are still to come—a bog garden and a 300-foot bamboo tunnel (controllable clumping types this time), for instance. But don't wait for their completion to visit the garden; it looks glorious right now. Though temperate plants tend to give up the ghost by August, tropicals are just getting started. Flowers are at their peak bloom.

The Arboretum of Los Angeles County is at 301 N. Baldwin Avenue in Arcadia. It is open from 9 to 4:30 daily. For details, call (818) 821-3222.

Portable trellis supports sweet pea vines while it hides clutter.

TEST-GARDEN TIPS

Lattice trellis for flowering vines

A screen and a growing place for vines: this trellis provides both. Bud Stuckey, *Sunset*'s test-garden coordinator, designed it to obscure views of compost piles and the like, while providing growing and display space for vines and a backdrop for photography.

Stuckey built the frame out of three 8-foot-long finished redwood 4-by-4 posts and four 41-inch-long pieces of 2-by-4 finished redwood. He beveled each post to a point at the top and painted each post's bottom section with a coat of wood preservative. Woodscrews hold the frame together, and 4-inch angle irons secure it at the corners.

Two 8-foot-tall by 4-foot-wide redwood lattice panels, each attached to the frame with four evenly spaced screws, are spray-painted brown. (Other options are to paint the trellis to match your house or to leave it natural.)

Stuckey moves the trellis around the test garden seasonally as needed. To keep the trellis portable, he sinks the posts in sand, not concrete. He digs three holes, each about 2 feet deep, fills them with about 4 inches of sand, and positions a post in each hole. Then he fills in the holes with more sand, packing it in firmly.

Annual vines cover the trellis: so far, Stuckey has grown sweet peas, morning glories, and nasturtiums on it.

NEW PLANT REPORT

The cool mandevillas

Mandevilla, for most of us, is synonymous with the hot pink trumpets of 'Alice du Pont'. But this popular patio vine with glossy green leaves has a cooler side, too. *M. boliviensis* has white flowers. And two new white-flowered varieties are expanding the options. 'Summer Snow', from Monrovia Nursery Company, has icy white flowers brushed with traces of blush pink. It is an excellent container plant when supported with a stake, frame, or trellis (it grows to 20 feet tall). Another white-flowering mandevilla to look for is 'My Fair Lady' (sometimes labeled dipladenia). It's the more compact (to 2 feet tall) and shrubbier of the two, making it well suited for hanging baskets. Both plants need rich soil and plenty of water during their growing period. 'Summer Snow' does better in partial shade. 'My Fair Lady' needs at least a half-day of sun. If you can't find these summer coolers, ask your nursery to order 'Summer Snow' from Monrovia, 'My Fair Lady' from Weidners' Gardens.

Snowy white trumpets touched with pink dangle from 'Summer Snow' mandevilla.

LANDSCAPING SOLUTIONS

Staging plants for maximum impact

Seattle garden designer Ben Hammontree is a master of horticultural stagecraft. He arranges plants—in containers and in garden beds—so that they form colorful combinations. For example, in the planting shown on page 192, he filled a large terra-cotta pot with pink and white petunias, trailing red and white *Verbena peruviana,* and deep purple heliotrope. Then he set the pot atop a 3-foot-tall "pedestal"—actually the stump of an old apple tree—which was quickly concealed by the mass of foliage and flowers spilling out of the pot. Rising behind the pot are the bright red blooms of 'Altissimo' rose, a climbing hybrid tea planted in a bed. This display lasts from early May well into October.

When Hammontree creates a container planting, he likes to crowd the plants a bit, squeezing in about 10 percent more plants than are normally recommended. The secret to maintaining the lush and verdant look of these plantings is plenty of water and food. During especially hot weather, Hammontree sometimes waters the plantings twice a day. He feeds them prodigiously with half-strength dilutions of fish emulsion or 15-30-15 liquid fertilizer twice, or even three times, a week.

GARDEN TOURING

Visit the green slopes of Vail

Nearly 10 years ago, a few committed gardeners persuaded the town of Vail, Colorado, to let them plant a display garden in front of the amphitheater in Gerald Ford Park. That project inspired them to add two more gardens.

In the display garden, rock plants grow in a peat bed, over rocky outcrops, and on gravel. The Mountain Perennial Garden has thousands of plants representing about 2,000 varieties. The Meditation Garden comprises mostly evergreens. Together, these side-by-side gardens make up the Betty Ford Garden. It's open from dawn to dusk every day. Admission is free.

Towers of flowers shoot up from *Acanthus mollis.*

PLANT PROFILE

Acanthus mollis: A Greek classic

When the ancient Greeks embellished the capitals of Corinthian columns with leaf motifs, they chose the foliage of *Acanthus mollis* as their model. Its noble leaves continue to win admirers. They are deeply lobed (a bit like a giant oak leaf) and can measure as much as 10 inches across and 2 feet long. The glossy leaves grow in dense clumps that send up flower spikes resembling huge asparagus stalks. These spikes, which can reach 7 feet or taller in cool, moist climates, are lined with buds that open into snapdragon-like blossoms tinged with cream, green, and purple. If you cut the flowers just before the color starts to fade and take them indoors to stand in water, they'll dry slowly, much as hydrangeas do.

This month, nurseries offer blooming plants in 1-gallon cans to set out immediately. *Acanthus mollis* is hardy in *Sunset* climate zones 4 through 7. Note that its big fleshy roots, once established, can be hard to dig out (some gardeners consider the plant invasive), so grow it in a place where it won't compete with other plants. Although the plant takes full sun, it gets biggest and greenest when grown in light to medium shade. *Acanthus mollis* grows best in loose, rich loam, and it works well in containers.

By Sharon Cohoon, Steven R. Lorton, Lauren Bonar Swezey

PACIFIC NORTHWEST
Garden Notebook
BY STEVEN R. LORTON

Inevitably, I'll walk round a corner of my house on a hot, sunny afternoon this month and come face-to-face with disaster: a big pot of colorful annuals with the flowers flopped over and the foliage shriveled up—all because I forgot to water. Through the years, I've caused enough of these disasters to make me appreciate sedums and sempervivums, two unthirsty plants that positively thrive in scorching summer weather. I grow these brilliant gems in big, shallow pots on sunny surfaces in both my Seattle and Skagit Valley gardens.

My friend Barbara Thomas taught me some great tricks to keep these plants looking gorgeous. Her secret ingredient is turkey grit—the stuff poultry farmers put out so the birds have the right amount of stones in their gizzards—which she buys by the 50-pound bag from feed stores. The grit is composed of granite with a consistency somewhere between fine gravel and sand. She blends 3 parts grit to 1 part fresh potting soil, then plants sedums and sempervivums in the mix. If she happens to be passing the pots with a hose or watering can, she gives them a squirt to rinse accumulated dust off the foliage. Every three to four weeks from April through October, she gives her pots of sempervivums and sedums a sprinkling of 15-30-15 liquid plant food. Her plants bloom like mad, and the succulent foliage really shows off in shades of burgundy, red, green, and celadon.

Thomas clips back blooms when they fade, pinches off spent rosettes, and thins crowded clumps to start new pots.

•

I confess: I'm a plant-aholic. My current obsession is dwarf conifers, and my appetite for them is ravenous. One of my all-time favorite nurseries for conifers is Wells Nurseries in Mount Vernon, Washington. The place is full of rich blue spruces, feathery gold cedars, and lush green pines. Most of the plants in the nursery were introduced by the family that owns the nursery—selected and propagated during the last 59 years. Take a look at the *Chamaecyparis nootkatensis* 'Pacific Arrow' that owner Neil Hall found growing on Vancouver Island, brought home, and propagated. It's hard to leave empty-handed. Wells Nurseries is just south of Mount Vernon on the east side of Interstate 5, at 424 E. Section Street (take exit 226). Hours are 8 to 5 Mondays through Saturdays. For information, call (800) 761-9355.

•

I'm goofy over a new daylily: 'Fragrant Light'. The leaves are bold and strappy, growing in clumps that stand 2½ feet tall or higher. The big flowers are pale yellow and slightly ruffled, with a strong but clean scent reminiscent of lily-of-the-valley. The plant reblooms with vigor.

THAT'S A GOOD QUESTION

Q: Is there really any benefit to a "green manure" cover crop for the dormant vegetable garden?
A: Whenever I've had the foresight to sow a cover crop, I've been pleased with the results. I'll plant one this month in my vegetable patch to hold down erosion this coming winter and boost soil fertility next spring. Leguminous cover crops, such as clover, fava beans, and vetch, extract nitrogen from the air and fix it in nodules that form on the roots. When I plant, I till a little lime into the soil (legumes produce more nitrogen in limed soil), let the soil rest a day or two, then broadcast seed and rake it in. The plants will grow through the winter. Next spring, when I plow, I'll turn the plants into the soil.

NORTHERN CALIFORNIA
Garden Notebook
BY LAUREN BONAR SWEZEY

Last year I installed a low-tech drip irrigation system in my front yard that uses ooze tubing with a battery-operated timer attached to a hose bibb. I just wanted a simple system that I could run while on vacation. Since then, I have renovated my backyard, and now I need a system I can count on to water my plants from spring through fall. My solution? A more permanent system that uses polyethylene tubing, drip emitters, and three automatic valves hooked up to a multistation automatic controller (one station for my small lawn, one for high-water-use plants, and one for low-water-use plants).

While checking into which products to use, I ran across ⅜-inch-diameter poly tubing (available by mail from the Urban Farmer Store, 415/661-2204). I tried it and liked it. Most poly tubing sold for drip systems comes in either ½- or ¼-inch-diameter sizes. The former is often used to bring water from the valves to the garden but also can distribute water directly to plants. The latter, "spaghetti" tubing, distributes the water to individual plants. I don't like to use ¼-inch tubing because it can be disrupted too easily by rakes, kids, and frolicking animals (although it's good for watering pots and for use with minisprays). And ½-inch tubing can be difficult to snake around plants and hide unobtrusively among the foliage. For a small garden like mine, ⅜-inch tubing is a happy medium. I use ½-inch tubing to bring water from the main line (it runs around the perimeter of the garden), and the ⅜-inch tubing to snake around plants. I use one or two drip emitters per plant (trees get multiple emitters). So far, so good!

•

Speaking of irrigation, outdoor container plants dry out fast in warm summer weather, especially when the containers are made of clay. When you go on vacation, you can help your small (4- to 8-inch) potted plants retain moisture by sinking them into soil up to their rims. (This also keeps them from blowing over.) Put them in a shady spot and tell your stand-in irrigator to give them special attention. Thirsty roots can pull all the available moisture out of a small amount of soil in very little time. To prevent large containers from drying out, group three or more together so the pots will shade each other, mulch the soil surface with an inch-thick layer of fir bark or pebbles, and add soil polymers (such as Broadleaf P4) to pencil-size holes poked into the soil.

THAT'S A GOOD QUESTION

Q: When is the best time to cut back penstemon (and other herbaceous perennials), and how far back should you cut?
A: Penstemon *can* start getting a bit rangy by midsummer. But whacking the plant back substantially now is not a good idea, says Joe Brosius of Magic Growers, a wholesale nursery specializing in perennials. Depriving a herbaceous perennial of most of its leaves while it is in an active growing stage prevents it from absorbing nutrients and can cause it to go into shock. A better solution, he says, is to snip out unproductive or unsightly stems—or stems that have finished blooming—a few at a time throughout the plant's growing season. Cut back to where there are bumps on the stems near the crown. When the penstemon stops blooming and goes dormant in late fall, it is safe to cut the whole plant back to a few inches from the ground. Salvia, rudbeckia, artemisia, coreopsis, and many other herbaceous perennials should be treated the same way. Other perennials, like nepeta and delphinium, can be cut back midseason for a second flush of bloom.

SOUTHERN CALIFORNIA
Garden Notebook

BY SHARON COHOON

Gardening here is heaven. Comparing notes with my mother back in Kansas every month about our respective gardens makes me well aware of that. Orchids in December, lettuce in February, roses in April. Meanwhile, Mom's still waiting for the ground to thaw. "It must be nice," she says enviously. And during those months I agree in spades.

But by the time August rolls around, I'm more aware of the flip side of gardening in paradise. "When do you get a break around here?" I grumble. Because it's hard to take one when your plants don't. This month, though, I'm declaring a moratorium. Not planting another thing. Turning on the sprinklers, picking up a book, crawling into the hammock, giving it a rest. Don't you want to do the same?

Two new gardening books would make excellent hammock fare:

Earthsong: How to Design a Truly Spectacular Natural Garden, by Chase Revel (Laservision, Carson City, NV, 1995; $29.95). The author, an artist who lives in Pacific Palisades, designed his hillside garden as a series of vignettes. In the book, he presents each scene with just a photograph or two and a spare page of text. You can pick it up, like a book of poetry, and start anywhere, or read it from cover to cover. Either way, you get the message—and lots of good ideas.

The Collector's Garden: Designing with Extraordinary Plants, by Ken Druse (Clarkson Potter, New York, 1996; $45). Frankly, few of us will ever achieve gardens equal to the ones in this book. We don't have the time, the land, the energy, or the necessary level of obsession. You won't covet these gardens—at least not in August—as much as you'll wish you could visit them. This book is the next best thing.

•

If, on the other hand, you really must plant—and that, I admit, was the case with me last year—try a cuphea. In August I planted false heather (*C. hyssopifolia*) and bat-faced cuphea (*C. llavea*), an irresistible plant that bears small, bright red flowers with tiny purple bat "ears." Both actually seemed to relish the heat. My very favorite cuphea, though, remains *C. micropetala,* a taller member of this family. Its yellow-orange tubular flowers look great in arrangements.

South African bulbs are also good to plant this month. Freesias, sparaxis, and ixia are beginning to arrive at nurseries. For a wide range of choices, visit the University of California Irvine Arboretum's annual South African Bulb Sale from 10 to 3 on August 24 and 25. (Call 714/824-5833 for directions and details.) Or buy the bulbs from Jim Duggan Flower Nursery; to request a catalog, send $2 to 1452 Santa Fe Dr., Encinitas, CA 92024, or call (619) 943-1658.

THAT'S A GOOD QUESTION

Q: When is the best time to cut back penstemon, and how far back should you cut?

A: Penstemon *can* start getting a bit rangy by midsummer. But whacking the plant back substantially now is not a good idea, says Joe Brosius of Magic Growers, a Pasadena wholesale nursery specializing in perennials. Depriving a herbaceous perennial of most of its leaves while it is in an active growing stage prevents it from absorbing nutrients and can cause it to go into shock. A better solution is to snip out unproductive stems a few at a time throughout the plant's growing season. Cut back to where there are bumps on the stems near the crown. When the plant stops blooming and goes dormant in late fall, it's safe to cut the whole plant back to a few inches from the ground. Treat salvia, rudbeckia, artemisia, and coreopsis the same way.

INLAND WESTERN STATES
Garden Notebook

BY JIM McCAUSLAND

Though August is hot, summer is winding down. Days are getting shorter, fruits and vegetables are ripening, and the breeze sounds a little rougher as it sighs through older, tougher leaves.

It's a good time to take stock of your garden. Dick Hildreth, director of education at Red Butte Garden and Arboretum in Salt Lake City, says that every gardener should keep a garden journal—a place to record successes, failures, and ideas for your next shot at the perfect garden.

I take notes on my computer day by day. I organize the notes in files by month so I can easily compare monthly entries from one year to the next. By doing this, I learned that some of my apples were alternate-bearing (heavy crop one year, light the next), and I realized that there were big swings in insect populations from year to year.

Other excellent gardeners I know hate computers. One, who swears she's not a Luddite, puts everything in spiral notebooks. She likes them because she can paste empty seed packets and plastic nursery tags onto the pages and make notes around them. I tell her that one good fire will vaporize her garden history. She tells me that one good power surge will send my data into the ether. While we're arguing, we're both becoming better gardeners because, as Dick Hildreth suggests, we're keeping records and comparing notes.

•

Garden cleanup must be one of the most underrated tasks. When I plant a tree, nobody notices. But if I edge the lawn and weed the front flower bed, everybody comments on how good my yard looks.

I used to edge the lawn with a shovel, grubbing out trespassing grass rhizomes with a hand weeder after I'd cut my Maginot Line. But as the number of my flower beds grew, the amount of weekly edging I did seemed to increase by hours. I finally started edging with a string trimmer. It does a fast and splendid job, though it turns my legs below the knees green with trimmings. I recommend a string trimmer, with this caution: never use it to kill a slug (the splatter factor would shock even Martin Scorsese).

•

Sometimes the summer lawn browns out because hot, dry weather puts the grass under stress. But other times, the lawn mower itself may be the culprit; after six months of steady use, the mower blades get as dull as the edge of a dinner plate. When it cuts, the mower frays the blades of grass, which quickly turn brown.

You can sharpen a mower blade, but if it's really dull, you can save yourself a lot of work by buying a new blade. If you have a mulching mower, be sure to buy a blade that's made specifically for your mower. Because the blades and decks of these mowers are aerodynamically designed, a generic replacement may not be as efficient.

THAT'S A GOOD QUESTION

Q: My oaks get swollen, tumorlike growths on their branches. Do these harm the tree? What can I do about them?

A: Those growths are called galls, and they serve as nurseries for various kinds of insects, which "sting" the twigs, branches, and leaves as they lay eggs in them. Galls range in size from peas to tennis balls, and although they appear on a wide variety of plants, they are most commonly found on elms, pines, roses, walnuts, and willows. They don't hurt the trees they live on. There's no control for galls other than pruning them out.

PACIFIC NORTHWEST
CHECKLIST
AUGUST

Sunset
Western Garden Book
CLIMATE ZONES

☐ 1–3 ☐ 4–7

PLANTING & HARVEST

☐ **ANNUALS.** It's not too late to pep up patios, planters, and beds with summer annuals like sunflowers and zinnias. By August, nursery supplies of sixpacks are pretty much gone, but annuals in 4-inch pots should be available. Set out plants immediately, water them well, and start feeding them with a complete liquid fertilizer.

☐ **FALL AND WINTER CROPS.** Sow seeds of cilantro, cress, endive, lettuce, radishes, scallions, Swiss chard, and turnips (for winter greens) any time this month. Late in the month, sow arugula, cabbage (for spring harvest), corn salad, mustard, and onions.

☐ **HARVEST HERBS.** Cut herbs in the morning, just after the dew has dried, when their flavor is at its peak. To air-dry herbs for later use, lay them out on a clean screen in a dry, shady place for two weeks or so.

MAINTENANCE

☐ **CLIP SPENT BLOOMS.** To keep blooms coming on annuals, and to keep perennials from channeling their strength into seed production, clip flowers as they fade.

☐ **FERTILIZE.** Annuals, long-flowering perennials, and container plants can all benefit from a good feeding. Use a complete liquid food once a month, or apply a half-strength solution about every two weeks.

☐ **COMPOST.** Add grass clippings, spent flowers, inedible vegetable parts, non-meat kitchen waste, prunings, and most pulled weeds to the compost pile. Turn the pile once a month, and if it begins to dry out, add enough water so the pile stays as moist as a wrung-out sponge.

☐ **DIVIDE EARLY PERENNIALS.** You can dig and divide bearded irises and Oriental poppies now. Replant the divisions immediately in soil amended with organic matter.

☐ **PROPAGATE SHRUBS.** Camellia, daphne, elaeagnus, euonymus, hebe, holly, hydrangea, magnolia, nandina, rhododendron, and viburnum can all be propagated by tip cuttings. Strip leaves off the lower end of the cuttings, dip them in rooting hormone, and put them in pots filled with a mixture of equal parts potting soil and sand. Water the cuttings and keep them in a bright spot but out of direct sunlight. Mist them daily, or create a moisture tent over the pot using a plastic bag and small stakes. Move the cuttings into a protected area before the first frost.

☐ **WATER WISELY.** Irrigate early in the morning: you'll conserve water by giving it a chance to soak into the soil instead of evaporating into thin air.

PEST & WEED CONTROL

☐ **BATTLE SLUGS.** Set out traps and saucers of beer in cool, shady spots. Set out bait near the places where they hide from the heat—rocks, house foundations, and ground covers—but be sure to keep pets and children away from the poisonous bait.

☐ **WEED.** Remove weeds before they go to seed, and save yourself some trouble next spring and summer. Weeds with immature seeds can go on the compost pile. Put plants with near-ripe seeds and aggressive roots (such as morning glory and nightshade) in the garbage can.

PLANTING

☐ **PLANT FOR SUMMER-FALL BLOOM.** Zones 7–9, 14–17: Some perennials that bloom from now into fall include achillea, aster, begonia, coreopsis, dahlia, daylily (some varieties), fortnight lily, common geranium, lantana, *Limonium perezii*, Mexican bush sage, scabiosa, and verbena (in zones 1 and 2, check hardiness—a few plants, such as *Limonium perezii* and Mexican bush sage, aren't adapted to your zones). For annuals, choose celosia, cosmos, Madagascar periwinkle, marigold, sweet alyssum, and zinnia.

☐ **PLANT A SHADE TREE.** For optimum cooling effect, plant a tree on the southwest side of the house in a spot where it will shade windows. Use a deciduous tree for shade in summer and sun in winter. Zones 7–9, 14–17: Try a camphor tree, Chinese hackberry, Chinese pistache, Japanese pagoda tree, ornamental pear, Raywood ash, or red oak. Zones 1 and 2: Try American hornbeam, Eastern redbud, honey locust, Japanese pagoda tree, little-leaf linden, or Marshall seedless green ash.

☐ **START COOL-SEASON CROPS.** Zones 7–9, 14–17: Start seeds of broccoli, brussels sprouts, cabbage, and cauliflower; they need six to eight weeks to reach transplant size. Sow seeds of carrots, chard, lettuce, peas, and radishes directly in the ground. Zones 1 and 2: Where frosts aren't expected until late

Sunset
CLIMATE ZONES

☐ Mountain (1-2)
☐ Valley (7-9)
☐ Inland (14)
☐ Coastal (15-17)

October, sow seeds of beets, carrots, radishes, and spinach; they should be ready by fall.

MAINTENANCE

☐ **HARVEST FRUITS AND VEGETABLES.** Check the garden daily to see what's ready. Search bean, summer squash, and tomato plants thoroughly so you don't miss ripe vegetables. If you want to preserve tomatoes by canning them, harvest while they're still firm; soft tomatoes may contain harmful bacteria.

Harvest corn when the tassels have withered and the kernels are well formed and squirt milky juice when punctured. Cut herbs—such as rosemary, sage, and thyme—for drying; hang them from the rafters in a clean, dry place.

☐ **TEND ROSES.** Zones 7–9, 14–17: To get good fall bloom from your rose bushes, give them plenty of water during August's hot days. Also, feed bushes with a complete fertilizer and an iron chelate to correct chlorosis (if necessary) and water them in thoroughly. Snip off old blooms or rose hips; lightly shape plants if necessary.

☐ **WATER.** August is usually one of our hottest months. If plants are watered by an automatic system, make sure that it's running often enough and long enough to water plants adequately. Check soil moisture by digging down with a trowel. If hand-watering, keep the hose in one place long enough to wet the soil; a quick sweep across a bed is not adequate.

PEST CONTROL

☐ **CONTROL SPIDER MITES.** These pests thrive during hot weather; look for stippling and possibly fine webbing on leaves. Spray the undersides of leaves with insecticidal soap or the more toxic malathion. To reduce the chance of infestation, periodically rinse dust and grime off leaves with a strong jet of water from the hose.

CHECKLIST
AUGUST

Sunset
CLIMATE ZONES

1-3 7-9 11 13 14-24

PLANTING

❑ **BUY AND PLANT BEARDED IRISES.** Iris rhizomes begin arriving in nurseries this month. Shop early for the best selection. Plant 1 to 2 feet apart in an area that gets at least a half-day of sun. In hot inland areas, bury the rhizome tops slightly to prevent sunburn. Closer to the coast, plant so rhizome tops show slightly above the soil surface. Water thoroughly immediately after planting.

❑ **PLANT SUMMER VEGETABLES.** Coastal gardeners (zones 22–24) can still add transplants of cucumber, eggplant, pepper, squash, and tomato. Look for fast-maturing varieties. Inland (zones 18–21) and low-desert (zone 13) gardeners can sow or transplant a final crop of beans or corn.

❑ **START ANNUALS FROM SEED.** Calendula, Iceland poppy, nemesia, snapdragon, stock, sweet pea, and many other cool-season annuals can be sown in flats after midmonth. (This is often the only way to obtain tall-stemmed varieties or a large quantity of a single color.) Keep flats in partial shade. By October—prime planting time—the seedlings will be ready to transplant into the garden.

❑ **START WINTER CROPS.** Coastal, inland, and high-desert (zone 11) gardeners can sow cool-season vegetables in flats at midmonth and transplant the seedlings to the garden in six to eight weeks. Good candidates include anything in the Brassicaceae family—broccoli, cabbage, cauliflower, kale, and mustard; root crops such as beets, carrots, onions, and turnips; head and leaf lettuces; and edible-pod peas.

MAINTENANCE

❑ **DIVIDE BEARDED IRISES.** Dig up old, overgrown clumps of bearded irises and divide rhizomes with a sharp knife. Discard woody centers. Trim leaves of remaining rhizomes to 6 inches. Replant divisions 1 to 2 feet apart.

❑ **RENEW MULCH.** Check the mulch—if it is less than 1 inch deep, add more compost or shredded bark to a depth of 3 inches. Keep mulch away from bases of tree trunks and plant stems.

❑ **DEEP-WATER TREES.** Use a soaker hose to deep-water mature trees before they show signs of drought stress such as unseasonal leaf drop.

❑ **FEED TURF.** Lightly feed warm-season turf grasses such as Bermuda and St. Augustine with high-nitrogen fertilizer.

❑ **CARE FOR ROSES.** Cut off spent flowers and hips to stimulate fall flowering. Cut just above a leaf node with five or more leaflets. (Inland gardeners should wait another month, until temperatures drop.) Remove dead, weak, or crossed canes as well. Feed with a complete fertilizer, mulch heavily, and water deeply and regularly.

PEST CONTROL

❑ **PROTECT HOUSE PLANTS.** Spider mites, scale, and thrips may attack during summer months. Mist plants frequently to increase humidity and reduce stress. Treat plant infestations with insecticidal soap or horticultural oil.

❑ **COMBAT LAWN GRUBS.** Irregular brown patches in summer lawns are often caused by beetle larvae, which feed on grass roots. Pull up sections of dead turf to expose roots. If you find grubs, treat the lawn with parasitic nematodes.

CHECKLIST
AUGUST

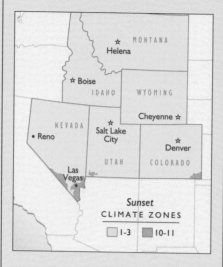

Sunset
CLIMATE ZONES
◻ 1-3   ▦ 10-11

PLANTING & HARVEST

❏ **PLANT IRISES, AUTUMN CROCUS.** Iris rhizomes and autumn crocus (*Colchicum*) corms are in nurseries now. Plant immediately. The irises will flower next year, the crocus within a month.

❏ **PLANT FOR FALL HARVEST.** Where frosts aren't expected until late October, sow beets, carrots, spinach, and radishes for fall harvest. In mildest climates, set out transplants of broccoli, cabbage, and cauliflower.

❏ **START GREENHOUSE CROPS.** Sow seeds of eggplant, peppers, and short-season tomatoes in early August in flats indoors or on a patio. When seedlings have two sets of true leaves, transplant them into pots at least 8 inches deep (12 inches for tomatoes). Transfer plants to greenhouse before nighttime temperatures fall below 55°. Keep the greenhouse between 60° and 80° during the day, 60° and 70° at night. To ensure pollination of eggplant and tomatoes, shake flowers to broadcast pollen from blossom to blossom.

❏ **SOW WILDFLOWERS.** Sow seed of annual and perennial wildflowers now for bloom next spring. Try bachelor's button, perennial blue flax, coreopsis, Mexican hat, poppy, prairie aster, Rocky Mountain penstemon, and yellow cone-flower. (In coldest areas, do this in September.) Cultivate soil lightly, spread seed, then mulch with ¼ to ½ inch of ground bark or other organic matter.

❏ **HARVEST FRUITS, VEGETABLES.** Pick beets, broccoli, bush beans, cauliflower, new potatoes, raspberries, strawberries, summer squash, sweet corn, tomatoes, and zucchini.

❏ **HARVEST HERBS.** Pick them in the morning, just after dew has dried. You can use most kinds fresh, but if you want to dry them and use them later, put them in a dehydrator, or place them on a clean screen in a dry, shady spot for about two weeks.

MAINTENANCE

❏ **DIVIDE PERENNIALS.** A good rule of thumb is to divide spring-flowering perennials in late summer or early fall, and fall-bloomers in spring. After delphiniums, German irises, Oriental poppies, and Shasta daisies bloom, divide large clumps. Dig up and cut the root mass into several sections using a sharp knife or pruning shears. Add organic matter such as compost to soil and replant perennials. While plants are out of the ground, clear the soil of weeds—especially grass and its runners. (In shortest-season areas, wait until spring to dig and replant.)

❏ **MAKE COMPOST.** As you pull out annuals and early vegetables, put them in the compost pile. Keep the pile well turned and as moist as a wrung-out sponge. By frost time, you'll have enough compost to dig back into empty garden beds.

❏ **PROTECT VEGETABLES.** High-elevation gardeners: use cardboard, glass, or row covers to protect vegetables from early cold temperatures. Set covers in place by late afternoon and remove before midmorning.

❏ **WATER SPROUTS, SUCKERS.** Vigorous shoots growing from the trunks or branches of birch, crabapple, hawthorn, lilac, Russian olive, and willow are water sprouts. Suckers grow from a plant's rootstock. Prune off both water sprouts and suckers.

PLANTING & HARVEST

❑ **PLANT VEGETABLES.** Beans, corn, cucumbers, squash, and tomatoes can all go in now for a late harvest. Near the end of the month, you can set out transplants of broccoli, cabbage, cauliflower, chard, and spinach; sow beets and carrots then as well. Mulch and shade the transplants to protect them from late summer's hot weather, and keep seedlings well watered.

❑ **HARVEST FRUITS AND VEGETABLES.** Gather whatever is harvestable to stop rot before it gets started, and keep rotten fruits from littering the ground below plants.

MAINTENANCE

❑ **CARE FOR LAWNS.** Mow the lawn often enough that you never have to remove more than a third of the grass blade at one time. Cut common Bermuda to about 1½ inches and hybrids to ¾ inch. Cut zoysia and St. Augustine to 1½ to 2 inches. Cut cool-season grasses such as fescue, buffalo grass, and Kentucky bluegrass to 2 to 3 inches.

❑ **CARE FOR ROSES.** To help roses get ready for a strong autumn bloom, acidify their soil with soluble sulfur (Disper-Sul), fortify it with a complete fertilizer, and apply iron chelate to correct chlorosis. Be sure to water everything in thoroughly.

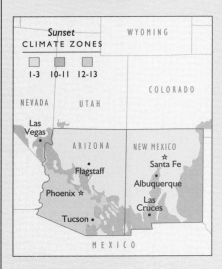

❑ **FERTILIZE SHRUBS.** Give them a half-strength application of complete fertilizer, watering it in well, to help them recover from heat stress.

❑ **KEEP COMPOST COMING.** Compost piles do a great job of breaking down weeds, grass, and vegetable waste as long as they're kept as damp as a wrung-out sponge. Turn the pile often to keep it well aerated. In this month's heat, you may have to water the pile every couple of days to keep it composting.

❑ **PREVENT FRUIT SPLIT.** Fruits such as citrus, melons, pomegranates, and tomatoes can split when monsoons (or irrigation) give them too much water after summer drought (their skins can't stretch enough to accommodate the extra water inside). To minimize this problem, keep the soil around these plants evenly moist as they mature.

❑ **PRUNE PEPPERS, TOMATOES.** You can encourage a fall crop on many kinds of spring-planted peppers and tomatoes by pruning them. Cut back tomatoes by about a third, and lightly prune peppers. Protect both with shade cloths to prevent sunburn on newly exposed stems.

PEST CONTROL

❑ **SOUTHWESTERN CORN BORERS.** If translucent patches are showing up on your corn leaves, skeletonizing them, corn borer larvae are likely responsible. They can also kill the plant's growing tip. Spray plants, especially where leaves join the stalks, with *Bacillus thuringiensis* (BT).

❑ **SPIDER MITES, WHITEFLIES.** Dislodge them by hosing off plants frequently, and follow up by spraying insecticidal soap to control infestations. Also, put out yellow sticky traps to catch whiteflies.

TEXAS

PLANTING

❑ **VEGETABLES.** In North and West Texas, you can sow beans, cabbage family members, collards, corn, cucumbers, potatoes, spinach, squash, and Swiss chard early in the month, and available transplants at the end of the month. In Central, South, and East Texas, do the same things, but two or three weeks later.

MAINTENANCE

❑ **MAKE COMPOST.** Haul garden waste to the compost pile, mixing weeds, lawn clippings, and nonmeat kitchen waste. Water and turn the pile regularly; it should become a wonderfully useful soil amendment within two months.

❑ **MULCH SEEDLINGS.** Apply a 2-inch layer of organic mulch around new seedlings. It will keep roots cool and hold in moisture. Don't let mulch touch seedling stems.

❑ **PROTECT VEGETABLE SEEDLINGS.** Row covers or latticework panels (available at building supply stores) suspended overhead can keep young seedlings from burning.

❑ **WATER.** Container plants, nursery stock, seedlings you just planted this year, and anything growing under house eaves need extra attention this time of year. Thoroughly drench the roots of permanent landscape plants with a soaker hose, deep-root irrigator, or hose running slowly into a watering basin dug around the plant.

PEST CONTROL

❑ **LAWN PESTS.** Chinch bugs can cause St. Augustine to dry out and die back, and microscopic Bermuda mites can do the same to Bermuda grass, giving it a classic shaving-brush look. The treatment for both pests is the same: an application of chlorpyrifos (Dursban) or Diazinon.

❑ **SPIDER MITES.** These are everywhere this time of year. Mottled leaves and fine webs give away the mites' presence; control them by spraying with a miticide.

❑ **WHITEFLIES.** Yellow sticky traps are the best control measure for these.

Lilac

"Every spring my aunt would invite my mom me to drive out to her farm and collect arm-fuls of lavender lilacs to tote back home, and the scent floated throughout our house."

—Ardice Eggert, Glendale, Arizona

Spring. Common, or French, lilac (*Syringa vulgaris*) is a shrub that does best where winters are cold (*Sunset* climate zones 1–11), but there are varieties (most called Descanso hybrids) for mild-winter climates (zones 12–16, 18–22). Nurseries usually carry varieties best suited for the local climate.

When we asked readers to name their favorite garden fragrances, we weren't prepared for the often poignant outpouring of responses that rolled in by the score from 15 states, Canada, and Mexico.

We heard from one woman whose long bout with amnesia was cured by an unexpected encounter with fragrant hyacinths, and from a couple whose lifelong romance was linked to a certain honeysuckle plant (when it was cut down, the man died).

Sifting through these odes to more than 150 different plants, we distilled readers' favorites down to the essential few on these pages. Grow them in your garden and breathe deep. But keep your ears open, too: when scented flowers

A guide to 18 scented flowers our readers can't forget

bloom, you'll probably notice a certain sentimental drift in your conversations.

Walking under the Hall's honeysuckle growing over the front porch of my house, a friend stopped suddenly and said, "I'm 10 years old again." Years from now, my daughter will probably stroll under another honeysuckle in some distant place, stop for a moment, and say the same thing. Such is the power of plant fragrances to insinuate themselves deeply into our pasts, and our futures, too.

UNFORGETTABLE
garden
fragrances

BY JIM McCAUSLAND • PHOTOGRAPHS BY PAUL HAMMOND

Jasmine and Jessamine

"That sultry, spicy, damp smell wafting into a tropical bedroom is without par. I have been romanced by night-blooming jasmine."

—Cecelia Smith, Honaunau, Hawaii

Spring/summer. Most of the plants in this group have a sweet, rather heavy fragrance.

• Night jessamine (*Cestrum nocturnum*, zones 13, 16–24), a shrub native to the West Indies, is the "night-blooming jasmine" described above. Its scent is powerful, too powerful for some. ("We used to call it night-blooming asthma," wrote Margaret Harris of Albany, California.) Plant it near a window so its scent can drift into the house on a summer evening.

• True jasmine (*Jasminum grandiflorum, J. officinale, J. polyanthum;* zones 5–9, 12–24) includes semideciduous and evergreen vines. Spanish jasmine (*J. grandiflorum*) and poet's jasmine (*J. officinale*) flower all summer; *J. polyanthum* (shown at left) blooms from early spring through summer.

• Star jasmine (*Trachelospermum jasminoides*, zones 8–24) is a common ground cover in California and the Southwest, but in the Pacific Northwest it's sold as an espaliered summer pot plant. Flowers are most strongly fragrant in the evening.

Rose

"The smell of roses is life.... My memories soar back to my grandmother's little rose garden I used to enjoy as a child."

—Jerri Johnson, Aloha, Oregon

Summer. Few plants have been as intensively bred as roses. One result of the breeding is that some varieties are heavily scented, while others have no fragrance at all. For this reason, the best time to buy these plants is in summer, when you can smell the roses. Different roses grow well in different zones. The best bet is to buy plants from a nursery that has a strong interest in roses.

Reader favorites include 'Electron', 'Fragrant Cloud', 'Fragrant Hour', 'Fragrant Memory', 'Garden Fragrance', 'Mister Lincoln', 'New Dawn', 'Nymphenburg', 'Perfume Delight', *R. rugosa* 'Hansa', 'Sunsprite', and 'Sutter's Gold'. 'Mikado' is shown at left.

DAPHNE

"The sweet odor of the daphne [is] powerful on damp mornings and subtle in the dry afternoons."

—Father Steve Norcross, Lebanon, Oregon

Winter/spring. *Daphne odora,* an evergreen shrub, grows in zones 4 through 10, 12, and 14 through 24, producing strongly fragrant clusters of pink flowers at the ends of its branches. *D. odora* 'Marginata' is shown. It doesn't take many daphne flowers to fill a room with sweet, almost citrusy fragrance. But daphne can be tricky to grow: the plant demands good drainage and, for some reason, often seems to thrive beside concrete walkways.

HONEYSUCKLE

"Their fragrance is…especially noticeable during the still of the night. Our master bedroom abuts the rear yard, and with the windows open, we never want to exhale!"
— Naomi Steele, Seattle

Spring/summer. Hall's honeysuckle (*Lonicera japonica* 'Halliana', zones 2–24), shown here, is probably the most popular of many wonderful honeysuckle species and varieties. Its sweetly scented white flowers, which grow on a 15-foot vine, change to yellow as they age. Use it as a ground cover or climbing vine, and plant it close to a path, window, or entry so you can enjoy its spring and summer flowers.
Giant Burmese honeysuckle (*L. hildebrandiana*, zones 9, 14–17, 19–24) produces huge, white, fragrant tubular flowers on fast-growing vines. It's a good choice for mild-climate gardens.

HELIOTROPE

"Its heavy, sweet fragrance evokes memories of high button shoes and bustles." —Jean Myer, Mountain View, California

Summer. Commonly sold as a summer annual, heliotrope (*Heliotropium arborescens*) is perennial in zones 8 through 24. Its fragrance can be fairly strong, something like vanilla with light grape overtones. It's a good plant to use in containers.

Where does fragrance come from?

Fragrance in flowers is nature's way of encouraging pollination. Just as fragrance draws people to take a deeper whiff, it lures insects to blossoms hidden by leaves and other plants. Some flowers are fragrant only at night and attract only night-flying pollinators, like moths, while others are more fragrant during the day and attract day-flying insects, like bees and butterflies. Yet some flowers perfume the air both day and night and attract both day and night insects.

The fragrance itself comes from essential oils called attars that vaporize easily and infuse the air with their scents. They are present in different combinations in different plants, but often they're markedly similar, which is why there are irises that smell like grapes.

·12 Other Memorable Scents·

Several readers associated fragrances with particular people or places (such as plumeria with Hawaii). Some examples:

• **Lavender** *(Lavandula angustifolia), summer. "My aunt would make lavender sachets for use in our clothes drawers. I can clearly remember using lavender-scented furniture polish and picking fresh lavender to put in my bedroom."*

—Elizabeth Reid, Redmond, Washington

• **Orange blossoms,** *spring. "Several years ago I had a boyfriend, Fred, who would take the sweet-smelling citrus blossoms and string them into a beautiful necklace…so I could wear it…and smell the incredible fragrance all day long. Still to this day, when I smell citrus blossoms, it reminds me of a very special relationship."*

—Tracy Mauldin, Sacramento

• **Sweet pea** *(Lathyrus odoratus), spring. "I was born in England…. My most vivid memories of scent come from roses, lavender, and sweet peas, all of which are in abundance in my own garden. [I never thought] I would be in America and able to indulge in planting and looking after a garden so large. Friends say, 'What a lot of work!' I say, 'What a lot of pleasure!'"*

—Elizabeth Reid, Redmond, Washington

These plants also won frequent praise for their fragrant flowers:

- Chinese wisteria *(W. sinensis), spring*
- Common butterfly bush *(Buddleia davidii), spring/summer*
- Gardenia, spring to fall
- Iris, spring (some rebloom in late summer or fall)
- Lily-of-the-valley *(Convallaria majalis), spring*
- Mexican orange *(Choisya ternata), spring*
- Peony, mid- to late spring
- Sweet alyssum *(Lobularia maritima), spring/summer in cold areas, all year in mild areas*
- Rhododendron ('Fragrantissimum' and 'King George'), spring

Pink-flowered Calluna vulgaris 'Mullion' (top left in the photo above) and two varieties of Erica cinerea (front) mound around gold-foliaged C. v. 'Aurea'.

A passion for
heathers

More than 200 kinds thrive in this garden near Mendocino, California

By Lauren Bonar Swezey

IT ALL BEGAN 10 YEARS AGO WHEN JIM Thompson and his wife attended a rhododendron show in Oregon. Heathers were offered at the plant sale, and knowing nothing about them, he purchased a few plants to bring home. "I soon discovered that our growing conditions are ideal for heathers," says Thompson. "They thrive in cool, moist air, well-drained, acid soil, and sun."

Now, Thompson's garden is a showplace of summer-blooming heathers, which include numerous kinds of *Calluna, Daboecia,* and *Erica.* The velvety tapestry of colors and textures covers more than half of his ½-acre front yard in Manchester, California, 30 miles south of Mendocino.

To give his flat lot the more visually interesting look of undulating hills, and to better set off the heathers, Thompson built up mounds of soil and planted the heathers on top. Ten to twelve plants of each variety are grouped together, and the various groups are mixed and matched by foliage and flower color.

Thompson buys just one plant of each kind, then takes stem cuttings to increase his collection. He usually takes the cuttings in late summer, sets them in an outdoor rooting bed filled with a mixture of half sand and half peat, and shades them with lattice. Six to eight weeks later, he moves the rooted cuttings to a box filled with potting soil that sits in full sun. Next fall, they're ready to go in the ground.

Undulating mounds of pink, red, and white heathers are at peak bloom in mid-to late summer. Swaths of gold-foliaged heathers lighten the composition.

CHAS McGRATH

Bell-flowered Daboecia cantabrica 'Rubra' intermingles with rose-pink Calluna vulgaris 'Peter Sparkes' (above left).
At right, flowers of white C. v. 'Kinlochruel' poke up through gold-foliaged Erica cinerea 'Golden Drop'.

CARING FOR HEATHERS

Since heathers thrive in poor soil—and Thompson's soil is sandy—compost alone nourishes his plants; it's mixed into the soil at planting time. (Add peat to alkaline soil to increase acidity.)

When transplanting heathers, Thompson avoids disturbing the roots too much. After knocking the plants out of nursery cans, he scores only the bottom and shoulders of the rootballs.

Heathers don't demand much water or fertilizer, but they need to be kept moist the first year. After that, Thompson waters his plants only once every three weeks. Even in warmer climates, heathers don't need much water, especially in loamy soils.

In fall after blooms fade, Thompson uses a hedge trimmer to clean off the old blooms, removing very little foliage. ∎

THOMPSON'S FAVORITE HEATHERS

The following 12 heathers have attractive foliage and flowers, transplant easily, and are not difficult to grow. Unless noted, all are summer bloomers. (Thompson is too humble to recommend a 13th favorite—*Calluna vulgaris* 'Forty-Niner Gold'. This gold-foliaged sport, which he found growing on one of his *C. v.* 'Long White' plants, is the only heather from the United States that's registered with the Heather Society in Great Britain.)

Calluna vulgaris 'County Wicklow': pink double flowers, 10 inches tall by 12 inches wide. "Should be in every heather garden," says Thompson.

C. v. 'Cuprea': lavender, coppery foliage, 18 inches by 18 inches.

C. v. 'Kinlochruel': white double flowers, 10-inch compact mound. "The best double white."

C. v. 'Peter Sparkes': rose-pink double flowers, 18 inches by 18 inches.

C. v. 'Silver Queen': pinkish lavender, woolly silvery foliage, 18 inches by 18 inches. "Contrast with deep green- or gold-leafed varieties."

Daboecia cantabrica 'Cinderella':

white with blush of pink, gray-green foliage, 18 inches by 18 inches. "A gold-medal winner in the Netherlands."

Erica carnea 'Vivellii': carmine-red late winter to spring, bronze foliage in winter, 6-inch by 18-inch spreading mat.

E. ciliaris 'Mrs. C. H. Gill': crimson, 18 inches by 18 inches. "Covered with flowers."

E. cinerea 'C. D. Eason': magenta, dark green foliage, 12 inches by 15 inches.

E. c. 'Eden Valley': lavender and white, plant grows 10 inches by 15 inches. "Very floriferous."

E. c. 'Golden Drop': amethyst, coppery gold foliage during summer, reddish

in winter, 6 inches by 12 inches.

E. vagans 'Mrs. D. F. Maxwell': cerise, 18 inches by 20 inches. "Indispensable for summer color."

THOMPSON'S FAVORITE
MAIL-ORDER SOURCES

If you can't find the heather varieties you want at a nursery, try one of these two sources (both offer free lists; send a self-addressed, stamped envelope).

Heather Heaven, Box 71, Fortuna, CA 95540; (707) 725-6384.

Heaths and Heathers, E. 502 Haskell Hill Rd., Shelton, WA 98584; (360)

Bananas!

These handsome tropicals are becoming the landscaping plants of choice in Southern California

By Sharon Cohoon

BANANAS ARE THE GODZILLAS OF the herb world. Some varieties shoot up 20 feet or higher. But bananas are not trees; they're herbaceous perennials, and thus they die back as part of their life cycle. What looks like a tree trunk is actually a flower stalk containing no more wood than the stem of an aster.

After the banana stalk produces a flower cluster that develops into fruit, the stalk dies. But new stalks quickly spring up from the underground rhizome to take the place of the one that died. Just think of the banana as a canna on steroids and you've got the picture.

Southern Californians are growing fonder of banana plants. When Laguna Hills Nursery in Lake Forest, (714) 830-5653, started carrying bananas seven years ago, it sold barely 30 plants a year. Last year it sold more than 300. Increasing interest in fruit-bearing plants of all sorts, and the wider availability of banana varieties with more cold tolerance than the commonly sold Cavendish types, explain some of the growth in sales. But bananas are also gaining appeal strictly as ornamentals.

Nothing creates a tropical mood better

than bananas—or does it as quickly—says Robert Ramirez, a Santa Monica designer and builder who always includes bananas in his landscape plans. And with their mostly vertical growth, bananas are ideal candidates for narrow, hard-to-plant stucco "canyons" between houses. Their broad leaves quickly screen out neighbors' windows, creating privacy while allowing in enough light to keep these corridors from seeming gloomy.

Banana leaves are surprisingly translucent. Sunlight makes them glow.

GARY MATSUOKA

Bananas like these spaces, too. They're protected from wind, and they enjoy the heat reflecting from the canyon walls.

Bananas are not quick crops. It takes 10 to 15 months of nearly frost-free weather to produce a flower stalk, then another 4 to 8 months for the fruit to develop and ripen. (Mild freezes will ruin leaves and/or stalks but not the underground corm.) But harvests are huge. A single stalk can produce a bunch of bananas weighing 30 to 60 pounds. Fruit flavor varies from strawberry-citrus to vanilla cream, according to variety, but is invariably sweeter and more complex than the flavor of standard supermarket bananas.

Bananas need ample water and fertilizer but are otherwise remarkably easy to grow. Their only significant enemy in Southern California is frost. Temperatures between 32° and 40° will kill the foliage, though the plant will quickly releaf. Temperatures much below 30° will kill the stalk as well. But as long as temperatures don't fall below 22°, the underground rhizome will survive and the plant will spring back. If you live inland, where winter frosts are likely, grow your banana in a large, wheel-equipped pot that you can move under the eaves or indoors in winter.

PLANTING AND CULTURE

For quickest results, buy a container plant already in leaf. For economy, plant a semidormant rhizome. Choose the warmest, most protected location in your garden, such as one with southeast exposure near a wall. (Dwarf bananas—up to 8 feet tall—can also be planted in large containers such as barrel halves, preferably on wheels so they're easy to move.)

Dig a hole 2 to 3 feet wide and 18 inches deep. Add organic matter such as compost, an all-purpose fertilizer, and supplemental potassium (Sul-Po-Mag or sulfate of potash) to the backfill mix.

Water the plant thoroughly and keep the soil moist until several new leaves appear. Continue to irrigate frequently—approximately once a week—as long as the plant is actively growing. (Growth slows down when temperatures dip below 54°.)

Bananas are heavy feeders. Continue to provide nitrogen and supplemental potassium regularly during warm weather. In winter, allow plants to dry between waterings, and stop fertilizing.

Prop up fruited plants with two poles to keep them from toppling in the wind. Harvest bananas individually as they ripen. When the stalks are fully harvested, cut them back to 3 or 4 feet. Allow the plants to reabsorb nutrients for a month, then cut off the remainder of each stalk.

After the old stalks are finished, smaller, younger stems (suckers) will spring up at the base of the primary stems. You can allow as many as three suckers to develop, but allowing only one sucker at a time to develop into a trunk creates the most interesting effect. ∎

BANANAS FOR EVERY NEED, EVERY TASTE

All-around favorites

'Raja Puri'. Small but very sweet fruit. Fruited plants need no support. Grows 8 to 10 feet tall.

'Dwarf Brazilian'. Delicious, pleasantly tart fruit that stays firm even when quite ripe. Plant tolerates wind and needs no staking. Grows 8 to 12 feet tall.

'Mysore'. Small, orange-fleshed fruit with intense flavor. Red trunks and undersides of leaves make this banana plant highly ornamental. Grows 15 to 18 feet tall.

'Ice Cream' (also called 'Blue Java'). Fruit looks exotic and, when fully ripe, tastes like ice cream or vanilla custard. Skins are silvery blue before ripening, then pale canary yellow. Grows 12 to 15 feet tall.

Hardiest varieties

David Silber, co-owner of Papaya Tree Nursery in Granada Hills, (818) 363-3680, has been growing bananas successfully for 12 years in *Sunset* climate zone 19. He recommends the following varieties for cold tolerance.

'Dwarf Orinoco'. Large, triangular plantain-style fruit, usually cooked but can be eaten fresh. This is the most cold-hardy variety for Southern California. Grows 7 feet tall.

'Cardaba'. A large, triangular banana, good both raw and cooked. Grows 12 to 16 feet tall.

'Manzano'. Slightly crisp and tart flesh. Fastest crop. Grows to 15 feet tall.

Most ornamental

'Dwarf Jamaican Red'. Trunk, leaves, and fruit skin are all reddish purple. Orange-fleshed fruit has strong banana flavor. Plant is tender and usually does best near coast. Grows 7 to 8 feet tall.

'Ae Ae'. Grown primarily for gorgeous white-and-gray-green variegated foliage. Trunk and fruit have similar coloration. Although it is usually cooked, fruit can be eaten raw. Best planted in partial sun. Not vigorous. Grows to 15 feet tall.

Varieties your kids will like

Cavendish varieties look and taste like the supermarket bananas most familiar to kids, only better. 'Valery' grows 10 to 15 feet tall; 'Williams', 8 to 12 feet; 'Grand Nain', 6 to 8 feet; 'Dwarf Cavendish', 4 to 6 feet. All of these varieties are cold-tender, particularly 'Dwarf Cavendish'.

An array of birdhouses turns a shingled wall into a garden gallery above a bed of snapdragons, assorted annuals, and perennials. For details on this unusual folk art display, see page 222.

216

SEPTEMBER

Garden guide 218

Checklists & garden notebooks . . . 223

Secrets of the garden masters 230

Tulips year after year, naturally . . . 238

Soft summer blues 241

Garlic revival 242

Putting the "snap" in snap peas . . . 246

CDs loaded with garden answers . . 247

GARDEN
Guide

Create a realistic dry creek bed

A dry creek bed meanders through clumps of ornamental grasses and perennials in this garden.

We're all more regimented than we think. That's why our attempts to simulate something—such as a dry creek bed—are so rarely convincing.

Artificial creek beds tend to be overdesigned and overarranged, says Owen Dell, a California landscape architect who specializes in dry creek beds. The tendency is to push all of the big boulders neatly to the edges, give each its own space, bury all to a uniform depth, and then wonder why our creation has all the poetry of an irrigation ditch. But even a small-scale dry creek bed running across a front yard can—if

done well—convey the ferocity of the real thing.

The secret to making a realistic creek bed, says Dell, is learning how to think like a river. The one pictured above, which Dell designed for Lloyd and Jeanne Gibbs of Solvang, California, illustrates his point. Dell recommends visiting some natural creek beds, especially ones similar in scale to what you want, before simulating one. Notice what the force of water does to the rocks. In nature, pebbles get washed toward shore, and boulders too heavy for the current to move end up in the

middle of the stream, not the reverse. Rocks get piled on top of each other in a mad jumble or lie half-buried in silt.

When you understand how the violent force of water shapes natural creek beds, says Dell, you are ready to mimic that "chaos" in your own garden.

As with any landscaping project, start with the major players. Site the largest rocks mentally. Turn them around in your mind before having them forklifted into place. Then do the same with mid-size and small rocks. In general, try to put things down the way they were picked up, advises Dell.

LANDSCAPING SOLUTIONS

Sweet peas twine on a cypress arch

As fanciful as it may appear, the arch of Italian cypresses framing the approach to Tim and Marguerite Lindsay's home in Sunland, California, was chosen for practical reasons. The arch frames a view of the nearby San Gabriel Mountains.

Tim chose a green living arch over one made of wood or iron because it would be softer-looking and cost considerably less. It took about one year for the pair of 5-gallon trees to grow tall enough to be tied together at the top with 12-gauge copper wire. Pruning maintains the arch's form and keeps it looking neat.

The arch also provides a platform for sweet pea vines. "I needed a sunny area to grow sweet peas, and I thought an arch could do double duty supporting them," says Tim. When the sweet peas have run their course, he plants cardinal climber (*Ipomoea quamoclit*), a summer annual vine. Any lightweight vine could be substituted for sweet peas in this scenario. But more vigorous vines like common morning glory (*I. tricolor*) are too heavy for a living arch to support.

Sweet peas ('Royal White' and 'Royal Scarlet') climb over an arch formed by two Italian cypress trees.

CONTAINER CULTURE

Ornamental asparagus steals the show

Some container plantings are carefully planned for a one-season show. Others evolve and change form through the years, much as people change appearance. The pot pictured at left falls into the latter category.

About five years ago, *Sunset* gardener and floral designer Kim Haworth planted the 22-inch pot with a Myers asparagus, some ivy, and sweet alyssum. In the following years, different gardeners added other plants and the annuals came and went, but the ornamental asparagus remained at center stage.

Last fall, the container came into its prime, strutting a striking combination of textures and colors. The fernlike lime green foliage of the Myers asparagus poked out among tall orange snapdragons; purple alyssum and purple trailing lobelia tumbled down one side of the pot. The planting positively glowed, especially in the low golden light of late afternoon.

Myers asparagus makes an ideal container plant that can be grown outdoors year-round in *Sunset* climate zones 12 and 13 and as an indoor-outdoor plant in colder climates.

Lush spikes of Myers asparagus wave toward orange snapdragons. Dainty purple alyssum and trailing lobelia soften the pot's edge.

JAMES FREDERICK HOUSEL

Colorful houttuynia: A ground cover worth taming

If you want a vivid ground cover for a garden bed, the brilliantly colored foliage of *Houttuynia cordata* is hard to beat. The trouble is, this plant is very aggressive. In just two years, a couple of plants from 4-inch pots can form a thick mass, and their runners may easily have spread 10 feet.

The photograph at left shows an excellent way to tame this beautiful plant. This houttuynia is planted in a slightly raised bed and bounded on all sides by a walk, which contains its shallow roots. This one is growing under a weeping blue spruce (*Picea pungens* 'Pendula').

The spruce, with its strong, deep roots, has no trouble at all holding its own in a bed with this rambunctious ground cover. The two plants' contrasting foliage textures and colors create a garden spectacle from mid-April until the first hard freeze, when the houttuynia dies down and disappears for the winter.

Houttuynia is hardy enough to grow in *Sunset* climate zones 1 through 9 and 14 through 24. Nurseries sell plants in 4-inch pots or 1-gallon cans. Before you purchase a plant, crush one leaf between your fingers and take a good whiff: the odd orange peel scent may not appeal to you. You can set out plants this month. Keep them well watered until autumn rains start.

To ensure lush growth next year, feed your plants in mid-February by broadcasting a complete granular fertilizer over the bed.

Red- and cream-splashed leaves of houttuynia contrast with the frosty needles of a weeping blue spruce.

Colorful lettuces with a delicate crunch

Lettuce is one of the most satisfying vegetables to grow. It's fast and easy to grow from seed, and as long as you take care to plant it at the proper time of year (fall or spring), water it regularly, and protect it from slugs and snails, you can't go wrong. The payoff, of course, is a bunch of colorful, tasty greens for salads.

Bud Stuckey, test garden coordinator at *Sunset*'s headquarters in Menlo Park, likes lettuce for another reason: some varieties are simply beautiful to look at. Stuckey combines them to make a temporary tapestry of green among other plants. His favorites for looks and flavor are these three particularly handsome crispheads.

'Reine des Glaces' is an apple green Batavian crisphead lettuce. Its tender, deeply cut leaves have crunchy ribs and form a small, loose head (rather than a tightly formed head like an iceberg-type crisphead).

'Rosy' is a gorgeous crisphead with burgundy-and-green leaves that develop into a small, well-shaped head. It's slow to bolt, making it a good choice for spring planting.

'Sierra' Batavian crisphead (also sold as a butterhead) has wavy, bright green leaves blushed with bronze. It forms a looser, more open head than 'Rosy' and, like leaf lettuce, can be picked a leaf at a time. It also tolerates heat much better than many lettuces.

The Cook's Garden (Box 535, Londonderry, VT 05148; 802/824-3400) offers 43 varieties of lettuce (including the three listed here) in four categories—butterhead, crisphead, looseleaf, and romaine. Free catalog.

NORMAN A. PLATE

Freshly cut heads of three handsome lettuces—'Rosy' (front), 'Reine des Glaces' (top), and 'Sierra' (right)—are ready for the salad bowl.

Spice up the garden with choice fall bloomers

Come fall, when gardening in other parts of the country is shutting down for the year, gardens in the coastal Northwest (*Sunset* climate zones 4 through 7) can still be full of colorful flowers if they contain the right plants. Last fall, we visited several nurseries to find out which plants were blooming. We were pleasantly surprised by the large number of perennials that bloom right up to the first hard frost, sometimes into November.

Some of the colormakers listed below put on their best show in the cool fall months. Others start blooming in spring or summer and continue nonstop. To prolong flowering, regularly clip off spent blooms.

Anemone hybrida (Japanese anemone). Maplelike leaves and arching stems 2 to 4 feet tall. White, pink, or rose flowers. Blooms in fall. Partial shade.

Aster. Many kinds. *A. frikartii* hybrids bloom the longest, from late spring to fall. Plants grow 2 feet tall. Full sun.

Gaura lindheimeri. Branching flower spikes 2¼ to 4 feet tall bear pink buds that open to white. Full sun.

Salvia. Many species bloom over a long period. Heights and flower colors vary. Full sun.

Sedum. Varieties of *S. spectabile* and *S. telephium* sport broad, dense flower clusters (often coral and deep pink) that appear in fall, brown when freezing weather starts, but stand tall through the winter. Full sun.

In the coastal Northwest, look for late-flowering perennials such as Japanese anemone (top center) and aster (center) in nursery cans this month.

A new bacteria threatens Southland oleanders

In 1994, hundreds of mature oleanders in the Coachella Valley began turning brown and dying. More recently, cases of oleander dieback also were reported in Irvine and Tustin. Experts first thought the cause was drought stress or salt burn. But the tip dieback and scorched-looking leaf margins turned out to be the result of something far less easy to correct: a new strain of the bacteria *Xylella fastidiosa.* According to Mike Henry, environmental horticultural adviser at the University of California Cooperative Extension in Riverside County, this bacteria has plagued the area for more than a century. It wiped out the Southern California grape industry in the late 1800s. But until now, no strain of the bacteria has ever attacked oleander.

The glassy-winged sharpshooter, a leaf-sucking exotic pest native to the southeastern United States that recently showed up in Southern California, is believed to be spreading the disease (as are the native sharpshooter species). Though oleander leaf scorch is currently limited to Riverside and Orange counties, the sharpshooters that spread it have been found in other areas, including Los Angeles and Ventura counties.

At present, no effective chemicals exist for controlling bacterial scorch in oleanders. The most important control is maintaining good plant health. Remove infected portions of the plant to help slow its decline. If possible, avoid setting out plants known to be potential hosts of *X. fastidiosa,* including Boston ivy, Virginia creeper, crape myrtle, and periwinkle (*Vinca minor*). If you encounter oleanders with scorch symptoms, contact your local cooperative extension office.

GARDEN ART

A showcase for birdhouse folk art

Some birdhouses aren't strictly for the birds. The ones that line the wall of Linda Terhark's garden, shown on page 216, function almost exclusively as decorative art. Terhark collected them during her travels. "They're one of my favorite forms of folk art," she says. "Each is handmade by a different crafts-person, and they're made for outdoors."

Altogether, 18 birdhouses are on display in the garden. Each one hangs from an eye screw or hanging clip that slips onto a nail driven into the wall. This mounting method makes it easy to take down the birdhouses—to rearrange or maintain them, or to clean out old nests. While these houses aren't arranged to attract avian tenants, every year a family of birds, usually swallows, nests in one or two while the rest stay vacant.

Terhark created a shadow-box effect by hanging the birdhouses in the open spaces between, beside, and above lattices mounted to the wall. The lattices are made of cedar 1-by-1s.

You can find handcrafted birdhouses in many garden boutiques and specialty catalogs. One good mail-order source is Smith & Hawken; call (800) 776-3336 for a catalog.

COOK'S CHOICE

Sow kale for a tasty cover crop

In the August Garden Notebook, there was a discussion of winter cover crops for the vegetable garden. Verna Van de Water of Maple Valley, Washington, uses kale as a cover crop. Any kale will work, but one of Van de Water's favorites is 'Dwarf Blue Curled Vates', an exceptionally hardy variety available from W. Atlee Burpee & Co. (800/888-1447). Sow kale early this month.

During the winter, the kale covers the soil, preventing erosion. And by early spring, Van de Water harvests all the kale greens her family can eat. Then she turns the remaining plants into the soil when she plows the garden to start a new planting season.

TIPS, TRICKS & SECRETS

How to make cut flowers from your garden last longer

If you ask a dozen florists or garden club aficionados how they prolong the life of cut flowers, you're likely to hear as many different answers as there are flowers ("sear the poppy stems" or "cut roses under water"). You'll get plenty of good plant-specific advice.

But what if you just want to go out into your garden and cut a few blooms for a mixed bouquet? Here's some advice from Michael Prihoda, instructor of floral design at South Seattle Community College.

Arrange to harvest the flowers early in the morning, before the blossoms become stressed by summer's heat and sun. Carry a container of lukewarm water with you, and as you cut each flower, plunge the stem immediately into the water.

Bring the flowers indoors as soon as possible, then recut the stems to suit the arrangement you want and strip all the leaves from the part of the stems that are going to be underwater or inside a container. If the flowers look at all limp, put the entire bouquet into the refrigerator for a few hours.

Display the bouquet in a place that doesn't get direct sunlight, and change the water about every three days. If you follow these steps, most of these garden blooms should last a week or even longer.

TOOL REVIEW

A riser that grows with your plants

During the growing season, healthy shrubs, flowers, and vegetables grow vigorously. What happens when the plants grow so big that they block the sprinklers that water them?

Try Just-A-Riser, a clever, manually adjustable riser that attaches to any standard irrigation system with stationary (not pop-up) shrub heads. Bill Marshall, owner of Redwood City Hardware in Redwood City, California, invented it.

As plants grow and block the spray, the riser can be raised by turning a slip nut joint, pulling up on the pipe, and retightening the joint. No tools are required. To lower the riser, just loosen the slip nut joint again.

To install Just-A-Riser, remove the existing riser, save the shrub head, and screw Just-A-Riser into the existing fitting. Keep all dirt out of the line. As soon as you've finished adding the new risers, but before you reinstall the shrub heads, flush the lines by turning on the water. After flushing, install the shrub heads on the risers.

Just-A-Riser comes in three adjustable sizes: 12 to 22 inches tall (about $6.50), 18 to 34 inches tall (about $7), and 24 to 46 inches tall (about $8). The risers are available at some hardware stores and home improvement centers. If you can't find them near you, call Redwood City Hardware at (415) 366-3917.

By Sharon Cohoon, Steven R. Lorton, Lauren Bonar Swezey

As plants grow up, Just-A-Riser slides to new sprinkling heights.

NORMAN A. PLATE

PACIFIC NORTHWEST
Garden Notebook
BY STEVEN R. LORTON

Lately I've come to look forward to September with as much enthusiasm as I do May. There are dozens of plants, including big, weedy-looking things, that bloom this month. And nowhere is the floral abundance of Indian summer more glorious for me than around my garden pond in Washington's Skagit Valley.

Through the years, I've tried to grow things that would spread or self-sow, and be able to hold their own with native plants, yet be of minimal interest to slugs and other pests. I've found some winners. For big, tough purple flowers, my favorites are 'Hella Lacey' asters, two eupatoriums (*E. maculatum* and *E. fistulosum*), and *Verbena bonariensis*. For yellow, my favorite is *Rudbeckia nitida,* which can grow 7 to 9 feet tall and is filled with flowers from now through autumn.

All of these plants are available in 1-gallon cans this month. Because September and October can be dry, I make sure the plants are well watered before they go into the ground. I plunge each nursery can into a big bucket filled with water, submerging the can for several hours, if not overnight. Then, when I dig the planting hole, I fill it up with water twice, letting it soak into the ground. After I've filled in the hole, I water again. The plants show little or no transplant shock, and the flowering ones hold onto their blooms.

•

We use a lot of basil at our house, but pickings have often been pretty slim by September. Then we discovered the basil 'Fino Verde Compatto'. It produces dense clusters of inch-long leaves on foot-tall plants. The neat thing about this basil is that it keeps its sweet flavor even after the plant has bloomed. So it extends our fresh basil season up to the first hard frost. You can order seed for planting next spring from Shepherd's Garden Seeds, 30 Irene St., Torrington, CT 06790; (860) 482-3638. A packet of seeds costs $1.95.

•

I wonder why people don't grow pole and bush beans much for drying anymore. It's so easy to do. This month, we'll pick our beans and lay them on newspapers on a covered back porch. In a few weeks, they'll be dry and we can shell and store them in glass jars (they're very ornamental). There's nothing like a soup made with homegrown beans.

THAT'S A GOOD QUESTION

Q: I've heard that September is the best month to divide and move hellebores. Isn't that a month early for dividing? .

A: In the Northwest, the traditional time to divide perennials is October (and also November in *Sunset* climate zones 4 through 7). Hellebores are an exception: in early autumn they experience a surge in root growth, so dig and divide them now. Keep the divisions well watered until autumn rains begin. The payoff will come early next spring, with a better show of flowers from established plants that will be prepared to withstand the summer ahead.

NORTHERN CALIFORNIA
Garden Notebook
BY LAUREN BONAR SWEZEY

One advantage of exercising outdoors is that I see a lot of gardens on my afternoon jogs. I enjoy seeing the kinds of plants people are growing and how they're using them. Not long ago I came upon two gardens next door to one another, each filled with colorful flowers. My first thought was: how pretty. But looking more closely, I realized that one was much more appealing than the other. Why? The color combinations. Pleasing in one garden, jarring in the other.

The less successful garden combined lavender, pink, and white stock with orange and yellow wallflowers and pink pansies. Ouch! Soft colors like pink and lavender spar with orange shades rather than embrace them. The neighboring garden, however, incorporated apricot and lavender *Primula obconica*, medium-purple pansies, and apricot and purple alyssum. Just a touch of white sweet alyssum brightened the composition here and there. Very nice.

Selecting colors can be a bit tricky when you start with young seedlings that aren't blooming. But you can always change plants that don't work.

•

For the San Francisco Landscape Garden Show each April, talented landscape architects and designers create magical gardens that provide visitors with great landscaping ideas. To honor their achievement, this year *Sunset Magazine* offered its first award of excellence for the best overall design and use of plant material. Landscape designer Scott Colombo of San Rafael, California, received this award for his display titled "Windows on Provence," pictured at right.

As one of three *Sunset* judges, I was impressed by the wonderful garden surrounded by ocher-colored walls. Its tiny, two-level courtyard edged with planting beds and filled with fragrant plants made me feel as if I had been transported to southern France. Colombo's use of a beautiful cork oak, olive and citrus trees, and grasses was exceptional and very appropriate for our Mediterranean climate. All great gardens contain some sort of water feature, and Colombo's had two. Particularly appealing was an urn fountain that gurgled in the center of the upper patio. I wanted to transplant it right into my own backyard. Although the garden space was only 20 by 30 feet, there were plenty of ideas to take home.

THAT'S A GOOD QUESTION

Q: I am attempting to grow sweet peas for the first time. Is it possible to do so in the heat of the summer in the Sacramento area?

A: Sweet peas, even varieties labeled "heat resistant," do not like heat. They thrive in the cooler months of fall and early spring. To get the longest-lasting flower show, sow seeds in full sun in late September or early October before the soil gets cold and soggy. Plants will develop through the winter, establishing a healthy root system. For climbing types, provide strong netting or a fence. By early spring, sweet peas will be ready to burst into bloom. For continuous bloom, harvest flowers regularly until heat knocks them out.

SOUTHERN CALIFORNIA
Garden Notebook

BY SHARON COHOON

"Clean your room—you'll feel better for it," my mother told me back when I was a sullen teenager. I ignored her advice most of the time, of course. But on those rare occasions when I took it, Mom proved right.

Now the same thing is happening with my garden. The good gardeners I turn to regularly for inspiration preach the same sermon this time of year: "You really ought to write about September being the time to clean up your garden before starting fall planting." But I always shut my ears to their advice because I didn't want to write about something I didn't want to do.

Last September, though, their message finally clicked, and I found myself thinning out a row of seriously overgrown India hawthorn. That looked so good I decided to cut back all my woody perennials while I was at it. Then I decided my ragtag collection of herbaceous perennials needed editing, and I yanked out everything I no longer adored.

When my "room" was finally clean, sure enough, I felt better. And not because virtue is its own reward. The payoff of cleanliness is emptiness. Grooming your garden results in new spaces for new plants—and a whole month to daydream about how to fill them. Listen to your mother. Go clean your room.

●

Three mail-order nurseries to inspire plant daydreams:

Heronswood Nursery, 7530 N.E. 288th St., Kingston, WA 98346. Where the gardeners who are always two or three plants ahead of you seem to shop. The fat catalog is a fun read. About *Polygonum japonicum* 'Spectabilis', for example: "Though it takes a small to medium-size nuclear device to rid one's self of this plant, if provided the proper place (consider your neighbor's garden), the effects of [the] foliage … [are] quite marvelous." The catalog costs $4.

Mountain Valley Growers, 38325 Pepperweed Rd., Squaw Valley, CA 93675. Herb lovers' heaven—so far ahead of the curve, you won't know how to use what you buy. Can anyone tell me, for instance, how to cook with Cuban oregano? The catalog is free.

Canyon Creek Nursery, 3527 Dry Creek Rd., Oroville, CA 95965. A small selection of choice plants well suited for dry climates but sometimes hard to find in retail nurseries. The fall-blooming sunflower, *Helianthus angustifolius*, is a good example. The catalog is $2.

THAT'S A GOOD QUESTION

Q: "Baby's tears are taking over my garden. How do I get rid of it?"
A: *Soleirolia soleirolii* may look delicate, but this tiny-leafed plant has developed a survival strategy that makes it tough to eradicate. If you try to pull it out, its fragile stems break, and any piece you overlook and fail to dispose of will quickly put down roots. So weeding doesn't really work. Your best bet, says Larry Amling, manager of Armstrong Garden Center in Torrance, is to use the herbicide glyphosate (Roundup). The hotter the weather, the better herbicides work, he says. So sizzling September is a great time to wage war. Allow the soil under your baby's tears to dry out before applying the herbicide, Amling advises. The thirstier the plant, the more liquid herbicide it will absorb. Be careful to protect any surrounding plants you want to keep (glyphosate kills any plant parts it touches). A large piece of cardboard makes a good barrier. And don't expect immediate results. It takes glyphosate about a week to do its job.

INLAND WESTERN STATES
Garden Notebook

BY JIM McCAUSLAND

Wherever you garden, September is a swing month. In my garden, the first chilly morning of the season comes now. As my lawn shakes off its summer bout with heatstroke, I encourage its rejuvenation with fertilizer and plenty of water. Then I head into the perennial beds and start dividing spring-flowering plants, so they'll have plenty of time to recover for next year's bloom.

●

At the end of every summer, I photograph my front garden. As I look at my photos of gardens past, I'm amazed at how much things have changed, and I get a good sense of where the garden is headed. Those photos helped convince me that a cute little English holly that came with the house was becoming an unruly monster; I cut it down. Another photo showed me that my asphalt driveway was too dominant visually; I solved the problem by lining it with birch bark cherries. Some gardeners get 8- by 10-inch color prints and draw in proposed new trees and shrubs right on the photos.

●

In my garden, fall is a labor-intensive season. I yank out spent summer vegetables, grind up woody plant waste, prepare beds for fall planting, and paint fences and outdoor furniture before winter sets in. To protect my hands, I wear leather gloves for these jobs. For comfort and durability, I prefer gloves made of elk skin, but supple, tough goatskin gloves are a good choice, too. Remember that leather gloves with a smooth finish (as opposed to suede-finished split leather) shed water better and don't catch thorns as easily. I pay $15 to $20 for good gloves, and get several years of hard wear out of them.

●

Running bamboos are beautiful and often hardy, but if you don't contain them, they can take over the whole garden. These aggressive and herbicide-tolerant plants spread by underground rhizomes that are hard to dig out. One way to contain running bamboos is to use 30-inch-wide, 40-mil plastic to form an underground barrier. You can order this material by mail for about $1.50 per running foot from Tradewinds Bamboo Nursery, 28446 Hunter Creek Loop, Gold Beach, OR 97444;(541) 247-0835; bambugib@harborside.com; price list is free. Or grow running bamboo in a half-barrel. This looks beautiful aboveground, but it also works sunk into the ground. A few of the bamboo roots may creep out, but they're easier to find, nip off, and strip out than the roots of an uncontained plant.

●

Horse manure is a cheap, widely available soil amendment, but if it hasn't been thoroughly composted, it may be loaded with viable weed seeds. Although sellers usually offer "composted" horse manure, as far as I can tell, that just means that at some point it was heaped into a pile. To make sure the manure is well rotted when you apply it, buy it now and pile it on an empty garden bed until spring.

THAT'S A GOOD QUESTION

Q: Can clumping palm trees be divided? How do you do it?
A: Many clumping palms (like *Caryota*, *Chamaedorea*, *Chamaerops*, *Ptychosperma*, and *Rhapis*) can be divided. Younger palms are easier to divide than older ones. The best way to start new plants is to divide the suckers from the mother plant. As soon as new fronds appear on the suckers, they are usually well rooted and ready to cut and replant.

PLANTING

❏ **BULBS.** Spring-flowering bulbs, including daffodils and tulips, will start filling nursery bins this month. Shop early to get the best selection. Get the bulbs you buy into the ground soon—before they dry out or rot.

❏ **BERRIES.** Ground covers, trees, and shrubs with attractive berries will start appearing in nurseries this month. Buy and plant them immediately, and keep the plants well watered to sustain the berry show.

❏ **PERMANENT PLANTS.** Now that the weather is cooling, fall planting can begin, especially in zones 1, 2, and 3. Shop for perennials, shrubs, and trees; they can go into the ground immediately. Keep plants well watered until fall rains come.

MAINTENANCE

❏ **CARE FOR LAWNS.** Lawns, especially ones that have been watered through the summer, surge into active growth in early fall. Feed them with about 1 pound of actual nitrogen per 1,000 square feet of turf. If the lawn has bare spots, rake up the soil, remove all weeds, sow new grass seed, cover seed with a light layer of new soil, and water it in well. The grass should be up and robust by next spring.

❏ **DIVIDE IRISES.** Siberian and Pacific Coast irises can be dug, divided, and replanted starting in mid-September. Use a sharp knife to cut clumps apart.

PACIFIC NORTHWEST
CHECKLIST
SEPTEMBER

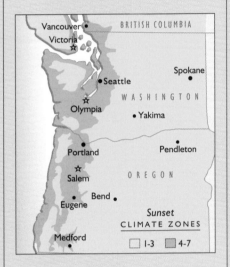

Sunset
CLIMATE ZONES
❏ 1-3   ■ 4-7

Replant immediately in rich, well-drained soil, and water transplants well. You can scatter a light application of complete granular fertilizer around each plant.

❏ **KEEP MAKING COMPOST.** Use vegetable waste, spent annuals, and prunings you accumulate this month to start a fresh pile. If you've kept the old pile moist and well aerated, the compost may be ready to use.

❏ **MULCH.** Cold weather will soon be a threat, especially in zones 1, 2, and 3.

Weed around vulnerable plants, then put down a layer of organic mulch (compost is excellent) to help insulate roots and minimize soil erosion.

❏ **TEND FUCHSIAS.** The season isn't over yet. Continue to pinch off spent flowers to keep them from maturing into seed pods. Water plants, keeping them continuously moist. Keep up with your feeding program.

❏ **WATER.** Be especially vigilant about watering plants in pots or under eaves.

❏ **WINTERIZE GREENHOUSES.** Before you know it, it will be time to bring plants into the greenhouse. Examine the watering and heating systems. Replace broken glass or plastic window panels. Clean out seedbeds and flats. Pull any weeds that have sprung up in planting beds, in floor cracks, or around the perimeter of the greenhouse.

PEST & WEED CONTROL

❏ **SLUGS.** The war is never-ending, especially in the mild climates west of the Cascades. Stick with your chosen battle plan, be it bait, beer traps, hand-picking, or a flock of pet ducks. As you're weeding, grooming, and pulling spent annuals this month, you'll run into clusters of slug eggs—little, milky spheres that look like pellets of controlled-release fertilizer. Use the tip of a trowel to crush them.

❏ **WEEDS.** Pull weeds now before they have a chance to set seed, and add them to the compost pile.

CHECKLIST
SEPTEMBER

PLANTING

☐ **PLANT NEW LAWNS.** Zones 1–9, 14–17: Toward the end of the month, sow seed or lay sod over soil that's been rotary-tilled and amended with plenty of organic matter. Zones 1 and 2: Plant new lawns early in September (at highest elevations, wait to plant seed until October; it will germinate in spring when the snow melts).

☐ **PLANT PERENNIALS.** Zones 7–9, 14–17: When the weather cools a bit, you can plant campanula, candytuft, catmint, coreopsis, delphinium, dianthus, diascia, foxglove, gaillardia, geum, Japanese anemone, penstemon, phlox, pincushion flower, salvia, scaevola, and yarrow.

☐ **PLANT VEGETABLES.** Zones 7–9, 14–17: Set out seedlings of cool-season crops such as broccoli, cabbage, cauliflower, lettuce, and spinach. Plant seeds of beets, carrots, leeks, onions, peas, radishes, and turnips.

☐ **REPLANT FLOWERPOTS.** Zones 7–9, 14–17: After the heat of summer, flowerpots may look bedraggled. To carry the pots through the remainder of the warm season, replant them with late-summer annuals such as salvia, marigold, and zinnia. Or wait until month's end to plant cool-season annuals such as calendula, Iceland and Shirley poppies, ornamental cabbage and kale, pansies, primroses, snapdragons, stock, sweet peas, and violas. Freshen the planting mix in pots, too.

Sunset
CLIMATE ZONES

☐ Mountain (1-2)
☐ Valley (7-9)
☐ Inland (14)
☐ Coastal (15-17)

☐ **SET OUT PERMANENT PLANTS.** Zones 7–9, 14–17: September marks the beginning of the fall planting season. Nurseries should be well stocked with a good variety of trees, shrubs, vines, and ground covers (wait until spring to plant frost-tender plants, such as bougainvillea and citrus).

MAINTENANCE

☐ **RENOVATE LAWNS.** Zones 7–9, 14–17: Late September is a good time to start on lawns. First dethatch, then aerate (both pieces of equipment can be rented), and finally fertilize lawns with a complete lawn fertilizer; water well. If you need to reseed bare patches, prepare the area by digging in organic matter, then pack down the soil, water well, scatter seed, and cover lightly with mulch. Water several times a day to keep the seed moist; cut back when new grass is well rooted.

☐ **DISBUD CAMELLIAS.** Zones 7–9, 14–17: To get huge, show-quality blooms in spring, remove all but one bud per stem.

☐ **DIVIDE PERENNIALS.** In Northern California's mildest climates, now through October is the time to divide many perennials, such as agapanthus, candytuft, coreopsis, daylily, and penstemon, that are overgrown or not flowering well (in zones 1 and 2, do it early in the month). Perennials can also be divided to increase the number of plants in your garden. Use a spading fork or shovel to lift and loosen clumps. With the shovel or a sharp knife, cut clumps into sections through soil and roots. Replant sections in well-amended soil; keep moist.

☐ **PICK UP FALLEN FRUIT AND LEAVES.** Inspect fallen fruit. If it's diseased or infested with insects and you don't plan to use it, bag and discard it. Also, clean up fallen leaves from the bases of fruit trees in case they're harboring diseases. It's best not to compost fruit and leaves unless you know your pile gets hot enough to kill the pests.

PLANTING

❑ **BUY AND PLANT BULBS.** Spring-flowering bulbs begin arriving in nurseries this month. Shop early while stock is fresh and selection is ample. Choices include anemone, babiana, daffodil, freesia, hyacinth, iris, ornithogalum, ranunculus, scilla, sparaxis, and tulip. In the high desert (zone 11), plant immediately. In all other zones, wait until the soil cools in October before planting most bulbs. South African bulbs like freesia, however, can be planted immediately.

❑ **CHILL TULIP BULBS.** For best performance in all areas except the high desert, chill tulip bulbs for six to eight weeks before planting. Store in a paper bag in the crisper section of your refrigerator. (Don't store with ethylene-producing fruit, like apples.) Plant after Thanksgiving.

❑ **PLANT SWEET PEAS.** For sweet peas by December, plant seeds now. Look for varieties designated "early flowering." To speed germination, soak seeds overnight before planting. Provide a wall, trellis, or several 6-foot poles for vines to climb.

❑ **PLANT FOR WINTER-SPRING COLOR.** For blooms by Thanksgiving, coastal and low-desert gardeners (zones 22–24 and 13, respectively) can set out cool-season annual seedlings starting in mid-September. Choices include calendula, English daisy, Iceland poppy, linaria, nemesia, pansy, snapdragon, and stock. Inland gardeners (zones 18–21) should wait until October to plant. Set out biennials, such as

foxglove and Canterbury bells, that you started from seed earlier this summer or buy in small pots at the nursery.

❑ **PLANT (OR SOW) COOL-SEASON VEGETABLES.** Coast and inland: After midmonth, set out seedlings of broccoli, brussels sprouts, cabbage, cauliflower, celery, chives, kale, and parsley. Sow seeds for beets, chard, chives, collards, kale, kohlrabi, parsnips, peas, radishes, spinach, and turnips. Plant garlic, onions, and shallots. High desert: plant lettuce, radishes, and spinach.

MAINTENANCE

❑ **PROTECT AGAINST BRUSHFIRES.** Dead vegetation adds fuel to flames. In fire-prone areas, before the onset of Santa Ana winds, cut and remove all dead leaves and limbs from trees and shrubs, especially those that grow near the house. Clear leaves from gutters and remove woody vegetation growing against structures.

❑ **FEED PERMANENT PLANTS.** Feed established trees, shrubs, ground covers and warm-season grasses, such as Bermuda. Repeat in a month. Coastal gardeners (zones 22–24) can also fertilize tropical plants with a fast-acting product one last time if needed. Don't feed California natives or drought-tolerant Mediterranean plants, and wait three to four weeks to fertilize new transplants.

❑ **SPREAD MULCH.** Hot fall days are hard on heat-sensitive azaleas, camellias, and gardenias. Protect these and other plants by renewing organic mulch in a layer as deep as 3 inches. Keep mulch away from the trunks of trees and shrubs.

❑ **PROTECT PLANTS FROM WIND.** Santa Ana winds usually blow this month. Take down hanging baskets to protect them from drying out in the hot winds. Support young trees with strong stakes and ties that don't girdle trunks.

WEED CONTROL

❑ **FORCE WEED SEEDS.** When preparing a new bed for planting, water to start weeds growing. As soon as weeds germinate, pull them out or remove with a hoe. When weeds are gone, new plants will have less competition for soil moisture and nutrients.

CHECKLIST
SEPTEMBER

Sunset
CLIMATE ZONES

☐ 1-3   ■ 10-11

PLANTING & HARVEST

❏ **PLANT BULBS.** Before the ground freezes, set out crocus, daffodil, hyacinth, *Iris reticulata,* and tulip bulbs. To protect them from soil temperature fluctuations, plant daffodils and tulips 10 to 12 inches deep and small bulbs 5 inches deep. If existing daffodils and tulips were crowded last spring, lift, divide, and replant them now.

❏ **FORCE BULBS.** Begin forcing amaryllis and narcissus now for Christmas bloom indoors.

❏ **PLANT LAWNS.** Early fall is ideal for seeding a lawn or laying sod. Just keep the grass well watered until cold weather stops its growth.

❏ **HARVEST FRUIT.** Pick fruit before it drops to the ground and rots. Harvest raspberries when the sun is high and berries are warm to the touch.

❏ **HARVEST VEGETABLES.** Cantaloupes are ready when skin is well netted and the fruit slips easily from the vine. Pick watermelons when tendrils near the fruit start to turn brown, and winter squash when rind colors and hardens. Pick cucumbers and summer squash any time. Pick everything that is ready before heavy frost is expected; for light frost, protect eggplant, peppers, and tomatoes with floating row covers.

MAINTENANCE

❏ **DIVIDE PERENNIALS.** In all but very highest elevations, lift and divide crowded clumps of bleeding hearts, daylilies, hostas, peonies, and Shasta daisies. To protect against ground freezing and heaving, mulch after replanting.

❏ **MULCH WINTER PLANTS.** If it freezes early where you live, lay down a 3-inch layer of organic mulch to protect roots from freezing. You can use straw, shredded leaves (run them through a lawn mower or shredder to keep them from matting when they get wet), or rough compost.

❏ **REBUILD SOIL.** As annuals and vegetables die, chop the plants into small pieces and work them into the open ground along with generous amounts of other organic matter, like compost. Use only healthy plants; discard any that are diseased or infested with insects. Adding organic matter now will loosen the soil, allowing you to work it earlier next spring.

❏ **LIFT SUMMER BULBS.** When foliage dies down, lift cannas, dahlias, and gladiolus. Let them dry for a few days, then store at 35° to 50° in a well-ventilated space. Store cannas and dahlias in sand, peat moss, or vermiculite. Leave containerized begonia tubers in pots.

❏ **WATER.** Pay special attention to plants growing under eaves and in containers.

❏ **WINTERIZE GREENHOUSES.** Scrub out seedbeds and flats with a weak dilution of bleach and water. Then check for damaged weatherstripping, broken glass, and torn plastic, and replace if necessary. Finally, check vents, filters, and heaters, replacing or repairing broken components before winter comes.

PEST & WEED CONTROL

❏ **PREVENT SNOW MOLD.** Spray lawns with a fungicide, such as benomyl, to prevent pink or gray mold.

❏ **WEED.** Hoe, pull, or spray weeds with an herbicide before they drop their seeds. Water well the day before spraying or pulling.

PLANTING

❑ **BULBS.** In the mountains (zones 1–3) and high desert (zones 10 and 11), plant spring-blooming bulbs of crocus, hyacinths, and tulips now. In the low desert, prechill these bulbs before planting (see the item at top right).

❑ **PERENNIALS.** In intermediate and low deserts (zones 12 and 13), start seed of carnations, columbines, coreopsis, feverfews, gaillardias, hardy asters, hollyhocks, lupines, penstemons, phlox, Shasta daisies, statice, and yarrows. They'll be ready for transplanting in about eight weeks.

❑ **COOL-SEASON CROPS.** As soon as temperatures drop below 100°, sow beets, carrots, celery, chard, endive, green onions, kale, kohlrabi, leeks, parsley, parsnips, peas, potatoes, radishes, spinach, and turnips. Sow lettuce and cabbage-family members (such as broccoli, cauliflower, and brussels sprouts) in flats now for transplanting into the garden in October.

❑ **WARM-SEASON CROPS.** If you plant beans and corn in intermediate and low-desert zones around Labor Day, you'll be harvesting both crops by Thanksgiving.

❑ **GROUND COVERS, SHRUBS, TREES.** In the high desert (zone 10), set out containerized permanent plants that aren't frost-tender. In intermediate and low desert zones, wait until October.

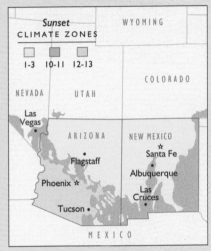

Sunset CLIMATE ZONES
◻ 1-3 ◼ 10-11 ◼ 12-13

MAINTENANCE

❑ **CARE FOR LAWNS.** If you plan to overseed your Bermuda lawn, stop feeding it. If you don't plan to overseed, apply high-nitrogen fertilizer now and water it in well to keep the Bermuda actively growing as long as possible.

❑ **FEED ROSES.** Water deeply, apply a complete fertilizer (preferably one that contains chelated iron), water again, and apply a 3-inch layer of organic mulch around the bases of plants.

❑ **PRECHILL SPRING BULBS.** In mild-winter areas, spring-blooming bulbs like crocus, hyacinth, and tulip need a few weeks of chilling to break dormancy and flower in spring. Buy these bulbs now, put them in paper bags, and store them in the crisper section of the refrigerator for at least six weeks until the soil cools down enough to plant, around Thanksgiving.

❑ **WATER.** Late-summer rain may help, but it may not be enough for ornamental plants, especially in sandy soil. Keep an empty coffee can or glass jar outside, checking and emptying it after each rain. It'll tell you how much precipitation fell, and can help you decide how much additional watering to do.

PEST CONTROL

❑ **SPIDER MITES.** Tiny mites give leaves a stippled look and leave fine webs among twigs and leaves. Dusty leaves attract mites, so keep plants free of dust by occasionally hosing off the leaves. Apply a miticide if necessary.

❑ **SOLARIZE FIREWOOD.** Green firewood (less than a year old) can harbor bark beetles that pose a risk to garden trees. Eliminate them by separating the wood into stacks no more than 4 feet high, wide, and deep. Cover the stacks with clear plastic. Bury the bottom edges of the plastic and tape the seams. Solar heat will do the rest, cooking the beetles inside within a few weeks.

TEXAS

PLANTING

❑ **SPRING BULBS.** Spring-flowering bulbs arrive in nurseries just after Labor Day. Shop early for the best selection. Look for crocus, daffodils, grape hyacinths, hyacinths, scillas, tulips, and a host of lesser-known bulbs.

❑ **PERENNIALS.** Moderate temperatures and, in most places, the coming winter rains make this a good time to plant most kinds of perennials, including campanula, candytuft, catmint, coreopsis, delphinium, dianthus, diascia, foxglove, gaillardia, geum, penstemon, phlox, salvia, and yarrow.

❑ **PERMANENT PLANTS.** Set out containerized trees, shrubs, and ground covers all over Texas this month. In light of the present drought, it's wise to select low-water-use plants, especially natives.

❑ **VEGETABLES.** Here's a schedule that works, wherever you garden. Sow brussels sprouts 14 to 16 weeks before frost; beans, cabbage, cauliflower, cucumbers, and peppers 12 to 14 weeks before frost; broccoli, chard, and kale 10 to 12 weeks before frost; and other cool-season crops (such as beets, carrots, lettuce, and peas) 8 to 10 weeks before frost.

MAINTENANCE

❑ **FERTILIZE LAWNS.** Apply about 1 pound of actual nitrogen per 1,000 square feet of turf.

❑ **MAKE COMPOST.** Compost the weeds, vegetable remains, bean vines, grass, and leaves that come out of your garden this month.

PEST CONTROL

❑ **CABBAGE LOOPERS.** Spray the biological control *Bacillus thuringiensis* on cabbage-family members (broccoli, brussels sprouts, cabbage, cauliflower, kohlrabi, and mustard) to kill the little green worms that eat their leaves.

❑ **WHITEFLIES.** Yellow sticky traps will thin their numbers.

City sidewalk meanders through Michael Barclay's woodland paradise in Kensington, California. At rear is a spectacular Rhododendron nuttallii 'John Paul Evans'.

SECRETS
❧ *of the* ❧
GARDEN
MASTERS

What does it take to make a gorgeous garden? Five passionate plant lovers reveal their secrets

Passionate gardeners have one thing in common—a need for plants in their lives. Their gardens are often filled with horticultural gems collected from specialty nurseries, botanical garden plant sales, and friends' backyards. Within this group of gardeners are the true masters: those who put plants together in such artful ways that they appear unstudied, almost spontaneous—as though planted by nature. On the following pages, we meet five such gardeners: Michael Barclay, creator of a lush woodland garden, Dan Heims, who skillfully weaves foliage plants into a living tapestry of green, Judy Wigand, who combines perennials with great flourish, and Gwen and Panayoti Kelaidis, alpine rock-garden enthusiasts.

BY SHARON COHOON, JIM MCCAUSLAND & LAUREN BONAR SWEZEY

"Some of us get so carried away, our lives and gardens become inseparable," says plantsman extraordinaire and garden designer Michael Barclay.

One glance at Barclay's ⅕-acre garden in the East Bay hills overlooking the San Francisco Bay tells you that this kindly, exuberant man is *obsessed*. You could call his garden the wild kingdom or the Garden of Eden: it doesn't contain a single patch of bare earth.

"When you're a collector nut, there's no cure. Even if I had more space to garden, it would look like this," he says, gesturing toward the layers of 1,800 species and varieties that make up his woodland garden.

Gardening has been in Barclay's blood since he was a boy in New York and his grandfather showed him how to grow vegetables. Although he didn't make a career of gardening until years later, those early lessons stayed with him.

The gardening bug resurfaced when he purchased his double-lot home in Kensington in 1968. "I knew nothing about West Coast gardening, but I couldn't wait to get a trowel in the ground. I really misunderstood the climate." He started with a tropical garden that "looked like Miami Beach."

Four years later, he lost almost everything in the big freeze of '72. "I was so miserable, I sat down and read everything about my climate zone and analyzed the few things that had survived." Barclay then decided that what the front yard needed was a woodland. But it contained only one spruce tree.

Now the woodland garden runs the length of his house, including the parking strip. "It's a crazy space, 126 feet long and 12 feet wide at its widest, so I wanted it to be playful." Before planting, Barclay dug out all of the soil and replaced it with an acid soil mix. During the next year or two, he spent every avail-

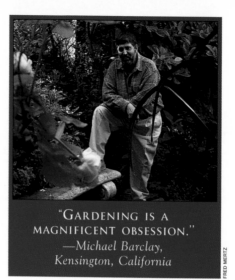

"GARDENING IS A MAGNIFICENT OBSESSION."
—*Michael Barclay,
Kensington, California*

FRED MERTZ

able cent on bags of oak leaf mold and soil blend for rhododendrons.

To develop quick shade, he planted some fast-growing conifers. Then, using 'Pink Pearl' rhododendron and common snowball as the lead colors, Barclay planted a pink- and white-flowered woodland garden accented with blue and purple.

He set out trees and shrubs "in as many heights as possible" to create density and layers. The top layer consists of flowering deciduous magnolias—*Magnolia* 'Iolanthe', *M. ashei,* and *M. watsonii*.

Next are the Japanese maples. "I adore the fernleaf fullmoon maple (*Acer japonicum* 'Aconitifolium') and tricolored *A. palmatum* 'Shishihengen'," says Barclay. Mixed among them are 60 species and varieties of rhododendrons.

Dwarf and slow-growing conifers add distinctive texture to the magnolias and rhododendrons. Barclay is especially fond of dwarf cryptomerias, such as 'Elegans' and 'Vilmoriniana', for their wonderful foliage color and texture.

The soil is crammed with bulbs, perennials, and woodland ground covers—species primroses and sweet woodruff. Three kinds of bulbs naturalize successfully in the garden—snowflake (*Leucojum*), Asiatic lilies and *Lilium regale,* and narcissus in cream, pink, salmon, or white.

Hellebores are favorites because of their early bloom, starting in October. The yellow, green, and white flower color of *Helleborus niger* 'Potter's Wheel' echoes the flower color of its neighbor 'Jury's Yellow' camellia.

The rest of Barclay's eclectic garden is filled with hundreds of plants. In the backyard, 'Altissimo' and 'Veilchenblau' roses intertwine over an old plum tree, and a mayten tree supports 'Cl. Cécile Brunner' ("the trees and shrubs become hat racks").

Also scattered about are fragrant shrubs such as *Daphne burkwoodii* 'Albert Burkwood', *D. caucasica, Michelia doltsopa,* and wintersweet. "You can hardly see wintersweet's flowers, but one January day walking in the garden an unearthly fragrance floats up in the air and you know it's in bloom."

BARCLAY'S SECRETS

✦ **Forget stakes.** Plant tall lilies such as *Lilium regale* behind rhododendrons. Grow clematis on other plants instead of structures. Let rhododendrons support them. Allow purple *Clematis* 'Jackmanii' to tangle with tall climbing roses, such as apricot yellow 'Jaune Desprez'. "You need a clematis you can cut almost to the ground every year or two when cleaning up your roses. *C.* 'Jackmanii' can easily handle it."

✦ **The best daphne.** *D. caucasica.* "Sometimes daphnes commit daphnecide, but [this one] doesn't."

✦ **The most fragrant rhododendrons.** Maddenii hybrids. They "grow almost better in the Bay Area than in their native climates of Burma and Vietnam." Favorite: *R. nuttallii* 'John Paul Evans'. "It has the largest flowers of any rhododendron." Other top choices are 'Mi Amor' and 'Else Frye'.

NORMAN A. PLATE (2)

Pure white Rhododendron 'Helene Schiffner' blooms in front of the rounded blue leaves of Cercidiphyllum magnificum 'Pendulum'.

Fifty-foot climbing rose
'Cl. Cécile Brunner' mingles
with a weeping mayten tree.
At right is purple 'Gypsy
Queen' clematis.

Foliage in various shades
of green and red creates a
rich tapestry in Dan
Heims's garden. In the
foreground, hostas spread
their oval leaves among
ferns and rare purple
Cordyline indivisa.

Like Cassius Clay sizing up Sonny Liston, Dan Heims sized up his new property 16 years ago: on a corner lot, little privacy, and terrible soil.

In Heims's corner was a lifelong interest in gardening. "My grandfather got me started," he says. "He was a Russian, and lots of Russians have their dachas surrounded by fruit trees, flowers, vegetables. He passed this love of gardening on to my mother, and then to me. It's never left." Also on Heims's side were a robust sense of design ("I call it Genuine 42nd and Cullen Design," he says, referring to his address, "because the ideas all originate here") and the landscape maintenance company he'd started years ago with a '57 Chevy pickup and a $10 lawn mower.

It was a battle, but in the end Heims won out. With flowers and big-leafed perennials concealing the roadside drainage ditch between the garden and street, and Japanese maples walling out the traffic, he has a peaceful retreat that's packed with his favorite plants. "I look at the Japanese maples along my property line in the morning and it's like a cathedral window, the light shining through red and green leaves, gold ones in fall," he says. Hostas and other shade lovers carpet the forest floor, clematis and roses clamber along deck rails and up trellises, and a red banana plant rises above it all during the warm months.

Perfume from at least a dozen different fragrant plants draws visitors through the garden. And yet the garden doesn't suffer from the junk-shop look that curses most other plant collections.

How did he orchestrate it all so well?

"I dealt with problems first.... Then I added aesthetics," says Heims. "I had kids, so paths needed to go in early, and I had to train the kids to stay on the paths." Then the plants went in.

"Every garden is an unending story," Heims says. "You just keep adding chapters."

"MY [GARDEN] IS ECLECTIC...
AN EXTREMELY LOVELY BLEND
OF TEXTURES AND COLORS."
—*Dan Heims, Portland*

HEIMS'S SECRETS

* **Can't-beat-it soil amendment.** "I mix a compost/sandy loam blend with 5 to 10 percent manure, complete fertilizer, and green sand, which is high in trace elements. An integral part of English gardens is muck, which is a fancy name for rotted manure. Some of the best plants I ever saw grew from the stuff. I always remembered what TV gardening expert Tom Halvorson said: 'If you have a garden and a dollar, spend 90 cents on soil and 10 cents on plants.'"

* **Place plants carefully.** "Don't plant bully plants beside wimpy plants." Put scented plants on a slope above the garden. That way "the fragrant air pools down below. I enjoy the perfumes mixing."

* **Unify your plantings.** "I mass plants that are roughly the same size. I can have a forest of Japanese maples, for example, all different types, but it still looks like one forest."

* **Keep up the problem patrol.** "I tour the garden for 10 minutes every day. When I see trouble, I approach it organically first, then go to chemical controls as a last resort. If you catch the first flush [of weeds] in spring before they go to seed, it's remarkable how easy weed control is the rest of the year. I also plant densely to exclude weeds, and help my neighbors with their weed control."

* **Favorite fertilizer.** "I like controlled-release formulas like Osmocote and Sierra Blend. Iron is an underused trace element, since it's gone in acid soils."

* **Favorite nursery.** Collector's Nursery in Battleground, Washington. "They have a phenomenal variety that runs from alpines to perennials to wildflowers and beyond."

* **Favorite tool.** "My ARS Switchblader pruners. They're lightweight and used for every purpose: pruner, trowel."

Flowering plants such as daylilies and alliums, which bear attention-getting pink globes, fill wide bed adjacent to garden path. Vines scrambling over lath fence and trees of various heights provide leafy backdrop.

From the day it opened, Judy's Perennials in San Marcos, California, has had mystique. People travel great distances to visit this small specialty nursery and its big demonstration garden—the proprietor's ½-acre yard. And not just because Judy Wigand always has great plants, though she does. They also come, we're convinced, hoping that Wigand's obvious garden mastery will somehow magically rub off. Well, pilgrims, we have bad news.

The secret behind this gardening mecca is simple: It's hard work.

Bob Brooks, the man responsible for turning Judy on to gardening, owned Cordon Bleu Farms, a mail-order daylily nursery next door to Wigand's home. He remembers hiring her to weed his 4-acre field after her teenage son quit, saying the job was too tough, and Brooks doubted she'd last the week. But Wigand soon convinced Brooks that she was up to the strenuous work. And, under Brooks's tutelage, the eager nongardener quickly became a passionate plant lover. "Bob taught me all the essentials," she says. "I learned to garden literally from the ground up."

Learning to propagate cuttings sank the gardening hook in even deeper. "The magic of getting roots to grow from a stick really excited her," says Bill Teague, another passionate gardener, who taught her to root penstemon cuttings.

Before long Wigand had propagated enough cuttings to convert her backyard from a dying avocado orchard into an exuberant flower garden. And Cordon Bleu customers began knocking on her garden gate asking if she had plants to sell. Which gave Wigand the idea that propagating plants as a business might earn her enough money for her next project, relandscaping her large front yard. And, when she did—hauling in truckloads of amendments, contouring the land, and doing the planting herself—the results were so spectacular that more customers came. And her nursery business was born.

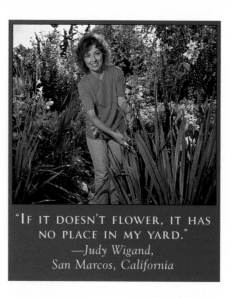

"IF IT DOESN'T FLOWER, IT HAS NO PLACE IN MY YARD."
—Judy Wigand,
San Marcos, California

What makes Wigand's front garden such a traffic stopper is the number of flowering plants blooming in it at any time. Not an inch is wasted on grass. Instead, Wigand has treated the 90-foot-square space as one big mixed border, with meandering pathways weaving through it. Plants billow and spill to the very edges of the property. Flowering shrubs rather than traditional evergreens provide the border's "bones." Geraldton waxflowers, spiraeas, shrub roses, buddleias, salvias, cassias, and blue hibiscus flower in fluid succession. Alstroemerias, asters, phlox, scabiosas, and hundreds of other perennials form the middle tier. And verbenas and other ground covers compete for the remaining space with babiana, nerines, and other South African bulbs.

Everything in Wigand's garden works as hard as she does. Spectacular flowers are only the first step toward admittance to this garden. Plants that are keepers must also have disease and drought resistance, a long bloom period (or be repeat bloomers), and freedom from fuss. "I don't have time for plants I have to dig up in winter or put ice cubes on to simulate a hard frost. There are too many plants that do well in our climate to bother with that.

"Gardening is fun," says Wigand. "I love it, and I hope to be still at it when I'm 80."

WIGAND'S SECRETS

⚜ **Use a simple color palette.** "I love purple," says Wigand. "I use lots of it. Also pinks. Plus bits of pure blue here and there. Some lemon yellow for punch. And lots of pure whites to divide colors and add sparkle."

⚜ **Tame lusty growers.** Instead of yanking out vigorous, shrubby plants like lavatera the minute they start to show character, prune them. Keep the height but clip off lower branches to create a more treelike shape. Then you can plant underneath and have two flowering plants in the space formerly occupied by one.

⚜ **Shop the plant sales.** Public gardens often discover good gardening plants long before nurseries do.

⚜ **If you find a plant you like, clone it.** Take cuttings from new treasures as an insurance policy before planting.

⚜ **Favorite weeding tool.** A hand weeder with a sharp, angled triangular blade on a 17-inch-long handle. "It makes weeding 10 times as fast."

⚜ **Favorite digging tools.** A spade with a heart-shaped blade on a 20-inch handle is "great for digging small holes."

Perennials include pink-flowered Cistus 'Victor Reiter', yellow 'Bitsy' miniature daylily, tall pink watsonias, and alstroemerias.

JOHN HUMBLE (2)

What happens when two plant zealots marry? If their gardening tastes differ, the honeymoon might be short. Fortunately, Gwen and Panayoti Kelaidis found their styles compatible. Both have a passion for alpine rock gardening.

In their backyard, Gwen, a trained botanist, created a magnificent rock garden "tapestry" using many small-scale rocks and plants ("nothing over 12 inches high"). Low berms of soil and rocks form a miniature mountain range around their lawn. It's meant to be viewed from above.

"A rock garden is the natural end point for a fanatic perennial gardener," says Gwen. "You can grow so many more [rock garden] plants in the same space." The plants in her garden come from all over the world. Panayoti is one of her best plant sources. "My husband's tapped in to all the best plantspeople in Europe. He's a good guy to know if you want plants," she says.

As curator of the Denver Botanic Garden's Rock Alpine Garden, Panayoti, a gardener turned botanist, describes himself as a plant fanatic. He experiments at the botanic garden, and in the process, he has introduced other Rocky Mountain gardeners to many new plants from central and western Asia, South Africa, the Mediterranean, and the West that thrive in Denver's challenging climate. Some of Panayoti's best-known introductions include purple ice plant (*Delosperma cooperi*), yellow ice plant (*D. nubigenum*), and *Veronica liwanensis*.

For their own garden, Gwen's favorite plants include cushionlike, white-flowered *Arenaria tetraquetra; Bolax glebaria* ("we call this AstroTurf"); matting and spreading daphnes (*D. cneorum* 'Eximia' and *D. c.* 'Ruby Glow'); various types of yellow-flowering, mat-forming *Draba;* sprawling, blue-flowered *Gentiana septemfida;* blue-flowered *G. acaulis;* white or pink *Lewisia; Thymus serpyllum* 'Elfin'; and shrubby *Viola delphinantha.*

She's fond of her river of sempervivums, which contains 14 kinds, such as 'Cordeur's Memory' and 'Cherry Frost'. She has at least 50 sempervivums in the garden ("no rock garden should be without them"). She would have grown more, but her husband made her throw out the ones with labels. "He's a plant purist."

"Rock gardeners are plant collectors. We grow things that may not look good to others. It's not the voluptuous side of gardening; we're not concerned just about flowers," Gwen says. ∎

Small rocks form miniature mountains in Panayoti and Gwen Kelaidis's Denver garden. Crawling between the rock outcrops and tumbling over ledges are fascinating textural plants.

STEPHEN COLLECTOR (2)

"PLANTS NEXT TO ROCKS ARE MUCH MORE BEAUTIFUL THAN A BUNCH OF PLANTS TOGETHER."
—*Gwen Kelaidis, Denver*

THE KELAIDISES' SECRETS

❦ **Imitate nature.** Create natural rock ridges instead of little pockets here and there. "The bones of the garden are the rocks. If they don't work, the garden isn't right."

❦ **Look for plants with great textures.** "Bun" (cushion) plants, such as *Draba rigida*, are particularly outstanding.

❦ **Tuck plants carefully into nooks and crannies** to look as if a seed hit a rock, then sprouted where it dropped. "Rock gardening is all about a plant's relationship with the rocks."

❦ **Most often used tool.** "A three-pronged hand cultivator. Every week or so, I scratch the gravel mulch to get rid of weed seedlings." (Gwen makes sure not to disrupt seedlings of her rock garden plants.)

Tulips year after year, naturally

*Plant species tulips this fall for flowers
next spring and maybe forever*

By Jim McCausland and Lauren Bonar Swezey

*Tulipa saxatilis
springs up every year
in this Northern
California garden.*

"COMPARISONS ARE ODIOUS," said a wise mother about her children. The same could be said about species tulips: they ought to be judged on their own merits, not against their bigger, showier descendants—hybrid tulips.

Tulips are native to the Mediterranean region and the Middle East, where plant breeders created the first hybrids centuries ago. When tulips reached Holland, breeders there continued to experiment, tulipomania swept the country, and hybrids came to dominate the market.

But in recent years, gardeners have been rediscovering the natural benefits of growing species tulips.

Tulipa clusiana 'Cynthia' bears candy-striped flowers on long stems.

First, species tulips generally have smaller flowers on shorter stems than hybrids. But their diminutive scale only emphasizes the delicate beauty of their flowers and foliage. They bear single or multiple flowers in bicolors or pure shades (lilac, crimson, orange, yellow, cream, and white), with leaves ranging from narrow, crinkly, and blue-green to broad with maroon bands.

Second, species tulips have the ability to naturalize and multiply in the garden, while their hybrid cousins usually peter out within a year or two. This ability makes species tulips an attractive long-term investment: at a cost of 25 cents to $1.15 a bulb (often cheaper than hybrids), they go on growing indefinitely, forming new bulbs after each spring bloom. .

HOW TO GROW THEM

Fall is the time to buy and plant species tulips. Choose a site that gets full sun in spring. Most species tulips originated in wet-winter, dry-summer climates like those of the West, so they do best in areas that don't get much, if any, summer water. To survive and naturalize, species tulips require very well drained soil. They thrive in rocky, gravelly, or sandy soil. They also do well in raised beds, on gentle slopes, and in containers.

In garden beds, put them up front so nothing will get in the way of their early-spring show. For the most effective display, plant at least two dozen bulbs of any species. Pack them close together—2 inches apart for the smaller bulbs, 5 to 6 inches for the larger—to create substantial blocks of color.

Plant bulbs at a depth equal to three times their diameter (about 1½ to 6 inches deep). Then let nature take its course; water only if winter rains don't come.

After blooming, new bulbs start forming. Feed at that time with a balanced fer-tilizer such as 12-10-18. Keep the soil moist but not wet until the foliage starts yellowing, then stop watering. The foliage can be removed when it dies.

WHERE TO BUY BULBS

Look for bulbs in garden centers, nurseries, and bulb catalogs. Mail-order suppliers offer the widest selection; order soon. Catalogs are free.

Daffodil Mart, 7463 Heath Trail, Gloucester, VA 23061; (800) 255-2852.

McClure & Zimmerman, 108 W. Winnebago St., Box 368, Friesland, WI 53935; (414) 326-4220.

Van Engelen, 23 Tulip Dr., Bantam, CT 06750; (860) 567-8734.

12 CHOICE TULIPS

Last year, we planted species tulips in *Sunset's* test garden in Menlo Park, California, and in a home garden in the Seattle area. The dozen species described here were chosen from those tested by virtue of their performances in our trials and a survey of experienced growers. The regions where the tulips originated are noted.

Tulipa bakeri **'Lilac Wonder';** Crete. One of our favorites, it bears open rose-lilac flowers with yellow centers on 6- to 8-inch-tall stems. Tiny blue-green leaves have burgundy edges. This is one of the few species suitable for Southern California.

T. batalinii; Asia Minor. One of the best dwarf species, it bears 3-inch-wide flowers in various colors on 4- to 6-inch stems. Thin leaves have wavy edges. This is a great species to plant in rock gardens. Named varieties include 'Apricot Jewel' (apricot-orange outside, golden inside),

Tulipa linifolia has satiny scarlet blooms with black centers.

'Bright Gem' (peach), 'Bronze Charm', 'Red Jewel', and 'Yellow Jewel'.

T. chrysantha (T. clusiana chrysantha); northwest India. Flowers have deep yellow centers and magenta outer segments; stems are 4 to 8 inches tall. Leaves are narrow and green. This tulip multiplies well.

T. clusiana; Afghanistan, Iran, Iraq. Flowers have deep purple centers, white inner petals, and broad crimson bands on outer segments; stems are 8 to 12 inches tall. Long, thin blue-green leaves have crinkly edges. This species spreads by underground stolons and multiplies well. *T. c.* 'Cynthia' has slender, elegant flowers on 8- to 14-inch stems; catalogs describe its blooms as ruby edged with chartreuse, but in our trials they were pale yellow with magenta on the outer petals.

T. kolpakowskiana; Central Asia, Afghanistan. Medium to soft yellow flowers with magenta outer petals bloom on 5- to 8-inch stems. Narrow, wavy-edged leaves lie flat.

T. linifolia; Central Asia, Iran, Afghanistan. This knockout has brilliant scarlet blooms with jet-black centers on 4- to 6-inch stems. Narrow blue-green leaves have crinkly edges. This species is a good choice for rock gardens.

T. praestans **'Fusilier';** Central Asia. Gorgeous medium-red flowers appear in clusters of three or four on 8- to 12-inch stems over broad green leaves.

T. pulchella violacea; Asia Minor. Classic tulip-shaped violet flowers emerge just above ground level on 3- to 4-inch stems. Narrow blue-gray leaves have straight edges. *T. p.* 'Persian Pearl' bears magenta flowers with yellow bases on 3-inch stems. Both are good for rock gardens.

T. saxatilis; Crete. Our favorite for mild climates, it bears big, showy lilac flowers with yellow bases on 12-inch stems. The plant spreads by underground stolons. Because it needs mild winters and warm summers, this species is one of the few suitable for Southern California.

T. tarda (T. dasystemon); Central Asia. Multiple star-shaped, yellow-and-white flowers bloom for a full month on 3- to 5-inch stems. Narrow leaves have bronze edges. The plant spreads by underground stolons.

T. turkestanica; Central Asia. This is the earliest species to bloom (late February to March), with multiple flowers that have creamy yellow petals, yellow throats, and red-brown marks on the outer petals, on 4- to 5-inch stems. The blue-green leaves are narrow.

T. vvedenskyi **'Tangerine Beauty';** Central Asia. Large, bright orange-red flowers appear on 1-inch stems; as blooms open wider, the stems lengthen to 4 to 6 inches. Leaves are silvery blue-green. ■

Soft summer blues

You dry hydrangea blossoms and lavender for long-lasting arrangements

NORMAN A. PLATE

FLOWER BEDS ARE AS RIPE FOR harvesting as vegetable plots over the next few months. An ample crop of blossoms awaits, ready to be snipped, dried, and turned into beautiful bouquets. Hydrangea blossoms—those big blue and pink puffs that are bouquets in themselves—make especially distinc-

ive arrangements when dried. The colors turn smoky, subtle, and cool. Designer: Françoise Kirkman.

WHAT YOU NEED

- **A CONTAINER** such as a basket, terra-cotta pot, or vase
- **FLORIST'S FOAM**
- **DRIED FLOWERS** such as hydrangea flower heads and lavender stems (if desired, also statice, larkspur, ornamental oreganos, and salvias)
- 4-inch-long wood **FLORIST'S PICKS** with wire ties to lengthen stems

STEPS

1. **Fill container** with blocks of florist's foam, cutting to fit with a long-bladed knife. Fill gaps around the sides with smaller pieces of foam.

2. **Insert the tallest hydrangea** upright in the center of the foam. Stem height should at least equal that of the container. If necessary, attach a florist's pick to extend stem length.

3. **Arrange remaining hydrangeas** at an angle so that flower heads overhang container rim. Cut stems slightly shorter than center stem to give the bouquet a rounded shape.

4. **Fill spaces** between hydrangea heads with lavender or other dried

flowers, pushing stems gently into the foam.

TIPS

- Harvest hydrangeas when the tiny true flowers at the center of the showy heads are fully open and as color is beginning to fade. If the flowers are too fresh when cut, they'll wilt. If possible, cut with 1-foot stems. Smash woody ends of stems with a hammer so they will absorb water. Place stems in a tall vase with 2 inches of water. Place vase in a dark corner of a well-ventilated room until water has evaporated and flowers are leathery, about a week. Hang upside down until completely dry, four or five days.

- Cut lavender stems when flower spikes are just beginning to open. Remove lower leaves, and tie stems into bunches. Hang bunches upside down and not touching each other in a warm, well-ventilated place until completely dry, four or five days.

- Dry larkspur, statice, ornamental oreganos, and salvias the same way as for lavender.

- Spray dried flowers with aerosol hair spray to make them less brittle. ■

By Sharon Cohoon

HANDLING HYDRANGEAS

Squash the hydrangea stems, then set them in water.

After the stems have absorbed all the water, hang them up to dry.

Insert blossoms in florist's foam, giving bouquet a rounded shape.

Garlic
revival

*Give ordinary cloves a rest and try growing these
rich, lively, vintage varieties*

Two dozen heads of roasted garlic and more than 50 raw cloves sit on the table. They represent nine varieties of garlic grown by Chester Aaron, a gardener and author widely known for his avid interest in this plant. None of these garlics is commercially significant. But most have an ancient lineage. Breathlessly, bravely, food professionals and farmers prepare to compare them.

Clove after clove, bite after bite, palates ride a wild roller coaster of intense sensations—rich and resonant, sharp and racy, piquant and hot, sweet and buttery— until they finally wither with garlic overload.

This gathering at Oakland's Oliveto Cafe and Restaurant is representative of many garlic tastings, including ones staged at *Sunset,* that have helped us pinpoint some of the most flavorful choices in this new garlic wave. Because even though Westerners have a measurable addiction to garlic, our options have been surprisingly limited. Of the 630 million pounds of garlic grown annually in California—most

By Linda Lau Anusasananan and Lauren Bonar Swezey

You may not find ruby-skinned 'Creole Red' garlic at your supermarket. But you can grow it in your own garden, along with other notable garlics that are savoring new popularity.

PETER CHRISTIANSEN

domestic supply—only two varieties, 'California Early' and 'California Late', make up the bulk of the crop, a quarter of which is consumed in-state.

It's this love that has stimulated richer garlic options. Garden hobbyists and specialized growers have rediscovered almost-forgotten varieties and expanded our resources for them. Many seed catalogs now offer dozens (one company has 400 varieties!). And garlic eaters are most likely to find these non-mainstream alternatives from late summer through late fall in farmers' markets, select produce markets, and natural food stores.

But with more garlic choices, the big questions are: which ones should you choose, and how do you know what you are getting?

GARLIC VARIETIES

The hundreds of varieties of garlic (*Allium sativum*) are divided into two subspecies, softneck (*A. s. sativum*) and hardneck (*A. s. ophioscorodon*). And neither should be confused with the massive elephant garlic (*Allium ampeloprasum*)—it's not a true garlic.

Most softneck garlics (including 'California Early' and 'California Late') are of the Artichoke group, which is named for the way the cloves form, not because of any kinship with artichokes. Each head consists of 12 to 20 cloves in overlapping layers. These are the most adaptable and easiest to grow.

The other softneck group, Silverskin, has heads that contain 12 to 40 cloves each—explaining, perhaps, why the late culinary bon vivant James Beard, along with the French, chose 40 cloves of garlic to go with a chicken. The skin colors of Artichoke and Silverskin range from white, creamy, or faintly pink to white with a brown blush. The peeled cloves of both groups are creamy to pale gold.

Hardneck garlics produce a woody flower stalk in late spring that grows 1 to 6 feet above the leaves and twists into a coil. As the garlic head forms, the stalk straightens. (Aboveground, the flower at the tip of the stalk develops many small bulblets, known as bulbils, which can be planted in the fall and used for garlic greens.) When the garlic head is mature, it is usually composed of a single circle of large cloves. The outer skin may be dull brown, red, or purple. The skin around the cloves is more intensely colored than the outer layers, but the cloves themselves are white. Of the three hardneck groups, Rocambole, with only 6 to 11 cloves per head, is the most acclaimed for flavor and ease of peeling.

TAMING GARLIC TO TASTE

Garlic's characteristic smell becomes pronounced when a compound in the garlic, alliin, meets the enzyme allinase, from which it has been separated by cellular membranes. When these membranes are broken—by chewing, pressing, or cutting—allinase comes into contact with alliin, forming the hot-tasting sulfur compound called allicin. The more

GARLICS THAT MEASURE UP

These five varieties of garlic are exceptional. But there are many more varieties to be discovered, each of which offers a range of flavor experiences.

PETER CHRISTIANSEN

'CELAYA PURPLE'
(hardneck, Rocambole). Raw, this garlic from Mexico is strong, with a lingering heat. Roasted, it's mild to strong and tastes a bit like an artichoke. The purple-streaked skin on the cloves is fairly easy to peel off, and the heads keep well for about three months. For best production, 'Celaya Purple' needs a cold winter and warm spring.

'CREOLE RED'
(softneck, Silverskin). This is one of the original red garlic varieties grown in America. Raw, it tastes slightly sweet at first, then follows with a lingering hot, peppery aftertaste. Cooked, it develops a rich, mild caramel quality with a touch of heat. The shiny pinkish red–skinned cloves are easy to peel. The heads keep well for three to four months. As a plant, 'Creole Red' performs best in mild-winter climates.

'INCHELIUM RED'
(softneck, Artichoke). This garlic was discovered on an Indian reservation. Says grower Chester Aaron, "Its mild, almost sweet flavor doesn't have a strong effect in cooking, but it's excellent raw on bruschetta." The skin on the cloves is white. The heads are large and store well for about six months. The plant grows almost anywhere.

'RED TOCH'
(softneck, Artichoke). The origin of this garlic is near Tochliavri in the Republic of Georgia. Some claim it has the perfect garlic flavor when raw. Roasted, it's mild and sweet. The skin on the cloves is streaked with red and pink. The large heads store well for about six months. This garlic grows readily in most places.

'SPANISH ROJA'
(hardneck, Rocambole). This garlic was introduced to the Portland area in the late 1800s. Raw, its flavor is mild to medium-hot with a piquant finish. Roasting emphasizes its robust side. Ron Engeland of Filaree Farm describes this variety as the one that epitomizes garlic flavor. The big, shiny reddish purple–skinned cloves are very easy to peel, and the heads keep well for about three months. The plant grows best in the Northwest and in Northern California.

thoroughly you crush the cells, as in a garlic press, the stronger and more pungent the results. The heat of cooking inactivates and eliminates the effects of allinase—mostly by driving away the volatile sulfur. Keep these techniques in mind to make garlic taste the way you want.

•**Hot and brash.** Use garlic raw, finely chopped or pressed. Use in salad dressings and aïoli.

•**Robust but not burning.** Chop garlic and cook briefly. (Take care not to scorch; this gives garlic an exceptionally bitter taste.) Use in cooked sauces and stir-fries.

•**Tame and mild.** Simmer whole cloves until soft and tender. Use cloves to pickle, eat plain, or add to dishes.

•**Sweet, nutty, and creamy.** Roast whole, unpeeled heads or slowly pan-brown whole, unpeeled cloves until garlic is very soft when pressed. Use when you want to eat quantities of garlic—as a spread for bread, for instance.

GROWING GARLIC AT HOME

Here are tips from the experts on growing garlic in home gardens.

•The best time to plant garlic in mild-winter climates is from mid-October through December: in Southern California, plant in November; in the Pacific Northwest, plant in October and November. In cold-winter climates, plant in late September.

•Choose a site that gets at least six hours of sun a day. Garlic—particularly Rocambole—prefers rich, well-drained soil full of organic matter. If your soil is clay-dense and poorly drained, grow garlic in raised beds. In heavy soils, the outer skin stains and the garlic may rot.

•To grow garlic in raised beds, fill beds with a good soil mix purchased from a garden supply company. In the beds or in the ground, mix in about a 2-inch layer of well-composted manure. Let the soil sit for about six weeks before planting, soaking it every four to five days.

•To plant, carefully separate the garlic cloves from the head, choosing cloves that are firm, unscarred, and unbroken. Keep in mind that large cloves produce large heads, small cloves produce small ones, and cloves from small heads also tend to produce small heads—especially in the hardneck varieties.

•Wet the soil thoroughly and plant cloves 6 inches apart in rows 6 to 8 inches apart, with scar (flat) end down. The tip of the clove should be 1 to 2 inches below the soil surface.

•Since different garlics mature at slightly different times, plant the same kinds of garlic together so that, at the end of the season, watering can be controlled.

•Fill the holes with soil, but don't tamp down. Soak the soil again. Cover the beds with a 6- to 8-inch-thick layer of mulch, such as straw, to help maintain the soil moisture and moderate soil temperatures.

•Garlic requires constantly moist soil. If rain isn't adequate, water when the soil several inches below the surface is almost dry. In mild climates, foliage growth starts in a couple of months.

•About March 1 (a week or two earlier in the south, later in the north), spray the foliage with a combination of fish emulsion and seaweed (kelp), and four weeks later, follow up with another application. Fertilizing after early May doesn't help heads grow.

•On Rocamboles, flower stalks appear in midspring. To get the largest head, cut off the stalk when it's 4 to 6 inches tall—either before or right at the time the first coil forms.

•To harvest garlic green, pull it in the spring when the heads are small and not distinctly formed. Plan to use immature garlic within several days; it's as perishable as green onions.

•Depending on the climate, garlic reaches maturity from late May to mid-July. Stop watering about two weeks before harvest—or when 25 to 30 percent of the leaves have turned brown. Harvest when 60 to 75 percent of the tops are brown.

•Get harvested garlic out of the sun immediately. Too much heat greatly impairs garlic's storage life. Brush the soil from roots (don't wash heads). Bundle stems together with string in groups of 5 to 10 heads.

•Hang garlic bundles for two to three weeks in a dry, shady, well-ventilated area that stays moderately cool (65° to

---

75°). Heads are cured when skins and stalks feel completely dry.

•It takes about two months for individual characteristics to fully develop. When garlics stand even longer, these differences grow more subtle, but Rocamboles may develop more of a bite.

•Store garlic at cool room temperature in a well-ventilated spot out of direct sun.

A DISH THAT DEMANDS GARLIC

Distinctive garlics bring individuality to dishes. But even supermarket garlics, with their fewer flavor nuances, work well. Here's a recipe that makes excellent use of some of the popular varieties.

And if a recipe calls for garlic cloves by the cupful, you cn also purchase and use refrigerated peeled fresh cloves.

Chicken with 24 Cloves of Garlic

Prep and cook time: About 1 hour

Notes: Two heads of a large-clove Artichoke or Silverskin variety or two heads of a small-clove Rocambole variety will yield about the right amount of garlic. 'Creole Red', 'Spanish Roja', and 'Celaya Purple' work well.

Makes: 4 servings

 1 tablespoon olive oil
 4 whole chicken legs (about 2½ lb. total), skin removed if desired
 ½ cup chicken broth
 ½ cup dry white wine
 24 large cloves garlic, peeled
  Parsley sprigs
  Salt and pepper

1. Coat a 10- to 12-inch frying pan (nonstick if chicken is skinned) with oil. Add chicken and cook, covered, over medium-high heat until browned, about 7 minutes. Turn pieces over, cover, and continue cooking until browned on the other side, 5 to 7 minutes longer. Uncover; pour off and discard fat.

2. Add broth, wine, and garlic. Cover the frying pan tightly and simmer for about 15 minutes. Turn chicken pieces over; continue to simmer, covered, until meat is no longer pink near bone, 10 to 15 minutes longer.

3. Transfer chicken and garlic to a platter. If necessary, boil juices, uncovered, over high heat until reduced to about ⅓ cup. Spoon juices over meat. Garnish with parsley sprigs. Add salt and pepper to taste.

Per serving: 388 cal., 51% (198 cal.) from fat; 38 g protein; 22 g fat (5.7 g sat.); 7 g carbo.; 133 mg sodium; 128 mg chol. ∎

NORMAN A. PLATE

Fresh from the garden, smooth-skinned snap peas are plump, sweet, and crunchy.

Putting the "snap" in snap peas

Sugar snaps are praised for their flavor, but watch out for mildew. We grew nine varieties, and here's what we found

SINCE THEIR DEBUT IN 1979, edible-pod snap peas have become *the* gourmet pea. In markets, their thick, crunchy-sweet pods command hefty prices—sometimes approaching $4 a pound. Fortunately, gardeners can grow their own.

One major drawback for gardeners in the West is powdery mildew. This fungus coats the leaves and stems with white spores and can wipe out a 'Sugar Snap' plant—the original All-America Selections winner and the old standby for flavor—before it produces much of a crop.

Some snap pea varieties are touted as mildew resistant. But do they stand up to such claims in the garden? We tested nine commonly available varieties. (Of the nine, four are not labeled as mildew resistant, and five are listed as resistant or partially resistant.) We planted one crop of each in March and a second in September and monitored each variety for mildew. Then a panel of experts from *Sunset's* garden and food staffs rated the varieties for flavor.

The bottom line? Snap pea varieties vary widely in flavor; some are crunchy-sweet, others watery and bland. For the snappiest peas, choose your varieties carefully or plant them in fall when mildew is less of a problem.

'SUPER SUGAR MEL': A TWO-TIME WINNER

In our spring planting, 3-foot-tall 'Super Sugar Mel' was a clear winner. Although it's not touted as mildew resistant, it showed no signs of fungus. And the flavor was rated one of the three best by our panel. The 3½- to 4-inch-long pods are sweet, crunchy, and juicy. The plant is also a top producer, since two pods develop per node.

A number of the other snap pea varieties in our spring planting succumbed to mildew, including 'Cascadia', which is supposed to have some resistance. Two favorites for flavor, 2-foot-tall 'Sugar Ann' and 6-foot-tall 'Sugar Snap', were almost completely covered with mildew by early June. 'Sugar Bon', 'Sugar Pop', and 'Super Snappy' didn't get mildew, but they weren't especially tasty. Most tasters rated them only somewhat sweet.

The fall planting fared much better. None of the snap peas developed mildew—even our flavor favorites 'Sugar Ann' and 'Sugar Snap', which had both succumbed to mildew in the spring. The one major drawback of 'Sugar Snap' and its new, flavorful, mildew-resistant sibling, 'Super Sugar Snap', was that the vines grew so tall that they were damaged significantly during the windy weather in January. ■

By Lauren Bonar Swezey

Icons lead users of the Garden Problem Solver to various troublemakers—pests, diseases, and weeds.

CDs loaded with garden answers

A pair of new compact discs can help you select plants, identify pests, discover remedies, and much more

YOUR SUMMER GARDEN MIGHT BE winding down, but gardening questions go on year-round in the West: How can you stretch the flower show into fall? What plants have the flashiest autumn foliage? What can you do about powdery mildew on roses and zinnias?

Two new CD-ROMs from Sunset Publishing Corporation can help you answer those questions: the *Western Garden* (1995, $49.95), based on the best-selling *Sunset Western Garden Book,* and the

As the photos on their boxes suggest, these two CDs cover an array of horticultural topics, from pruning techniques to beneficial insects such as bees.

Garden Problem Solver (1996, $39.95). These CDs are interactive storehouses of garden information, enhanced with video, audio, scalable color photos, and powerful built-in search features.

LOOKING FOR PLANTS?

The *Western Garden* CD contains an encyclopedia of more than 6,000 plant species listed by common name and genus. If your computer has sound capability, you can hear the preferred pronunciation of each plant name: is it *clem*atis or clem*a*tis? A click of the mouse tells all.

If you have only a general idea of what plant you want, use the Plant Selector to click on any category (trees, shrubs, vines, and so forth) and characteristics (bloom season, height, and color). Then enter your zip code and you'll get a customized list of plants that thrive in your climate zone (this CD uses *Sunset*'s 24 Western climate zones).

As you identify plants you like, you can add them automatically to an electronic Garden Notebook to print out or review later.

Another useful feature is Quick Tips—videos that demonstrate various gardening techniques. Click on the daffodil video, for example, to see how a *Sunset* gardener plants daffodils in big containers, packing the bulbs in so tightly that they touch.

GOT A PROBLEM?

Owning the *Garden Problem Solver* is like having a Master Gardener on hand to answer questions. The CD offers advice on when to plant and how to maintain a healthy garden, and tells what to do when problems strike.

Advice on what to do in your garden and when to do it is listed in a Garden Calendar. Use the calendar to assign specified tasks to certain days, or to add notes tailored to your own gardening schedule. (This CD uses USDA climate zones.)

The *Garden Problem Solver* is loaded with color pictures that can be enlarged. You can use the photos to identify insect pests or to look at symptoms, like scab on apples, to discover the organism that causes them. Weeds are also covered in this section.

If you already know what the problem is, you can go straight to the solution. For example, if your roses have black spot, you can quickly find out that the recommended chemical control is the fungicide captan.

You can preview an abridged version of the *Garden Problem Solver* on the Internet by navigating to Time-Warner's Virtual Garden site at http://www.timeinc.com/vg.

THE TECHNICAL STUFF

Both of these CD-ROMs are sold in home and garden centers, at software stores, and through Sunset Publishing Corporation (call 800/829-0113). They come in versions for Windows-based and Macintosh computers.

If you use Windows 3.1 or Windows 95, you'll need at least a 486 processor at 25 MHz, 8 megabytes of RAM, an SVGA monitor (640 by 480, 256 colors), a Windows-compatible sound device, and a double-speed CD-ROM drive.

For Macintosh, use at least System 7.0.1, a 68030 processor at 25 MHz, 8 megabytes of RAM, a 256-color display, and a double-speed CD-ROM drive. ■

By Jim McCausland

Alpine plants mold themselves snugly around well-placed rocks in this sloping entry garden.
For details on the plan and plantings, see page 252.

OCTOBER

Garden guide......................250

Garden notebooks 255

Garden checklists.................257

The world in a garden...........262

Smoke trees light up the garden ..265

A tale of two lilies................266

Herbs for the whole year.........269

Flower discoveries 270

SUNSET'S
GARDEN
Guide

Set among desert plants, a pyramid is one of the geometric shapes that catch the eye in this Phoenix landscape.

Colorful geometry in a desert garden

"It's a modest little garden," says landscape architect Steve Martino of the one (shown above) he designed in Phoenix. "But everything is very studied and refined. I took all of the things I like and put them into one garden."

The colorful sculptures and walls were inspired by the famous Mexican landscape architect Luis Barragán, the sunken garden by ancient ruins in the Southwest, and the water channel by those used in Moorish architecture.

Martino also wanted to give owner

Jay Hawkinson something unexpected. "Jay is an art director and likes offbeat things and colorful geometric forms, like spheres, cubes, and triangles," says Martino. So he used a geometry theme.

The garden is bordered by the walls of a housing development. Martino hid these walls by adding new ones inside them. A low lavender-mauve wall that runs part of the length of the garden provides extra seating. A channel between the walls carries water from a fountain to a pond. A shade structure made of

brightly colored fabric hung from metal poles shelters the patio from the hot desert sun.

The garden contains few plants, but each one is placed where its form shows off to best advantage. Some of Martino's favorites are *Bauhinia congesta*, brittlebush, *Penstemon parryi*, *Lycium andersonii*, prickly pear cactus, quail bush (*Atriplex lentiformis*), and *Verbena gooddingii*. In spring, palo verde trees brighten the garden with their yellow flowers. The plants attract wildlife such as quail.

250 OCTOBER

Crown imperial: Regal form, peculiar scent

Ever since crown imperial (*Fritillaria imperialis*) was introduced in the 16th century, gardeners have had strong opinions about this hardy spring-blooming bulb.

They generally agree that it has a regal bearing, with flower stalks that rise to 4 feet topped by a "crown" of tufted leaves over a head of bright yellow, orange, or red flowers. But some gardeners are put off by what they perceive as character flaws. For example, after it's planted, crown imperial may skip a year's bloom before it gets back in sync. Its scent has been delicately described as "foxlike" by some and bluntly compared to rotten meat by others. In any case, you'll want to plant it in an open area.

Crown imperial grows in *Sunset* climate zones 1–7, 15–17. Set out bulbs this month in well-drained soil in a spot that gets full sun or partial shade, and don't disturb them. The plants will bloom in April or May, depending on where you garden.

Look for *F. i.* 'Lutea' or 'Lutea Maxima' for yellow flowers, *F. i.* 'Aurora' or 'Rubra Maxima' for red-orange blooms. One good mail-order source is McClure & Zimmerman, Box 368, Friesland, WI 53935; (414) 326-4220.

Fritillaria imperialis 'Aurora' wears a necklace of red flowers beneath a leafy crown.

'Sunshine' gazania bears multicolored blooms in an array of vibrant shades.

Gazanias sport jazzier blooms

Clumping gazanias, which form mounds of evergreen leaves, now come in a wider range of colors and flower sizes. Bud Stuckey, test garden coordinator at *Sunset*'s headquarters in Menlo Park, California, planted some from seed and found that one called 'Sunshine' bears particularly jazzy blooms on compact 6-inch plants. The 4-inch-wide flowers come in an array of circuslike patterns and bright colors— orange, yellow, burgundy, and pink, with darker stripes and defined markings in the center of the bloom. Each flower can have four or five sharply defined colors.

Other gazanias are subtler. Sundance Mixed has 4- to 5-inch-wide blooms, but the color range spans only yellow to rust. The plants grow 10 to 12 inches tall.

Talent Mixed bears 2½-inch-wide flowers in shades of copper, mauve, orange, white, and yellow. The plants grow 8 inches tall and have silvery white foliage.

Gazanias are perennials in *Sunset* climate zones 10 through 13; grow them as summer annuals in zones 1 through 3. Start seeds in flats (in cold climates wait until spring). Transplant into 4-inch containers when the seedlings have several sets of leaves. When the plants are sturdy and well established, set them out in the ground. Use clumping gazanias as small-scale ground covers or temporary fillers.

'Sunshine' is available from Park Seed, Cokesbury Rd., Greenwood, SC 29647; (800) 845-3369. Sundance Mixed and Talent Mixed are available from Thompson & Morgan, Box 1308, Jackson, NJ 08527; (800) 274-7333.

Thousands of daffodils create ribbons of blooms in spring atop Boot Hill.

COMMUNITY ACTION

"Daffodil Hill" comes to Livermore

Weedy Boot Hill in Livermore, California, was an eyesore. For several years, members of the Livermore–Amador Valley Garden Club wanted to cover the dry, barren slope with daffodils. But three years ago, when Jacquie Williams-Courtright, owner of Alden Lane Nursery, returned from a nursery convention excited by a community daffodil project, the idea took off.

With the nursery's encouragement and financial help, the garden club really put its shoulder to the project and made it work. Club members were so enthusiastic they expanded their efforts into Pleasanton, Dublin, and Sunol. The Daffodil Valley Project was born. The first blooms appeared in spring 1995.

Each autumn, garden club members, community organizations, and private citizens donate money or time to plant thousands of daffodils in the area. Local residents are also encouraged to plant daffodils in their own gardens.

At Boot Hill, club members planted 22,000 daffodil bulbs—mostly 'California Trumpet', 'Early Cheer', 'Fortune', and 'Ice Follies'. Another 75,000 bulbs have been planted in other parks and public areas, and 100,000 have been sold to the general public.

This year at district, state, and national garden club conventions, the Livermore–Amador Valley Garden Club received seven awards for civic landscaping.

In late October, the garden club will plant 5,000 more daffodils on Boot Hill (at Stanley Blvd. and Wall St.). City of Livermore employees will also be helping out as part of their Make a Difference Day. The club is also encouraging members of the community to help plant daffodil bulbs—and to help supply bulbs for the project.

Bulbs can be ordered now for this year's planting. For more information about the Daffodil Valley Project, call project manager David Oakley at (510) 846-4038.

LANDSCAPING SOLUTIONS

A rock garden transforms a front yard

Too steep to mow, Gary Necci's front garden in Seattle seemed like a hopeless candidate for landscaping. But by tackling his problems one at a time, Necci was able to create a rock garden that became the talk of the neighborhood (see photo on page 248).

First, Necci gained some privacy by planting a row of Austrian black pines (*Pinus nigra*) along the sidewalk. The pines also set the tone for the alpine rock garden he had in mind.

Before placing the rocks that anchor the garden, Necci laid out two alternate paths from the sidewalk to the house. These earth-and-rock walkways also provide easy access to the whole garden.

The rocks, mostly rhyolite from a local supplier, were arranged by hand into a series of small planting terraces. Before he set out plants, Necci prepared the soil around the rocks by mixing decomposed granite with an enriched planting mix.

Necci's garden scheme called for plants of different colors and textures to creep over the rocks and collide with each other. He used several kinds of hebes, heathers, and thrifts (*Armeria*) and dozens of kinds of thyme, although he likes red-flowering best, for both its intensity and its length of bloom. He used Scotch moss for its strong chartreuse color.

Plants that tend to get leggy, like hebe and heather, are sheared to keep them looking groomed and to force them to conform with the rounded contours of the rocks. Overhead sprinklers provide water when it's needed.

The spirit of the land returns

"It smells like the chaparral," say visitors to Scott Goldstein and Lauren Gabor's all-native garden. *Salvia clevelandii* is the obvious top note, but many subtler aromas—ceanothus, artemisia, coyote mint, and meadow rue—enrich the perfume.

Goldstein and Gabor's garden is also luring back native fauna. "Birds, butterflies, and insects I've never seen before are coming to the garden," says Goldstein. "And lately a red-tailed hawk has been hovering overhead."

Creating a habitat convincing enough to attract indigenous wildlife may be the ultimate reward of a native garden, says Goldstein. "It's more than just pretty flowers. It's about capturing the spirit of the land."

The 60- by 100-foot garden is divided into two habitats. A "fantasy meadow" on one side is planted in blue grama grass and sedge and thickly sown with California wildflowers. Coastal chaparral plants cover the other half.

Several mature trees rescued from residential development sites, including a rare Engelmann oak, are the foundation plants. Native perennials and annuals grow on "islands" under each tree, and decomposed-granite pathways wind among the islands.

As natural as it all looks, building this native habitat wasn't easy. Some indigenous plants transplant to the drought-tolerant garden readily enough, says Goldstein. Sages, for instance. "I've yet to lose one," he says. Woodland plants do, too. And, surprisingly, most trees. But many natives resent being moved. You must dislodge them from their containers gingerly, being cautious not to disturb their roots. Then you have to gauge their water needs nervously for several seasons. Don't drown them, but never let them dry out either. "Let natives wilt and you've lost them," says Goldstein. "They need more irrigation than other plants to get established."

Nurse natives through one or two summers, though, and you can safely ignore them. No need to amend the soil; they like it already. No fertilizer, please; it just weakens them. And no water other than rain required.

Nothing left to do, says Goldstein, but inhale the chaparral.

Leaf shape affects ornamental cabbage

Ornamental cabbage and kale do a great job of filling fall and winter containers with colorful foliage in shades of red, pink, and white. As you shop for plants, remember that leaf shape can tip you off to the plants' potential long-term performance. Varieties with large, smooth leaves show the most weather damage and rot fastest. Kinds with frilly leaves have less surface area, so they stand up better in foul weather, hold less water, and are less likely to rot. Also, dark leaves hold up better than light leaves.

Salvias and lupines form a floral island under a rescued oak. Paths that wind around the garden recall hiking trails in wild chaparral country. Near the gate, the dead stump of a toyon provides a pillar for native clematis and morning glory vines.

A bulb planter's best friend

Y ou're planning the biggest bed of daffodils or tulips ever and faced with the daunting task of planting hundreds of bulbs. There's a tool perfectly suited to the task—a dibble, or dibber. Using one of these instead of a trowel can save you a lot of time and help prevent a sore wrist, if not carpal tunnel syndrome.

A dibble is essentially a sharp-pointed conical probe with a handle. You push it down into the soil to form a tapered hole; the amount of force you exert determines the depth of the hole. In addition to planting bulbs, some gardeners use dibbles to bore holes for planting sixpack-size annuals.

Dibbles (called dibbers in Canada) come in many shapes and sizes and are made out of various materials, including wood and metal. They range in price from about $15 for a small one to $30 for a larger one (plus about $5 for shipping). Three different dibbles are shown in the photo at left. The one with the curved handle is available from A. M. Leonard, Box 816, Piqua, OH 45356; (800) 543-8955. The wooden model and the metal version with the red handle are available from Dig This, 102-45 Bastion Square, Victoria, B.C., Canada V8W 1J1; (604) 385-3212.

Three styles of dibbles are all designed to poke planting holes for bulbs.

NORMAN A. PLATE

'Rubrum' belongs in the lily hall of fame

A lthough the new Asiatic and Oriental hybrid lilies are causing a stir, as we report on page 266, an old-fashioned favorite has proven its worth as a late-summer performer—*Lilium speciosum* 'Rubrum'. This lily bears loose clusters of fragrant flowers that open on sturdy 5-foot stalks in August and September. The 6-inch-wide crimson-and-white blossoms have deeply curved petals with crimson dots. A spidery bouquet of unusually long stamens dangles in the center of each bloom.

Many nurseries and bulb catalogs sell this lily. One good mail-order source is White Flower Farm, Box 50, Litchfield, CT 06759; (800) 503-9624. Plant bulbs this month or next spring as soon as you can work the soil. Grow them as you would Asiatic or Oriental lilies.

NORMAN A. PLATE

'Rubrum' lilies have long, dangling stamens.

Synchronized spring bloom in Salt Lake City

T he Temple Gardens in Salt Lake City put on one of the West's best early-spring shows, with flowering bulbs such as crocus, daffodils, and tulips popping into bloom through a mix of colorful bedding plants, including aubrieta, candytuft, English daisies, forget-me-nots, pansies, primroses, snapdragons, and violas. All these plants are chosen by head gardener Peter Lassig for their reliable spring performance, even after winter temperatures plunge to –20°.

Lassig's trick for synchronizing bloom is simple: when the bulbs are planted this month, sixpack-size bedding plants are also set out—giving the plants seven or eight weeks to get their roots established before the ground freezes, usually in early December.

To coax bedding plants into bloom early, Lassig puts row covers over the transplants right after Thanksgiving. Protected in this way, they start flowering in early April, a full month ahead of their usual bloom time in open ground.

Grow aspens for clattering hearts of gold

O ur September travel story on where to see aspens in all their fall glory may have tickled your curiosity about how they do as garden trees. Quaking aspen (*Populus tremuloides*) can be grown in Sunset's climate zones 1 through 7, but the tree is most successful—and easiest to find in nurseries—in zones 1 through 3.

In the garden, aspens rarely grow taller than 25 to 30 feet. In spring and summer, the heart-shaped leaves dangle on long stems, and the slightest wind sets them shivering. In autumn, of course, the leaves turn that famous shade of gold. In winter, the naked branches and gently contoured trunks with smooth, silvery gray bark look beautiful against the wall of a house, a stand of dark conifers, or the open sky.

As in the wild, aspens love moist places in the garden, so they're perfectly happy along a stream or pond. If you don't have a natural water source in your garden, plant them in a low spot and irrigate them generously in dry weather. Nurseries sometimes sell aspens in containers, and you can also start them from seed or cuttings. Aspens send up suckers, which form handsome clumps. If suckers grow out of bounds, dig them up and start new groves.

By Sharon Cohoon, Steven R. Lorton, Jim McCausland, Lauren Bonar Sweeney

PACIFIC NORTHWEST
Garden Notebook

BY STEVEN R. LORTON

Cotoneasters are widely admired for the brilliant red and orange berries most varieties bear in autumn. But this month, I'll again be dazzled by a more bewitching member of the cotoneaster family that grows in my Skagit Valley garden. *C. hebephyllus* bears black berries the size of small pearls, and its velvety dark green leaves look as if they've been edged in sterling. The foliage is green on top and fuzzy underneath, with silvery hairs that stick out around the leaf edges. When the leaves catch the low autumn sun, the whole plant sparkles. *C. hebephyllus* forms a vase-shaped plant, with black stems that shoot up about 12 feet tall and stretch 10 feet wide. This deciduous cotoneaster grows in all Northwest climate zones.

I was introduced to this plant by Mareen Kruckeberg, who owns MsK Nursery north of Seattle. She has a number of these cotoneasters as well as many other rare and unusual plants. The nursery is open only by appointment; call (206) 546-1281.

•

My family enjoys eating the pumpkins and winter squash we grow, all the way from harvest through May. After we cut them from the vine (leaving a few inches of stem), we wipe them off with a dry cloth and put them on a layer of newspapers four sheets thick in the crawl space under the house. We leave plenty of space between the fruits so air can circulate around them. The temperature in the crawl space ranges from the mid-40s to the low 50s, so freezing isn't a factor. Our main problem is mice, which love to gnaw on the pumpkins and squash (as well as the potatoes we store there). To control the mice, we set four to six mousetraps around the stored produce. Early in the season, we trap about two mice a week. Then the mouse invasion slows, but we keep the traps baited and ready. I've tried all kinds of bait, including peanut butter, but the mice can't resist mozzarella cheese.

•

THAT'S A GOOD QUESTION

Q: When you plant bulbs, do you put anything special in the planting hole, like the fabled "pinch of bonemeal"?

A: I like to keep things simple. After I've dug the hole, I toss in about a teaspoon of complete (16-16-16) granular fertilizer and stir it into the loose soil; then I put the bulb in place and cover it with soil. My spring-flowering bulbs look pretty great. As for bonemeal, it's a good natural amendment, and some gardeners sprinkle the stuff like fairy dust. Bonemeals usually contain 3 to 5 percent nitrogen and as much as 12 percent phosphorus.

NORTHERN CALIFORNIA
Garden Notebook

BY LAUREN BONAR SWEZEY

Sometimes I run across good gardeners in the most unlikely places. On a balmy evening not long ago on a stroll along the Embarcadero in San Francisco, my family and I came across historic Fire Station 35 (Engine 35, Fireboat 1). My 2½-year-old son wanted to see the fire engines. I glanced around the building and, to my surprise, discovered a veritable flower factory growing beside it. Firefighter Tim Fewell saw us snooping around and invited us through the gate. He was the one who had started the gardening bug at the station. He began by planting flowers in a few barrels. Soon his fellow firefighters Terry Walling and Cameron Buckle were building him raised vegetable beds in the empty side yard. Now Fewell and his buddies produce veggies for the entire crew.

"We have 16 tomato plants—mostly Italian types that were started from seed by an Italian lady friend," says Fewell. "I told the guys from the other firehouses to stop by, I have plenty of tomatoes!" He also grows basil, dill, eggplant, peppers, and zucchini.

What's the secret to this bountiful garden? The soil. When Fewell started the garden, the soil was sandy clay that compacted in the beds. A friend (the owner of Marin Sanitary Service) sent over a truckful of compost. "I also use a lot [read once a week] of Miracle Gro on the flowers," says Fewell. The "guys" put in an automatic drip system for Fewell, so the garden gets watered even when duty calls. Most important, it gets "plenty of TLC."

•

Every year when bulb-planting season comes around, I get a thrill out of thumbing through the glossy colored pictures in bulb catalogs. One of the challenges of catalog shopping is picking colors that work well together and matching bloom times, if you want them to coincide. It's particularly difficult with tulips because of their huge color range and many groupings, from Darwin hybrids to Fringed types. On top of that, the color reproduction in catalogs can be off, so even with careful planning, coordinating is usually hit and miss.

I select tulips by looking for colors that appeal to me and reading the descriptions. If the tulips are in the same category, the timing usually works. It gets trickier when you choose from more than one category, because bloom times aren't always listed.

Last season I tried 'Attila', a violet purple Triumph tulip, with 'Shirley', a white Triumph tulip etched with purple. Even though the purples looked identical in the photos, they weren't. 'Attila' was more reddish purple. 'Shirley' was a knockout, though. As the flower matured, the grape coloring on the petal edges slowly spread through the white, giving the tulip a purple blush. This year I'm trying 'Dreaming Maid', a Triumph tulip that is "all shades of violet, edged with white," combined with another Triumph tulip, 'White Dream' (both from Dutch Gardens, 800/818-3861).

THAT'S A GOOD QUESTION

Q: Four dogs play on our common grassy area: our neighbor's three males and my female. My neighbor says the brown spots in the grass are caused by my female's urine. Is there a difference in chemistry between female and male urine?

A: "Dogs are dogs," says veterinarian Alice W. Wolf, of Texas A & M University. "The concentration of chemicals in the urine is the thing, not the sex. Males usuallly urinate on upright objects (shrubs, flowers), so may be less harmful to lawns behaviorally if not chemically."

SOUTHERN CALIFORNIA
Garden Notebook

BY SHARON COHOON

Plant fanatics are dangerous companions. Hang out with them for a day and you inevitably head home with a Jeepful of plants to shoehorn into an already crowded garden. Leaving their company sans plants is about as likely as walking out of a patisserie empty-handed when you have a sweet tooth. Their enthusiasm is irresistible. That's my excuse anyway.

My latest failure to resist temptation started in Jan Smithen's garden in Upland. A gardening instructor at the Arboretum of Los Angeles County, Smithen puts her knack for spotting great new plants and combining them expertly to good effect in her own garden. *Salvia sinaloensis*, a low mound of gray-green foliage topped with tall flower spikes in a gorgeous shade of dark violet-blue, is a good example. Smithen gave this Mexican species a prominent place in the front of her border and backed it monochromatically with gray-leafed ballota and 'Lochinch' buddleia. "Sinaloensis is a must-have if you love purple," she said, knowing I do. So I took an extra salvia off her hands.

Another plant new to me that I spotted in Smithen's garden was *Geranium* 'Stanhoe'. She used it to edge a decomposed-granite pathway. The geranium looked as if it had been custom-designed to complement the granite's blonde tones. Though 'Stanhoe' has sweet tiny, pinkish white flowers, its leaves are its main attraction. They're small and heart-shaped, in a subtle, hard-to-describe color. "Gray-green dipped in café au lait?" suggested Smithen. After that description, how could I refuse a division?

A few days later I visited Tom Piergrossi in Encinitas and got into more trouble. Piergrossi is a landscape designer who propagates a lot of his own plant material. I made it past his variegated gaura, variegated ajuga, and even a gorgeous variegated calamondin citrus. But not past a variegated version of fortnight lily. (Funny how a small change can make an old plant newly interesting.) "I don't have room for this," I said. "Don't worry," said Piergrossi. "Everyone who sees it will want it, and you'll always be dividing it." I bought one.

Visiting Smithen's and Piergrossi's gardens convinced me you don't have to settle for ordinary landscaping plants. There are thousands of extraordinary plants to choose from. You may have to search a bit to find them, but the chase is half the fun. Happy hunting.

For information about Smithen's gardening classes, call (818) 447-8207. For information about Piergrossi's plants (he opens his backyard for wholesale business on Mondays), call (619) 753-3208.

Public gardens provide great opportunities for plant chasing. Most offer fall plant sales this month or next. Check your local newspaper's garden calendar for sales, or call the gardens directly.

THAT'S A GOOD QUESTION

Q: How do you get catmint (*Nepeta faassenii*) started in a neighborhood full of cats?

A: Cats do find *Nepeta* irresistible. My own two tomcats nuzzled a dozen tender young catmint seedlings to death before Jan Smithen told me how to foil them by barricading the plants with bamboo barbecue skewers, pointed ends up. It works. You can usually remove the skewers when the plants mature. Cats don't seem to be as attracted to older plants. I've also found that studding the skewers generously throughout a newly seeded vegetable or annual bed keeps cats from using it as a litter box. Don't skimp, though, or they'll just weave through them. (Thorny rose prunings work, too. Cats see them, decide not to tangle with them, and head the other way.)

INLAND WESTERN STATES
Garden Notebook

BY JIM McCAUSLAND

Lately I've tried to restrain my tendency to pigeonhole plants according to their traditional roles and instead look at each one's unique qualities and potential uses. For example, I'd always considered oregano to be an herb, but when I saw a row of dwarf oregano plants used as a low border, I realized that they looked better than boxwood and were fragrant, too.

When I started admiring the qualities of fruit trees, I came to regard the Asian pear as one of the best ornamentals around, even without its golden fruit. I would not have said that when my tree was young and growing in a rather disorganized manner. But it has matured into a graceful tree that takes well to pruning, and I've become one of its great boosters.

•

With fall's cooler weather, I'm less thirsty, so I'm inclined to water my plants less. But I've been burned by that tendency—and so have my plants. To be on the safe side, I check soil moisture every couple of days by using a trowel to turn the top 2 inches of soil over. If it's moist, I wait; when it's dry, I water long and deeply.

•

When I select bulbs from the bins at a garden center, I'm looking for two things: the largest bulbs of any variety (because larger bulbs usually deliver more and larger flowers) and bulbs that look like most of the other bulbs in the bin. Just like shirts on the sale table of a department store, bulbs get mixed up by browsing customers, and if you aren't careful, that row of red tulips might wind up being red and yellow, short and tall, or maybe not even tulips at all.

•

If you live where winters are mild enough to grow cabbage and other cole crops, you'll have those pretty white butterflies that produce the green worms that eat holes in the leaves. I've found that my kids are the best control for cabbage butterflies: I give them badminton rackets and let them swing away. The butterflies have some amazingly effective evasive maneuvers, but the kids manage to swat enough of them to make a difference. If you don't want to go after the butterflies, you can kill the worms by spraying plants with the biological control *Bacillus thuringiensis*.

THAT'S A GOOD QUESTION

Q: I have been wrestling to green up a lawn in very hard clay soil. I have been watering heavily, but … it seems the moisture is penetrating less than an inch [and] little or no air is getting to the roots. I was planning on aerating again in the fall, and my father suggested filling the holes with sand. Is this a good idea? Also, I have used gypsum to loosen flower beds in the past. Is this something that could help my lawn?

A: Aeration, sand, and gypsum will help a little. Gypsum can make soil more crumbly and permeable to air, roots, and water, but gypsum isn't very soluble and it doesn't easily penetrate far enough to do much good. The best long-term solution is a complete renovation. Get a soil test to learn whether you'll need to add gypsum, calcium sulfate, or other nutrients before you replant the lawn. Then hire a bulldozer service to "cross-rip," or loosen, the soil 12 to 18 inches deep. Till 3 inches of organic matter and any other amendments into the top 6 inches of soil, level the ground, and replant the lawn.

PLANTING

❏ **BULBS.** Plant crocus, daffodils, grape hyacinths, hyacinths, scilla, and tulips this month. If you buy bulbs from bins, look for ones that are firm and plump; plant them in the ground immediately. It's not too late to order bulbs from mail-order suppliers.

❏ **PERENNIALS.** Hardy perennials in 4-inch pots and 1-gallon containers can go into the ground this month. Water them well until fall rains take over.

❏ **WILDFLOWERS.** For bloom in spring, broadcast seed early in the month over weed-free rock gardens, hillsides, and fields. If possible, lightly rake seeds into the ground and cover with a 1/4-inch layer of organic matter.

❏ **GROUND COVERS.** Set out transplants in well-cultivated, weed-free soil enriched with plenty of organic matter. Most plants from 4-inch pots, when spaced 6 to 12 inches apart, will form a solid mat in a year or two. Water plants well until fall rains begin.

❏ **TREES AND SHRUBS.** Fall planting gets them off to a good start. Keep them well watered through the first winter: in most cases, freezing weather is harder on thirsty plants, causing leaf burn and killing marginally healthy ones.

MAINTENANCE

❏ **DIVIDE PERENNIALS.** From now into November is the best time to dig and divide perennials. Dig around large clumps with a spade or shovel, then pry

PACIFIC NORTHWEST
CHECKLIST
OCTOBER

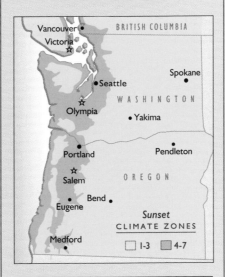

them out of the ground. A chunk the size of a dinner plate will easily divide into four pieces. Amend the soil in planting holes, replant divisions, and water them well.

❏ **FERTILIZE LAWNS.** The autumn feeding is the most important one of the year. Fertilizing now helps the grass build a strong root system that will take your lawn into the next season. Apply 1/2 pound of actual nitrogen per 1,000 square feet of turf.

❏ **PREPARE PLANTING BEDS.** After clearing spent flowers and vegetables out of beds, enrich the soil with organic matter but leave it in a rough state. During the coming winter, alternate cycles of freezing and thawing weather will break down the clods of soil.

❏ **ADD TO COMPOST.** Keep piling on fallen leaves, grass clippings, prunings, and spent annuals. Add this new material to the stuff that is already "cooking" on the compost pile. If the pile is dry, water to keep the decomposing matter as moist as a wrung-out sponge. By next spring, the finished compost will be ready to spread on beds.

❏ **CARE FOR HOUSE PLANTS.** Plants that have been summering outside need to come in now. Before you bring them indoors, look for signs of disease and stowaways like insects and slugs. Remove damaged or yellowed foliage. With the hose nozzle set for a fine mist, shower the dust off leaves. Scrub the pots and water plants well. Give foliage plants their last feeding now. Continue to feed winter-blooming plants.

PEST & WEED CONTROL

❏ **BATTLE SLUGS.** Whatever your method—handpicking, slug traps, or bait—go at it full bore. If you use poison bait, place it where it won't be a threat to children or pets.

❏ **WEED.** Pull them before they set seed, and put them on the compost pile. You'll want weed-free beds going into the winter and before you put down a seasonal layer of organic mulch.

NORTHERN CALIFORNIA
CHECKLIST
OCTOBER

Sunset
CLIMATE ZONES
☐ Mountain (1-2)
☐ Valley (7-9)
☐ Inland (14)
☐ Coastal (15-17)

PLANTING

☐ **PLANT BULBS IN CONTAINERS.** Zones 7–9, 14–17: For a grand show in spring, fill pots with potting soil so tops of bulbs sit 4 to 5 inches below the pot rims. Firm the soil and set bulbs closely together on top. A 16-inch flared pot will hold 40 to 50 tulips, daffodils, or hyacinths. Cover with soil, leaving about 2 inches at the top for watering space. Set in a cool, shady area, wet the soil, and mound with wood shavings or other mulch; dampen again. Move pots into full sun when leaves develop. Flowers will appear about four months after planting.

☐ **PLANT NEW PERENNIALS.** Zones 7–9, 14–17: This is a good time to plant hardy perennials, but it's especially important to get early bloomers such as candytuft, campanula, columbine, coral bells, delphinium, and foxglove in the ground so there's enough root growth to support a good spring flower show. For the best value, plant from sixpacks or 4-inch pots.

☐ **PLANT VEGETABLES.** Zones 7–9, 14–17: By October, it's too late in most areas to set out crops that need a long time to mature, such as broccoli, cabbage, and cauliflower. But there's still time to plant onions, radishes, spinach, and turnips. Lettuce can be planted year-round in many parts of zone 17.

☐ **SET OUT GARLIC.** Zones 7–9, 14–17: Plant in rich, well-drained soil. Break bulbs apart into individual cloves and plant scar end down. Cover regular garlic with about 2 inches of soil, ele-

phant garlic (not a true garlic, but a bulbing leek with mild garlic flavor) with 4 to 6 inches. Press the soil down firmly and water. Irrigate if the weather is dry.

☐ **SET OUT TREES.** Zones 7–9, 14–17: Fall is the best time to set out trees. For shade in summer and sun in winter, choose a deciduous tree (ash, Chinese tallow tree, honey locust, liquidambar, oak, redbud). Evergreen trees (acacia, eucalyptus, fruitless olive, tristania) provide greenery all year.

☐ **SOW WILDFLOWERS.** To get the best show in spring, sow wildflowers now. To prevent weeds from overrunning the flowers, choose an area that's free of weeds and weed seeds, or kill them in advance. In zones 7–9 and 14–17, you still have time to "pregerminate" (germinate in advance) the weed seeds to get rid of them: water the soil so seeds germinate, then hoe or spray with a contact herbicide.

MAINTENANCE

☐ **CARE FOR PERENNIALS.** Cut back old, straggly plants almost to the ground. Work compost or soil conditioner into any bare spots. Divide and replant plants that are crowded and not performing well, using pruning shears or a saw for fine-rooted plants like yarrow and a shovel for tough plants like daylily.

☐ **CLEAN UP DEBRIS.** To reduce the number of sites that harbor insects and diseases during winter, pull weeds and spent annuals and vegetables. Clean up all fruit and leaves. Compost only pest-free plant debris. Add other material to your city's compost collection, if it has one (commercially made compost normally gets hot enough to kill insects and diseases), or toss.

☐ **DIG OR MULCH CORMS AND TUBERS.** After foliage dies, you may want to dig tuberous begonias, dahlias, and gladiolus for winter storage. If you leave them in the ground, they can rot (especially in poorly drained soil). Remove foliage, shake off soil, and store them in a cool, dry place. Some gardeners find wooden wine boxes perfect for storing bulbs.

OCTOBER

PLANTING

❏ **PLANT NATIVES.** Ceanothus, Matilija poppy, woolly blue curls, and other plants native to California are used to getting water in winter. Plant them now and let them take advantage of rains to develop deep roots before summer. Rosemary, cistus, lavender, and other plants adapted to a wet winter–dry summer climate are also easier to establish if planted now.

❏ **SET OUT BULBS.** Plant anemone, daffodil, ranunculus, and the South African bulbs that thrive here—such as babiana, freesia, homeria, ixia, sparaxis, and watsonia. Buy tulip and hyacinth bulbs now, but before planting, chill for four to six weeks in the refrigerator (stored in paper bags in the crisper, away from apples).

❏ **PLANT COOL-SEASON ANNUALS.** Coastal, inland, and low-desert gardeners (zones 22–24, 18–21, and 13, respectively) can set out transplants of calendulas, English daisies, Iceland poppies, lobelia, nemesia, ornamental kale, pansies, snapdragons, stock, and violas.

❏ **SOW ANNUAL SEEDS.** Many cool-season annuals planted by direct seeding grow fast and give better results than transplants. Coastal and low-desert gardeners can sow baby blue eyes, forget-me-nots, linaria, Shirley poppies, and sweet peas now. For more ideas, see page 270.

❏ **PLANT COOL-SEASON CROPS.** Coastal and low-desert gardeners can continue to plant beets, broccoli, brussels sprouts, carrots, cauliflower, chard,

SOUTHERN CALIFORNIA
CHECKLIST
OCTOBER

Sunset CLIMATE ZONES

collards, kale, head and leaf lettuces, pak choi, peas, radicchio, radishes, spinach, and turnips.

MAINTENANCE

❏ **CUT BACK GERANIUMS.** To encourage regrowth during the winter, cut back garden geraniums (*Pelargonium hortorum*) by a third to a half. Make straight cuts just 1/4 to 1/2 inch above joints, leaving several healthy leaves on each branch.

❏ **DIVIDE PERENNIALS.** Dig, divide, and replant perennials growing in crowded clumps. Asters, daylilies, gloriosa daisies, helianthus, Shasta daisies,

and yarrow are likely candidates.

❏ **FEED ROSES FOR WINTER BLOOM.** Coastal and low-desert gardeners can promote a final bloom cycle by giving roses one last feeding early this month. Continue to water well and deadhead.

❏ **SOAK AZALEAS AND CAMELLIAS.** How well these shrubs grow now will determine how much they flower next spring. Give them a thorough, deep watering and cover the soil around them with several inches of mulch (keeping it away from the plants' crowns). Mist the foliage during Santa Ana winds.

❏ **PREPARE FOR SANTA ANA WINDS.** Prevent branch breakage by thinning top-heavy trees such as jacaranda. When winds are predicted, give trees, shrubs, and ground covers a deep soaking. And once the winds come, mist plants frequently—especially vulnerable plants in containers and hanging baskets. Stake newly planted young trees.

PEST CONTROL

❏ **MANAGE INSECT PESTS.** When the temperature drops, aphids and whiteflies seem to multiply. Dislodge them from plants with blasts of water from a hose, or use an insecticidal soap.

❏ **CONTROL SNAILS AND SLUGS.** To guard against snails, put collars or sleeves around vulnerable plants, and copper bands or screens around beds. To control their numbers, set out traps at night or handpick pests in the morning or evening.

CHECKLIST
OCTOBER

PLANTING & HARVEST

❑ **PLANT BULBS.** Plant spring-flowering bulbs in well-prepared soil, then mulch to prevent hard freezes from heaving the young bulbs out of the ground this winter.

❑ **PLANT PERMANENT PLANTS.** Set out ground covers, trees, shrubs, and perennials. As winter approaches, many nurseries reduce their stock of container plants; take advantage of low prices. Plant by the end of October. In the highest elevations, wait until spring.

❑ **SOW WILDFLOWERS.** For bloom in spring, broadcast seed early in the month over rock gardens, hillsides, and fields. If possible, lightly rake and cover with a 1/4-inch layer of organic matter. (In areas where winters are cold but snow cover is minimal, sow seed in spring.)

❑ **PREPARE PLANTING BEDS.** For earlier planting next spring, hand-spade beds now, working in generous amounts of organic matter such as compost or manure. Leave soil rough so it will absorb moisture through winter; the freezing-thawing cycle will break apart clods.

❑ **HARVEST TOMATOES.** If a killing frost threatens (usually on a still, clear night), either protect plants with row covers or harvest fruits and bring them indoors to ripen. Tomatoes that are dark green won't ripen, but those that are starting to show yellow or red will continue to ripen indoors at room temperature.

❑ **STORE PRODUCE.** Beets, carrots, turnips, and potatoes keep best when stored at 35° to 45° in lightly damp sand. Onions and shallots need cool but dry storage in mesh bags or slotted crates. Leave a 2-inch stem on winter squash and pumpkins; store at 50° to 60°. Store apples and pears in separate containers indoors at about 40°. Pick

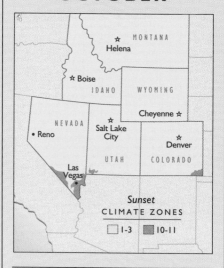

Sunset
CLIMATE ZONES

❑ 1-3 ■ 10-11

broccoli and brussels sprouts before a killing frost. Carrots, kale, horseradish, parsnips, and turnips can tolerate heavy frost, and well-mulched plants can stay in the ground all winter.

MAINTENANCE

❑ **CUT BACK PERENNIALS.** After the first hard freeze, cut back flowering perennials such as aster, campanula, daylily, phlox, and veronica to about 2 inches above the ground.

❑ **DIVIDE RHUBARB.** For improved production, divide and transplant overcrowded rhubarb roots after the first killing frost. Water occasionally to supplement rains until the first heavy snow.

❑ **CLEAN UP.** Collect diseased plant refuse, tie it up in plastic bags, and discard. Compost other plant material except leaves from ash, cottonwood, maple, oak, poplar, and willow, since these leaves do not break down readily (use them as mulch).

❑ **MULCH PLANTS.** After a hard freeze, spread 2 to 3 inches of compost, straw, or other organic matter to protect bulbs, perennial flowers and vegetables, permanent plants, and strawberry beds. Mulch conserves soil moisture and helps minimize freezing and thawing of soil, which can heave plants out of the ground.

❑ **PROTECT YOUNG TREES.** Bright winter sunlight can make young tree trunks split and crack along their south sides. Protect them with a coat of white latex paint or a layer of tree wrap or burlap. After trees are three or four years old, the bark should be thick enough to prevent sunburn.

❑ **WATER.** After leaves have fallen, water deciduous trees deeply, but only when the temperature is above freezing. Also water evergreens and spread mulch around them to retain moisture before the ground freezes.

❑ **FLUSH IRRIGATION SYSTEMS.** To prevent mineral buildup and cracked tubing, flush drip systems before the soil freezes. Remove end caps from main lines, turn the water on for a few minutes, then shut it off. Drain all the water out, then replace the end caps. If you have an ooze-type system, store tubing in a dark, protected place for the winter.

❑ **WINTERIZE LAWN MOWERS.** Once the grass stops growing, properly store your lawn mower, following the manufacturer's instructions. Most mowers need their gas and oil drained, blades cleaned or replaced, and moving parts lubricated.

PEST CONTROL

❑ **PINE-BARK BEETLES.** Before spring, burn all firewood cut from pines killed by pine-bark beetles. Otherwise, newly hatched beetles may fly into your healthy pine trees and infest them when the weather warms.

SOUTHWEST
CHECKLIST
OCTOBER

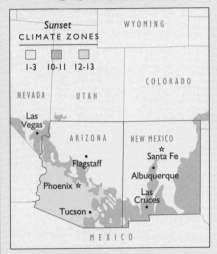

Sunset CLIMATE ZONES

1-3   10-11   12-13

PLANTING

☐ **BULBS.** Plant amaryllis, anemone, calla, crocus, daffodil, harlequin flower, oxalis, ranunculus, and watsonia. In climate zones 12 and 13, prechill bulbs of crocus, hyacinth, and tulip by storing them in the refrigerator for at least six weeks before planting.

☐ **COOL-SEASON ANNUALS.** In zones 12 and 13, try seedlings of calendula, dianthus, English daisy, Iceland poppy, lobelia, nemesia, ornamental cabbage and kale, pansy, primrose, schizanthus, snapdragon, stock, and viola. In zones 10 and 11, plant seedlings of aubrieta, candytuft, English daisy, forget-me-not, primrose, snapdragon, and stock.

☐ **PERENNIALS.** Plant right away for spring bloom. Water them well until their roots get established.

☐ **COOL-SEASON CROPS.** In zones 12 and 13, try beets, cabbage and other cole crops (bok choi, broccoli, brussels sprouts, cauliflower, Chinese cabbage, kale, kohlrabi), carrots, chard, endive, garlic, lettuce, onions, parsley, peas, radishes, and turnips.

☐ **STRAWBERRIES.** Plant any time after midmonth for a crop next spring. 'Sequoia' and 'Tioga' are easy to get and do well in the low desert. In the high desert, try 'Fort Laramie' and 'Ogallala'.

☐ **GROUND COVERS.** In zones 12 and 13, try *Acacia redolens,* Baja and Mexican evening primroses, *Dalea greggii,* dwarf rosemary, gazania, lippia, low-growing junipers, snow-in-summer, and verbena. In zones 10 and 11, there's still time to plant low-growing junipers.

☐ **NATIVE PLANTS.** This is the best month of the year to start all kinds of native plants, from trees and shrubs to grasses and wildflowers. To prepare wildflower seedbeds, cultivate the soil at least as deep as one spade blade and amend it with organic matter, broadcast the seeds, and rake them in. Then let nature take over.

☐ **TREES AND SHRUBS.** Plant all kinds except frost-tender ones such as bougainvillea and hibiscus (set them out next spring). When planting trees and shrubs from nursery cans, loosen the soil at least as deep as the rootball and five times as wide.

☐ **OVERSEED LAWNS.** Mow Bermuda grass lawns closely (about ½ inch), overseed with perennial ryegrass, and water deeply.

MAINTENANCE

☐ **TEND ROSES.** Prune them back by about a third, feed, and water to encourage one more round of bloom by Christmas.

☐ **WATER.** If nature doesn't provide water, irrigate the plants you've sown or planted this fall. Check soil moisture with a trowel; water after the top inch of soil has dried out.

☐ **WEED.** Before they set seed, hoe weeds off (if they're young and shallow-rooted) or pull them out (if they're mature). But don't put flowering weeds into the compost pile or they'll set seed and come back to haunt you next year.

TEXAS

PLANTING & HARVEST

☐ **PLANT SPRING BULBS.** Buy and plant bulbs as soon as they become available in nurseries. In the Houston area and South Texas, prechill bulbs of crocus, hyacinth, and tulip by storing them in the refrigerator for at least six weeks before planting.

☐ **PLANT COOL-SEASON CROPS.** Set out seedlings of cabbage, broccoli, kale, and other cole crops.

☐ **PLANT PERENNIAL HERBS.** Set out chamomile, chive, English lavender, oregano, parsley, thyme, winter savory, and rosemary (with protection from frost when necessary).

☐ **PLANT PERENNIALS, BIENNIALS.** Plant columbine, hollyhock, dianthus, Shasta daisy, foxglove, iris, penstemon, perennial verbena, violet, yarrow, and grasses.

☐ **HARVEST CROPS.** Summer-sown beans, lettuce, and radishes should be mature and ready to pick. As soon as fall-sown seedlings of carrots and lettuce come up, thin plants, saving the baby carrots and lettuce you thin to use in salads.

MAINTENANCE

☐ **DIVIDE PERENNIALS.** Dig and divide perennials such as bee balm, daylilies, and Shasta daisies to revitalize the plants.

☐ **FEED LAWNS.** Apply 1 pound of actual nitrogen per 1,000 square feet of turf. Fertilize newly seeded winter lawns after six weeks of growth.

☐ **TEND ROSES.** Feed plants and water them deeply to encourage a round of fall bloom.

PEST CONTROL

☐ **INSECTS AND SNAILS.** As fall flowers and vegetables start putting out tender new growth, aphids, whiteflies, and snails often move in to feast. Hose aphids and whiteflies off plants, then spray for remaining insects with insecticidal soap. Control snails by setting out poison bait where it won't present a threat to children and pets.

Mohamed Shaffi (above) waters gandana. Below, Mitch Nakashima stands by his trellis made of recycled materials. At right, community garden members including Shiva Azimi, Fadieh Haddad, and Santos Gonzales display the "fruits" of their labor.

RENEE LYNN

The
world in a
garden

On a few acres in Northern California, 108 families from 12 countries grow vegetables

by LAUREN BONAR SWEZEY

I t's a warm summer morning. Cris and Sandra Ortiz are relaxing under a large shade tree—the only tree on Hayward Community Gardens' sunny, 7-acre property in Hayward, California. Cris, who is president of the board for the gardens, is talking about *gandana,* an Afghani relative of the onion with a mild leek flavor.

He leads me to his plots, pointing out the 26 tomato bushes, dozens of 'Blue Lake' beans, Japanese and Pakistani cucumbers, squash, zucchini plants, and an unusual-looking plant called *apio* (Puerto Rican potato). This member of the celery family has celery-like leaves and potato-like roots. "You can boil the leaves for tea; it puts you to sleep," says Cris. "The root is delicious in soup or mashed like a potato."

Down the path that borders plots of familiar and unfamiliar vegetables, Mitch Nakashima is harvesting Japanese cucumbers and tending pole beans. Soon Ghulam Durani strolls by, headed for his plot of Afghani vegetables. He shows me a baby dill-like plant. "We are people from the mountains," says Durani, "and every plant has a medicinal use. This one cleans the blood."

Strolling through these gardens is like visiting many of the agricultural communities of the world squeezed into one place. Some 442 people from 108 families—representing 12 ethnic groups—grow crops here. You'll find rows of corn, green beans, and tomatoes, as well as a wonderful array of less common vegetables, such as taro and sugarcane.

Like many other community gardens around the West, this garden is about much more than vegetable plots.

"Many of the people at our community garden are immigrants," says Cris. "Everyone learns from each other here. We trade vegetables and recipes. It helps [us] integrate."

The
gardens
and their
gardeners

RENEE LYNN

Cris Ortiz, who emigrated from Puerto Rico 34 years ago, tends 4½ plots at the community garden. Some of the vegetables he keeps for his family, but the rest he sells at the community garden's vegetable cart near the entrance. The proceeds help pay the garden's water bill. "Cris is here day and night," says treasurer Betty Chaffin. "He knows everyone and what they plant. The gardens couldn't operate without him."

Ortiz collects and saves his own vegetable seeds at the end of each season. "For tomatoes, I just take seeds out, wash and dry them, and then store them in a jar. I cut open cucumbers and scoop out the seeds."

Ortiz takes me over to visit with Fadieh Haddad (shown above), an elderly Jordanian he calls "Mama." Dressed in a long skirt and apron, with her hair tucked under a colorful bandanna, Mama's tending beans. She doesn't speak English, but she cheerfully shows us her vegetable plot. Mama brought seeds of runnerlike beans from the old country, Ortiz explains.

Mitch Nakashima, a Japanese American from Hawaii, takes special pride in the appearance of his garden plot. All of the vegetables are neatly arranged and, whenever possible, strung up on trellises to save space. He even prefers to trellis his Japanese 'Long Green' cucumbers, because then "I can see all of the fruit," says Nakashima.

His cucumber trellis is actually a tent made with 2-inch wire mesh. He plants the seeds at its base and allows the vines to crawl up both sides. Nakashima's bean trellis is made from recycled wood and string. "I use a lot of recycled materials—I never throw anything away." He even recycles twist ties to attach the vines to the trellises.

When Nakashima starts seeds, he doesn't just plant a few for his own plot. He sows a packet in containers and passes out 2-inch potted plants to anyone at the garden who wants them.

Besides growing standard vegetables such as asparagus, 'Blue Lake' beans, 'Butterfruit' corn, and seedless 'Oregon Pride' and 'Siletz' tomatoes, he also grows special Asian vegetables. "Japanese pumpkin ('Kabocha') is like an acorn squash—sweet in flavor—but it's green. I chop it up and cook it with meat." Another unusual favorite of Nakashima's is bur-

dock (*gobo* in Japanese), a 3-foot-long, sweetly pungent root vegetable shaped like a parsnip. "I plant it in May and harvest it in November. Japanese [eat] it for New Year's."

During the cool season, Nakashima plants broccoli with different maturity dates so his harvest doesn't come all at once. 'Packman' matures in 85 days, 'Shogun' in 102.

Chico Rios came to Hayward from Jalisco, Mexico, 15 years ago. Each Saturday he spends all day tending his plot while two of his children, Veronica and Angel, play in the garden and, on hot days, soak in a bright blue barrel of water.

Gardening is one of Rios's favorite pastimes, and he does it well. His plot is a home away from home, complete with a shed that has an arbor attached. The arbor not only provides shade on hot days but also holds up rambunctious vines of chayote and *chilacayote* (a special Mexican squash). His beds are immaculately tended and edged with wood to make them easier to water, and "so the kids don't step in the plants," says Rios.

All year, the beds are filled with a huge assortment of vegetables. What does he do with them all? "I feed my family of 10 and give them away to friends," says Rios with a broad grin.

During the summer, Rios grows three kinds of corn for making tortillas and tamales ("someone gave me seeds from El Salvador"), beans for drying, cilantro, 'De Arbol' and 'Fresno' hot chilies, white and yellow sweet peppers, sugarcane ("we chew it for the juice"), tomatillos, and 'Better Boy' and 'Early Girl' tomatoes.

In early spring and fall, Rios grows broccoli, cabbage, cauliflower, garlic, lettuce, onions, and peas. He puts the arbor to good use again by hanging the garlic and onions to dry.

Nomi Vardy retired in California about 13 years ago after living in Russia and Germany most of her life. "I always had pieces of land in Russia. I came to America and had no land. Then I read in the newspaper that I could garden here [at the community garden]," she says.

Vardy grows what she calls "Russian food," along with potatoes and sunflowers. "I brought over a sunflower with extra-big seeds—they're too big for the birds to eat," she says. She also likes diversity. She grows and dries tomatoes, raspberries, and zucchini to send to relatives in Russia. "They have nine months of winter, so they grow almost no vegetables."

Vardy often spends three to four hours at a time in the garden. "Everyone who wants to live longer has to work in the garden and play sports. I swim an hour twice a week. I'm so tired from gardening and then go in the cold water—it feels wonderful." ■

The Hayward Community Gardens, founded in 1975 by Connie Hawkins, occupies city-owned property that's leased to Pacific Gas & Electric Company. The gardeners depend on funds from HUD, donations from members, and profits from the sale of vegetables. Membership (for Hayward residents with low and middle incomes) is by application. The garden, at 25051 Whitman Street, is not open to the public, but anyone can buy fresh vegetables at its stand between 8:30 and 2 on Saturdays year-round.

To start your own community garden, the nonprofit San Francisco League of Urban Gardeners (SLUG) offers a 16-page booklet explaining how to go about it. The first few pages provide a definition and history of community gardening. The succeeding pages explain how to get started and how to find land and identify owners. A 22-page companion booklet discusses managing and organizing the garden. To order the booklets, send $5 for each to SLUG, 2088 Oakdale St., San Francisco, CA 94124; (415) 285-7584.

Smoky with lavender blooms, Cotinus coggygria has bluish green leaves, which echo the blue fescue grass growing beneath it.

SANDRA IVANY

Smoke trees light up the garden

Their flowers and leaves add color, sound, and motion

IN THE WORLD OF MAGIC, A PUFF OF smoke is often used for dramatic effect. The plant world has its magicians, too, and the smoke tree (*Cotinus coggygria*) is one of the most flamboyant performers. The tree produces so many puffs that it all but disappears.

Starting in late spring or early summer, this shrubby deciduous tree is covered with flower clusters that resemble puffs of pink or lavender smoke. And the smoke seems to get even thicker as the fading flowers send out stalks covered with fuzzy purple hairs. The whole show lasts a month or longer before the flower clusters shrivel and drop.

But that's only part of the tree's magic act. In summer, the leaves—in various shades of bluish green, burgundy, and deep purple—shimmy and rattle on inch-long stems when stirred by the slightest breeze. Then in fall, the foliage turns gold, orange, or red, depending on the variety.

Smoke tree grows naturally as a densely branched shrub to 15 feet tall, and it can be trained into a single-trunked tree

that reaches 25 feet tall with a nearly equal spread. Its roundish leaves measure 1½ to 3 inches long. *C. coggygria* has bluish green leaves. *C. c.* 'Royal Purple' has rich purple leaves, and *C. c.* 'Velvet Cloak' has very dark purple leaves; if you plant either of these varieties where low morning or evening light can shine through them, the leaves glow like garnets. *C. c.* 'Grace' has softer purple leaves that turn brilliant scarlet in autumn.

A lesser-known species, *C. obovatus,* has a form much like that of its cousin *C. coggygria,* but its leaves are two to three times larger. The foliage of *C. obovatus* stays green through summer, then turns a spectacular orange in autumn.

In the landscape, smoke trees make excellent accent, background, or contrast plants. Ones with burgundy or purple leaves make striking foils to green- or silver-leafed plants. Many gardeners cut trees back annually or every few years to create a thicket of shrublike switches. You can also espalier plants along a sunny garden wall.

Smoke tree is hardy enough to grow in all *Sunset* climate zones. It takes full sun, thrives in poor or rocky soil, tolerates some drought, and resists oak root fungus. It needs no fertilizer and only infrequent water but does require good drainage. Many nurseries sell plants in 1-gallon or larger containers. Fall is prime planting time. ∎

By Steven R. Lorton

The incandescent leaves of Cotinus obovatus catch fire in the fall.

MICHAEL THOMPSON

ASIATIC HYBRIDS. *In June and July, their vivid blooms glow at the hot end of the lily spectrum. Clockwise from top right: 'Windsong', 'Hello Dolly', 'Yellow Gold' (also at top left), 'Camelot'; 'Juanita' is in the center.*

A tale of two lilies

Asiatic and Oriental hybrids are superstars of the summer garden.
Plant them now for blooms next June into September

By Jim McCausland
Photographs by Norman A. Plate

ORIENTAL HYBRIDS. *From mid-July, they flaunt blooms in shades of pink, rose, and white. Clockwise from top right: 'Heartbeat',
'Fellowship', 'Little Girl', 'Mona Lisa', 'Friendship', 'Geisha'. Most are descended from the gold-band lily, shown in center.*

A T THE LONDON FLOWER SHOW OF 1862, the crowd was abuzz over a plant that had just been imported from Japan: the gold-band lily (*Lilium auratum*). Only the tiger lily (*L. lancifolium*), brought from China in 1804, had ever created as big a stir among English gardeners.

Excitement about these lilies grew on both sides of the Atlantic, and eventually breeders created two great lines of hybrids: the Orientals (descended from *L. auratum* and *L. speciosum*) and the Asiatics (descended from *L. lancifolium* and other east-Asian species).

In the United States, Jan de Graaff of Oregon Bulb Farms started hybridizing lilies in the 1930s. Thanks to him and to other breeders, we can now fill our gardens with the beauty of lilies from late spring through summer. Asiatics reign in June and July, and Orientals take over from mid-July into September.

In the past, the chief drawback to growing Asiatic and Oriental hybrids was their susceptibility to viruses. But with today's vigorous hybrids and disease-free bulbs, viruses aren't the problem they once were.

ASIATICS

Most of the Asiatic hybrids have upward-facing flowers and work best when packed into containers or a perennial border, where they surpass other lilies with their vibrant mass of color. Asiatic

Good companions in a container planting are 'Heartbeat', a dwarf variety of Oriental lily, and creeping phlox.

lilies, buy short Asiatic varieties and plant them in containers filled with good potting soil; or plant *L. speciosum,* a parent of the Orientals, which seems to do well in this area.

Lilies grow best in full sun or filtered shade in hot-summer climates. To stay healthy, they need a moderate amount of winter chill and fast-draining soil with plenty of organic matter.

In warm-winter areas, where freezing temperatures are rare, plant prechilled bulbs. After the first year, your refrigerator can supply the "winter" chill: just dig up lily bulbs after foliage dies down, shake the dirt off the bulbs, and refrigerate them in a plastic bag with damp peat moss or sand until roots start to sprout. Replant in January.

In the garden, plant bulbs of both Asiatics and Orientals 8 inches deep (deeper in lighter soil, shallower in heavier soil). To provide a cool root run for lilies, many gardeners plant them where they can push up through heathers or ferns. Lilies and shrub roses also make excellent companions because they bloom at the same time.

In containers, plant five bulbs under 4 to 6 inches of fast-draining mix in pots at least 1 foot deep and 16 inches in diameter. Provide protection against frost for container plantings in cold-winter areas.

Lilies need two feedings per year (once when buds emerge, and once after flowering) with a relatively low-nitrogen fertilizer such as tomato food. Divide plants every three or four years.

SOURCES
Most growers offer collections of two or three dozen Asiatic or Oriental hybrids that put on a long bloom show in a range of colors. Here are four mail-order sources; catalogs are free.

B & D Lilies, Box 2007, Port Townsend, WA 98368; (360) 385-1738.

Jackson & Perkins, Box 1028, Medford, OR 97501; (800) 292-4769.

Wayside Gardens, 1 Garden Lane, Hodges, SC 29695; (800) 845-1124.

White Flower Farm, 30 Irene St., Torrington, CT 06790; (800) 503-9624.

A good reference is *The Gardener's Guide to Growing Lilies,* by Michael Jefferson-Brown and Harris Howland (Timber Press, Portland, 1995; $29.95).

hybrids make great cut flowers as well. For those reasons—and for their dependability—they've become the most widely grown lilies in the garden world.

If you're a seasoned gardener, you may have grown 'Enchantment' (a classic old orange) and perhaps 'Connecticut King' (yellow) for indoor arrangements. Newer hybrids really expand your choices. Now you can buy much shorter plants like the knee-high Pixies for containers, the beautiful, midsize L.A. hybrids (see facing page), and jumbo-flowered varieties like 'Camelot' and 'Hercules'.

Colors still include good oranges ('Eloise') and yellows ('Joanna'), but they also take in whites ('Nepal' is a good one) and reds (try 'Hello Dolly' and 'Tristar'). You'll even find gorgeous pink varieties like 'Bright Eyes' and 'Sorbet' with speckled white centers.

For an Asiatic with great virus resistance and down-facing blooms, try 'Ariadne', with spotted dusty rose flowers.

ORIENTALS
Orientals grow a foot or two taller than Asiatics, and they bear large, richly fragrant flowers in the pink, rose, and white range. Most Orientals have blooms that face downward, although breeders have developed upward- and outward-facing varieties, too.

For all-around performance, it's hard to beat 'Casa Blanca'; its fragrant, 10-inch white blooms make fine cut flowers. 'Sans Souci' (pink-spotted white) stays short enough to use in big containers. The Imperial strain bears dinner plate–size flowers in crimson, silver, gold, or pink. 'Mona Lisa' has outward-facing, soft-pink flowers with white edges.

If you like a touch of red in your lilies, try 'Fellowship', whose white petals each have a red stripe down the center, or 'Friendship', whose dark red, white-edged flowers face up at you.

There are other Orientals with upward-facing flowers: 'Star Gazer', which was the first one bred, has spotted, red-orange petals that shade to pink at the edges; reddish pink 'Strawberry Shortcake' and pale purple 'Heartbeat' have similar flowers on smaller plants.

Oriental hybrids seem to be more susceptible to viruses than Asiatic hybrids, so virus-resistant varieties are well worth seeking out. The deep red 'Black Beauty' (a classic cross with *L. henryi*) is wonderfully vigorous and floriferous.

PLANTING TIPS
Lilies grow everywhere in the West. You can order bulbs of all kinds now for planting in fall (in most mild-winter areas), winter (in Southern California, low and intermediate deserts, and South Texas), or spring (in cold-winter areas). However, in the Southwest, where mild winters and alkaline soil work against

MEET THE L.A. HYBRIDS

The L.A. hybrids are named not for Los Angeles, but for their parents: a *Lilium longiflorum* mother and an Asiatic father. These hybrids are vigorous, usually virus-resistant, and long-blooming (some flower for a full month), and most have a light fragrance. Although they benefit from winter chill, L.A. hybrids don't need as much of it as some other lilies.

Aladdin lilies make up part of this group. Mostly in the white, yellow, pink, peach, and orange color range, they include several virus-resistant hybrids, such as 'Aladdin's Beauty' (shown below), 'Aladdin's Sun' (yellow), and 'Aladdin's Quest' (pink). Bred in Oregon, the Aladdins are exclusive to B & D Lilies (see sources).

'Aladdin's Beauty' is one of the L.A. hybrids bred at Cebeco Lilies in Oregon.

Other growers also offer a number of L.A. hybrids. 'Arizona' (pink), 'Eternal Flame' and 'Evening Star' (orange), 'Salmon Queen' and 'San Jose' (salmon orange), and the Showtime series are all worthy plants; look for them in nurseries and mail-order catalogs.

L.A. hybrids can be damaged by late spring frosts, so it makes sense to choose later-blooming varieties if you garden where cold weather lingers. ■

Herbs for the whole year

Four easy ways to preserve fragrant leaves

AS THE GROWING SEASON DRAWS to a close, taking advantage of your herb garden's bounty or of great herb buys can be overwhelming, even if you're an ambitious cook. The simplest solution is to preserve the herbs. It's easy, you have options, and although some home-dried herbs have less color than their commercial counterparts, their tastes are comparable.

The old-fashioned method, air-drying, is enjoyable and simple enough to be a child's project. Faster ways to dry herbs are to use a dehydrator or a microwave oven. Freezing retains the leaves' fresh flavor best.

Stored as directed here, these herbs will be good for a year or more.

The first step. Rinse herbs well in cool water, then dry on towels or blot dry.

Air-drying. Different herbs dry at different rates, so bundle just one kind of herb at a time. Make bundles no larger than about ¾ inch thick at the stem end. Tie stems securely with cotton string, twine, or raffia, leaving enough of the strand loose to form a loop for hanging.

Hang bundles, leaves down, in a warm (but not above 90°), dry place away from direct sunlight and where air can circulate freely around each bundle. It takes 7 to 10 days (longer in cool or moist climates) for the leaves to become crisp enough to crumble. To protect herbs from dust, remove leaves and store them airtight.

Dehydrator drying. Arrange herb leaves in a single layer on dehydrator screen trays. Place in a dehydrator set at 115° to 125° and dry until leaves are crisp enough to crumble. The time required varies, depending on leaf size and the dehydrator's efficiency. If the dehydrator is moderately full, small leaves (such as thyme, oregano, and rosemary) may be ready in four to five hours, but start checking at four; larger leaves, like basil, mint, and sage, take longer. Drying takes longer in a full dehydrator. Store cool leaves airtight.

Microwave drying. Line a microwave-safe platter with microwave-safe paper

Tie herb sprigs together at stem ends, then hang in a well-ventilated area to dry.

towels. Arrange ½ to 1 cup herb leaves in a single layer (they can overlap slightly) on the towels. Cover herbs with another paper towel. Heat small leaves in a microwave oven at full power (100 percent) for one minute, large leaves for two minutes. Then heat at 30-second intervals until leaves are dry and crisp enough to crumble, two to four minutes total. Keep an eye on the process, and if the paper starts to darken or smoke, turn off the power at once but leave the door shut for at least a minute to avoid a flare-up. Let the leaves cool, then seal airtight.

Freezing. For freshest flavor, freeze leaves just plucked from the stems. Lay leaves in a single layer on baking sheets. Freeze, uncovered, until leaves are rigid, about an hour, then quickly pour them into freezer containers and return at once to the freezer. The frozen leaves won't stick together. Pour out what you need; crumble or chop while frozen.

Woodier leaves like rosemary and thyme darken slightly when thawed, but fleshier, more tender leaves like basil, mint, and sage get very dark—fresh leaves do the same when cooked.

If you plan to use the herbs to make pesto or herb butters, color matters. Blanch leaves before freezing to preserve their color.

To blanch, immerse leaves, a handful or two at a time, in boiling water just until they turn brighter green, two to three seconds. Immediately skim leaves from the water and immerse in ice water until cold. Drain dry on towels. Freeze as directed for unblanched herbs. ■

By Christine Weber Hale

Surprising faces in the flower world are (clockwise from top): 'Purple Queen' corn cockle; pale pink 'Beauty Mix' lavatera; fluffy pink double poppy; and rich rose 'Ruby Regis' lavatera.

Flower discoveries

Mauve poppies? Rosy red forget-me-nots?
Grow such offbeat treasures from seed

By Sharon Cohoon

WHY GROW ANNUALS FROM seed? There are at least a dozen practical reasons. Saving money, for instance. Seed packets may not be the bargain they were a few years ago, but they're still cheaper than planting from sixpacks. Another reason is hardier plants. Annuals from seed are typically stronger, taller, and more productive than transplants. Seeds also offer more options in flower colors. Shirley poppy seedlings, for example, are usually sold in mixed colors in nurseries, but perhaps you would rather have them exclusively in shades of pink. Enjoying blooms earlier than your neighbors is another advantage. Sow seeds at the optimum time—right now in most areas—and you'll have flowers well before gardeners who wait to plant from sixpacks.

But the best reason to grow annuals from seed is really for the sheer joy of discovery. Flowers you won't commonly see in nurseries unfurl like little miracles—with unusual colors, shapes, and markings. They're the kind of flowers that make visitors to your garden exclaim, "Wow, I've never seen that before. What is it?"

Seeds of unusual varieties are presents that unwrap themselves and shout, "Surprise!" And it's as true on your hundredth sowing as it is on your first.

Give yourself some presents this year. We did. We combed through seed catalogs, ordered every variety that struck our fancy, and tried them all out in our test garden. The surprises we liked best are listed below.

All grow well in beds and borders. Sow seeds in weed-free soil that's been well amended with organic matter such as compost, then raked smooth. Follow directions on package labels. ■

Brilliant colors splash the heart of 'Zulu Prince' African daisy (top right) and 'Bright Eyes' flax (right).

NORMAN A. PLATE

11 SPRING DISCOVERIES

Initials after each listing indicate seed sources (listed below).

1. African daisy (Arctotis hybrid) 'Zulu Prince'. Spectacular daisy-petaled flower reminiscent of an exotic feather necklace. White with black center and purple and yellow inner rings. Good cut flower. 2 feet tall. SC

2. Corn cockle (Agrostemma githago) 'Purple Queen'. A deep violet version of the more common lilac-rose-colored annual. Long, graceful stems. Grassy gray-green foliage. Excellent cut flower. 2 to 3 feet tall. SS

3. Flax (Linum grandiflorum) 'Bright Eyes'. Similar to scarlet flax but sporting ivory flowers with chocolate centers. Excellent filler plant. 1 foot tall. TM

4. Forget-me-not (Myosotis sylvatica) 'Carmine King'. Unexpected rosy red rather than true blue. 6 to 8 inches tall. TM

5. Lavatera (L. trimestris) 'Beauty Mix'. A semidwarf lavatera. Pastel mix of salmon, rose, pink, and white. Many flowers are delicately striped. 2 to 3 feet tall. SS

6. L. t. 'Ruby Regis'. Rich rose-colored, chalice-shaped flowers with a satiny texture. Maple-shaped leaves. Multibranched. 3 to 6 feet tall. SS

7. Nemesia (N. versicolor) 'Blue Gem'. Small deep blue, trumpet-shaped flowers. Endearing, bushy plant for front of border. 8 to 10 inches tall. TM

8. Poppy (Papaver commutatum) 'Lady Bird'. Single scarlet flowers with black central blotches. 18 inches tall. TM

9. Papaver laciniatum. Huge (5-in. diameter) double flowers that are deeply frilled. Solid white, pink, crimson, rose, and salmon shades. 2 to 3 feet tall. TM

10. P. rhoeas 'Angels Choir'. Shirley poppies in antique shades with wavy double flowers. 2 to 2½ feet tall. TM

11. P. r. 'Mother of Pearl'. Shirley poppies in antique shades—mauve, pastel blue, lilac, peach, dusty pink, gray. 2 to 5 feet tall. TM

SEED SOURCES

SC: Seeds of Change, Box 15700, Santa Fe, NM 87506; (888) 762-7333.

SS: Shepherd's Garden Seeds, 6116 Highway 9, Felton, CA 95018; (408) 335-6910.

TM: Thompson & Morgan, Box 1308, Jackson, NJ 08527; (800) 274-7333.

Dress up your Thanksgiving table with fall leaves, berries, and flowers from your garden.
For details on assembling this striking bouquet, see page 277.

NOVEMBER

Garden guide......................274

Garden notebooks 277

Garden checklists.................281

Taming wildflowers 286

Diminutive daffodils..............291

gardenguide

NORMAN A. PLATE

Painting with spring flowers

Fill a border with a multicolored blend of tulips, nemesias, violas, and Iceland poppies

by LAUREN BONAR SWEZEY

A riot of color fills the flower border in Charles and Jackie Davis's Piedmont, California, garden from the first of February to mid-April. The hot color medley of yellow, orange, and red shown at left is a "very cheerful, gaudy palette," says landscape designer Bob Clark of Oakland, California. The border was planted last fall and photographed in spring.

Violas in dark and soft yellow and mixed nemesias carpet the ground, with Iceland poppies and five kinds of tulips popping up through them. The flower colors play off one another, unifying the planting. Yellow violas and nemesias complement yellow 'Big Smile' and 'Olympic Flame' tulips, red nemesias echo the red in 'Kingsblood' tulips, and orange nemesias reflect the color of the orange Iceland poppies.

Each season, a different color palette changes the mood of this flower bed. Clark develops his planting schemes so there's a blend of colors at every level—from plants as low as 4 inches to ones as tall as 30 inches. Taller tulips are planted at the back of the border, while shorter tulips bloom in front. To prolong the season, he also includes tulip varieties that bloom at different times.

When a border packs in as much color as this one, the background should be kept simple. "Always have a foliage foil [such as green] for the color, so things don't look disorganized," Clark says.

Before planting, prepare the bed by tilling compost or another organic amendment into the soil. In mild-winter areas of Arizona and Texas, prechill tulip bulbs in the refrigerator; plant annuals first, then interplant tulips among them. In cold-winter areas, plant tulip bulbs in fall, but wait until spring to interplant seedlings of Iceland poppy and nemesia.

gear

The neat thing about tip bags is that they don't tip. (The name doesn't come from the bags' refusal to be knocked over; *tip* is British for garden trash.) These sturdy woven-polypropylene bags have broad bases that keep them securely upright so they won't tip over and spill their contents. They also have wide mouths—thanks to plastic bands in the rims—which make them easy to fill. And their handy carrying loops are convenient for hanging the bags up and out of the way as soon as their job is done.

Sunset's test garden coordinator, Bud Stuckey, liked the tip bag he tried out in our test garden so much that he picked up another for home use—the supreme compliment.

Tip bags are available in three sizes: small (14 inches tall, 12 inches across, $20); medium (18 inches tall, 23 inches across, $24); and large (18 inches tall, 30 inches across, $27). The medium and large sizes are available at most Smith & Hawken stores; all sizes are available through the catalog (800/776-3336). — *Sharon Cohoon*

'Scentimental' is a blushing beauty

This 1997 All-America Rose Selection winner, a floribunda, could as easily have been named "Unpredictable." Its cherry-and-cream blossoms never turn out the same way twice. Some flowers are predominantly red with white swirls; others, just the reverse. For further caprice, sometimes the cream comes blushed with pink. Because all variations share the same sweetly old-fashioned form and scent, gardeners aren't likely to mind not knowing exactly what to expect from each bud. The variability in this award-winning rose's personality is just one of its many charms.

The unpredictable coloring and cup shape of this variety's blooms come from its garden rose ancestry, says its hybridizer, Tom Carruth,

Unthirsty plants for dry times

Fall planting takes on a whole different character when you're in the midst of a killer drought, as much of the Southwest and Texas is now. As old plants and lawns parch, replace them with drought-tolerant trees, shrubs, and ground covers. These still need water, especially during their first year, but in the long run, they need less water to look good.

Most nurseries carry a few drought-tolerant plants, but here are some mail-order sources to add to your choices. These firms offer a wide selection of seeds and plants, although not all of them are drought tolerant.

Agua Viva Seed Ranch, Route 1, Box 8, Taos, NM 87571; (800) 248-9080. Plants and seeds of drought-tolerant native perennials and wildflowers. Catalog free.

Aztekakti/Desertland Nursery, Box 26126, El Paso, TX 79926; (915) 858-1130. Cactus, desert plants. Catalog $1.

Desert Nursery, 1301 S. Copper St., Deming, NM 88030; (505) 546-6264. Cactus and succulent plants. Send a self-addressed, stamped envelope for a price list.

Northplan/Mountain Seed, Box 9107, Moscow, ID 83843; (208) 882-8040. Seeds of trees, shrubs, and wildflowers from the mountain and intermountain West. Native seed list $1.

Plants of the Southwest, Agua Fria, Route 6, Box 11A, Santa Fe, NM 87501; (800) 788-7333. Native plants of all kinds. Catalog $3.50.

Wild Seed, Box 27751, Tempe, AZ 85285; (602) 276-3536. Seeds of Southwest natives. Price list free.

— *Jim McCausland*

director of research at Weeks Roses in Upland, California. 'Ferdinand Pichard', a hybrid perpetual dating from 1921 and still considered one of the best striped roses, is one of its grandparents. But the rose's frequency of bloom comes from its more modern parents: 'Playboy' and 'Peppermint Twist'. Additional virtues of 'Scentimental' are good disease resistance and an attractive rounded growth habit.

'Scentimental' will start appearing in nurseries this month. If you can't find it locally, ask your nursery to contact Weeks Roses (800/992-4409), the wholesale grower responsible for introducing it.— *S. C.*

COOK'S *choice*

Plant shallots now for soup next year

Anyone who cooks with shallots or uses them in a soup will tell you that these onion relatives have their own delicate flavor. In the Northwest's mild-winter areas (zones 4 through 7), you can get an early start on shallots, just as you can garlic, by planting bulbs this month. In colder zones, 1 through 3, plant in early spring.

Many nurseries carry shallot bulbs. Plant the bulbs (pointed ends up) 2 inches deep in rich, quick-draining soil in a spot that gets full sun. During the winter, the bulbs will establish themselves, and when spring arrives, the plants will go into high gear. When the tops turn yellow in late spring or early summer, pull the bulbs—two to eight plump ones will have formed. They're delicious when eaten fresh. Like garlic heads, shallot bulbs store well if kept in a cool, dry place. — *Steven R. Lorton*

TIPS *and* **SECRETS**

A recipe for starting moss

Cast-stone statues, landscape rocks, and other objects look older—and usually better—if there's a bit of moss growing on them. You can wait for moss to grow naturally, or you can hasten the process by using a moss-starting recipe.

Seattle landscape architect Bob Chittock has a proven formula: He dissolves a lump of native blue clay or porcelain clay (available at craft shops) in 3 cups of water until the mixture has the consistency of a thick milkshake. Then he mixes the clay suspension with 1 cup of undiluted liquid fish fertilizer and 1 cup of moss that he has gathered (sidewalk cracks are good spots to collect moss). Thoroughly whip the mixture in an old blender, then paint it onto the object with a brush.

If the object is in a shady, moist place, you should see a patina of moss by spring. — *S. R. L.*

The flowers and foliage of these three plants blend beautifully.

GREAT *gardens*

Native Sons

Purple smoke tree, Santa Barbara daisy, and variegated agave may seem like an unusual plant combination. But these three, which grow together in a demonstration garden at Native Sons Wholesale Nursery in Arroyo Grande, are beautifully compatible.

Smoke tree (*Cotinus coggygria*) is so popular with gardeners in England that you'd never know it's also remarkably drought resistant. Originally from Southern Europe, it has a Mediterranean plant's typical tolerance for aridity. Its lack of thirst makes it an excellent companion to Santa Barbara daisy (*Erigeron karvinskianus*), a Mexican native.

Dave Fross of Native Sons wanted to see a third texture in the demonstration garden, so he moved the variegated agave here to see how its sculptural qualities would affect the composition. He liked what he saw and left it, pot and all. The container makes the agave more of a focal point, creating a stronger vignette, he says. Its swordlike leaves arch out of the pot in a way that causes the plant to resemble a fountain. The container should restrict root growth so the agave doesn't overplay its part.

The bronzy foliage of the smoke tree is a handsome foil for the pale pink-to-white flowers of the Santa Barbara daisy, and the muted green and cream colors of the agave act as bright accents.

The combination, predicts Fross, should have a long run. — *S. C.*

Pacific Northwest Garden Notebook

by **STEVEN R. LORTON**

Many nongardeners tend to think of October as autumn and November as winter. We gardeners know better—November is a wonderful autumn month, too. True, a few deciduous trees are naked by now, and most perennials are frost-nipped, but the show is far from over. I'm always amazed by the sweet gum trees (*Liquidambar styraciflua*) that line my street in Seattle. They drop a leaf here and there starting in late October, but I've seen lots of leaves on these trees as late as Christmas. I plan to add some sweet gums to my garden in the Skagit Valley, and when I do, I'll follow the advice I give friends: Always buy plants for autumn color when they are in autumn color.

Although nurseries often sell these trees labeled only as liquidambar, there are many varieties. *L. s.* 'Burgundy' will give you deep purple-red fall color. Or you might get *L. s.* 'Palo Alto', which turns orange red to bright red. And *L. s.* 'Festival' puts on its autumn show in shades of yellow, pink, peach, orange, and red. Buy those plants whose leaves you like best.

•

For autumn flowers, get a *Schizostylis coccinea* (commonly called crimson flag or Kaffir lily). This delicate, summery-looking plant is plenty tough. I grow it in the Skagit Valley, and I've cut its flower spikes to take indoors for Thanksgiving. Its grassy foliage reminds me of iris leaves. Its star-shaped, 2½-inch flowers line the stalks like gladiolus blossoms. If seed pods are allowed to form, you can crush them, drop them into some well-tilled soil, and cover them up. Next spring, spindly little shoots that look like weed grass will spring up—and you'll be looking at a little nursery of baby plants.

•

I haven't started a worm bin yet, but I've been thinking about it because everyone I know who's been using worm castings is squirming with delight. I've started my education process by subscribing to *Worm Digest*. This quarterly newsletter is put out by the Edible City Resource Center in Eugene, Oregon, a nonprofit organization that promotes sustainable organic agriculture. To subscribe, send $12 to Worm Digest, Box 544, Eugene, OR 97440. The center's Web site address is http://www.applied3d.com/worm/.

•

When ever-shorter November days curtail puttering in my Seattle garden, I head to the Center for Urban Horticulture on the University of Washington campus. From 4 to 7:45 on Mondays, the Washington Garden Clinic is held at the center; Master Gardeners are on hand to answer questions. For information, call (206) 543-8616. In the same building, the Miller Horticultural Library stays open until 8 P.M. Mondays. It has an incredible collection of references, including gardening books, magazines, newsletters, and hundreds of seed, bulb, and plant catalogs.

THAT'S A GOOD QUESTION

Q: When do I plant trillium bulbs, and where do I get them?

A: Most gardeners plant trilliums in spring, setting out blooming plants from 1-gallon cans. The plants grow from thick, fleshy rhizomes. You can also plant the rhizomes now in rich, quick-draining soil in a shady location where they won't be disturbed. One mail-order source for rhizomes is Bosky Dell Natives, 23311 S.W. Bosky Dell Lane, West Linn, OR 97068; (503) 638-5945. Rhizomes start at $5 each, plus shipping.

A bouquet from your garden

Beautiful holiday table settings call for striking bouquets. And in many part of the West, you can find plenty of great bouquet-making materials right outside the back door.

Two days before Thanksgiving last year, we asked *Sunset* gardener and floral designer Kim Haworth to create an arrangement using flowers and foliage from *Sunset's* gardens (see photo on page 272). While our gardens are large (7 acres), the kinds of flowers, berries, and leaves that Haworth discovered are typical of those that put on a fall show in many residential gardens.

Haworth chose purple as her base color, since many of our fall-flowering plants—including *Limonium perezii*, Mexican bush sage, and *Origanum laevigatum* 'Hopley's'—bear lavender to purple flowers. For accents, she used the orange-red berries of *Cotoneaster lacteus* and the orange flowers of lantana and lion's tail (*Leonotis leonurus*). Pin oak leaves fill in the gaps. "When I finished, the design looked too dull," says Haworth, "so I popped in bright yellow gloriosa daisies (*Rudbeckia* 'Indian Summer')." If you don't grow any of these plants, substitute clippings from special plants in your own garden.

The asymmetrical arrangement is low so diners can see over it. Big leaves and flowers are confined to its base; wispy flower spikes add interest at the top. Florist foam anchors them in the low bowl. This arrangement will last four to seven days in a moderately cool home.

Other great fall-bouquet makers include asters, cosmos, Japanese anemones, gaillardia, and gerberas. And don't overlook the colorful foliage of shrubs such as smoke tree (*Cotinus coggygria*) or purple hop bush (*Dodonaea viscosa* 'Purpurea').

— *L. B. S.*

gardenguide

The gentler side of "the Rock"

Gardens on Alcatraz? It may not seem possible, but roses, pink-flowered ice plants, and callas have grown on "the Rock" for more than a century. A new book, *Gardens of Alcatraz* (Golden Gate National Parks Association, San Francisco, 1996; $14.95), chronicles the history of these gardens.

The 96-page paperback is sure to delight plant lovers and history buffs, and to enrich an Alcatraz visit. Essays by author John Hart, landscape architect Michael Boland, and plant and horticulture expert Russell A. Beatty describe the rich tapestry of plants—from fruit trees to natives—that softened the Rock's austere contours, as well as the gardeners who tended them. Vivid photographs by amateur photographer Roy Eisenhardt show some of the 145 kinds of plants still growing there.

"The story of the gardens of Alcatraz is a compelling account of men and plants brought together on an island uninhabitable by either," writes Beatty. The first gardens were planted here at the end of the Civil War era, when military officers brought soil to the Rock and lined their picket fences with cannonballs; inmates tended plots during the federal prison years. The penitentiary closed in 1963, but many of the plants have continued to thrive on their own, providing a sprinkling of color.

November is a good time to trek through the Rock's gardens. But if you can't get there, pick up a copy of *Gardens of Alcatraz* in bookstores, or order it through the National Park Store by calling (415) 433-7221.

— *Rizza Yap*

Northern California Garden Notebook

by LAUREN BONAR SWEZEY

I visit gardens and nurseries a lot, and in my wanderings I often come across plantings so unique that I can't help sharing them. Oakland designer Archie Days's succulent dish gardens are works of art.

Days uses a wide variety of containers—"everything and anything from secondhand stores," he says—including glazed pottery, rocks, rusted metal, and wood. A single container or multiple containers stacked together might form the base of his compositions. He packs succulents in the containers so closely that they stay small and tight like bonsai. The overall effect is very sculptural.

Days started making his dish gardens by chance five years ago. With limited space for his collection of succulents, he began potting various kinds together. Friends and acquaintances liked what they saw, and after giving a number of the dish gardens away, Days started selling them.

The dish gardens are easy to care for; they require watering only about once a week, and periodic grooming (removing debris that falls on them). Unlike many container gardens, they're long-lived, lasting five years or more before they outgrow the containers.

Days's creations are available at the Dry Garden in Oakland (510/547-3564). You can also buy them directly from Days (510/632-5313). Prices range from $20 to $100 each.

NOW'S THE BEST TIME TO BUY CHINESE PISTACHE

Chinese pistache (*Pistacia chinensis*) is generally considered a desirable tree for patios, lawns, and streetside plantings because of its beautiful fall foliage color and its moderate size. But I've discovered that not all pistache trees are created equal.

Several years ago, the City of Palo Alto planted two pistache trees in the parking strip in front of our house. After a couple of years, I noticed that one tree had developed a much better form than the other. The nicely shaped tree is male, and the gawky, thin-canopied tree is female. From late spring to midsummer, the female puts much of its energy into producing berries, which seems to affect the growth and lushness of the tree. By fall, berries have begun to drop everywhere, making a mess. In spring, numerous seedlings pop up in my planting beds. The female tree doesn't develop good fall color either—its leaves just turn a dull yellow, then drop.

Chinese pistache trees are usually grown from seedlings. When you buy one, it might be either male or female, and it may or may not produce good fall color. So if you plan to shop for a Chinese pistache, do so in fall. That way, you can choose the leaf coloring you like, such as crimson, orange, scarlet and yellow tones, and also pick a male tree without berries.

THAT'S A GOOD QUESTION

Q. I have been looking for the 'Mermaid' rose for years with no luck, and wonder where the Schlegels (May '96 issue, page 62) ever found it?

A. The American Rose Society in Shreveport, Louisiana (318/938-5402), will supply sources for any rose in its *1996 Handbook for Selecting Roses*. 'Mermaid' can be purchased by mail from the Antique Rose Emporium in Brenham, Texas (800/441-0002); catalog is $5 (free with order). Roses cost $11.95 (bareroot), plus shipping.

Southern California Garden Notebook

by **SHARON COHOON**

Butterflies, so the song goes, are free. They flit into your yard, sip a little nectar from your flowers, and split. And their aerial ballet doesn't cost you a penny. But a new butterfly emerging from a chrysalis is a rarer performance. I had seen a butterfly break out of its case once—an awe-inspiring sight—and I dearly wanted an encore. But to watch that again, I was expecting to pay a price.

To begin with, I'd have to plant butterfly-host plants, sacrificing garden space I could have used for a strictly ornamental plant. (Each butterfly species has just a few plants its larvae can feed on; if you don't have these plants in your garden, the butterfly goes elsewhere to lay its eggs.) Then, once the eggs had hatched into hungry caterpillars, I'd have to stand back and watch them nibble holes in the foliage of those host plants, ugly though the scene might be.

I planted passion vine—baby food for Gulf fritillaries. The adults arrived in squadrons. Eggs were laid. Purple-and-orange caterpillars hatched. But to my surprise, all the little monsters disappeared, leaving only the tiniest trace of damage to my *Passiflora caerulea.* So I added baby's tears for red admirals, dill and fennel for anise swallowtails, and milkweed for monarchs. But the same thing happened. Most of the caterpillars I invited for dinner ended up as somebody else's lunch. Birds, spiders, ants, dragonflies, and parasitic wasps all preyed on them. My host plants showed few traces of caterpillar jaws. Yet I salvaged at least one undamaged chrysalis each season to watch it come to life. Another free performance, as it turns out.

So if you've been imagining that harboring host plants would lead to the mass destruction of your garden, stop worrying. Based on my experience, the caterpillars take all the risks. The least we can do is provide food. Plant some milkweed this month. Host a caterpillar party.

Of course, you could take the easy route. For $3 to $4, you can buy a chrysalis from the Monarch Program. Set it on your desk, wait for a butterfly to emerge, and "prepare to be humbled," says program director David Marriott. A few dollars more will buy two caterpillars, a host plant, and the opportunity to watch the entire metamorphosis. There's a catch, though—you have to pick up your order at the program's office in Encinitas (or meet the $25 mail-order minimum). Consider the visit an opportunity to see the Butterfly Vivarium, a charming netted structure housing several species of butterflies in all stages of life. Kids love this place, so take your children along. The program's primary purposes are research and education, however, so the office doesn't have regular visiting hours. But Marriott is happy to schedule appointments. For information, call (800) 606-6627. For a brochure and price list, write to Box 178671, San Diego, CA 92177.

THAT'S A GOOD QUESTION

Q. How can you use the herbicide glyphosate (Roundup) in tight places without endangering nearby plants?

A. Andie Paysinger faced this situation in raised herb beds in her Lancaster, California, garden. Hand-pulling had not been very effective in these hard-to-weed areas, but spraying glyphosate in such tight quarters seemed risky. Her solution was simple but ingenious. Cutting the bottoms off plastic bottles (such as 2-liter soft drink containers) converts them into highly focused herbicide delivery systems, Paysinger discovered. Place the bottomless bottle over a weed, insert the Roundup nozzle into the top, and spray. Wait a second or two for the spray to settle, lift the bottle, and move to the next weed. When applied this way, glyphosate leaves neighboring plants dry. Paysinger has been using this method for two years and hasn't lost an herb yet.

FALL PLANTING

Dig-your-own pansies in Encinitas

Long before pony packs appeared on the nursery scene, growers started pansies in open fields and dug them up just before taking them to market. Though it wasn't as efficient as modern methods, the field system had its benefits. Plants developed bigger, healthier rootballs. And a large field of multicolored pansies made a fine sight.

In Southern California, Weidners' Gardens in Encinitas brings back the tradition of field-grown pansies, but with a twist—at Weidners', customers do the digging. Yet the nursery gets no complaints. Seeing all those colors together in the field really seems to inspire customers' creative juices, Mary Weidner says. Some people bring their own containers and plant up a color bowl on site.

Dig-your-own season begins around November 1 and continues through the third week in December or as long as the pansies hold out. But even though more than 25,000 pansies are planted for the event, don't dawdle. Get there early, advises Weidner. Once the season begins, customers dig up more than 1,000 pansies a day. "They go fast." A wide variety of colors is available, including 'Imperial Pink' and 'Jolly Joker'.

Cost per pansy is approximately $1.10, with discounts for volume purchases. Weidners' supplies tools and carrying boxes (bring your own gloves). The nursery is at 695 Normandy Road in Encinitas. Hours are 9:30 to 4:30 daily except Tuesdays. For additional information, call (619) 436-2194.
— *S. C.*

gardenguide

JOHN RIZZO

New plants from the old Soviet Union

When states of the former Soviet Union opened up, Oregon nurseryman Jim Gilbert was quick to fly over for a look. He knew that plant breeding in the Soviet Union had often taken a very different direction from breeding in the West, and he wanted to see what new plants would adapt well to North American gardens.

Gilbert brought back many edible plant species that we'd never heard of, and many we knew, though not as serious food sources.

Among his finds were mountain ash (*Sorbus aucuparia* 'Rabina' is shown above), a honeysuckle with edible berries that Gilbert named honeyberry (*Lonicera kamchatika*), magnolia vine (*Schizandra chinensis*), and goumi (*Eleagnus multiflora*), a relative of the Russian olive with fruits that look somewhat like pie cherries.

We were especially taken with highbush cranberry (*Viburnum opulus*), whose white flowers and brilliant red berries allow it to stand on its own as an ornamental.

Most of these plants are well-suited for the West's coldest climates. For a catalog, send $2 to One Green World, Box 1080, Molalla, OR 97038; to order, call (503) 651-3005.   —*J.M.*

Westerner's Garden Notebook

by **JIM McCAUSLAND**

I've always liked November best of all the months, perhaps because it's so low-key. Summer is long gone and winter storms are on the way, it's true, but the garden doesn't demand much beyond light weeding—and watering if rains delay their arrival. Whatever you've planted for spring, be it color or crop, uses winter to send out roots in preparation for the spring growth push that's still months away.

It's an especially good time to tend summer-worn tools. I broke the handle of a favorite spade—one of those industrial-strength English numbers—and was amazed at how easy it was to replace. I simply bought a new handle and rivet from the mail-order place that sold me the spade years ago, drilled out the old rivet, and refitted the new rivet and handle in minutes.

•

I've noticed that fall seems to bring tree toppers out of the woodwork. They try to tell you that if you don't take the tops out of your trees, a winter storm could blow any of them down—on you or your property. It's a badly flawed message. Topped trees grow back multiple tops, all of which are thinner, weaker, and often leafier than the single trunk they replaced, increasing the risk that the top will blow out in the future. Topping also makes the trees look profoundly ugly. Instead, have a professional arborist—somebody who doesn't top trees—remove enough of the side branches to open up the tree so wind can blow through, not against, it.

•

The advent of winter stimulates my interest in indoor plants. I'm especially fond of the Thanksgiving and Christmas cactus—hybrids from the *Schlumbergera* tribe—because they have such wonderful blooms in a broad spectrum of color. I tried to keep track of which was Thanksgiving cactus, which was Christmas cactus, and which were hybrids, but then I learned that most have been so heavily hybridized that their lineage has all the certitude of a scrambled egg. Now I just buy colors I like: salmon, white with a touch of pink, red, and so forth. Water them occasionally and fertilize around bloom time and you'll have a plant that will fill a washtub in 20 years.

•

If you live in cold country, the winterization process is important for garden equipment, especially drip irrigation systems. To protect them from freezing, either drain them or install a weeper valve (it automatically drains lines after each use). If your drip system isn't permanently installed and you can take it up without making an impossible tangle of spaghetti tubing, store it in the garage, away from the sun and harsh weather, for the winter.

Even hose-watering systems need attention. Detach and drain hoses and sprinklers and store them in the garage. Once, I forgot to uncouple a hose from my "freezeproof" hose bib. When the water in the hose froze, it expanded into the bib, which then burst at the valve.

THAT'S A GOOD QUESTION

Q: I am reluctant to use salt on my driveway this winter because of the bordering plants and grass. I heard that fertilizer can be used to de-ice surfaces. What is the most economical and efficient way to do this?

A: Fertilizer works because it contains salt, which, in concentration, burns plants just as plain salt does. Try sand instead, or dig shallow gutters along your driveway to carry off salt-laden meltwater. Don't use sand on wood decks or polished masonry, which can be scarred. Instead, try sawdust.

Planting

☐ **ANNUALS.** Sow hardy annuals such as candytuft, clarkia, larkspur, linaria, and wildflower mixes now in weed-free, well-tilled soil. Seeds sown in fall will germinate and flower earlier than the same seeds sown in spring.

☐ **BULBS.** There's still time to get spring-flowering bulbs into the ground this month. Crocus, daffodils, and tulips are the obvious choices, but even at this relatively late date, nurseries will still be filled with alliums, anemones, scilla, and even more exotic candidates.

☐ **CAMELLIAS.** You'll find Sasanquas in nurseries, in bloom this month in zones 5–7. Buy and plant immediately. It works well espaliered under the eaves of houses, where blossoms are protected from the pelting rain.

☐ **CONIFERS.** You'll find dozens of ready-to-plant conifers in containers at nurseries. With leaves off deciduous trees and shrubs, it's easy to see where a conifer or two would enliven your winter garden. And it's not too early to start shopping if you want a living Christmas tree. Buy the plant and let it stand in a bare spot in the garden, so you can decide where you want it after the holidays. Bring it indoors after Thanksgiving for its Yuletide stint. Keep contained conifers well watered.

Maintenance

☐ **CUT BACK MUMS.** When the last flowers fade, cut back chrysanthemums to within 6 inches of the ground. They'll send up new growth next spring.

☐ **DIVIDE PERENNIALS.** In zones 4–7, November is still an excellent month to dig and divide perennials. Our mild, rainy winters will encourage new roots to develop, and the plants will zoom into action next spring. Circle clumps with a shovel or spade and pop them out of the ground. A dinner plate–size clump will divide into three parts. Replant divisions. Old, knotted roots and worn-out stalks can be put on the compost pile.

☐ **GROOM BORDERS.** As frost brings plants down, cut them back. Leave 4 to 6 inches of neatly trimmed stalk sticking up to protect the plant's crown through the winter and to remind you where the plant is when you're preparing beds next spring. Clear out debris from beds (it harbors slugs and other pests). There are some plants that you'll want to leave standing for winter interest: the large sedums, baptisia, ornamental grasses, and iris are all candidates. Weed thoroughly. Spread a layer of mulch over beds—2 inches is a good thickness.

☐ **GROOM LAWNS.** Mow and edge the lawn one last time, and rake up fallen leaves and other debris. Nothing is quite as annoying as looking at a shabby lawn all winter when it's too wet and cold to get out and do anything about it.

☐ **MAKE COMPOST.** Prunings, grass clippings, pulled plants, and raked leaves all go on the compost pile. Turn it one last time for the season.

☐ **PRUNE TREES, SHRUBS.** Remove dead, diseased, and injured wood. Step back and eye the plant for form. Prune out branches that cross, ones that are closely parallel, and anything else that detracts from a handsomely shaped plant.

Pest control

☐ **SLUGS.** Continue to bait, set out beer traps, and handpick these slippery varmints. If you get them now, next spring your foliage won't look as if it's been riddled with buckshot.

Planting

☐ **CHOOSE TREES FOR FALL COLOR.** Zones 7–9, 14–17: For attractive fall color in mild climates, try Chinese pistache, Chinese tallow tree, crape myrtle, ginkgo, Japanese maples, liquidambar, persimmon, Raywood ash, redbud, and sour gum.

☐ **PLANT ANNUALS.** Zones 7–9, 14–17: For instant color, you can still buy 4-inch-size plants (it's probably too late to set out sixpack-size plants; they'll just sit and sulk until spring). Gently loosen the roots before planting them in the ground or in a container.

☐ **PLANT FOR PERMANENCE.** Zones 7–9, 14–17: November is a good time to plant cold-hardy ground covers, shrubs, trees, and vines. Wait until spring to set out tender plants, such as bougainvillea, mandevilla, and princess flower. Bare-root roses and trees start appearing in nurseries next month: plan ahead to determine what your garden needs. Make sure to choose a tree that will fit the size of your garden space.

Maintenance

☐ **CARE FOR HOUSE PLANTS.** As days get shorter, house plants may not get as much light as they need. Most house plants need bright but indirect light. If a plant is sitting in a dark corner, move it to a brighter area (closer to a window, for example). Plants may need

Sunset
CLIMATE ZONES
☐ Mountain (1-2)
☐ Valley (7-9)
☐ Inland (14)
☐ Coastal (15-17)

less water as the days grow cooler (unless the house is kept warm), but they still need periodic light applications of fertilizer.

☐ **CLEAN UP DEBRIS.** Pull up what's left of summer annuals and vegetables that have stopped producing. To help eliminate overwintering sites for insects and diseases, rake up leaves and pick up fallen fruit. Add debris to the compost pile (except diseased plants and weeds that have gone to seed).

☐ **COMPOST.** Start a simple compost pile by layering greens (grass, plant debris, and weeds without seed heads) with browns (straw, dried leaves). Or build a simple wire one: bend a 4-foot-tall piece of 12- to 14-gauge wire fencing into a cylinder about 4 feet across and hook the cut edges together. To fill,

chop up materials and alternate a 2- to 8-inch-thick layer of brown material with a 2- to 8-inch-thick layer of green material, watering each brown layer as you go. You can also top each brown layer with a shovelful of manure or soil to help heat up the pile. Keep the pile evenly moist and, for faster composting, aerate the pile by turning it every few weeks or so.

☐ **DIVIDE PERENNIALS.** Zones 7–9, 14–17: Dig out and separate overgrown clumps. To break apart delicate roots, use your hands; for tougher roots, use shears, a pruning knife, or a shovel. To divide agapanthus and fortnight lily, you may need to force them apart with a spading fork. Add organic matter to the soil, and replant.

☐ **WATER.** If rains are infrequent or absent, water landscape plants, lawns, and vegetables often enough to keep the soil moist. But if rains do come regularly, don't forget to turn off your automatic sprinklers.

Pest control

☐ **SPRAY FRUIT TREES.** Zones 7–9, 14–17: After leaves have fallen, spray peaches and nectarine trees with lime sulfur to control peach leaf curl. For brown rot on apricot trees, spray them with a fixed-copper spray. Spray on dry days when no rain is predicted for at least 36 hours. Cover the stems and trunk thoroughly.

Planting

☐ **PLANT COOL-SEASON ANNUALS.** Coastal, inland, and low-desert gardeners (zones 22–24, 18–21, and 13, respectively) can set out African daisies, calendulas, Iceland poppies, ornamental cabbage and kale, nemesias, pansies, snapdragons, stock, violas, and other early-blooming annuals. For shady areas, try cineraria, primrose, and cyclamen.

☐ **CONTINUE TO PLANT BULBS.** Spring-flowering bulbs that don't require prechilling can be planted now. South African bulbs such as babiana, freesia, homeria, ixia, and sparaxis are the best choices for naturalizing. Adapted to wet winters and dry summers like ours, they thrive here. To create natural-looking plantings, toss handfuls of a single kind of bulb over a planting area, then plant where the bulbs fall. Other bulb choices include anenome, calla, daffodil, oxalis, and ranunculus. Plant quickly, though, if you garden in the high desert (zone 11).

☐ **PLANT COOL-SEASON VEGETABLES.** Coastal, inland, and low-desert gardeners can choose from arugula, beets, bok choy, broccoli, brussels sprouts, cabbage, carrots, cauliflower, chard, collard greens, garlic, kale, kohlrabi, leeks, lettuce, onions, peas, radicchio, spinach, Swiss chard, and turnips.

DEBRA LAMBERT

Sunset
CLIMATE ZONES

1-3 7-9 11 13 14-24

☐ **PLANT PERENNIALS.** Perennials still have plenty of time to establish a healthy root system before winter chill in coastal, inland, and low-desert gardens. Look for coral bells, daylilies, delphiniums, foxgloves, penstemon, salvias, scabiosa, and yarrow.

☐ **SOW WILDFLOWER SEEDS.** Broadcast seeds by hand over weed-free soil. Rake the area lightly to cover seeds with soil. Keep the soil consistently moist until seeds germinate and winter rains take over.

Maintenance

☐ **CLEAN UP.** As summer annuals and vegetables decline, pull and toss them into the compost bin. Remove decaying flowers and leaves from beneath perennials and shrubs to eliminate hiding places for slugs, snails, and sowbugs, as well as overwintering spots for fungus diseases.

☐ **PRUNE CANE BERRY PLANTS.** Old canes of blackberry, boysenberry, and loganberry should be cut back to the ground. Leave the smooth-barked canes that grew this year to bear fruit next year. Wait until December or January to cut back the canes of low-chill raspberries.

☐ **TEND CHRYSANTHEMUMS.** Support still-blooming plants with stakes and ties. After they bloom, cut back plants, leaving 6-inch stems. Lift and divide old clumps; cut roots apart and discard woody centers, then replant.

Pest and weed control

☐ **MANAGE CABBAGEWORMS.** The white butterflies flitting through your cabbage patch are laying eggs that will hatch into leaf-chomping caterpillars. Control damage by using floating row covers to exclude the butterflies. Or spray the uncovered plants with *Bacillus thuringiensis,* focusing the spray carefully on the cabbageworm larvae.

☐ **CONTROL SNAILS AND SLUGS.** Hand-pick snails in the early evening or morning. Or use barriers (row covers or copper stripping), baits, or traps. Pay special attention to seedlings and tender-leafed plants; these are favorite foods for snails.

☐ **STAY AHEAD OF WEEDS.** Pull out annual bluegrass, chickweed, groundsel, shepherd's purse, and spurge as quickly as they emerge.

Planting

☐ BULBS. Nurseries and garden centers are well stocked with all kinds of spring-flowering bulbs now. Buy before they have been picked over. Plant all kinds immediately in cold-winter areas, but prechill tulips, hyacinths, and crocus for six weeks if you garden in the desert; the crisper section in your refrigerator works nicely for this.

☐ WILDFLOWERS. Put them in weeded and prepared beds, water well, and watch, weeding out anything that wasn't in your mix. (When you sow wildflower beds, also sow a small amount of the same seeds in a flat of sterile soil so you'll have a reference plot. Otherwise, you won't know weeds from flower seedlings.)

Maintenance

☐ BRING IN HOUSE PLANTS. If you haven't done it yet, bring tender plants into the house for the winter. Check plants for insects, rinse them off in lukewarm shower water, and put in a place that gets plenty of light.

☐ DIG AND STORE DAHLIAS. Stop watering a few days before digging dahlias, then carefully unearth them with a spading fork. Discard tops, brush off dirt, and let tubers cure for a few days in a dry, frost-free place. Then store them in boxes of peat, vermiculite, or sand.

Sunset
CLIMATE ZONES
☐ 1-3   ☐ 10-11

☐ GROOM LAWNS. This month will be your last chance to clean up your lawn. Mow one last time, rake leaves before they mat and smother the grass beneath, and edge. Once serious frosts set in, growth slows or stops for the winter.

☐ GROOM PERENNIALS. Be judicious as you cut back perennials, leaving ones that, though they don't have their summer colors, do have seed heads or dried flowers for winter interest (and bird food).

☐ MAKE COMPOST. As the weather cools off, you can speed up the composting process by grinding plants before you throw them into the compost pile. If you have a lot of fallen leaves, for example, go over them with your mower, then dump the bag full of shredded leaves into the compost pile.

☐ MAINTAIN TOOLS. Your last act in the fall garden should be to put an edge on all your tools, from hoes and shovels to pruning shears, then wipe them down with oil (machine oil for metal parts, linseed oil for handles) and store them in a dry place for the winter.

☐ MULCH EVERYTHING. Put a 3- to 4-inch layer of organic mulch around half-hardy plants, on bulb beds that might otherwise heave during hard winter frosts, and under trees and shrubs.

☐ PRUNE TREES, SHRUBS. After leaves fall from deciduous trees, you can prune. Do your work on a mild day (not when it's subfreezing), removing dead, diseased, and injured branches, water sprouts, and crossing or closely parallel branches. Then prune for shape.

Pest and weed control

☐ INDOOR PLANTS. Examine house plants for aphids, scale, spider mites, and mealybugs. Rinse infested plants with lukewarm shower water, then spray with insecticidal soap.

☐ WEEDS. Now is the time to go through the garden and hoe the fall crop under. Throw weeds into the compost pile if they don't have seed heads or flowers, and replace them with mulch.

Planting

□ **ANNUALS.** In sunny places, put in ageratum, aster, bells-of-Ireland, calendula, candytuft, clarkia, cornflower, foxglove, larkspur, lobelia, painted daisy, petunia, phlox, snapdragon, stock, sweet alyssum, and sweet pea. In shady places, set out dianthus, English daisy, pansy, primrose, and viola.

□ **WILDFLOWERS.** Sown now, these should come up fairly quickly. Try blackfoot daisy (*Melampodium leucanthum*), California desert bluebell (*Phacelia campanularia*), desert globemallow (*Sphaeralcea ambigua*), fire-wheels (*Gaillardia pulchella*), Mexican hat (*Ratibida columnifera*), Mexican tulip poppy (*Hunnemannia fumariifolia*), and owl's clover (*Orthocarpus purpurascens*). If rains are infrequent, keep seed plots moist until plants are at least 2 inches tall.

□ **VEGETABLES.** Sow or plant asparagus, beets, broccoli, brussels sprouts, cabbage, carrots, cauliflower, celery, endive, garlic, kale, kohlrabi, leeks, lettuce, mustard, parsley, peas, radishes, spinach, Swiss chard, and turnips.

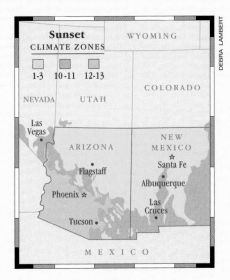

□ **BERMUDA GRASS.** Mow your warm-season lawn at about ½ inch and then overseed it with 10 to 20 pounds of rye seed per 1,000 square feet. You can use annual or perennial rye grass; the difference is that the coarser-leafed annual rye costs less and needs more frequent mowing than its perennial cousin does. About a month after sowing, fertilize your new grass to help it fill in quickly.

□ **TREES, SHRUBS.** This is the best time of year to plant hardy trees and shrubs, including acacia, cassia, *Cordia boissieri*, desert spoon, fairy duster, mesquite, oleander, palo verde, *Salvia greggii*, and Texas ranger. Water them in well. They'll be in a much better position to handle next summer's heat than spring-planted nursery stock.

Maintenance

□ **CULL SPLIT CITRUS.** Most kinds of citrus grow faster this month—so fast that fruit can split. Be sure to pick off and discard split fruit, which attracts fungus and insects to otherwise healthy trees.

□ **PRUNE AND FEED ROSES.** Remove faded flowers, pruning lightly as you go. Take out dead, diseased, crossing, and injured canes, and prune for shape. Then apply a complete fertilizer and water it in well to encourage a flush of winter flowers.

Pest control

□ **APHIDS.** Blast them off new growth with a hose, then spray plants with insecticidal soap. Soap sprays work best if diluted with distilled water.

Planting

□ **BULBS.** In north, east, or central Texas, plant immediately. If you live along the Gulf Coast or in South Texas, bulbs may not get enough chill to flower well, so put crocus, hyacinth, and tulip bulbs in the refrigerator for six weeks, then plant.

□ **PERMANENT PLANTS.** If the ground doesn't freeze deeply or long where you live, you can plant almost any kind of tree, shrub, or ground cover now. Considering the drought, it makes sense to plant drought-tolerant varieties. Water well the first year. They'll have the winter to send out roots and should grow well next spring and summer.

□ **VEGETABLES.** In south, central, and coastal Texas, you can still plant mustard, garlic, leeks, onions from seed, peas, and turnips. You can also start

salad crops and cabbage-family members from seedlings.

Maintenance

□ **CARE FOR INDOOR PLANTS.** As winter light levels fall, watch indoor plants for light deprivation. If they start losing leaves, and new growth becomes weak and stretched out, try supplementing daylight with artificial plant lights.

□ **PICK SPLIT CITRUS.** When citrus trees take up moisture too quickly after a dry summer, fruit tends to split. Pick split fruit right away, before fungus and insects move in.

Pest control

□ **APHIDS.** Cool-season aphids are at work on ornamentals in mild-winter parts of Texas. When you see aphids, blast them off with a jet of water from the hose or, in worst cases, hit them with insecticidal soap, diazinon, Dursban, malathion, or Orthene.

□ **THRIPS.** Common on permanent plants like roses and mums, thrips can be controlled with diazinon, malathion, or systemics like Orthene. ◆

Taming wildflowers

Forget grand meadows. Today's wildflowers
grow attractively in small beds and even in pots.
New seed mixes make it possible

A dozen or so years ago, it was a romantic notion: wildflower seeds packaged in cans could create instant meadows. Gardeners across the country, sparked by visions of dazzling blooms and meadow grasses carpeting their backyards, bought into the dream. And cans of these promising seed mixes flew off nursery shelves.

Then reality hit. Gardeners—especially in the West—didn't find their backyards large enough for meadows. And many of the mixes contained mostly grass seed; the grasses and weeds usually grew faster than the wildflowers. In most cases, the meadows weren't pretty sights.

These days, gardeners want seed mixes that provide impressive floral displays through a long season. Seed companies are responding by blending seeds for specific uses—to attract birds and butterflies, for cut flowers, for shade, and for fragrance—and providing for a succession of blooms by combining annuals and perennials.

Wildflower gardens no longer need acres of land to look attractive. You can plant them in more confined spaces—in small planting beds, around mailboxes, in raised beds, and even in containers. Such areas are easy to plant, weed, water, and keep cleaned of old flowers.

With today's seed mixes, it's even possible to sow wildflowers among perennials in a bed or border, or between newly planted shrubs as temporary fillers.

"It's a carefree style of gardening that's colorful and gives a tremendous bang for the dollar," says Michael Landis, owner of the Wildflower Seed Company in St. Helena, California, and designer of numerous wildflower gardens. "And you can bring that carefree style indoors when they're used as cut flowers."

In many areas of the West, November is prime time to sow wildflowers, so plants have time to get well established for strong bloom in spring.

CUTTING GARDENS AND MORE

Landis often uses wildflowers as most gardeners would use bedding plants ("but they're a lot less expensive"). He sows an annual cut-flower mix in raised beds, where the soil is good, plants are easy to maintain, and flowers are convenient to cut. He plants his bird-and-butterfly mix near the edge of a patio where the flowers—and the wildlife they attract—can be enjoyed. And he uses his woodland mix in the light shade under high trees (no wildflower mix is suitable for dense shade). Since a mix contains perennials such as ox-eye daisy, Landis says the show is often

Baby blue eyes fill a 20-inch-wide pot in spring. They're the first plants from a seed mix to bloom.

by JIM McCAUSLAND *and* LAUREN BONAR SWEZEY

NORMAN A. PLATE

What's a wildflower?

When you think of wild-flowers, you probably think of blooms that carpet hillsides for a few weeks every spring. With that in mind, it seems that wildflower mixes should be simply blends of those kinds of flowers, right?

Wrong.

"In the early 1980s," one grower told us, "our wildflower mixes ran heavily to native wildflowers. But we learned that people really just wanted easily grown flowers with a long bloom season. Now that's what we give them."

Do they ever. Today's wild-flower blends are as well orchestrated as great opera. Working with both perennials and self-sowing annuals, producers create mixes that start flowering early in spring. If the seed is sown according to directions, successively taller tiers of annuals take over as the season progresses, with perennials pushing up underneath (some of those perennials bloom later the first year). A good wildflower mix will provide you with flowers almost from spring to autumn.

In the second year, the plant palette changes. Many of last year's annuals come back, but not those whose seeds couldn't survive the winter. All the surviving perennials come back, gradually pushing out the annuals. "This is a great way to start a perennial garden," an Oregon seedsman told us.

The third, fourth, or fifth year is usually the last for wildflower gardens. They're often defeated as grasses, which are hard to pull out without tearing up the annuals, take over.

If you want to try growing a marathon wildflower garden, build it around perennial and annual selections that are strongly self-sowing in your area.

Cosmos, godetia, and Shirley poppies add a splash of color around this mailbox near Washington's Hood Canal.

more spectacular the second year.

Ken and Donna Erickson of Port Orchard, Washington, created an island of wildflowers that doubles as a cutting garden. It's situated in their backyard and provides a handsome background for their vegetable garden's mostly green plants.

Becky Schaff of Moon Mountain Wildflowers in Carpinteria, California, uses wildflowers more liberally in her small Santa Barbara front yard. She sows them between Mexican bush sage and rockrose. The planting "is so spectacular, people stop and take photos," says Schaff. "And my neighbors are starting to redo their landscapes with wildflowers now."

Because she wants her front yard to always look good, she sows seeds year-round (not just in fall). A succession of bloom keeps her in wildflowers for about nine months (the colder the winter, the fewer months successively planted wildflowers can bloom). The key to attractive wildflower beds, she says, is to keep them maintained. If you let them go, they'll look ragged fast.

Schaff's major planting is in September or October. She tills the soil between existing perennials, then sows the seeds. Her first flowers appear in January. To keep flowers coming, she waters once or twice a week, removes faded flowers constantly, and tosses any seeds they've set back into the soil.

Around May, when the first show starts to fade, she pulls out dead annuals such as linaria and shakes the seeds around the garden beds. She cuts back perennials and long-blooming annuals such as dianthus, evening primrose, and rudbeckia so they'll rebloom.

To extend the bloom show into fall, Schaff overhauls her wildflower plantings in July. She pulls out faded annuals, then tills the bare soil and reseeds with quick annuals such as African daisy and flax (*Linum*). Her quietest blooming period is in November and December.

GETTING STARTED

When you see the fabulous displays of California poppies and goldfields growing in the desert, you'd think they could grow like that anywhere. But it just isn't so. In the wild, such displays

WILLIAM B. DEWEY

Deep red Shirley poppies, orange California poppies, and scarlet flax bloom profusely in midspring in Becky Schaff's small Santa Barbara front yard.

WORKHORSES *of* WILDFLOWER SEED MIXES

	ANNUALS	PERENNIALS
EXOTICS	Baby snapdragon (*Linaria maroccana*)	Dame's rocket (*Hesperis matronalis*)
	Bachelor's button (*Centaurea cyanus*)	Foxglove (*Digitalis purpurea*)
	Blue flax (*Linum grandiflorum*)	Russell hybrid lupine (*Lupinus*)
	Cosmos (*Cosmos bipinnatus*)	Shasta daisy (*Chrysanthemum maximum*)
	Scarlet flax (*Linum grandiflorum* 'Rubrum')	Siberian wallflower (*Erysimum hieraci-*
	Shirley poppy (*Papaver rhoeas*)	*ifolium*)
		Yarrow (*Achillea millefolium*)
NATIVES	Baby blue eyes (*Nemophila menziesii*)	
	Blue lupine (*Lupinus succulentus*)	California poppy (*Eschscholzia californica*)
	Calliopsis (*Coreopsis tinctoria*)	Coreopsis (*Coreopsis lanceolata*)
	Chinese houses (*Collinsia heterophylla*)	Gloriosa daisy (*Rudbeckia hirta*)
	Clarkia (*Clarkia unguiculata*)	Purple coneflower (*Echinacea purpurea*)
	Godetia (*Clarkia amoena*)	
	Indian blanket (*Gaillardia pulchella*)	
	Tidytips (*Layia platyglossa*)	

NORMAN A. PLATE

Bountiful harvest from one wildflower mix (see below) includes bachelor's button, calendula, clarkia, cosmos, and zinnia.

Inert matter isn't necessarily bad. Because tiny seeds can be difficult to sow evenly, producers often mix them with rice hulls or some other extender that makes it easy to see where you've scattered seed.

Timing varies by region. Planting in fall or winter is best in mild-winter climates. Commercial wildflower growers in Lompoc, California, sow in December, for example. In the Northwest and cold-winter climates, spring planting is usually more successful: fall plantings are subject to too much winter kill.

After you've sown the seed, rake it lightly into the soil, then water well. To help you identify weed seedlings, sow some seed in a nursery flat at the same time you sow the rest in the ground. After seedlings emerge in the garden, compare them with the seedlings growing in the flat. They should be identical. Any seedlings that show up in the garden but not in the flat are probably weeds. Pull them.

Water and weed regularly during the growing season and feed twice with a complete fertilizer (controlled-release is a good choice). Cut back wildflowers as they fade, but let them go to seed if you want a repeat show next year.

Bloom time depends on planting time. You can make multiple sowings to get three peaks of bloom in long succession. Sow some seed in one bed in fall, for example; sow again in spring about a month before the average date of the last frost, in an adjacent bed. And finally, sow some seed in a third bed after the last frost.

WHERE TO BUY SEED

Nurseries and garden centers often sell a variety of mixes. Some even sell seed out of barrels in fall. If you can't find what you want near you, you can order by mail. Most catalogs offer seed suitable for a wide variety of climates.

Clyde Robin Seed Company, Box 2366, Castro Valley, CA 94546; (510) 785-0425. Catalog free.

Moon Mountain Wildflowers, Box 725, Carpinteria, CA 93014; (805) 684-2565. Catalog $3.

Plants of the Southwest, Agua Fria, Route 6, Box 11A, Santa Fe, NM 87501; (800) 788-7333. Catalog $3.50 (price list free).

Wildflower Seed Company, Box 406, St. Helena, CA 94574; (800) 456-3359. Catalog free.

Wild Seed, Box 27751, Tempe, AZ 85285; (602) 276-3536. Catalog free. Seeds for the Rocky Mountains, Great Basin, and Sonoran Desert. ◆

are subject to the whims of weather and may not come back like that every year. Wildflower seeds give a vastly superior performance in well-prepared, weeded, and watered garden soil. Plant them in waste places and you'll get scruffy-looking, short-lived plants. That's also usually the case if you plant under trees (especially oak, eucalyptus, pine, and walnut).

Prepare wildflower beds as you'd prepare soil for a vegetable garden: dig or till in a 3-inch layer of rotted manure or compost, then level the soil surface and water. After about three weeks, hoe or pull the weeds that come up. Then you're ready to plant.

Check the guidelines on the package first, but in general, scatter seed at the rate of about 1 ounce per 300 square feet (that's 50 to 100 seeds per square foot!). Knowing the ingredients listed on the can or packet will help. If you buy a 12-ounce can that contains 75 percent inert matter and 25 percent seeds, you've just bought 3 ounces of seed and should sow accordingly.

What's in a wildflower mix?

Wildflower mixes typically contain about 60 percent annual flowers and 40 percent perennials. As many as half the seeds in the box (but usually fewer) are likely to be American natives. Familiar annuals and perennials make up the rest.

Many wildflower mixes are specialized in one way or another: there are mixes of extra-short flowers or cut-flower blends, shade-tolerant wildflowers, and go-for-broke mixes that contain nothing but annuals good for one spectacular, single-season show. Depending on the type of mix, the seed content might be weighted more toward one type of flower than another. A bird-and-butterfly mix might contain more rocket larkspur than a cut-flower mix, for example.

But many of the same seeds appear in mix after mix, no matter what the focus of the blend is. We analyzed the labels of eight mixes from five different suppliers. The chart on page 290 shows some of the seeds that appear in many mixes; don't be surprised if you find alyssum, calendula, zinnia, and other familiar flowers as well.

ROBERTO SONCIN-GEROMETTA

Six-inch-tall 'Hawera' thrives between paving stones. Design: Bob Clark, Oakland.

Diminutive daffodils

Just inches tall, with compact flowers, they're perfect for tiny spaces

"Good things come in small packages," so the old saying goes. And when it comes to daffodils, small is certainly good.

Diminutive varieties, which grow only 4 to 6 inches tall, can fill a garden with an elegance that can't be matched by their taller cousins. They come in a range of flower shapes, from a trumpet to a dandelion form. Each bulb, depending on size and variety, can produce two or three bloom stalks, and each stalk may sport a single flower or a cluster.

"They're like wildflowers once they find their happy spot," says Becky Heath

of the Daffodil Mart. Plantings increase in size from year to year, forming bushy clumps of leaves and flowers.

In mild-winter climates, buy bulbs at nurseries this month, or order them by mail for planting as soon as possible. Plant the bulbs at a depth equal to three times their diameter in a spot that gets full sun and has well-drained soil.

HOW TO USE THEM

Flowers as small as these need special plantings to show them off. Plant bulbs in clusters of half a dozen or more at the front of a border, in a rock garden, in

small containers, or among low-growing plants such as candytufts, Johnny-jump-ups, pansies, and *Vinca minor.* They combine well with other little bulbs such as *Anemone blanda,* grape hyacinths, and species tulips. Brent Heath, also of the Daffodil Mart, plants 'Hawera' daffodils with *Tulipa bakeri* 'Lilac Wonder' in a strawberry jar.

WHERE TO BUY BULBS

Daffodil Mart, 7463 Heath Trail, Gloucester, VA 23061; (800) 255-2852.
McClure & Zimmerman, Box 368, Friesland, WI 53935; (414) 326-4220. ◆

by LAUREN BONAR SWEZEY

SUNSET'S *top 8* PICKS

Catalogs often lump small daffodils together under one heading—"miniatures"—but these diminutive types might actually be jonquils, species, or other forms.

Narcissus 'Baby Moon'. Sweetly fragrant yellow flower has six distinct (not overlapping) petals. Three to five blooms per stem.

N. bulbocodium conspicuus. Bright yellow flower resembles a hoop petticoat, with a megaphone-shaped cup and reedlike petals.

N. 'Hawera'. Small, pale yellow bell-shaped cup has swept-back petals. Produces as many as six stems per bulb and seven blooms per stem.

N. 'Little Beauty'. Creamy white flower with a yellow cup. Usually one flower per stalk.

N. 'Minnow'. White petals surround a bright yellow cup. Three to five flowers per stem.

N. pseudonarcissus pumilus plenus 'Rip Van Winkle'. Bright yellow double flowers look like dandelions. One flower per stem.

N. 'Sundial'. Bright yellow flat-cupped daffodil looks like a round sundial. One or two flowers per stem.

N. 'Tete-a-Tete'. Bright yellow petals surround a darker cup. One to three flowers per stem.

Savor the season with a visual feast of produce and greenery.
Wreath-making tips start on page 306.

DECEMBER

Garden guide.......................294

Garden notebooks 297

Garden checklists.................301

Bountiful wreaths..................306

The abundant table...............310

Sunshine in a box.................314

Miniature trees for tabletops......315

Bamboos for the great indoors....316

gardenguide

NORMAN A. PLATE (2)

Edible ornaments for the birds

Trim a tree with fruits, seeds, and other avian treats

by JIM McCAUSLAND

L ast winter Bud Stuckey, *Sunset's* try-anything-once test garden coordinator, decided to give birds a present, so he decorated an outdoor tree with ornaments made of fruit and seeds.

By any standard, the edible ornaments were a big hit. From the human point of view, it was fascinating to see the tree covered with various small songbirds every morning. From the avian standpoint, the ornaments provided a needed dietary boost during the lean winter months. Within 10 days after the tree was trimmed, birds had stripped it of all the edibles.

If you'd like to duplicate this project, you have two options: decorate a live tree in a container or in the ground, or take your cut Christmas tree outdoors after the holidays and redecorate it.

Our menu is designed to satisfy both fruit-eating and seed-eating birds.

For the fruit eaters, Stuckey strung garlands of dried apples, bananas, hawthorn berries, and cranberries onto sewing thread and covered wire loops with fresh grapes and peanuts. He wired orange slices to the branches.

For the seed eaters, he tied stalks of ornamental wheat onto the branches, along with ears of ornamental corn and broom corn. The *pièce de résistance,* as far as the birds were concerned, was peanut butter–coated pinecones encrusted with wild birdseed mix and hung with florist's wire.

THE MENU
• Dried apples, bananas, hawthorn berries, and cranberries
• Fresh grapes and oranges
• Raw whole peanuts, wild birdseed mix
• Ornamental wheat
• Ornamental and broom corn
• Peanut butter–smeared pinecones

A recipe for home-baked soil

A ny serious gardener can always use a fresh supply of potting soil. For a practical gift, you can give your own "house blend." Here's my no-longer-secret recipe:

2 parts fine compost
2 parts coarse sand
1 part garden loam
1 part leaf mold

Thoroughly blend the compost, sand, loam, and leaf mold. The mixture can be used immediately for potting container plants. But if it is going to be used to start seeds or to root cuttings, you'll need to sterilize it first. Spread the mixture out in baking pans and pour ½ cup of water over the soil. Bake it in a 180° oven for no less than two hours. (Note: higher temperatures will destroy valuable components of the soil.) Heating soil can be a stinky process, so open the windows and doors in the kitchen to air it out.

Let the soil cool, then pour it into a bucket or a heavy-duty plastic bag and tie on a ribbon. — *Steven R. Lorton*

tools

Who needs leaf blowers—which do no more than move leaves from one spot to another, along with clouds of dust, pollen, and pollution (not to mention noise)—when curvaceous new rakes are making the chore of clearing up leaves much easier, quieter, and more thorough?

The Mongoose Rake (soon to be renamed Landscaper Tough), shown here, has a lightweight handle that helps reduce back strain, and its cushioned grip helps prevent blisters. Manufactured by Ames Lawn and Garden Tools, it retails for about $15 at hardware stores.

True Temper Hardware's Snake Rake is similar, but is equipped with a button that adjusts the handle's length to your height. It costs around $16. Both rakes come in various sizes, with either metal or plastic tines. — *Rizza Yap*

Mini roses: cute but fragile

M iniature roses in 2-, 4-, and 6-inch pots have become widely available at nurseries, florists, and even grocery stores during the last few years. Small leaves and dozens of gorgeous little pink, red, salmon, white, or yellow blooms per plant make these roses almost irresistible. Their small size makes them inexpensive and ideal for housewarming or thank-you gifts. The 2-inch pots are also perfect for decorating individual place settings for parties.

But how well do they hold up indoors in the small pots? Will they continue to bloom for long?

We bought a few plants last Christmas and monitored their growth

indoors. Eventually, the roses rebelled against the low light and dry indoor air. The soil in the 2-inch and 4-inch pots dried out too fast (though the plants can rot if they're overwatered, especially when the light is too low).

One company's 2-inch self-watering pots kept the plants evenly watered for the first couple of weeks, as long as the reservoir never dried up. But the wick that was supposed to draw water from the reservoir into the rootball didn't always work.

The plants didn't produce many new buds indoors. But given regular moisture and fairly bright light, existing flower buds continued to open.

The secret to a long and happy life for these roses is diligence. Allow the plants to finish their bloom cycle, then plant them outdoors in the ground or in larger containers that are easier to keep watered (in cold-winter climates transplant them into larger pots and keep indoors until spring). Given the right light and room to spread, they'll eventually grow into 18- to 24-inch-tall plants. — *Lauren Bonar Swezey*

gardenguide

Fragrant Northwest evergreens

Traditional conifers have pungent scents that we associate with the holidays. But other evergreens, including a number of Northwest natives, can spice up wreaths, swags, and greenery-filled urns. Prowl your garden or shop nurseries for richly fragrant plants such as native Oregon myrtle (*Umbellularia californica*), sweet bay magnolia (*Magnolia virginiana*), rosemary, and sages like *Artemisia tridentata,* the aromatic sage that flourishes east of the Cascades. — *S. R. L.*

GIFTS *for the* GARDEN

A tiny bath for little birds

A birdbath can be as simple as a round bowl set out among plants, or as decorative as garden art. The bath shown below is both; easy to nestle among plants, it is sculptural, too. Its design was inspired by Native American petroglyphs found in the Grand Canyon.

Hand-cast in concrete with a weather-resistant limestone aggregate, it's 13 inches long and 3 inches deep. The inside of the bowl is textured to give the birds more grip. Petroglyphs embellish three corners. Designed by George Carruth, it's available by mail from Carruth Studio, 1178 Farnsworth Rd., Waterville, OH 43566; (800) 225-1178. The model shown costs $63 (including shipping). — *L. B. S.*

NORMAN A. PLATE

STEPHEN FREDERICK

DECORATING

A wisteria that's all lights

Last December at the Bellevue Botanical Garden in Washington, a shining arbor strung with "wisteria" vines set the landscape aglow. Gardeners anywhere can easily re-create this display on a sturdy arbor.

Light up a dormant wisteria or grapevine that's already in place. Or take a tip from the display above and create vines by twisting clusters of prunings (wisteria, honeysuckle) or even rope. Fasten 4-foot sections of prunings together and secure them with plastic ties or plastic-coated wire (never use exposed metal wire). Then wind the vines through the arbor and tie them in place. Next, weave strands of miniature white lights through the vines to highlight them. Each 4-foot section of vine takes three 50-bulb strands.

Finally, form "flower" clusters by bunching up purple and yellow lights—three 50-bulb strands for each cluster. You can use extension cords to connect the lights to a power source (usually three strands of lights per cord), but don't exceed the manufacturer's recommended wattage capacity.
— *Colleen Foye Bollen*

Pacific Northwest Garden Notebook

by STEVEN R. LORTON

The day after Thanksgiving, we always have a big family argument. That's the day we get our Christmas tree. There's no disagreement about the species: we all like a noble fir (*Abies procera*). But my son, John, and I go for the tallest tree on the lot. My wife, Anna Lou, starts sorting through the 5-footers: "Now doesn't this look nice? It won't shed so many needles." Negotiations can last up to two hours. We usually end up with a 7- to 8-foot tree. But last year, John and I spotted an 18-footer that would fit neatly under the 25-foot ceiling in the great room of our house in the Skagit Valley. While John held onto the tree, expounding its virtues to his mother, I sneaked off and paid for it. Cheerfully ignoring the huffy silence, we tied the tree to the car roof and headed back to the house.

When we got the tree home, we filled a 5-gallon plastic bucket with plain water and set that inside an empty plastic garden grub tub (to catch any spills or leaks). We cut off the lowest limbs, sawed off 2 inches from the bottom of the trunk, and put the tree in the bucket of water in a cool corner of the room. We put several large stones in the water around the bottom end of the trunk to hold it steady inside the bucket and secured the tree in three places along the trunk with strong wire looped through sturdy screw eyes we'd put in the wall at 5-, 10-, and 15-foot intervals above floor level. From installation to take-down time (the first week in January), we added water three times. We never had a greener tree with less needle drop. On New Year's Day, my wife actually muttered, "This is the prettiest tree we've ever had." And John and I simultaneously thought, "20 feet in '96!"

I like to give my gardening friends stocking-stuffer gifts—packets of seeds, a bottle of liquid plant food, a ball of good garden twine. This year, they're going to get a bar of Grandpa's Wonder Pine Tar Toilet Soap, which has been around since 1878. I've used this stuff all my life, and no other soap does a better job of taking grass and weed stains off my hands. It also has a soothing effect on thorn nicks and nettle stings. After a long, cold, wet day in the garden, I fill the tub with hot water, and soak and lather (the soap's odor is almost medicinal); once I dry off, I feel clean as a cowboy on Saturday night. I've even used it on our dog, Rio, and she emerges flea-free. Some drugstores and many health food and organic cosmetic shops carry this soap. If you can't find it, ask your favorite drugstore to order it.

THAT'S A GOOD QUESTION

Q: I once heard you give a talk in which you mentioned the "Rule of Threes" for putting together pots of mixed live plants for holiday decorations. What is that rule?

A: To keep mixed pots from being a jumble of unrelated elements, stick with a total of three colors in foliage, bloom, and ribbon (or other ornament) and don't use more than three kinds of plants in each pot. For example: If you want to pair a pink poinsettia with paper white narcissus, you've already got three colors—pink and white in the flowers, and green in the leaves. You could add a solid green fern or two as a foliage filler. And if you put a ribbon in the mix, it should be the same pink as the poinsettia or white like the narcissus.

Northern California Garden Notebook

by LAUREN BONAR SWEZEY

Every now and then I'm reminded of the importance of special childhood memories. The other day I received a letter from Jean Taggart of San Francisco in response to our recent article (June 1996) on peaches. Our article, it seems, brought back memories from the 1930s of her family's fruit ranch on the Feather River. "One orchard was devoted to the 'J. H. Hale' peach," she wrote, "one of the most beautiful, flavorful, juiciest peaches I've ever eaten. They were huge ... freestones with a beautiful red center. All summer our principal desserts were peach cobbler or peach ice cream." Yum! I could almost taste the sweet, succulent fruit. In fact, my own fond memories of peaches came flooding back. Many summers ago on a family vacation to the Northwest, my mother had us stopping at every fruit stand from Oregon to Idaho looking for a peach that tasted as good as those she had savored as a child at her relatives' orchard in Vancouver, Washington. Unfortunately, no peaches ever quite measured up, but I'll never forget the journey.

After reading Taggart's letter, I was determined to find this peach tree for her. I searched and found the variety listed in a mail-order catalog from Sonoma Antique Apple Nursery (4395 Westside Rd., Healdsburg, CA 95448; 707/433-6420). The catalog's blurb describes 'J. H. Hale' as "still one of the best yellow-fleshed freestone peaches." Taggart later told me she doesn't have room to plant a tree, but hopes to find an orchard that might still be producing this variety so she can "journey into her past." But I'm hooked. If I can find a spot in my garden, I think I'll try 'J. H. Hale'.

MARINA THOMPSON

A SIGN OF CHRISTMAS TREE FRESHNESS

Several years ago in Phoenix, I noticed that some Christmas tree lots were displaying their trees in water-filled reservoir stands. The practice made lots of sense: it kept the trees fresh in spite of the drying desert air. Two Christmases ago, I discovered that Woolworth's Garden Center in Palo Alto also stores its Christmas trees in water. So I've been buying my trees there. They are always very fresh, and they seem to stay fresh longer than trees I've purchased that were simply nailed to wooden stands. If you can find a nursery that sells trees in water, I'm sure you'll be pleased with their lasting quality. If your nursery hasn't adopted this practice, you might encourage it to start.

THAT'S A GOOD QUESTION

Q: Where can I find a good selection of old-fashioned roses available by mail?

A: Northern California is home to many outstanding rose growers, and many sell old-fashioned roses by mail. *Heritage Rose Gardens,* 16831 Mitchell Creek Dr., Fort Bragg, CA 95437; (707) 964-3748 (catalog $1.50). *Mendocino Heirloom Roses,* Box 670, Mendocino, CA 95460; (707) 937-0963 (catalog $1). *Petaluma Rose Co.,* Box 750953, Petaluma, CA 94975; (707) 769-8862 (catalog free). *Regan Nursery,* 4268 Decoto Rd., Fremont, CA 94555; (510) 797-3222 (catalog $3). *Roses, Wine & Evergreens,* 3528 Montclair Rd., Cameron Park, CA 95682; (916) 677-9722 (free list with self-addressed, stamped envelope). *Vintage Gardens,* 2833 Old Gravenstein Highway S., Sebastopol, CA 95472; (707) 829-2035 (catalog $5).

Southern California Garden Notebook

by **SHARON COHOON**

Our weather is more like Majorca's than Massachusetts's. So most of the gardening books available can hinder as much as help us. They tell us how to garden on the East Coast or in England, where it rains all year long and the soils tend to be acidic. We, on the other hand, get all our rainfall in the winter and have soils that are alkaline. That's why, when a thoughtful book by a local gardener comes out—filled with advice on how to garden under these conditions—you shouldn't hesitate. Grab it. Such jewels are rare.

52 Weeks in the California Garden, by Robert Smaus, an editor at the *Los Angeles Times,* is one of those books. Every page is full of great tips. In the December chapter, for instance, you'll find out how pros like those at Sherman Gardens in Corona del Mar keep their annuals in peak production, why this is a good time to cut back perennials, which ones to cut back and how far, and why most birdhouses only succeed in attracting the same kind of feathered ruffians that hang out at McDonald's.

At $16.95, this book's a bargain. And after holiday shopping, haven't you earned a treat? If you don't find *52 Weeks* at bookstores or nurseries, call (800) 246-4042 to order (in which case it costs $15.95 plus shipping).

FOR GARDENERS IN SOUTHERN CALIFORNIA'S DESERTS AND MOUNTAINS

All gardens in Southern California don't enjoy Provence-like conditions. The weather in Idyllwild and Big Bear, for instance, can be more like conditions in Colorado. *The Undaunted Garden* should prove useful to gardeners in these Southern California regions. The author, Lauren Springer, lives in the Colorado foothills, where she gar-

dens with only 12 inches of rainfall a year, a soil pH above 8, greater temperature extremes than either Big Bear or Idyllwild, and pounding hailstorms. And as the numerous photos of her garden prove, Springer does it beautifully. The book comes from Fulcrum Publishing in Golden, Colorado, and costs $29.95 hardbound. Call (800) 992-2908 to order.

Gardening in Cathedral City, on the other hand, is more like gardening in Tucson. Two helpful books for desert gardeners are *Desert Gardening: Fruits and Vegetables* and *Desert Landscaping*. Both are by Tucson author George Brookbank. The first is published by Fisher Books, in Tucson, and costs $17.95. To order, call (800) 255-1514. The second is from the University of Arizona Press, also in Tucson, and costs $22; call (800) 426-3797 to order.

THAT'S A GOOD QUESTION

Q: "Why am I having so much trouble getting my new roses established? The old ones did fine in this spot."

A: Gary Matsuoka at Laguna Hills Nursery in Lake Forest hears this question so often he developed a name for the problem: Anemic Rose Replant Syndrome. Rose beds five years and older contain an extensive system of fine roots that are hard to remove, he says. When the left-behind roots begin to die, they fill the soil with root-decaying organisms. New roses spend most of their energy the first few years combating these organisms. If you want to continue planting roses in the same spot, remove the top foot of soil to get rid of the roots. Replace it with fresh topsoil. If the replacement roses are bare-root, consider growing them in containers for a year or so before planting them in the ground.

Westerner's Garden Notebook

by **JIM McCAUSLAND**

For several years, my family's preference has alternated between living and cut Christmas trees. In principle, I like the living ones, but my wife objected to the insects they brought in. It was hard to get creepy-crawlies out from underneath the heavy wooden tree box before we brought it inside. Two years ago we switched to cut trees, and now like them very much. But we've noticed a big difference in how fast they dry out. Those that suck water out of the stand's basin the fastest (like grand fir) seem to stay fresh the longest, while those that take it up more slowly (any tree whose cut base has callused over) dry out the fastest. To keep water uptake high, saw the bottom inch off any cut tree you buy, minutes before you put it in its stand.

If you plan to buy a living Christmas tree, get one that thrives in your climate—Douglas fir in the mountains, Afghan pine (*Pinus eldarica*) in the desert, for example—so that, when it outgrows its container and is too big to bring in the house again, you can plant it outdoors successfully.

•

Last winter, I foolishly advised readers to just toss plants like azaleas and poinsettias after the holidays, because I believed they had a poor survival rate. I still believe that about poinsettias, but Sally Braddy set me straight on the subject of azaleas. Her azalea blooms at least half of every year in the south window of a bright room in Fort Collins, Colorado. She feeds it every month or two, waters whenever the soil surface dries out, and keeps it in its original 8-inch pot. In summer, she sometimes puts the azalea on a cottonwood-shaded deck outside, where it gets more light and fresh air. Variety unknown, this evergreen azalea is in its fifth year.

•

If it freezes hard where you live, as it occasionally does in my garden, think about the birds that winter in the neighborhood. With a fast metabolism and no free water available, they've got a problem. I give them drinking water by dumping a couple of teakettlefuls of boiling water on the birdbath ice first thing every morning. It cools down very quickly as it melts the ice, so there's no danger to the birds, and at times I've had chickadees waiting a few feet away so they could drink as soon as I backed off. I've also tried a birdbath heater, but it seemed more trouble than it was worth.

THAT'S A GOOD QUESTION

Q: I read somewhere else that you could throw old sod upside down into a pile and then make it into a berm. I wonder if you have ever done that?

A: I've used sod to make a berm, and it works fine. After you stack the sod upside down, however, the grass will grow out its sides. Kill it by covering the sod with black plastic for at least two months. As sod decomposes—a two-year process—it settles, so don't plant large shrubs or trees in it during that time, or they're liable to lean as the berm settles. To speed up the decomposition process, sprinkle granular fertilizer between layers as you lay down the sod. As soon as you can easily dig a planting hole in the berm (perhaps a year later), it's ready to plant. If you're just going to put a ground cover or flowers on the berm, you can cover it with 6 inches of soil and plant it after a year.

Planting and shopping

☐ **BUY CAMELLIAS.** Winter-flowering plants are now in great supply. Slip plants in their nursery cans into larger decorative pots for holiday display. For a more festive touch, deck the branches with lights and ribbons. Plant them after the holidays.

☐ **HOUSE PLANTS.** In addition to poinsettias, nurseries are stocked with amaryllis, azaleas, cyclamen, and paper white narcissus. Group several plants (including foliage plants like ivy) together in a large pot, or cluster plants in nursery pots in a large basket. Keep the plants well watered and away from heat sources. Snip off faded blooms and yellowing leaves.

☐ **TREES AND SHRUBS.** In zones 4–7, all but marginally hardy trees and shrubs can go into the ground this month. Water them thoroughly after planting.

Maintenance

☐ **GROUND-LAYER EVERGREENS.** In zones 4–7, you can propagate new evergreen shrubs by using a technique called ground-layering. First, scrape away a fingernail-size bit of bark on a small branch that is close to the ground. Dab the wound with rooting hormone and stake the branch to the ground or put a rock or brick on top of it to hold it down. The scraped part of the branch should be in direct contact

with the soil, but the leafy top should be free. Keep the branch well watered as it develops roots. Next fall, you can sever the branch from its parent and transplant it.

☐ **INSPECT STORED BULBS.** Check frost-tender bulbs, corms, and tubers; discard any that show signs of rot. Dahlias are the exception: cut out the damaged spots, dust them with sulfur, and store them apart from other tubers.

☐ **KEEP ON COMPOSTING.** Post-storm debris, leaves left over from autumn cleanup, and seasonal greens that have wilted can all go on the compost pile. If you have a compost shredder, saw the old Christmas tree into manageable lengths, then grind the pieces up. Before you shred your wreaths and swags, be sure to remove any wires.

☐ **PRUNE FOR HOLIDAY GREENS.** Now is an excellent time to prune conifers and broad-leafed evergreens. Use the cut greens indoors for decorations. Remove—and dispose of—dead and diseased branches first. Next, take off branches that cross or are too closely parallel. Thin plants to show off their form. Make your cuts where you won't leave ugly stubs.

☐ **SAND ICY WALKS.** After sweeping or scraping ice off walkways, scatter sand freely over the surface. Unlike salt, sand won't harm plants. But don't use sand on decks, since it will scar the wood.

☐ **TEND GIFT PLANTS.** During the holidays, make sure poinsettias, Christmas cactus, cyclamen, and kalanchoe have good light and regular water, and keep them out of drafts. Feed flowering plants monthly until blooms drop. Treat poinsettias as short-term living bouquets: when their colorful bracts fade and leaves start to drop, toss them out.

☐ **WATER.** Pay attention to plants in containers. In most cases, well-watered plants are better able to withstand freezing weather than drought-stressed ones. New Zealand flax and silk tree (mimosa) are two exceptions that like to be on the dry side when temperatures plunge.

Planting

☐ CHOOSE CAMELLIAS. Zones 7–9, 14–17: Select *Camellia sasanqua* and early-flowering *C. japonica* while they're blooming. Sasanquas are good choices for espaliers, ground covers, informal hedges, and containers; they tolerate a fair amount of sun. Some are upright, others spreading or vinelike. Choices include 'Egao', 'Rainbow', 'Shibori Egao', and 'Yuletide'. Japonicas are handsome as specimen plants and espaliers. Look for 'Alba Plena', 'Elegans' ('Chandleri Elegans'), 'Daikagura', 'Debutante', 'Magnoliaeflora', 'Nuccio's Carousel', 'Nuccio's Gem', and 'Wildfire'.

☐ PLANT FRUITS AND VEGETABLES. Zones 7–9, 14–17: Late this month, nurseries begin selling bare-root artichokes, asparagus, berries, grapes, and rhubarb. Buy and plant early in the month while roots are still fresh. If the soil is too wet to plant, temporarily cover the roots with moistened mulch to keep them from drying out, or plant in containers.

☐ SHOP FOR BARE-ROOT ROSES. Zones 7–9, 14–17: Bare-root roses start appearing in nurseries this month. Shop while selections are good. Choices may include climbing roses, floribundas, hybrid teas, and shrub roses. If you can't find what you're looking for at nurseries, try one of the mail-order sources listed on page 298.

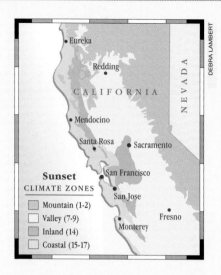

Sunset
CLIMATE ZONES
☐ Mountain (1-2)
☐ Valley (7-9)
☐ Inland (14)
☐ Coastal (15-17)

DEBRA LAMBERT

☐ SHOP FOR INSTANT COLOR. Zones 7–9, 14–17: Most nurseries have a good supply of 4-inch pots of color; you can cluster these in large containers or in the ground. Choose azaleas, calendulas, Christmas cactus, cineraria, cyclamen, English primroses, fairy primroses, kalanchoe, pansies, *Primula obconica,* and snapdragons. Protect Christmas cactus and kalanchoe from frost.

Maintenance

☐ FEED ANNUALS. Zones 7–9, 14–17: Even though the weather is cool and foliage growth has slowed, annuals need nutrients for root development. Feed with a complete fertilizer once a month or fish emulsion every two weeks or so.

☐ FILL HUMMINGBIRD FEEDERS. Zones 7–9, 14–17: These birds stay in Northern California through winter. Since flowers are scarce in most gardens now, it's important to keep your feeder filled; clean and refill it every few days.

☐ KEEP CUT CHRISTMAS TREES FRESH. To prolong the freshness of a cut tree, saw an inch off the bottom of the trunk, then store the tree in a bucket of water in a shady area outdoors until you're ready to bring it indoors. Before setting the tree in a stand, saw another inch off the bottom of the trunk. Use a stand that holds water and keep the reservoir full (check daily the first week). Keep the tree away from heaters and avoid hot-burning tree lights.

☐ WAIT TO PRUNE ROSES. Zones 7–9, 14–17: As roses become a bit bedraggled, it can be tempting to prune them right away. But it's still too early. And if the weather is mild, plants may still even produce a few flowers. Wait to prune until January and February.

Pest control

☐ APPLY DORMANT SPRAY. Zones 7–9, 14–17: To smother overwintering insect eggs and pests such as aphids, mites, and scale, spray deciduous flowering and fruit trees as well as roses with dormant oil after the leaves have fallen. For complete coverage, spray each tree's branches, branch crotches, and trunk, as well as the ground beneath its drip line.

Planting

☐ **BUY BARE-ROOT PLANTS.** Coastal, inland, and low-desert gardeners (zones 22–24, 18–21, and 13, respectively) can plant bare-root this month. Roses arrive at nurseries first. Shop early for the best selection. Also look for deciduous fruit trees, berries, grapes, and perennial vegetables such as artichokes, asparagus, rhubarb, and strawberries. Plant as soon as possible. If the soil is too wet for immediate planting, cover the roots with soil or plant temporarily in containers. Do not allow the roots to dry out.

☐ **BUY CAMELLIAS AND CYMBIDIUMS.** Now, while plants are in bloom, is the best time to select the flower colors you want. Most nurseries are stocked with *Camellia sasanqua* and early-blooming *C. japonica*. Cymbidium season is in full swing, too.

☐ **PLANT NATIVES.** Unless the soil is soggy, this month is still a good time to plant California natives and other drought-resistant plants. If rains are light, water regularly to get plants established.

☐ **PLANT WINTER ANNUALS.** Coastal and inland gardeners can fill in bare spots in the garden with cool-season annuals purchased as blooming plants. Low growers such as sweet alyssum, dwarf calendulas, pansies, and violas will fill in more swiftly and provide

quicker color than taller plants like stock and snapdragons.

☐ **PLANT WINTER VEGETABLES.** Choices include beets, broccoli, brussels sprouts, cabbage, carrots, cauliflower, lettuces, kale, peas, spinach, Swiss chard, and turnips.

Maintenance

☐ **CARE FOR CHRISTMAS TREES.** To prolong the freshness of a cut tree, trim an inch or so off the base of the trunk, place the tree in a stand that holds water, and keep the reservoir full (check daily the first week). If you're not ready to set up the tree indoors immediately, store it in a bucket of water in a shady place outdoors. Keep a living tree outdoors until shortly before the holiday. Be sure to water it regularly so the rootball doesn't dry out. Limit the tree's indoor time to two weeks or less. Keep all trees away from

heaters and avoid hot-burning tree lights.

☐ **FERTILIZE.** Fertilize fall-planted trees, shrubs, and ground covers. For steady growth, also feed winter vegetables and annuals.

☐ **PRUNE.** Cut branches of holly, juniper, nandina, pittosporum, podocarpus, pyracantha, and toyon; save the clippings for decorations. Cut back to the side branches or to about ¼ inch above buds.

Pest control

☐ **APPLY DORMANT SPRAY.** As soon as their leaves fall, spray deciduous flowering and fruit trees with dormant oil to smother overwintering scale, mites, and aphids. For fungal diseases such as peach leaf curl, mix lime sulfur or fixed copper into the oil. Spray the branches, crotches, and trunk, as well as the ground beneath the tree's drip line. If it rains within 48 hours of spraying, repeat the treatment. Spray again in January at the height of dormancy and in early February at first bud swell.

☐ **PREVENT BEETLE DAMAGE.** Prune eucalyptus, pine, and other trees susceptible to bark beetles now, while borers are inactive. Chip the prunings or cover the firewood tightly with a tarp to prevent beetles from laying eggs. (Beetles lay eggs on both dead and live wood.)

Planting

☐ **PROPAGATE HOUSE PLANTS.** As house plants get leggy in winter's low light, you can cut off elongated stems and root them in water for potting up later. Try this with dracaena, Chinese evergreen, and philodendron.

Maintenance

☐ **CARE FOR GIFT PLANTS.** If you plan to keep the azalea, cyclamen, kalanchoe, ornamental pepper, paper white narcissus, and other small gift plants that are so popular during the holidays, give them plenty of light, regular water and food (especially while they're blooming and setting fruit), and keep them out of drafts. Most plants will take poor conditions for a few days—as centerpieces in low-light places, for example—but give them optimal conditions again as soon as possible after the holidays.

☐ **CARE FOR LIVING CHRISTMAS TREES.** While they're indoors, keep trees away from fireplaces and heater vents. Water regularly; for slow, cool, even irrigation, cover the soil surface with a layer of ice cubes. Take your tree to a sheltered place outside immediately after Christmas to let it acclimate. If it's well below freezing where you live, put the tree in a cool, light, and protected place (such as an unheated porch) until temperatures start rising above freezing every day. Then put it outside.

DEBRA LAMBERT

Sunset
CLIMATE ZONES
☐ 1-3   ▦ 10-11

☐ **TEND TO INDOOR CACTUS.** Allow spring-flowering indoor cactus to dry off from mid-December through February, then water and apply a weak solution of fertilizer every second watering. Keep your cactus in a bright spot to encourage bloom.

☐ **RECYCLE CUT CHRISTMAS TREES.** Recycle your tree: grind it up for mulch or cut it into 2-foot lengths, stack it, and use it for firewood.

☐ **CHECK STORED BULBS, PRODUCE.** Look over stored summer bulbs (like begonias and glads), throwing out ones that are rotting. You can save imperfect dahlia tubers by cutting out bad spots, dusting with sulfur, and storing them away from the others. Also check stored squash, apples, and other produce, discarding any that show signs of rot.

☐ **FEED THE BRUSH PILE.** Leaves can go into the compost pile, but larger debris—downed branches, twigs, and bunches of pine needles, for example—should go in a brush pile.

☐ **MULCH.** It's not too late to put a 3- or 4-inch layer of mulch over perennial, bulb, and shrub beds that might be damaged by alternate cycles of freezing and thawing.

☐ **SAND ICY WALKWAYS AND PATIOS.** Sand is a better choice than salt for use around plants, since it's nontoxic and can be swept into the garden when the ice is gone. However, don't use sand on decks: it scars wood.

☐ **WATER.** When the temperature is above freezing, water dry spots in the garden. When sustained subfreezing weather returns, well-watered plants stand a better chance of surviving.

Pest Control

☐ **CHECK INDOOR PLANTS.** Look for early warnings of trouble, such as honeydew on leaves or the rims of pots (often from scale insects) or fine webs between twigs (spider mites). If you find these, treat the plants quickly. Put a plastic bag around the container and wash the whole plant in lukewarm shower water. Then treat it with an insecticidal soap or a pesticide that's specific to the pest you're fighting.

Planting

☐ **ANNUALS AND PERENNIALS.** You can plant calendula, candytuft, cyclamen, dianthus, Iceland poppy, larkspur, pansy, petunia, primrose, snapdragon, stock, sweet alyssum, and viola. If you live in a frost-free place, set out bedding begonias and cineraria as well. All these are sold in cell-packs.

☐ **BARE-ROOT PLANTS.** Berries and roses are usually the first to come in, followed by fruit trees and perennial vegetables like asparagus, horseradish, and rhubarb. Keep roots from drying out by wrapping them in wet burlap or packing them in damp sawdust between nursery and garden, then plant as soon as you get home. If the roots dry out, the plant dies.

☐ **BULBS.** As early as possible this month, plant daffodil, gladiolus, ranunculus, and prechilled tulip bulbs. (If you are prechilling the tulips yourself, plant only after they've had at least six weeks of refrigeration.)

☐ **NATIVES.** Set out nursery stock, water in well, and mulch. Then watch the weather: if you don't get much winter rain, follow up with regular deep watering to help roots get established.

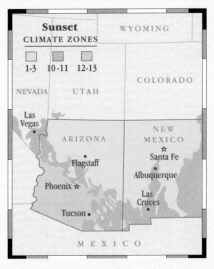

☐ **PEPPERS, TOMATOES.** Sow seeds of peppers and tomatoes in a warm indoor spot now. Give them plenty of light, regular watering, and light fertilizing; transplants will be ready for the garden by late February or early March.

Maintenance

☐ **CARE FOR GIFT PLANTS.** If you plan to keep the azalea, cyclamen, kalanchoe, ornamental pepper, paper white narcissus, and other small gift plants that are so popular during the holidays, give them plenty of light, regular water and food (especially while they're blooming and setting fruit), and keep them out of drafts. Most plants will take poor conditions for a few days—as

centerpieces in low-light places, for example—but give them optimal conditions again as soon as possible after the holidays. Treat poinsettias as short-term living bouquets: when their colorful bracts fade and leaves start to drop, toss them out.

☐ **FEED DECIDUOUS FRUIT TREES.** They benefit greatly from winter fertilizing. For trees at least four years old, apply 9 pounds of 10-10-10 fertilizer now, then 3 more pounds right after harvest.

☐ **PRUNE FOR HOLIDAY GREENS.** When you cut evergreens for swags and wreaths, you're pruning. Make each cut just above a side branch, thinning the tree or shrub evenly as you work. While you're at it, remove dead, diseased, and injured branches; to finish the job, prune for shape.

Pest control

☐ **SPRAY DORMANT PLANTS.** Spray roses and deciduous flowering and fruit trees with horticultural oil to smother such overwintering insects as scale, mites, and aphids. You can also control brown rot, peach leaf curl, and shot hole by mixing lime sulfur or fixed copper into the oil. Spray all parts of the tree, especially crotches and furrowed bark.

Planting

☐ **START SEEDLINGS.** In South Texas, after midmonth start seeds of cool-season flowers (such as calendulas, English daisies, pansies, and snapdragons) and vegetables (such as cabbage, cauliflower, and spinach) indoors for transplanting into the garden in February.

Maintenance

☐ **CARE FOR LIVING CHRISTMAS TREES.** While they're indoors, keep trees away from fireplaces and heater vents. Water regularly; for slow, cool, even irrigation, cover the soil surface with a layer of ice cubes. Take your tree to a sheltered place outside immediately after Christmas to let it acclimate. If it's well below freezing where you live, put the tree in a cool, light, protected place (like an unheated porch) until

temperatures start rising above freezing every day.

☐ **MULCH.** In cold-winter parts of Texas, it's not too late to spread mulch

over bulb and perennial beds and over the root zones of permanent shrubs (especially ones that are borderline hardy in your area).

☐ **TEND INDOOR CACTUS.** Allow spring-flowering indoor cactus to dry off from mid-December through February, then water and apply a weak solution of fertilizer every second watering. Keep your cactus in a bright spot to encourage bloom.

Pest control

☐ **APPLY DORMANT OIL.** When the temperature is above freezing and no rain is predicted for at least 48 hours, spray dormant oil onto fruiting and flowering deciduous trees and shrubs. It will kill eggs and overwintering larvae, so you'll have fewer problems next season. ◆

Savor *the* Season

Bountiful wreaths

FOREST-AND-GARDEN WREATHS COMBINE LUSH
FOLIAGE WITH COLORFUL FRUITS AND VEGETABLES

by **PETER O. WHITELEY**

photographs by **KEVIN CANDLAND**

"You need wonderful things to play with," says Sonoma, California, floral designer Valerie Arelt about the art of wreath making. We asked her to show us what she would do if the ingredients included seasonal fruits and vegetables. Arelt, noted for imaginative arrangements that have the lush, informal appearance of an English cottage garden, created three densely packed wreaths for the front door, entry hall, dining table, or mantel.

"The more unusual textures you can find, the more interesting the wreath," says Arelt. This is her overriding principle in looking for holiday wreath materials. On the following pages, we show you how to use Arelt's techniques with your choice of seasonal materials— from the garden, woods, nursery, or grocery store.

In a sculptural study of colors and textures, the warm tones and round lushness of citrus contrast with spiky gray-green pine and fir needles, set off by the velvety copper backs and shiny green tops of magnolia leaves.

Fail-safe tips for creating a ravishing wreath

Just take it one
cluster at a time

Small bouquets are the starting point of every wreath. Strip the leaves and needles from the last few inches of the stems so they can be gathered and tied with twist ties or florist's wire.

Vary the colors and textures of the bouquets to make rich-looking wreaths. Three color groupings—in the photos above, left, and right—form the basic building blocks for small wreaths.

This visual feast (also shown on page 292) mixes unexpected forms—Japanese eggplant, red pears, turnips, quinces, green apples—with muted greens of bay and rosemary.

Begin each wreath by lashing a bouquet to a wire frame with a continuous strand of florist's wire. Keep the wire taut and short. Add bouquets progressively around the ring.

Impale large, thick-skinned fruit (lemon, at top) with lengths of stiff, straight wire and tie onto the frame. For slender items (such as ornamental chilies), wrap twist ties around stems.

Florist's picks with wire can be tied to fruit with stems. Or poke picks into small, fleshy fruit. Place fruit individually to accent or fill in holes in arrangements.

WHAT YOU NEED

• Heavy-gauge wire or a plastic ring from a craft or florists' supply store. For small wreaths, you can make your own frame from a wire coat hanger by cutting off the hook and overlapping and twisting the cut ends together. For larger wreaths, use a double metal or plastic ring (frame) to keep the weight of the greenery and attached fruits and vegetables from bending or distorting the rings.
• A spool of coated florist's wire
• A pack of straight, 18- to 24-gauge stem wire
• Florist's picks
• A pack of green twist ties
• Picture frame wire

ARELT'S FAVORITES

• *Foliage:* camellia, cedar, citrus leaves, eucalyptus, fir, magnolia, pine
• *Fresh herbs:* bay, oregano, rosemary, sage, tarragon, thyme
• *Fruits:* grapes, green and Lady apples, kumquats, lemons, limes, oranges, pears, persimmons, pomegranates, quinces, tangerines
• *Vegetables:* artichokes, broccoli, brussels sprouts, chilies, garlic, Japanese eggplant, leeks, onions, peppers, radishes, red potatoes, shallots, turnips
• *Berries:* cranberries, eucalyptus, holly, pepper, privet, toyon
• *Nuts and cones:* acorns, hazelnuts, pecans, pinecones, walnuts

• *Dried materials:* barley, decorative grasses, ornamental corn, wheat, hydrangeas, roses

ASSEMBLING A BOUNTIFUL WREATH

1. Sort the different materials into separate piles. Remove leaves from the lower 3 inches of all cut branches, then place the stems in water so they will remain fresh.

For all wreaths, create a rich, leafy background texture, then add decorative elements. The background should blend three or four different textures of greenery. (For the large wreath shown at left and on the cover, Arelt chose short branches of pine, fir, citrus, and bay.)

2. Start your wreath by creating fan-shaped clusters of the mixed foliage and smaller items: the clusters should be small enough to hold in one hand. Tie them together with twist ties or the stem wire. Make enough clusters to cover the ring.

For small tabletop wreaths, begin with a basic greenery cluster—one made of bay, rosemary, and thyme, for example—then add color to each cluster. (Arelt creates three basic color groupings, such as a red-and-purple cluster of shallots, small red pears, and baby pomegranates; a white cluster of garlic; and an orange cluster of small chilies or decorative peppers and kumquats.) Remember to keep all of

the smaller elements in scale with each other.

3. Attach clusters to the ring using the spool of coated florist's wire. Wrap the wire tightly around the gathered stems and keep it taut, but do not cut the wire until all the clusters are added. The leaves of each successive cluster should overlie and mask the stems of the cluster previously secured. Work progressively around the ring until the stems of the last cluster are covered by the leaves of the first.

4. Attach individual fruits, vegetables, and other materials next, using the basic three techniques illustrated in the photos above. To determine the placement of large elements (like artichokes, lemons, or peppers), think of a triangle and place these key colors or textures at three points around the circle. Avoid a stiff, mechanical appearance by unevenly massing the smaller fruits. akeep the heaviest pieces of fruit close to the wire base, and insert the fruit so it radiates outward as the leaves do.

5. Finally, attach a sturdy loop (made from heavy picture frame wire) to the back of the wreath for hanging. For large, heavy wreaths, equally space two loops near the top center.

Arelt's wreaths last about three weeks outdoors, 10 days indoors.

For other holiday decorating tips, check out Arelt's video: *The Glorious Art of Christmas Decorations,* $29.95, plus $4.95 shipping; call (800) 752-6896. ◆

The abundant table

PLUCK FRUITS FROM YOUR GARDEN AND ADD
A FEW FLOWERS FOR A TABLE DECORATION
AS RICH AS A STILL-LIFE PAINTING

by **LAUREN BONAR SWEZEY**

Grand holiday dinners call for equally grand
centerpieces. The three arrangements on these
pages were created by floral designers who
drew their inspiration from Della Robbia
sculptures, Flemish art, and nature. They
combine fruit and foliage that you might find
growing in your own backyard this time of
year. Or you can substitute fruit from the
grocery store. (For maximum freshness,
assemble your centerpiece
no more than
one day before
your dinner.)

NOEL BARNHURST

NORTHERN CALIFORNIA *harvest*

"This is my version of Della Robbia, but it's less contrived, more spontaneous," says designer Jeffrey Adair of J Floral Art in Menlo Park. "The fruit isn't evenly spaced, and the design is more naturalistic." Adair created the elongated triangle arrangement with acacia, camellia, juniper, privet, redwood, and sumac foliage. Lady apples, persimmons, pomegranates, red 'Comice' pears, and walnuts provide the color and drama.

How to create a sumptuous centerpiece

Five easy steps to a handsome arrangement for your holiday table

Set a moist block of florist's foam on a plate (a low bowl, bread pan, or pedestal dish will also work). Secure the foam with green florist's tape as shown.

Build the basic shape first, using foliage. Poke snippets into the sides of the foam to hide the plate (shown are glossy camellia leaves).

PACIFIC NORTHWEST *native*

The textures, fragrances, and colors of the Northwest's foliage inspire the designs of Bud Gulbranson of R. David Adams Flowers in Seattle. "Although we often think of the holidays as a time of glitz and glitter, I also enjoy using subtle plant materials ... coupled with fresh fruits or vegetables." Bay, cotoneaster, heather, holly, ivy, mahonia, pine, variegated privet, rosemary, and Western cedar form the base. Redtwig dogwood sticks, nigella pods, cones, red 'Comice' pears, and red radishes add color and texture.

SOUTHERN CALIFORNIA *subtropical*

Whimsical is how designer Jacob Maarse of Pasadena describes his citrus extravaganza. The design is a partial oval; camellia foliage forms the base, citrus is the filler, and bird of paradise flowers take flight around the perimeter. Maarse found many of these materials in his backyard, including the 'Buddha's Hand' citrus ('Fingered' citron). A surprising touch: he cuts open a few citrus and breaks open some pomegranates to reveal their brightly colored flesh and seeds.

Insert thick-stemmed flowers—like these bird of paradise blooms—into foam before filling in with smaller-stemmed materials; they'll create the outline.

Poke the end of a 4-inch-long skewer—a sturdy stick or branch cut at an angle on each end—into each fruit. Or use green florists' picks.

Attach the fruit by slipping its stick end into the foam. Then add finishing touches, such as camellia blossoms and more foliage, to fill the empty spaces.

Washington navel oranges and 'Eureka' lemons are cushioned in excelsior.

Sunshine in a box

Shipping homegrown fruit is easy, if you learn the rules and pack well

The holiday gifts your relatives and friends might appreciate most may be right in your own backyard. Oranges, persimmons, and 'Meyer' lemons plucked from your trees could be as welcome as a ray of sunshine to those living in areas where these crops aren't as plentiful.

Don't have any crops in your backyard? Consider purchasing exotic fruit like blood oranges from a local farmers' market to ship as presents. They're still a treat.

First, a caveat; then some tips.

RESTRICTIONS

Before attempting to mail any fruit, find out whether the U.S. Department of Agriculture or your state's agricultural department restricts shipping the kind of fruit you want to send from your area (call your county agricultural commissioner). Until July of this year, for instance, sending tree fruit from Southern California was prohibited because of a Mediterranean fruitfly quarantine. And there may still be restrictions on specific crops in some other areas in the West.

by **SHARON COHOON**

It's also possible that the state you want to ship to may have restrictions on incoming fruit. Rules in Arizona, California, Hawaii, and Texas are particularly stringent.

PACKAGING

Heavy corrugated-cardboard boxes or equally strong containers are best for shipping all fruit. When packaging the fruit, separate each piece from its shipping mates with generous quantities of plastic foam peanuts, shredded newspaper, excelsior, or other cushioning material. Also cushion the bottom, sides, and top of the shipping container (three inches of the material should be sufficient to protect the contents). Pack the fruit tightly enough so that it cannot shift or rotate in transit, which causes bruising. Remember that the softer the fruit, the more easily it can bruise.

Include enough cushioning material so that it has to be compressed slightly when you close the carton, immobilizing the fruit. An alternate method is to place pieces of fruit in the fiber trays that professional growers use to ship apples and pears (supermarkets sometimes give them away). Fruit does not slip easily when cradled in these trays, though it still needs to be cushioned to keep it from bruising. Soft-skinned fruit such as apples, pears, and persimmons can be wrapped in tissue paper to prevent abrasion during shipping.

Nuts don't really need cushioning because their hard shells provide protection. Still, you may want to include packaging for an attractive presentation. To keep out moisture, seal nuts in zip-lock plastic bags before packing.

If you're shipping fruit to areas with subzero winter temperatures, use foam bubbles to provide some insulation. Lining the carton with a sheet of heavy plastic large enough to fold over at the top—a plastic trash bag, for instance—will also help insulate your crop. (Perforate the bag in a dozen or so places before using it to line the carton.)

SHIPPING METHODS

The best way to ship your fruit depends on the fruit's perishability. If you're shipping fruit that begins to ripen the minute you take it from cold storage—

such as pears—it's worth the extra cost to speed it on its way. Next-day delivery is ideal but pricey. (Shipping costs vary by courier, so try to do some comparison shopping.)

For most fruit, second-day delivery is a good compromise between economy and speed. Ship to a work address if no one is customarily at home during the day. If no one is home to sign for the package, it could sit in a warehouse until it can be redelivered. Also, try to ship on a Monday or Tuesday, avoiding Friday ship dates—a package left on a doorstep could be exposed to bad weather all weekend. ◆

FRUITS *and* NUTS *that* SHIP WELL

Fruits and nuts suitable for shipping as holiday presents vary from region to region. Here's a sampling.

Fruits: apples, avocados, grapefruits, guavas, kiwi fruit, kumquats, lemons, limes, oranges, pears, persimmons, pineapples, and pomegranates.

Nuts: almonds, chestnuts, hazelnuts, pecans, pistachios, and walnuts.

HOW *to* HARVEST *for* SHIPPING

Pick only perfect fruit. Eliminate any pieces of fruit with bruises or scars; they're more likely to rot in transit.

Ship fully ripe lemons, limes, grapefruits, other citrus. They will not mature further after picking.

Pick and ship green any fruit that softens significantly with ripening, such as avocados, kiwi fruit, pears, and persimmons. If they're already softening, don't ship them.

Package immediately any fruit that ripens within a few days after being removed from cold storage, such as kiwi fruit and pears, and ship via the fastest method available.

Miniature trees include (clockwise from top right): two Italian stone pines, two dwarf Port Orford cedars, and a rosemary.

Miniature trees for tabletops

These evergreens stand less than a foot tall. Buy several for a table

When I was a kid, Christmas trees were 5- to 10-foot-tall conifers such as pine, fir, or spruce—or squat 3-footers—that you bought at Christmas tree lots. Then dwarf Alberta spruce trees started to appear in nurseries in gallon cans as miniature living Christmas trees. But now, *really* tiny trees are available in such places as grocery stores and floral shops. You can pick up an Italian stone (blue) pine just 6 inches tall in a 3-inch pot, or even a dwarf Port Orford cedar (*Chamaecyparis lawsoniana* 'Woodii') in a 2- to 6-inch-wide container, to decorate a windowsill or other tight place.

Some of these trees are sold decorated with ornaments and candy canes. But it's much more fun to buy them undecorated and dress them up yourself. A festive bow or a string of lights and red berries can brighten them; gold stars and a beautiful angel can give them elegance and grace. And bunched together, they suggest a miniature forest.

Like any other living Christmas tree, these gems need special handling if you want to keep them growing for future Christmases. If your tree is displayed indoors for the entire holiday season, give it bright indirect light, advises Lucho Bianchi, head grower at Nurserymen's Exchange in Half Moon Bay, California. Also, don't let the plant sit in water or allow the soil to dry out. After the holidays, acclimate the plant to the outdoors by placing it on the patio or in another protected area for a few weeks. Trees growing in small containers should be transplanted into larger containers. ◆

by LAUREN BONAR SWEZEY

Bamboos for the great indoors

Plants that mind their manners in containers

Growing gracefully in ornate containers, these three bamboos are, from left, Sasaella masumuneana albostriata, Gintai-azumaneza, and Arundinaria anceps 'Pitt White'.

Graceful as grass, elegant as Japanese brush paintings, and strong as wood, bamboo is a remarkable garden plant. Remarkable, too, is that gardeners haven't caught on to bamboo's value as a house plant.

Plant bamboos in 16-inch pots and set them against plain walls or windows—bamboos will grow anywhere as long as they get enough light.

Bamboos display amazing variety: some have variegated leaves, others striped stems, and others exotic forms.

But for indoor plants, no attribute is more important than size. In the garden, bamboos can become huge. At right we list 10 smaller-scale bamboo plants and give their indoor heights and light requirements.

HOW TO HOUSE-TRAIN BAMBOO

There are several ways to restrain bamboo without topping plants. Start by allowing bamboo to become potbound. This isn't a good practice for most plants, but it's fine for bamboo, containing the growth of both clumping and running types. Also, since bamboos tend to be heavy feeders, you can restrict growth by applying controlled-release fertilizer every four months, beginning when new growth starts.

Bamboo culms (the stems) emerge from the ground with the same diameter they'll have when they're grown; break off the large culms, but let the smaller ones grow.

New leaves can appear in any of three seasons, depending on the type of bamboo. Clumping types (which grow rather tightly massed) produce leaves in summer, in autumn, or whenever plants are watered after a long dry spell. Running types (which can grow new shoots several feet from the main grove) usually produce leaves in spring.

As new leaves grow, old leaves fall off. This is the messiest season for bamboos; set them outdoors if the weather allows.

SOURCES

Many nurseries carry a few kinds of bamboo. You can also order plants by mail; good sources include Bamboo Giant, Box 422, Capitola, CA 95010, (408) 685-1248; Bamboo Sourcery, 666 Wagnon Rd., Sebastopol, CA 95472, (707) 823-5866; and Tradewinds Bamboo Nursery, 28446 Hunter Creek Loop, Gold Beach, OR 97444, (541) 247-0835. ◆

by **JIM McCAUSLAND**

10 BAMBOOS *for the* HOUSE

HIGH LIGHT
(more than 6 hours sun per day)

Arundinaria anceps 'Pitt White', 12 feet. The tall, slender culms are covered with thin, delicate foliage. Running type.

Buddha's belly bamboo (*Bambusa ventricosa*), 3 to 6 feet. The swollen culms that account for its common name appear only when it's potbound. Clumping type.

Mexican weeping bamboo (*Otatea acuminata aztecorum*), 8 feet. Extremely thin leaves are ⅛ inch wide, 6 inches long. Clumping.

MODERATE LIGHT
(4 to 6 hours sun per day)

Gintai-azumaneza (*Pleioblastus chino murakamianus*), 4 to 6 feet. Upright plant with variegated leaves, some of which are pure white. Running.

Marbled bamboo (*Chimonobambusa marmorea*), 2 to 4 feet. The cream-and-purplish new culms eventually become black. Running.

LOW LIGHT
(less than 4 hours sun per day)

Big-leaved bamboo (*Indocalamus tessellatus*), 2 to 3 feet. Leaves are 8 to 24 inches long. Running.

Dwarf whitestripe bamboo (*Pleioblastus variegata*), 1 to 2 feet. Bold white stripes mark the leaves. Running.

Hibanobambusa tranquillans 'Shiroshima', 4 to 6 feet. One of the most striking variegated bamboos. Running.

Pleioblastus shibuyanus 'Tsuboi', 2 to 5 feet. An upright plant with white stripes on its leaf centers. Running.

Sasaella masumuneana albostriata, 4 to 6 feet. Variegated new leaves turn green by fall. Running.

Article Titles Index

Abundant table, 310–313

Backyard poultry, 112–113
Bamboos for the great indoors, 316
Bananas, 213–215
Beautiful pots, 158–161
Bellflowers that will brighten any garden, 136–137
Bloom-again bearded irises, 110–111
Blooming branches for winter bouquets, 42–43
Bok choy: The tender, tasty green, 116
Bountiful wreaths, 306–309

California geology in miniature, 71
Camellias for a longer flower show, 47
CDs loaded with garden answers, 247
Celebrate summer with fresh-flower wreaths, 182–185
Clematis: A three-season guide to floral beauty, 80–81
Conifers that won't outgrow you, 44–46

Diminutive daffodils, 291

Easy-care herb pot, 79

First gardens, 62–70
Flower discoveries, 270–271
For the love of lavender, 108–109
Four fabulous shrubs, 26–28

Garden checklists, inland western states
January, 15
February, 40
March, 60
April, 92
May, 128
June, 156
July, 180
August, 202
September, 228
October, 260
November, 284
December, 304
Garden checklists, Northern California
January, 13
February, 38
March, 58

Garden checklists, Northern California (cont'd.)
April, 90
May, 126
June, 154
July, 178
August, 200
September, 226
October, 258
November, 282
December, 302
Garden checklists, Pacific Northwest
January, 12
February, 37
March, 57
April, 89
May, 125
June, 153
July, 177
August, 199
September, 225
October, 257
November, 281
December, 301
Garden checklists, Southern California
January, 14
February, 39
March, 59
April, 91
May, 127
June, 155
July, 179
August, 201
September, 227
October, 259
November, 283
December, 303
Garden checklists, Southwest (includes Texas)
February, 41
March, 61
April, 93
May, 129
June, 157
July, 181
August, 203
September, 229
October, 261
November, 285
December, 305
Garden checklists, Texas. See Garden checklists, Southwest
Garden for the senses, 186–187
Garden Guide
January, 8–11
February, 32–36
March, 52–56
April, 84–88
May, 120–124
June, 146–150
July, 170–174
August, 194–196
September, 218–222
October, 250–254
November, 274–280
December, 294–296

Garden notebooks, inland western states. See also Garden notebooks, westerner's
January, 15
February, 40
March, 60
April, 92
May, 128
June, 152
July, 176
August, 198
September, 224
October, 256
Garden notebooks, Northern California
January, 13
February, 38
March, 58
April, 90
May, 126
June, 151
July, 175
August, 197
September, 223
October, 255
November, 278
December, 298
Garden notebooks, Pacific Northwest
January, 12
February, 37
March, 57
April, 89
May, 125
June, 151
July, 175
August, 197
September, 223
October, 255
November, 277
December, 297
Garden notebooks, Southern California
January, 14
February, 39
March, 59
April, 91
May, 127
June, 152
July, 176
August, 198
September, 224
October, 256
November, 279
December, 299
Garden notebooks, westerner's. See also notebooks for specific regions
November, 280
December, 300
Garlic revival, 242–245
Grow lingonberries for evergreen ground cover or tart fruit, 140
Guide to natural soil enrichers, 29

Hardy exotics, 25
Herbs for the whole year, 269

How to shop for the right potting mix, 165–166

Is 'Blue Lake' still the best bean, 115
It's gloating time, 16–21

Juicy-crunch pears that look like funny apples, 48–49

Keys to organic gardening success, 106–107

Landscaping, South African–style, 189
Lusher-looking impatiens, 141

Miniature trees for tabletops, 315

Nectar bar for butterflies, 191
New cutting garden, 94–101
New perennials fast—for free, 134–135
No space? Grow orchids in your trees, 117

Palms that won't grow up to be headaches, 138–139
Paradise for plant lovers, 102–104
Passion for heathers, 210–212
Putting the "snap" in snap peas, 246

Raise a bed of great vegetables, 72–74

Scoop out a little pawpaw fruit, 142
Secrets of the garden masters, 230–237
Shade plants with a sunny look, 105
Smoke trees light up the garden, 265
Soft summer blues, 241
Space-saving watermelons, 114
Stewartias crown the garden with regal form, summer flowers, 188
Sunshine in a box, 314

Tale of two lilies, 266–269
Taming wildflowers, 286–290
Terra-cotta to treasure, 162–165
Terrorists in your tomato patch, 190
Thyme to plant, thyme to spare, 167
Tulips year after year, naturally, 238–240

Unforgettable garden fragrances, 204–209
Until there's a perfect strawberry, try 'Seascape', 75

Wander among wildflowers, 143
Where rhodies grow for the glory, 76–78
"Wild," wonderful, and robust rugosas, 22–24
Window box renaissance, 130–133
World in a garden, 262–264

General Subject Index

Acacia baileyana, for indoor display, 8, 42
Acanthus mollis, 196
Achillea, 176
Acidanthera, 126
Agapanthus orientalis 'Storm Cloud', 171
Agave, variegated, 276
Aglaonema modestum, 40
Alcatraz gardens, book about, 278
Aloes for winter color, 8–9
Anemone hybrida, 221
Annuals
    the perfect summer, 59
    surprise discoveries from seed, 270–271
    in wildflower mixes, 286–290
    winter color from, 16–17
Apples, fruit drop in, 152
Aquilegia fragrans, 54
Arugula selvatica, 34
Asian pear, 48–49, 256
Asparagus fern, Meyers, 219
Aspen, quaking, 254
Aster, 221, 223

Baby's tears, invasive, 224
Bacillus thuringiensis, 127, 190, 256
Bald cypress, 12
Balloon flower, 151
Bamboos
    containing running, 224
    as house plants, 316
Bananas for fruit and foliage, 213–215
Bare-root, 37
    advantages of, 37
    preplanting care, 15
Bark, colorful, 18–19
Basil, postfrost variety, 223
Beans
    for drying, 223
    pole, rated, 115
Bear's breech, 196
Bellflowers, 136–137
Berm made from recycled sod, 300
Berries, colorful, 18–19
Birds
    birdhouses as garden ornaments, 222
    edible tree ornaments for, 294
    tiny birdbath for little birds, 296
    water supply for, in cold climates, 300
Blackberries, pruning, 12
Blueberries, new super-size, 147
Blue spruce, underplanting for, 220
Bok choy, 116
Books. *See* Garden publications
Breath of heaven, pink, 28
Buddleia, 55, 191
Bulbs. *See also* specific bulbs
    bonemeal for, 255
    choosing from nursery bins, 256
    dibbles for planting en masse, 254

Bulbs *(cont'd)*
    for late planting in Southern California, 10
    prechilled, 10
    synchronizing spring bloom, 254, 255
Butterflies by mail-order, 279
Butterfly bush
    to attract butterflies, 191
    new species (*B. crispa*), 55

Cabbage, ornamental, 253
Cactus for the holidays, 280
Camellias, long-blooming, 47
Campanula, 136–137
Catmint, 176, 256
Catproofing a planting area, 256
Cauliflower, new green, 173
Cedar tree litter, 151
Cersis canadensis, 56
Cherry
    dwarfing rootstocks for sweet, 34
    new purple-foliaged flowering, 9
Chickens for the back yard, 112–113
Chinese evergreen, 40
Chinese pistache, shopping for, 278
Christmas
    gift plants, second lives for, 15, 295, 300
    gifts for gardeners, 295, 297
    tree care, 297, 298, 300, 315
Chrysanthemum coccineum, 124
Citrus fruit drop control, 152
Cleanup, garden, 198, 224, 275
Clematis
    grown up trees, 89
    three-season guide to, 80–81
Coleonema pulchrum, 28
Coleus, heat-loving, 121
Columbine, new fragrant, 54
Compost, 58, 91, 165, 175
Conditioners, soil, 29
Conifers, 44–46, 87, 197, 315
Container planting
    bamboos, 316
    conifers for, 315
    designing for drama, 196
    easy-care herb pot, 79
    handmade clay pots, 162–165
    hanging basket tips, 124, 175
    matching plants to pots, 158–161
    Myers asparagus for, 219
    Nemesia fruticans for, 148
    potting mix, selecting the right, 165–166, 175
    protection for during vacations, 173, 197
    "rule of threes" for mixed pots, 297
    vegetable, 176
    window box tips, 130–133
Coreopsis verticillata 'Moonbeam', 58
Cornus florida, 56
Corylus hybrids, new, 33
Cotinus, 265, 276
Cotoneaster hebephyllus, 255
Cover crops, 197, 222
Crape myrtle, 56
Crataegus phaenopyrum, 56
Crimson flag, 277
Crop rotation, 74, 88
Crown imperial, 251
Cuphea, heat-loving, 198
Cut flowers
    blooming branches as, 42
    floating pansies, 53
    foliage as substitute for, 99

Cut flowers *(cont'd)*
    gardens for, 94–101
    harvesting and conditioning tips, 101, 222
    holiday table settings, 277
    recommended plants for, 100–101
    tips for florist roses, 13
Cypress, bald, 12

Daffodil
    massed plantings of, 35, 252
    miniatures for tiny spaces, 291
    postbloom foliage care, 57
Daisies, painted, 124
Daphne, 207, 232
Daylilies
    hotline for, 91
    recommended new, 152, 197
    'Stella de Oro', 37
Decorations for home and garden, 182–185, 222, 277, 294, 296, 306–313
Deerproofing, 120, 151
Digitalis, 86
Diseases
    black spot, 148
    camellia petal blight, 47
    fusarium wilt, 190
    powdery mildew, 148
    verticillium wilt, 190
    Xylella fastidiosa attacking oleanders, 221
Dogwood, flowering, 56
Dormant oils. *See* Horticultural oils
Drought-tolerant plants
    for containers, 197
    cuphea, 198
    mail-order sources for, 275
    for Pacific Northwest, 197
    shrubs for hot climes, 26–28
    three good companions, 276
Dry creek beds, landscaping, 218
Drying plants, 153, 241, 269
Dwarf conifers, 44–46
Dwarfing rootstock for sweet cherries, 34

Earthworms, 39, 63, 277
Eastern redbud, 56
Electronic gardening. *See* Garden publications
Epimedium, cutting back, 37
Erica
    caniculata 'Rosea', 28
    a passion for, 210–212
Erigeron karvinskianus, 276
Erosion control, 149
Eupatorium for pond edges, 223
Evergreen pear, 56

Fall bloomers for the Pacific Northwest, 221
False heather, 198
Fertilizing
    in combination with lime, 92
    with fish pellets, 124
    on holidays, 37
Floral exhibits, 58, 91, 223
Flower beds, tips for starting, 92
Flowering cherry, 9
Flowering dogwood, 56
Flowering quince, for indoor display, 42
Foliage
    of bulbs, postbloom, 57
    for cut arrangements, 99

Foliage *(cont'd)*
    holiday decorating with, 277, 306–313
    landscaping for color with, 44–46, 89, 105
    new color for flowering cherry, 9
Foraging for wild edibles, book about, 127
Forsythia, for indoor display, 42
Foxgloves, naturalizing from seed, 86
Fragrant plants, 127, 204–209, 232, 235, 296
Fritillaria imperialis, 251
Front yard landscaping, 55, 120, 172, 230, 252
Fruit. *See also* specific fruits
    decorating with, 307–313
    as gifts, shipping, 314–315
Fruit trees
    apple, June fruit drop on, 152
    Asian pear, 48–49, 256
    branches, for indoor display, 42
    citrus, fruit drop on, 152
    fungus on, 38
    pawpaw, 142
    source for antique, 298
    top ten for taste, 10
Fuchsias, 11, 90

Galium odoratum, 86
Garden publications, recommended
    books, 14, 38, 53, 174, 175, 176, 198, 278, 299
    electronic, 174, 175, 190, 247
    newsletters, 151, 277
Garden structures
    birdhouses as folk art, 222
    blooming-walled pavilion in San Marcos, CA, 150
    making moss to cover, 276
    pressure-treated wood for, 90
    trellis ideas, 68, 195
Gardens, public, and display nurseries
    Alcatraz gardens (San Francisco, CA), 278
    Arboretum of Los Angeles County (Arcadia, CA), 195
    Betty Ford Garden (Vail, CO), 196
    Franceschi Park (Santa Barbara, CA), 8–9
    J. Paul Getty Museum gardens (Malibu, CA), 59
    Martha Springer Botanical Garden (Salem, OR), 122
    Meerkerk Rhododendron Gardens (Greenbank, WA), 76–78
    Mendocino Coast Botanical Garden (Fort Bragg, CA), 170–171
    Mount Pisgah Arboretum (Eugene, OR), 143
    "nursery-crawling" in Sonoma County, CA, 102–104
    Streisand Center for Conservancy Studies (Malibu, CA), 150
    Wooden Shoe Bulb Co. (Woodburn, OR), 84–85
Garlic
    book about, 175
    harvesting tips, 175
    new varieties, 242–245
Gaura lindheimeri
    for fall blooms in Pacific Northwest, 221
    new form of, 54

Gazanias, new clumping, 251
Geraniums, 127
Gladiolus care for yearly blooms, 126
Grasses, ornamental, winter cleanup for, 34–35
Ground covers
  amid recycled concrete paving, 69
  cutting back, 37
  nonstop blooming, 54
  taming houttuynia for, 220
  under pines, 86

Hanging baskets. See Container planting
Hazelnut hybrids for cold climates, 33
Heather, 210–212
Heliotrope, 209
Hellebores, dividing time, 223
Hemerocallis, 37
Herbicide
  glyphosate (Roundup), 224, 279
  high-potency, low-residue (Finale), 56
  precautions and tips for using, 128, 279
Herbs. See also specific herbs
  drying and freezing, tips for, 269
  easy-care pot for, 79
Himalaya honeysuckle, 125
Holly, new evergreen, 54
Honeysuckle, 208
Horticultural oils, 11, 38
House plants. See Indoor gardening
Houttuynia cordata, 220
Hydrangea, drying, 241

Ilex, 54
Impatiens
  new double, 54
  New Guinea, 141
Indoor gardening
  azaleas, 300
  bamboos, 316
  cactus, 280
  cutting back for fuller growth, 40
  poisonous plants, book about 28
  root-pruning and repotting, 11
  transplanting gift plants outdoors, 15, 295
  tropical paradise on a grand scale, 32
Inland western states, gardening information and ideas for
  garden checklists & notebooks. See Article Titles Index
  master secrets for an alpine rock garden (Denver, CO), 237
  region-specific book about, 299
  synchronizing spring bloom in Salt Lake City, 254
Insecticidal soap, tips for using, 86
Insect identification, book about, 176
Insect pests. See Pests
Insects, beneficial
  dormant sprays for, 11
  natural enemies of giant whitefly, 124
  patience with, 152
  praying mantids, 176
  trichogramma wasps, 127
Ipomoea tricolor, 88
Iris
  bearded, repeat-blooming, 110–111
  companions for, 124
  hotline for, 91

Iris (cont'd)
  indigenous to Pacific Coast states, 87
  Siberian, feeding and dividing, 148
Irrigation
  adjustable sprinkler riser for, 222
  drip systems, 197
  in fall, 256
  of hanging baskets, 175
  of lawn, minimizing, 175
  of new seedlings, 128
  oscillating sprinkler, improved, 174
  tips for fall, 256
  where to start with installing, 70
  winterizing systems in cold climates, 280
  of young trees, 149

Japanese larch, 89
Jasmines, true and false, fragrant, 206

Kaffir lily, 277
Kale, 222, 253

Lagerstroemia indica, 56
Larix kaempferi 'Diana', 89
Lavender
  drying, 241
  for Southern California, 108–109
Lawnmowers, importance of sharp blades for, 198
Lawns
  dog damage to, 255
  edging beds in, 176, 198
  eliminating, 92
  on hard clay soil, 256
  irrigation in drought conditions, 175
Leptospermum scoparium, 28
Lettuces for looks and flavor, 220
Lilacs, 204
Lilies
  Asiatic and Oriental hybrids, 266–269
  L. speciosum 'Rubrum' for dependable late-summer bloom, 254
Lily-of-the-Nile, new deeper blue, 171
Lime, application on lawns, 92
Lingonberries, 140
Liquidambar styraciflua, 277
Lonicera, 208

Magnolia, for indoor display, 43
Mandevilla, 39, 196
Manure, 29, 60, 224
'Meyer' lemon, avoiding fruit drop on, 152
Morning glories, 88, 150
Moss, grow-your-own patina of, 276
Mulch, help in calculating amounts of, 121
Mushroom compost, proper use of, 175

Narcissus, 35, 57, 252, 291
Nasturtium, new variegated-foliage, 54
Native plants
  all-native garden tips, 253
  for backyard wilderness (Newark, CA), 69
  in coastal ravine (San Juan Capistrano, CA), 34

Native plants (cont'd)
  at Earthside Nature Center (Pasadena, CA),
  in Mount Pisgah Arboretum (Eugene, OR)
  new seed mixes for smaller-space "wildflower" display, 286–289
  shared with South Africa, 189
Nemesia fruticans, 148
Nepeta faassenii, 176, 256
Newsletters. See Garden publications
New Zealand tea tree, 28
Northern California, gardening information and ideas for
  bare lot to beautiful in a year (Hollister), 64–65
  beginners' organic adventure in Berkeley, 62–63
  California geology in miniature in an El Cerrito backyard, 71
  community garden blends cultures in Hayward, 262–264
  "Daffodil Hill" comes to Livermore, 252
  daffodils run wild in Saratoga, 35
  English country garden on rugged slope (Mill Valley), 66
  garden checklists & notebooks. See Article Titles index
  garden for the senses in Oakland, 186–187
  heathers, perfect blooms for cool coastal climes (Mendocino), 210–212
  little-known botanical garden jewel (Fort Bragg), 170–171
  master secrets for a woodland garden (Kensington), 232–233
  "nursery-crawling" in Sonoma County, 102–104
  painting with spring flowers in Piedmont, 274
  private, deerproof front garden in Carmel Valley, 120–121
  succulent dish gardens are works of art (Oakland), 278
  texture and form in the winter garden (Oakland), 20
  three-tiered cutting garden (Pasadena), 96–97
  wilderness meadow in the suburbs (Newark), 69
Northwest. See Pacific Northwest
Nurseries, specialty
  for conifers (Mount Vernon, WA), 197
  drive-in, 36
  for fruit trees (Healdsburg, CA), 298
  for rugosa roses (St. Paul, OR), 22

Oaks
  galls on, 198
  underplanting, 151
Orchids
  chocolate-scented Oncidium, 33
  epiphytic, 117
  for outdoor gardens, 25
Oregano hedge, 256
Organic
  beginners' flower and vegetable garden, 62–63
  fertilizer, new on market, 124
  gardening techniques, 106–107
  soil enrichers, 29, 175
  weed controls, 70, 92

Pacific Northwest, gardening information and ideas for
  fall bloomers for, 221
  fragrant evergreens for holiday decorations, 296
  garden checklists & notebooks. See Article Titles index
  holiday centerpiece from the garden, 312
  irises indigenous to, 87
  keys to organic gardening success (Seattle), 106–107
  master secrets for a foliage garden (Portland, OR), 234–235
  mixed cutting garden in Seaview, WA, 98–99
  native plant arboretum near Eugene, OR, 143
  public rhododendron testing gardens (Whidbey Island, WA), 76–78
  rock garden transforms a front yard (Seattle), 252
  shady forest glen in Vancouver, B.C., 194
  spring madness in Bellevue, WA, 122
  tropical paradise indoors (Bainbridge Island, WA), 32
  white-flowered oasis in Seattle, 146–147
  winter color with bark and berries (Kingston, WA), 18–19
Palms
  dividing clumping, 224
  low-maintenance, 138–139
Pansies, dig-your-own, 279
Paperbark maple, protecting from passersby, 56
Paths, an assortment of garden, 69
Pawpaws, sweet and hardy, 142
Peach trees, spraying for fungus, 38
Penstemon, cutting back, 197
Peppers
  bell, harvesting, 176
  cool-summer chilies, 54
  low-heat jalapeños, 56
  new mini varieties, 36
  super-hot source, 85
Perennials
  cutting back herbaceous, 197, 198
  dividing, 223
  for erosion control, 149
  a long-blooming nemesia, 148
  propagation from stem cuttings, 134–135
  tough, self-sowing, 223
  in wildflower mixes, 286–290
Pesticides and organic controls
  Bacillus thuringiensis, 127, 190, 256
  for geranium budworm, 127
  herbicide, new (Finale), 56
  horticultural oils, 11, 38
  insecticidal soap tips, 86
  repellent for deer and rabbits, 151
  sticky traps, 175, 190
  for whitefly, 124, 175
Pests
  aphid, 152
  cabbage butterflies, 256
  fuschia mites, 90
  geranium budworm, 127
  glassy-winged sharpshooter on oleanders, 221
  spider mites, 87

Pests (cont'd)
    tobacco hornworm, 190
    whitefly, 124, 175, 190
Petunias, AAS winners for 1996, 9
Photos, for garden planning, 224
Pines
    ground cover under, 86
    pinching to control growth, 148
Pistacia chinensis, 278
Platycodon grandiflorus, 151
Poinsettias, postholiday survival rate, 300
Poisonous indoor plants, book about, 38
Pole beans rated, 115
Populus tremuloides, 254
Potatoes, unusual, 57
Powdery mildew control, 148
Propagation, 125, 134–135
Pruning
    potted plant roots, 11
    rhododendrons, 122
    roses, 10
    tips for, 15, 152, 173
Prunus serrulata, 9
Pumpkins, 125, 254
Pussy willow, for indoor display, 43
Pyracantha, trellis-trained, 68

Radishes, specialty, 10
Rain damage, preventing, 14, 58
Raised-bed gardening, 72–74, 90, 174, 176
Records, garden, importance of keeping, 198
Rhododendrons
    "most fragrant," 232
    planting tips, 123
    pruning, 122
    ratings of, 76–78
    transplanting, 125
Rock gardens, 237, 252
Root-pruning potted plants, 11
Roses
    AARS winner, 1997 ('Scentimental'), 275
    advice about, free, 91
    alfalfa as fertilizer for, 39
    American Rose Society, 278
    aphid control research, new, 152
    bare-root buying tips, 11
    blues and lavenders, new, 85
    climbing, disease-resistant varieties, 38
    common planting errors with, 13
    companion perennials for, 123
    as cut flowers, tips for, 13
    fragrant, 59, 206
    grown for colorful thorns, 36
    long-blooming varieties, 123
    miniature gift plants, caring for, 295
    old-fashioned, sources for, 57, 298
    pink hybrid teas, best, 91
    powdery mildew control, new research on, 148
    problems replanting in old beds, 299
    rootstock explained, 12
    rugosa, 22–24
    sources for obtaining any rose, 278
    spraying, 10
    unusual trellis for, 68
    wet weather care for, 58
    winter maintenance, 10

Rotating crops, 74
Rugosa roses for nonideal climates, 22–24

Sage. See Salvia
Salvia
    AAS winner for 1996, 9
    fall blooms for Pacific Northwest, 221
Santa Barbara daisy, 276
Santolina chamaecyparissus, 173
Schizanthus, window-box care, 130
Schizostylis coccinea, 277
Sedum, 197, 221
Seeds
    advantages of planting from, 151
    offbeat annuals from, 270–271
    tomato and pepper, experimenting with, 13
Sempervivum, growing in containers, 197
Shade plants
    care in summer, 194
    for a coastal ravine, 34–35
    forest glen in Vancouver, B.C., 194
    variegated foliage for a sunny look, 105
Shallots, 276
Shrubs
    alfalfa pellets and meal for, 39
    recycled "collars" to protect, 149
    tough and unthirsty, for hot climes, 26–28
Small-space gardening, 172
Smoke tree, 265, 276
Snap peas, mildew-resistant, 246
Soap, insecticidal, 86
Soil
    adding sulfur to, 58
    "can't-beat-it" soil amendment, 235
    enrichers, natural, 29
    high salt content in, 55, 175
    home-baked recipe for gift-giving, 295
    improving in new housing tracts, 70
    potting mix, choosing the right, 165–166
    turkey grit for potting soil, 197
Solarization, soil, 70
Soleirolia soleirolii, 224
Sorrel, 39
South African natives for California, 189, 198
Southern California, gardening information and ideas for
    bacterial scorch on oleanders, 221
    bananas for fruit and foliage, 213–215
    drive-in nurseries in, 36
    dry creek bed design tips (Solvang), 218
    fall planting for winter color (Pasadena), 16–17
    field-grown pansies for the digging in Encinitas, 279
    four fabulous shrubs for, 26–28
    framing garden "paintings" in Laguna Beach, 52
    garden checklists & notebooks. See Article Titles Index
    holiday centerpiece from the garden, 312
    lavenders for, 108–109
    master secrets for a perennial garden (San Marcos), 236

Southern California, gardening information and ideas for (cont'd)
    Mediterranean natural in Laguna Niguel, 67
    native plantings solve ravine landscape puzzle (San Juan Capistrano), 34
    nursery, recommended (San Marcos), 152
    orchids, outdoor (Santa Barbara), 25
    perennial erosion control in Occidental, 149
    region-specific book about, 299
    rose-and-perennial prize-winner in Tehachapi, 123
    rugosa roses suitable for, 22
    tropical forest in Arcadia, 195
Southwest, gardening information and ideas for
    garden checklists. See Garden checklists, Southwest, in the Article Titles Index
    geometric shapes in a desert garden (Phoenix, AZ), 250
    mail-order sources, 275
    region-specific book about, 299
    sun-loving coleus for Texas summers, 121
    winter color in a courtyard garden (Phoenix, AZ), 21
Soviet Union, plant finds in the former, 280
Spruce, dwarf Alberta, 87
Stewartia for understated majesty, 188
Strawberries, new, 35, 75
Succulents, 278
Sulfur, adding to soil, 58
Supports, natural, 219, 232
Sweet gum, 277
Sweet peas, 90, 223
Sweet woodruff, 86
Syringa, 204

Taxodium distichum, 12
Thymes for cooking, 167
Tomatoes
    determinate vs. indeterminate, 60
    new, for hot climates, 86
    pests and diseases of, 190
    when to plant, 59
Tools and equipment
    adjustable sprinkler risers, 222
    child-size garden tools, 147
    "collars" for newly planted shrubs, 149
    dibbles (dibbers) for bulb plantings, 254
    downspout sleeves, 14
    easy hanging basket liner, 124
    fall tool care, 280
    favorite, of garden masters, 235, 236, 237
    flexible plant stakes, 173
    landscape fabric, 70
    leather gloves, 224
    pine tar soap for cleanup, 297
    preservative for drying flowers, 152
    rakes, curvaceous new, 295
    spray tank, pumpless, 36
    sprinkler, improved oscillating, 174
    "tip" bags for garden cleanup, 275
Transplanting tips, 40, 253
Tree peony, new black-red, 54

Trees. See also specific trees
    buying for autumn color, 277, 278
    Christmas tree care, 297, 298, 300
    largest specimens, book about, 174
    litter from, 138–139, 151
    miniature, for tabletop decor, 315
    native oak care, 151
    small, 56
    topping, results of, 280
    young, watering plan for, 149
Trillium, 277
Tulips
    acres blooming in Oregon, 84
    coordinating, 255
    prechilled, for late planting in Southern California, 10
    species, 238–240

Vegetables
    cover crop for, 197, 222
    crop rotation of, 74, 88
    exotic, in Hayward community garden, 262–264
    family groups named, 88
    front-yard, 55
    mixed with ornamentals in front yard, 55
    mouseproofing, 255
    new seed varieties, 13
    raised beds for, 72–74, 90
    starting in cool weather, 13
Verbena canadensis for nonstop bloom, 54
Vines
    clematis in three seasons, 80–81
    fast-growing, colorful, 126
    Himalaya honeysuckle, 125
    on a living support, 219
    as structures for holiday lights, 296
    supporting against walls, 89
Virtual Garden (Internet web site), 174

Washington thorn, 56
Water gardening
    conservatory for, 32
    plants for pond edges, 223
    "pond-erosa" replaces lawn in Downey, CA, 172
Watering. See Irrigation
Watermelons for small gardens, 114
Weeds
    edible, 127
    nonchemical controls for, 70, 92
Westringia 'Wynyabbie Gem', 28
White-flowered garden, 146–147
Wildflowers. See Native plants
Wildlife
    attracting with plants, 150, 191, 253, 279
    holiday edible tree ornaments for, 294
Window box renaissance, 130–133
Winter color, 8, 16–21, 110
Wreaths
    fresh-flower in summer, 182–185
    holiday season, ideas for, 306–309

Yarrow, 176

Zinnias
    for cool, moist summers, 151
    perfect for cutting ('Yoga'), 59
Zucchinis for small gardens, heirloom, 88